Effective Tcl/Tk Programming:
Writing Better Programs with Tcl and Tk

Addison-Wesley Professional Computing Series

Brian W. Kernighan, Consulting Editor

Ken Arnold/John Peyton, *A C User's Guide to ANSI C*

David R. Butenhof, *Programming with POSIX® Threads*

Tom Cargill, *C++ Programming Style*

William R. Cheswick/Steven M. Bellovin, *Firewalls and Internet Security: Repelling the Wily Hacker*

David A. Curry, *UNIX® System Security: A Guide for Users and System Administrators*

Erich Gamma/Richard Helm/Ralph Johnson/John Vlissides, *Design Patterns: Elements of Reusable Object-Oriented Software*

Erich Gamma/Richard Helm/Ralph Johnson/John Vlissides, *Design Patterns CD: Elements of Reusable Object-Oriented Software*

David R. Hanson, *C Interfaces and Implementations: Techniques for Creating Reusable Software*

Mark Harrison/Michael McLennan, *Effective Tcl/Tk Programming: Writing Better Programs with Tcl and Tk*

S. Keshav, *An Engineering Approach to Computer Networking: ATM Networks, The Internet, and the Telephone Network*

John Lakos, *Large-Scale C++ Software Design*

Scott Meyers, *Effective C++, Second Edition: 50 Specific Ways to Improve Your Programs and Designs*

Scott Meyers, *More Effective C++: 35 New Ways to Improve Your Programs and Designs*

Robert B. Murray, *C++ Strategies and Tactics*

David R. Musser/Atul Saini, *STL Tutorial and Reference Guide: C++ Programming with the Standard Template Library*

John K. Ousterhout, *Tcl and the Tk Toolkit*

Craig Partridge, *Gigabit Networking*

J. Stephen Pendergrast Jr., *Desktop KornShell Graphical Programming*

Radia Perlman, *Interconnections: Bridges and Routers*

David M. Piscitello/A. Lyman Chapin, *Open Systems Networking: TCP/IP and OSI*

Stephen A. Rago, *UNIX® System V Network Programming*

Curt Schimmel, *UNIX® Systems for Modern Architectures: Symmetric Multiprocessing and Caching for Kernel Programmers*

W. Richard Stevens, *Advanced Programming in the UNIX® Environment*

W. Richard Stevens, *TCP/IP Illustrated, Volume 1: The Protocols*

W. Richard Stevens, *TCP/IP Illustrated, Volume 3: TCP for Transactions, HTTP, NNTP, and the UNIX® Domain Protocols*

Gary R. Wright/W. Richard Stevens, *TCP/IP Illustrated, Volume 2: The Implementation*

Effective Tcl/Tk Programming:
Writing Better Programs with Tcl and Tk

Mark Harrison
and
Michael McLennan

ADDISON-WESLEY
An Imprint of Addison Wesley Longman, Inc.

Reading, Massachusetts   Harlow, England   Menlo Park, California
Berkeley, California   Don Mills, Ontario   Sydney
Bonn   Amsterdam   Tokyo   Mexico City

The publisher offers discounts on this book when ordered in quantity for special sales. For more information please contact:

Corporate & Professional Publishing Group
Addison-Wesley Publishing Company
One Jacob Way
Reading, Massachusetts 01867

Library of Congress Cataloging-in-Publication Data

Harrison, Mark.
    Effective Tcl/Tk programming : writing better programs with Tcl and
Tk / Mark Harrison and Michael McLennan.
        p.   cm. — (Addison-Wesley professional computing series)
    Includes bibliographical references and index.
    ISBN 0-201-63474-0
    1. Tcl (Computer program language)   2. Tk toolkit.   I. McLennan,
Michael.   II. Title.   III. Series.
QA76.73.T44H37   1998
005.13'3—dc21   97–32246
                                                    CIP

Cover art by: Michael McLennan

ISBN 0-201-63474-0
Text printed on acid-free paper
1 2 3 4 5 6 7 8 9—MA—0100999897
First printing, November 1997

To Maria, Maxwell, and Katie
—Michael McLennan

To Ellen, Allegra, and Alexander
—Mark Harrison

For making it all worthwhile.

Contents

Preface

It's easy to get started with Tcl/Tk. Just follow the steps in Appendix A to obtain the `wish` program and start it up. Then type in a few lines of code, like this:

```
% button .b -text "Hello, World!" -command exit
⇒ .b
% pack .b
```

You'll see the Hello, World! button appear as soon as you enter the `pack` command. On Windows 95, it will look like this:

You don't have to edit any makefiles or fight with a compiler. You don't need to know everything about the X window system or the Microsoft Foundation Classes. You don't need to wade through pounds of confusing documents to find symbols, such as XA_FONT_NAME. Instead, you type a few lines of Tcl code and immediately see the results.

As you learn more about the Tk widgets, you can write lots of simple programs. With a text widget and 100 lines of Tcl code, you can put together a program for sending electronic mail (e-mail) messages. With a canvas widget and 200 lines of Tcl code, you can create a simple drawing editor.

A few other Tcl/Tk books will help you get started. John Ousterhout's *Tcl and the Tk Toolkit* starts with a complete overview of the Tcl language and then goes on to describe each of the Tk widgets. The book even describes how to add new functionality to Tcl/Tk by integrating your own C code into the `wish` program. Brent Welch's book *Practical Programming in Tcl and Tk* is another good source of Tcl/Tk code examples.

After reading one of the introductory Tcl/Tk books, you will be well acquainted with the nuts and bolts. But you may not yet have a good understanding of how they fit together to make an application.

We wrote this book to pick up where the others leave off. We assume that you understand some of the Tcl language and that you've written a few simple Tcl/Tk programs. If not, you can pick it up as you read along. But instead of explaining the basics, we focus on areas that are commonly misunderstood—such as the `pack` command, the `bind` mechanism, and the canvas widget. We not only explain how these things work but also show how you can use them to build powerful applications.

- We explain how the packer works and then show how you can use it to create a tabbed notebook that displays "pages" of widgets.
- We explain how binding tags work and then show how you can use them to handle the modes in a drawing editor.
- We explain how the canvas works and then show how you can use it to build a progress gauge, a color wheel, and a calendar.

Along the way, we describe the lessons that we've learned from developing many thousands of lines of Tcl/Tk code. We show you software architectures and programming techniques that will make your Tcl/Tk code easier to maintain. For example, we show how to

- Create client/server applications
- Package Tcl/Tk code into libraries of reusable components
- Use lists and arrays as data structures
- Handle common quoting problems

Above all else, we try to present a holistic view of application development. In Chapter 1, we show you how to go about designing an application—from the initial concept to a working prototype to a finished product. Throughout the book, we develop several useful applications: a desktop calculator, a drawing editor, and a daily calendar that will store all of your appointments. In Chapter 8, we show you how to add polish to your finished applications and how to deliver them to customers.

In the course of this book, we develop more than two dozen useful components, including a toolbar, a paned window, a balloon help facility, and a confirmation dialog. We provide complete source code for these components. You can download this software from the site **http://www.awl.com/cseng/books/efftcl/**. We encourage you to study these examples and to use them to build your own Tcl/Tk applications!

All of the examples in this book have been carefully designed to work with all recent versions of Tcl/Tk, including:

- Tcl 7.5 / Tk 4.1

- Tcl 7.6 / Tk 4.2
- Tcl 8.0 / Tk 8.0

The examples should work with later releases as well.

Most of our experience with Tcl/Tk comes from UNIX-based systems, so you will see a lot of references to UNIX throughout the book. But Tcl/Tk is not limited to UNIX systems. The Tcl 8.0 / Tk 8.0 release works cross-platform on UNIX, Windows 95/NT/3.1, and Macintosh systems. Almost all of our examples work identically on all three platforms. (Of course, some examples rely on such programs as `/usr/lib/sendmail`, which are available only on a UNIX system. Those examples will not work cross-platform without some modification.) Throughout the book, we've included screen snapshots from the various platforms to highlight the cross-platform capability.

Acknowledgments

Many people have made this book possible. Thanks to John Ousterhout and his team at Sun Microsystems for creating such a marvelous toolkit. Thanks to Mike Hendrickson, John Fuller, and the staff at Addison Wesley Longman for their encouragement and support in producing this book. Thanks to Brian Kernighan for nudging us in the right direction and for his careful reviews and helpful comments. Thanks to Don Libes, Jeff Korn, Jeffrey Hobbs, and Jim Ingham for uncovering a number of weak spots in our material. Thanks to Evelyn Pyle for her meticulous copyediting and for smoothing out the wrinkles in our grammar. And thanks to all of the other reviewers who have made this work stronger: Ron Hutchins, Raymond Johnson, Steve Johnson, Oliver Jones, Joe Konstan, David Richardson, Alexei Rodriguez, and Win Treese.

Mark Harrison would like to thank his many colleagues at DSC Communications Corporation for their involvement and for their practical suggestions about incorporating Tcl into mission-critical products. In particular, Mark Ulferts and Kris Raney were especially helpful in this regard.

Michael McLennan would like to thank Sani Nassif for getting him started with Tcl/Tk; George Howlett for teaching him much of what he knows about software; John Tauke for making Tcl/Tk development a legitimate business activity at Bell Labs; Kishore Singhal, Prasad Subramaniam, and the management at Bell Labs for supporting this work; Barb and Jim McLennan for their love and support; Joan Wendland, his friend and mentor; and Maria, Maxwell and Katie, for making him smile.

Mark Harrison
Michael McLennan
September 1997

Chapter 1
Building Tcl/Tk Applications

Most people can pick up the fundamentals of Tcl/Tk programming in a couple of hours and can be writing small programs to do real work in a few days. But at that stage, people start asking different kinds of questions: How do I plan larger applications? What's the best way to lay out and develop my screens? How can I package and distribute my application?

In this chapter, we'll describe the thought process involved in laying out a small application from start to finish. We'll build a small drawing program, starting with a hand-drawn idea. We'll build a quick prototype to see whether we like the look and feel of the program. We'll add some bindings and procedures to finish the implementation. We'll also show you how to plan your development so that most of your code can go into libraries. This will help you to reuse the code, making your applications easier to build and maintain.

1.1 Application-building process

How do you build an application using Tcl and Tk? The usual process can be summarized as follows.

1. Think about how you want your application to look. Sketch some pictures of the main windows and dialog boxes. It helps to study some books on graphics display and human interface design. We list some of our favorite books in Appendix B.

2. Identify the Tk widgets that can be used to compose the various elements of your sketches. Occasionally, you may want a widget that is not directly available in Tk. For

example, you may want a tabbed notebook or a progress gauge. You can build such things by using Tk widgets as component parts. The canvas widget and the text widget are both quite helpful in this regard (see Chapter 4 and Chapter 5 for details). You may be able to find what you're looking for in your own code library or at the Tcl/Tk archive site on the Internet (http://www.NeoSoft.com/tcl/).

3. Write the Tcl/Tk code to create the various widgets and pack them together to look like your sketches. This can be done quickly, and it allows you to experiment with the look and feel of your screens. In some cases, you might have "light" versions of some screens that are not fully featured. For example, you might start with a stripped-down print dialog rather than the final production dialog with all of the bells and whistles. Of course, if you have a production-quality dialog in your library, you can drop it in from the beginning.

Note: *If you're doing this development for someone else, now is a good time to get some early feedback on the overall design.*

4. Figure out what components or procedures are good candidates to be made into library routines. Set up the library infrastructure as detailed in Section 8.2. A bit of planning now can save quite a lot of time at the end of your project.

5. Add behavior to your program by adding commands to your widgets. If a widget does not have an option to support the behavior you want, you can add the behavior with the `bind` command (see Chapter 3 for details).

   Your program may be able to leverage other programs to do its work. For example, a drawing program might use the system printing command—like the `lpr` command on many UNIX systems—in order to send its output to the printer (see Chapter 7 for details).

6. Add any finishing touches to your program. Look for widget options with hard-coded settings that could be soft-coded in the option database, as discussed in Section 8.1.1. Add some balloon help to your application, using the code from Section 6.7.2. If your application takes a long time to start up, add a "loading" placard, like the one in Section 8.1.3, to let the user know that your program is running.

7. Test your program like crazy. If you have a syntax error in your Tcl code, you won't find it unless you execute the code.

8. Package your program so that it can be easily distributed and installed (see Chapter 8 for details). Pay attention to this step. This will be the first experience that your customer has with your program. Make that experience a good one!

1.2   A small application

Let's step through this process to build a small application—a "sketchpad" program that will let you draw pictures and doodle with the mouse. We'll start with a simple sketch of the overall design and gradually improve it to a finished application.

1.2.1   Designing the application

Let's begin by analyzing the features we want our sketchpad program to have. Since we want to keep our example small, we'll concentrate on a few key features.

- You can draw on the sketchpad by pressing the mouse button and moving the mouse around.
- You can clear the drawing area.
- You can select the pen color.
- You can see the x- and y-coordinates of the mouse.
- You can exit the application.

Next, we need to figure out how to provide the controls for these features. When you're designing a new application, think about other programs that you've used, and try to model your program after them. For example, most applications have a menu bar at the top with a series of pull-down menus. This lets you organize the features of your program in a way that is easy for the user to explore. If you look carefully, you'll notice that many applications have File, Edit, and View menus. The File menu has entries for loading and saving files, along with the Exit entry. The Edit menu usually has such entries as Cut and Paste. And the View menu has things to control toolbars, zooming, and perhaps a grid or rulers. If you follow these conventions, millions of users won't need a manual, because they will intuitively understand your application.

Figure 1.1 shows our first idea of what the sketchpad will look like. We will have a menu bar on top with two pull-down menus. The File menu has an Exit entry, and the Edit menu has a Clear entry to erase the drawing area.

It's a bad idea to put anything but menus in the menu bar. So we'll have another line below the menu bar, showing the pen color and the location of the mouse. The drawing area will go below that and will take up the majority of the screen.

There are lots of ways to control the pen color. When you're deciding on a feature like this, think about all of the possibilities and weigh the trade-offs. We could add an entry widget, for example, and let you type in a color name. But many users would grumble about all of the typing, and they might misspell the color names. We could provide a list-box with all of the color names, but that would take up a lot of space on the main window. We could pop up a dialog box with a color wheel. Most people understand this intuitive way of selecting colors. But if you build the application with this and try it out, you'll find that changing colors is a bit of a chore. You have to bring up the dialog, drag the marker on

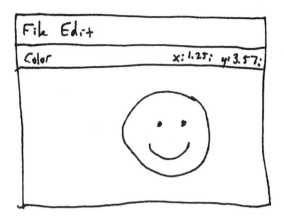

Figure 1.1. Sketch program, initial ideas.

the color wheel, and dismiss the dialog. If all you need are some simple colors, such as red, green, and blue, the color wheel is a bit much.

For this application, we'll use a color menu with choices such as black, white, red, green, and blue. This provides a compact way of selecting colors that is fast and easy. We can start with this and add the color wheel later on if it is needed.

1.2.2 Designing the screen

First, we need to decide what Tk widgets we can use to build the controls shown in Figure 1.1. We can handle the drawing area with a canvas widget. Wherever you click on the canvas, we'll add a small square of color. We can use a label widget to display the x- and y-coordinates as you move the pen around the canvas.

The menu bar is a frame with some menubuttons packed into it. Each menubutton has its own menu widget that contains the menu entries.

We'll use another menubutton and its associated menu to control the pen color, as we discussed earlier. If we want to add a color wheel later on, we can build it with another canvas widget. We'll show you how to do this in Section 4.4.

Now it's time to lay out the screen. Figure 1.2 shows the basic approach. We look for widgets that should be grouped together, and we add frames to handle the grouping. This makes our packing job easier, as we'll see in Section 2.1.4. We can use one frame to group the menubuttons together, forming a menu bar. We can use another frame to group the pen color with the pen location. We pack these all together in the main window, with the menu bar frame on the top, followed by the pen control frame and the canvas.

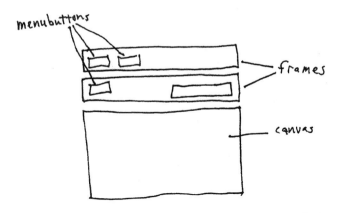

Figure 1.2. Laying out the screen elements.

1.2.3 Prototyping the screen

Now let's put some rudimentary code in place in order to see our general screen layout. The first cut of the code is pretty straightforward. We create the menu bar and pack it into the main window like this:

```
frame .mbar -borderwidth 1 -relief raised
pack .mbar -fill x
menubutton .mbar.file -text "File" -menu .mbar.file.m
pack .mbar.file -side left
menu .mbar.file.m
.mbar.file.m add command -label "Exit"


menubutton .mbar.edit -text "Edit" -menu .mbar.edit.m
pack .mbar.edit -side left
menu .mbar.edit.m
.mbar.edit.m add command -label "Clear"
```

At this stage, we're concerned only with how the program looks—not how it works—so we leave out things like the -command option for the menu entries.

We create the pen color menu and pack it like this:

```
frame .style -borderwidth 1 -relief sunken
pack .style -fill x

menubutton .style.color -text "Color" -menu .style.color.m
pack .style.color -side left
```

```
menu .style.color.m
.style.color.m add command -label "Black"
.style.color.m add command -label "Blue"
.style.color.m add command -label "Red"
.style.color.m add command -label "Green"
.style.color.m add command -label "Yellow"
```

We create the pen location label and pack it like this:

```
label .style.readout -text "x: 0.00 y: 0.00"
pack .style.readout -side right
```

And we create the drawing area and pack it like this:

```
canvas .sketchpad -background white
pack .sketchpad
```

Figure 1.3 shows the result, which looks passable at this stage of development. If we were building this application for someone else, we should get approval for the design. The customer may want to change things, and that may affect how the application works. We should get the customer's reaction to this design before spending too much time fleshing it out.

Figure 1.3. Sketch program, first cut.

1.2.4 Library analysis

Before we finish coding this application, we should look for ways to simplify the task. Whenever we find the same combinations of widgets appearing again and again, we can write a procedure to create them.

For example, suppose we were planning to add an option to set the background color of the drawing area. We might need another color menu for this. We could duplicate the code for the pen color menu and make a few changes, like this:

```
menubutton .style.bg -text "Background" -menu .style.bg.m
pack .style.bg -side left


menu .style.bg.m
.style.bg.m add command -label "Black" -command {set bg black}
.style.bg.m add command -label "Blue" -command {set bg blue}
.style.bg.m add command -label "Red" -command {set bg red}
.style.bg.m add command -label "Green" -command {set bg green}
.style.bg.m add command -label "Yellow" -command {set bg yellow}
```

But instead, we should make a procedure to create color menus, like this:

```
proc cmenu_create {win title cmd} {
    menubutton $win -text $title -menu $win.m


    menu $win.m
    $win.m add command -label "Black" -command "$cmd black"
    $win.m add command -label "Blue" -command "$cmd blue"
    $win.m add command -label "Red" -command "$cmd red"
    $win.m add command -label "Green" -command "$cmd green"
    $win.m add command -label "Yellow" -command "$cmd yellow"
}
```

This procedure takes three arguments, which are the three things that change for each color menu: a widget name, a title for the menubutton, and the command that's executed whenever you select a color. We could use this procedure to create two color menus for our application, like this:

```
cmenu_create .style.color "Color" {set color}
pack .style.color -side left


cmenu_create .style.bg "Background" {.sketchpad configure -bg}
pack .style.bg -side left
```

Notice that the commands we passed in to handle color changes are not complete commands. They are only the first part of a command, which we call a *command prefix*. We set up each of the entries in the color menu to append its color name onto the end of the command prefix, so each entry does something different to set the color.

Obviously, having a procedure saves us a lot of coding and also reduces the chance that we'll make a mistake the next time we add a color menu to this application. If we ever decide to improve the color menu, we can make all of our changes in one procedure.

A component like the color menu would be useful in many other applications. We might spend a little more time making it look nice and wrapping it up with a good set of procedures. We'll do this in Section 8.2.3. When we're finished, we'll end up with a color menu that you can create like this:

```
colormenu_create .style.color
pack .style.color -side left
```

Since we have this code at our fingertips, we might as well drop it into the sketchpad
application at this point. These two lines replace the menu code that we showed earlier.
When we add marks to the canvas, we'll ask the color menu for the current color, like this:

```
set color [colormenu_get .style.color]
```

If we put the color menu procedures into a Tcl/Tk library, we can reuse them in future
projects. We'll develop lots of components throughout the course of this book. All of them
follow the design patterns described in Section 8.2.

1.2.5 Adding behavior to the program

Now we'll take the skeletal application that we used for the prototype and fill in some code
to give the program behavior. One of the simplest things to do is to fix the File menu so
you can exit the application. We just need to add an `exit` command to the Exit entry, like
this:

```
.mbar.file.m add command -label "Exit" -command exit
```

Next, we can fix the Edit menu to handle the Clear entry. As we'll see in Chapter 4,
you can erase a canvas by telling it to delete all of its items, like this:

```
.mbar.edit.m add command -label "Clear" -command {
    .sketchpad delete all
}
```

The trickiest bits of code have to do with the sketching. The canvas does not support
sketching by default. We must attach new behaviors to it, using the `bind` command. We'll
explain bindings in much more detail in Chapter 3, but the basic idea is this: Whenever
something happens to the canvas or any other widget, it receives an event that describes
what happened. For example, when you click the left mouse button on the canvas, it
receives a `<ButtonPress-1>` event. By default, the canvas ignores these events, but we
can use the `bind` command to register a script that will handle them.

First, we'll take care of displaying the pen location as the mouse pointer is moved
around on the canvas. We do this by binding to the `<Motion>` event, like this:

```
bind .sketchpad <Motion> {sketch_coords %x %y}
```

Moving the mouse over the portion of the screen occupied by `.sketchpad` will generate a
series of `<Motion>` events. Each event represents the position of the mouse pointer, sam-
pled at a given instant of time. If the mouse is moved slowly, there may be an event at each
pixel along the path, but normally, the coordinates are somewhat separated.

With the `<Motion>` binding in place, Tk will substitute the x- and y-coordinates for
each event in place of the %x and %y fields and will then call the `sketch_coords` procedure. The `sketch_coords` procedure looks like this:

```
proc sketch_coords {x y} {
    set size [winfo fpixels .sketchpad 1i]
    set x [expr $x/$size]
    set y [expr $y/$size]
    .style.readout configure \
        -text [format "x: %6.2fi  y: %6.2fi" $x $y]
}
```

To display the new coordinates, we change the text of the label .style.readout. We could report the pixel coordinates directly, but it is probably more meaningful to the user if we convert them to something like inches. We use the winfo fpixels command to find out how many pixels it takes to make up 1 inch on the sketchpad, and then we scale the *x*- and *y*-coordinates by this value. We need to report only two significant figures after the decimal point—after all, the user is not a computer! So we use the format command to build a nice string, such as "x: 1.49i y: 2.51i", and this is what we display in the label.

Next, we need to handle the drawing operation. We'll create the illusion of drawing with a pen by adding squares to the canvas as we move the mouse. To do this, we need to bind to two events: We bind to <ButtonPress-1> so that clicking the mouse button puts a blob of "ink" on the canvas; we also bind to <B1-Motion> so that the pen will "paint" as you hold down the mouse button and move around:

```
bind .sketchpad <ButtonPress-1> {sketch_box_add %x %y}
bind .sketchpad <B1-Motion>     {sketch_box_add %x %y}
```

Tk replaces %x and %y with the location of the mouse at the time of the event and then calls the procedure sketch_box_add, which is defined like this:

```
proc sketch_box_add {x y} {
    set x0 [expr $x-3]
    set x1 [expr $x+3]
    set y0 [expr $y-3]
    set y1 [expr $y+3]
    set color [colormenu_get .style.color]

    .sketchpad create rectangle $x0 $y0 $x1 $y1 \
        -outline "" -fill $color
}
```

We want to draw a square 6 pixels by 6 pixels centered on the (*x*,*y*) coordinate. So we subtract 3 pixels from *x* and *y* to get the upper-left corner of this square, and we add 3 pixels to get the lower-left corner. We get the current pen color by calling colormenu_get with the name of our color menu. We'll see exactly how this works in Section 8.2.3, but for now you can assume that it returns a color name, such as black, red, or green. Finally, we put the little square of ink on the canvas by creating a rectangle. We're careful to set the outline color to the null string, overriding the black outline that you get by default.

1.2.6   Adding finishing touches

Now that we have the basic sketchpad program working, we should spend a little time adding some spit and polish. As you're finishing each of your applications, keep the following ideas in mind.

First, look carefully at each of the windows in your application.

- Are the widgets all squashed together? Are any of the widgets crowded near the border of the window? If so, you should add some padding to the `pack` and `grid` commands, using the `-padx` and `-pady` options, as described in Section 2.1.2.

- Does each window have a good title above it? You can set the title of the window by using the `wm title` command, as described in Section 6.3. For example, you can set the title of the sketchpad program by adding a line of code like this:

```
wm title . "sketch"
```

Next, look for any hard-coded widget options in the program. It's okay to hard-code the `-text` option of a label or the `-command` option of a button. But if you find colors and fonts that are hard-coded, think about moving them to the option database. If you hard-code a font name, a user who doesn't have that font won't be able to run your program.

In the sketchpad program, for example, we hard-coded the background color of the canvas like this:

```
canvas .sketchpad -background white
```

But what if the user wants a background that is black or antique white? It's better to create the canvas, like this:

```
canvas .sketchpad
```

and to add a resource to the option database, like this:

```
option add *sketchpad.background white startupFile
```

This sets the background resource for any widget named `sketchpad` to white. In this application, there is only one sketchpad, but we could generalize it to support lots of sketch pads, and they would all be white. We'll talk more about the option database and how all of this works in Section 8.1.1.

Next, think about adding keyboard accelerators to the menus. Exploring a menu is fine for a novice, but experienced users get tired of pulling the same menus down again and again. It's a good idea to provide keyboard shortcuts for common operations, such as cut and paste.

Finally, add some online help to your program. You could add a Help menu with a list of topics and use a text widget to display help files. We'll see some code that handles this in Section 5.3.

Or you could use the balloon help facility described in Section 6.7.2. For example, we can add balloon help to the sketchpad program with a few simple commands:

```
balloonhelp_for .style.color {Pen Color:
Selects the drawing color for the canvas}
```

```
balloonhelp_for .style.readout {Pen Location:
Shows the location of the pointer on the drawing canvas (in inches)}
balloonhelp_for .sketchpad {Drawing Canvas:
Click and drag with the left mouse button to draw in this area}
```

When you rest the mouse pointer on the pen color menu, the pen location label, or the canvas, a window will appear with one of the brief descriptions shown here. As you can see, adding balloon help is not a lot of work, and it makes it easy for new users to pick up your program.

You could also add an About... entry to the File menu. This brings up a dialog showing your name as the author, a copyright notice, and a telephone number for technical support.

With all of these improvements, our simple sketchpad looks like a full-fledged application. You can see the final product in Figure 1.4.

Figure 1.4. Final sketchpad application, with balloon help showing.

The same script will run cross-platform on UNIX, Windows 95/NT, and Macintosh systems. Under Windows, it looks like a Windows application; on the Mac, it looks like a Mac application, as you can see in Figure 1.5. In Chapter 9, we'll discuss portability issues and offer some guidelines that will help make your scripts portable across all three platforms.

1.2.7 Testing the program

Before you deliver your program to anyone, you must test it thoroughly. If you're used to programming in C or C++, you're used to having the compiler catch many mistakes for you. But Tcl will not catch your mistakes until runtime. Everything is interpreted, so you have to execute the code to find out that something is wrong. You must exercise all of your

                    (a)   (b)

Figure 1.5. The sketchpad application runs cross-platform on (a) Windows 95/NT and (b) Macintosh systems.

procedures, all of your loop bodies, and all of the branches of your conditionals. If you don't, your customers may find bugs for you and may stop being your customers!

As you're testing, look for the following problems.

- Try resizing each of your windows. This will uncover errors in packing and gridding (see Sections 2.1.5–2.1.6, and Section 2.2.3). As an example, consider our sketchpad program. When we compress the window as shown in Figure 1.6(a), everything looks fine. But when we expand the window, we uncover a packing error. Instead of getting bigger, the drawing area keeps its normal size, and we get dead space around the edge of the window. We can correct this by packing the canvas to expand and fill.

  Run your program at different screen resolutions. Does your program look good at a 640 × 480 screen resolution?

  If your windows have a minimum size, or if you want to prevent resizing, you can talk with the window manager (see Section 6.3.2).

- Check your key bindings. When you press the Tab key, does the focus highlight border shift the way you want it to? If not, you should change the order of your pack and grid commands to reflect the order for tab traversal.

  Does anything break when the CapsLock and NumLock keys are turned on? In particular, test your menu accelerators.

- What happens if you dismiss a dialog by using the Quit or the Close option from the window manager instead of clicking on the usual OK or Cancel buttons? Can you bring

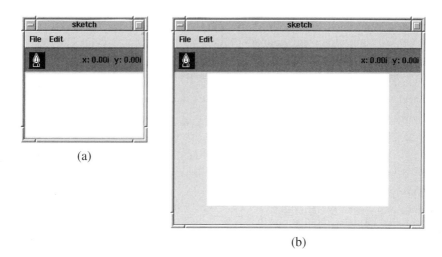

(a)

(b)

Figure 1.6. Sketchpad application with the main window (a) compressed and (b) enlarged. A packing error is uncovered.

that window back up? If not, you need to handle the WM_DELETE_WINDOW protocol, described in Section 6.5.

- If your application uses files, try reading from a nonexistent file. Try writing to a file that you can't overwrite or writing to a file when the disk is full. If you get the Tcl error dialog, you should add some catch commands to handle errors more gracefully (see Section 6.4).

- Try running your application on Windows and Macintosh platforms. Do the windows still look good?

  This test will also help you recognize any assumptions that you may have made about the operating system. If you're relying on UNIX programs, such as rm or lpr, for example, you'll notice right away on the other platforms.

1.2.8   Packaging the program

At this point, your program is finished, tested, and ready to ship. How do you put it in the hands of your customer? There are a few possibilities.

- Your customers already have the latest version of wish installed on their machines. The program may have come bundled with the operating system, or the customers may be using the program for their own projects. In this case, you need to distribute just the script files for your application.

- Your customers don't have `wish`, and they don't want to know about it. In this case, you need to build the `wish` program for their platforms and send them a full-blown distribution, along with your script files. Your customers can unpack your distribution on their machines and run an "install" program to put the executables and the support files in place. In Section 8.3, we'll show you how to write the install program as a `wish` script. After all, you're sending them a `wish`, so you might as well take advantage of it.

- Your customers are occasional users, with access to the Internet. In this case, you can package your application to run inside a Web browser. You just set up a Web page with a reference to your application and put the application script on the Web server. We'll show you how to do this in Section 8.4. When a customer displays your Web page, the browser will automatically download the application script and begin executing it. Browser programs like the Netscape Navigator have a plug-in module that supports this behavior. As long as your customers have the plug-in module installed, they can run any Tcl/Tk applications that you publish.

    Instead of popping up as another window on the desktop, the application will be embedded right in the Web page that the customer is viewing. But aside from that, it will look like an ordinary Tcl/Tk application. And it will be running on the customer's machine, so it won't be slowed down by network traffic. This scheme works best when your application is small (so it can be downloaded quickly) and when you're trying to reach lots of customers who are occasional users.

For our simple sketchpad program, we'll assume that the customers are people fooling around with their new Tcl/Tk installations. So we just need to send them our script. But the final version of our sketchpad also used some library procedures for the color menu and the balloon help and a special bitmap for the pen color. This is typical of many applications. More often than not, you'll find that your customer needs lots of different files to run your application. We'll show you how to create a complete distribution and how to install it in Section 8.3.

Now that you understand the overall development process, we'll explore the finer points of Tk. As we go along, we'll try to capture our ideas in library procedures that you can use in your own applications. If you want to obtain this code, you can download it from the Web site mentioned on page xiv.

Chapter 2
Packing, Gridding, and Placing Windows

You can create a widget as follows:

```
button .b -text "Exit" -command exit
```

But you won't see the widget on the screen until you use another command to position it. You can pack the widget into the bottom of the window, like this:

```
pack .b -side bottom
```

Or, you can put the widget on a virtual grid, like this:

```
grid .b -row 0 -column 0
```

Or, you can place the widget at a particular screen coordinate, like this:

```
place .b -x 10 -y 25
```

The `pack`, `grid`, and `place` commands are the three *geometry managers* in Tk. Each of these commands supports a different model for positioning widgets. The `pack` and `grid` managers have particularly good models, automatically adjusting the layout whenever a window changes size.

In this chapter, we'll examine each of the three geometry managers and show how you can use them to arrange the widgets in your application. Along the way, we'll build many common window arrangements.

We'll also show how you can use the existing geometry managers to build new ones. For example, we'll use the `pack` command to create a notebook that lets you flip through many different "pages" of widgets. We'll use the `place` command to build a paned window with an adjustable sash. These examples not only help you to understand how the geometry managers work but also give you useful code that you can use in your own applications.

2.1 Using the `pack` command

You can use a series of `pack` commands to position the widgets within a window. But you don't give absolute positions for each widget; rather, you give a recipe for laying them out. Before you can write one of these recipes, you must understand how the packer works.

2.1.1 Cavity-based model

Suppose you want to build a simple dialog like the one shown in Figure 2.1. It has a label with the `error` bitmap, another label with a text message, a separator line, and a Dismiss button.

Figure 2.1. Widgets are packed into position to create a simple dialog.

The code to create these widgets looks like this:

```
label .icon -bitmap error
label .mesg -text "Print job failed:
Printer is off-line
or out of paper"
frame .sep -width 100 -height 2 -borderwidth 1 -relief sunken
button .dismiss -text "Dismiss" -command exit
```

There is no "separator" widget, but we can use an empty frame to create the illusion of a separator. We give the frame a height that is exactly twice its border width, so all you can see is its border. And we give the frame a sunken relief, so it looks like a grooved line.

Of course, all of these widgets will be hidden off-screen until we position them with a geometry manager. To get the layout shown in Figure 2.1, we can use the following series of `pack` commands:

```
pack .dismiss -side bottom
pack .sep -side bottom
pack .icon -side left
pack .mesg -side right
```

Each `pack` command positions a widget within its parent window. The entire parent window is treated as an empty cavity. Widgets are packed around the edges of the cavity—

the `top`, `bottom`, `left`, and `right` sides—according to the order of the `pack` statements. As each widget is packed, the cavity gets smaller and smaller, shrinking toward the interior.

The packing process for these commands is illustrated in Figure 2.2. In this case, we are packing four widgets into the main window of the application. We start in Figure 2.2(a) with an empty cavity. The first `pack` command puts the Dismiss button along the bottom edge of the cavity, as shown in Figure 2.2(b). The white area along the bottom edge is referred to as the *parcel* of space allocated for the widget. Notice that the parcel for the Dismiss button occupies the *entire* bottom edge. This is a general feature of the `pack` algorithm. Each widget occupies an entire edge of the cavity, and the area that is left over becomes the cavity for the next `pack` command. When we pack the separator line along the bottom edge, it appears just above the Dismiss button, as shown in Figure 2.2(c).

Notice what happens when we pack the icon in on the left side, as shown in Figure 2.2(d). If you look carefully, you will notice that its parcel extends from the top of the window to the top of the separator line. The icon does not occupy the entire left edge of the window but rather the entire left edge of the cavity at the time that it was packed. This is a subtle distinction, but it can affect the way you lay things out. In this case, the icon will be centered in the area above the separator line, which is what we wanted. If instead we want the icon to be centered along the left edge of the window, we would have to pack it in first, so it would get the entire left edge.

Finally, we pack the message label in on the right side of the cavity, as shown in Figure 2.2(e). This leaves the cavity between the icon and the message for any other widgets that we might happen to pack.

Just before the window appears, the `pack` algorithm performs one last step: It makes the window just big enough to display all of the widgets packed within it. In effect, it "shrink-wraps" a window around its contents, as shown in Figure 2.2(f). This default size is called the *natural size*, or the *requested size*, for the window.

The real strength of the packer lies in this last step. Suppose we change the font on the Dismiss button, making it slightly larger. Or, suppose we put a long paragraph of text into the message label. The packer will automatically adjust the layout to compensate for such changes, and will make the window the proper size to display its contents. If we later pack in more widgets, the packer will again adjust the layout and will expand the window to accommodate them.

2.1.2 Packing options

In the previous section, we set out to build the window shown in Figure 2.1. We managed to get the widgets in their proper places, but the result shown in Figure 2.2(f) doesn't look quite right. For one thing, the widgets are packed together too tightly. This makes the window look cramped and makes the message difficult to read. Also, the separator line should go all the way across the window, from one side to the other, and the error icon should be up a little higher, so it sits in the upper-left corner of the window.

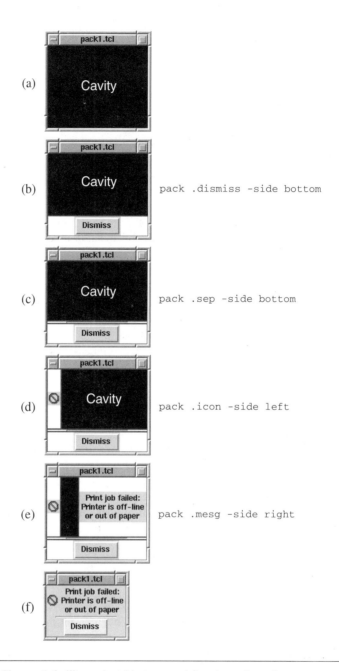

Figure 2.2. The pack facility packs widgets around the edges of a cavity.

All of these things are easy to fix if we add a few options to adjust the packing. We use the -padx and -pady options to add some extra space around each widget. You can see this in Figure 2.3(a) as the shaded area around each widget. We add 4 pixels above and below the Dismiss button and 4 pixels above and below the separator line. We add 8 pixels all the way around the error icon and the message. A little extra padding greatly improves the appearance of the window, as you can see in Figure 2.3(b).

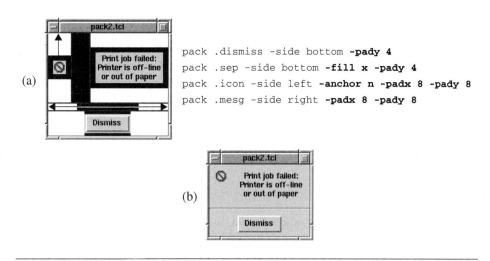

(a)

```
pack .dismiss -side bottom -pady 4
pack .sep -side bottom -fill x -pady 4
pack .icon -side left -anchor n -padx 8 -pady 8
pack .mesg -side right -padx 8 -pady 8
```

(b)

Figure 2.3. Using options to tweak the packing. (a) Diagram of the widget parcels. (b) Screen snapshot of the final result.

Next, we want to fix the position of the error icon. By default, each widget is centered within the parcel of space that the packer allocates. If we want the error icon to sit near the top of the window, we can anchor the icon at the top of its parcel, using the -anchor option. We use -anchor n to anchor on the "north" side of the parcel. You can anchor on any other side of the parcel or in any of the corners, using all of the directions on a compass: n, s, e, w, ne, nw, se, and sw.

In some cases, changing the -anchor option has no effect. For example, since the error icon is packed in on the left side, its parcel has extra space only on the top and bottom. The icon cannot shift left or right, only up or down. Setting -anchor e or -anchor w does nothing in this case. Similarly, setting -anchor ne or -anchor nw is the same as setting -anchor n. When you first start using the packer, this can be confusing. If you blindly add a few different anchor settings, you may not see any change on the screen. When this happens, walk through the `pack` algorithm for your window and diagram the parcels as we did in Figure 2.2. Once you understand how the parcels are laid out, you will understand how you can anchor the widgets within their parcels.

Finally, we want to fix the separator line. Instead of anchoring it on one side of the parcel or the other, we can use the -fill option to have it extend all the way across its parcel. By default, widgets are packed with -fill none, so they retain their normal size. You can use -fill x to make a widget fill horizontally, -fill y to make it fill vertically, or -fill both to make it fill in both directions. In this case, we use -fill x, since we want the separator line to extend horizontally across the window.

In some cases, changing the -fill option has no effect. For example, since the separator line is packed in on the bottom side, its parcel has extra space only on the left and the right. If we used -fill y instead of -fill x, the separator line would remain centered in the parcel. The separator line would try to fill in the vertical direction, but it would have nowhere to go. If we used -fill both, the widget would fill horizontally and would try to fill vertically, but it would have nowhere to go. The effect of -fill both would be the same as -fill x. Again, when you first start using the packer, this can be confusing. And again, you should walk through the pack algorithm and diagram the widget parcels to understand the various -fill settings for each parcel.

2.1.3   Packing order

The order of your pack commands is extremely important. The *packing order* determines the order in which widgets are added to the cavity. If you change the packing order, you may get results very different from what you expected.

In the previous example, the packing order was .dismiss, .sep, .icon, and .mesg. Suppose we change the packing order by rearranging the pack commands as shown in Figure 2.4(a). This changes the layout completely, as shown in Figure 2.4(b). Even though we packed the Dismiss button on the bottom, it somehow appears in the middle of the window!

This is easy to understand if you diagram the widget parcels, as we did in Figure 2.4(c). In this case, we pack .icon first along the left edge, followed by .mesg along the right edge. At this point, the cavity that remains is between them. When we pack .dismiss and .sep on the bottom, they appear on the bottom side of this cavity, which is really in the middle of the window. If we were to pack any other widgets in this window, they would appear in the cavity that remains, which is just above the separator.

2.1.4   Hierarchical packing

At this point, you might be starting to think that the packer is evil. And if you had to spend most of your time figuring out a clever packing order, it would be. But there is a better way of using the packer, one that eliminates most of the headaches.

To see the problem clearly, let's tackle a really difficult problem with the packer. Suppose you want to create a window like the one shown in Figure 2.5(a). Four buttons—A, B, C, and D—are all arranged in a square. We could handle this problem with the grid com-

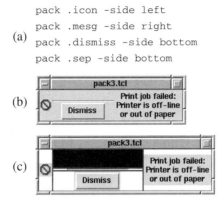

Figure 2.4. Changing the order of `pack` commands changes the packing. (a) A different series of pack commands. (b) Resulting screen snapshot. (c) Diagram of the widget parcels.

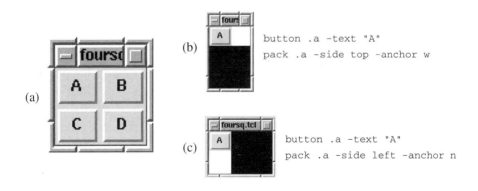

Figure 2.5. A difficult job for the packer. (a) Desired layout. (b) Packing the first widget on the top won't work. (c) Packing the first widget on the left side won't work either.

mand, which we'll talk about later in this chapter. But for the moment, assume that we must use the packer.

Suppose that we pack A in first on the top side, as shown in Figure 2.5(b). Remember, the packer allocates an entire side for each widget that we pack. If we pack A along the top, there is no way that we can pack B in the same parcel, next to it. B would be packed in the cavity area, which is drawn in black. Instead, suppose that we pack A in on the left side, as shown in Figure 2.5(c). Again, the packer allocates the entire side for **A**, and there is no way that we can pack **C** below it in the same parcel.

There is a better way to solve this problem. We add some frames to make our packing job easier, as shown in Figure 2.6. Each frame acts as a container for a group of widgets. We create a frame called `.f1` and pack **A** and **B** into the frame on the left side. We create another frame, called `.f2`, and pack **C** and **D** into it on the left side. We then pack the two frames into the top of the main window. Just before the window appears, the packer shrink-wraps everything down to a minimum size, and we get the arrangement we were looking for in Figure 2.5(a).

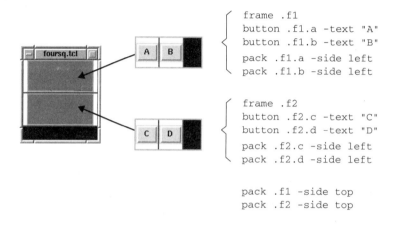

```
frame .f1
button .f1.a -text "A"
button .f1.b -text "B"
pack .f1.a -side left
pack .f1.b -side left

frame .f2
button .f2.c -text "C"
button .f2.d -text "D"
pack .f2.c -side left
pack .f2.d -side left

pack .f1 -side top
pack .f2 -side top
```

Figure 2.6. Adding some frames can simplify packing.

Each frame has its own cavity and its own packing order. The main window also has a separate cavity and a separate packing order. In the two frames, we pack everything from left to right, so it is easy to keep track of the packing. In the main window, we pack everything from top to bottom, so again, it is easy to visualize the final result.

Notice that when we introduced the two frames, we renamed the widgets to be children of these frames. Instead of having a widget named `.a`, we have a widget named `.f1.a`. There is a way to avoid this: You could use the `-in` option of the `pack` command to pack a widget into a sibling frame, but we don't recommend it. Doing so can lead to problems with the window-stacking order that are difficult to understand and to debug. It is better to make each widget a child of the frame or the toplevel that contains it.

It is easier to handle an arrangement like Figure 2.5(a) with the `grid` command. But you can use the strategy that we've shown here to handle many other packing problems. Suppose that you want to build a dialog like the one shown in Figure 2.7. The widgets in

this dialog don't really line up on a grid, so the `grid` command won't help in this case.
The dialog has an icon and a message along the top edge. These widgets would be easy to
pack if we grouped them together in a frame. The dialog also has two buttons along the
bottom edge. We should put these widgets in their own frame, too.

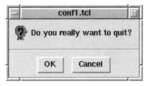

Figure 2.7. A confirmation dialog.

The code to create the confirmation dialog looks like this:

```
frame .top
label .top.icon -bitmap questhead
label .top.mesg -text "Do you really want to quit?"
pack .top.icon -side left
pack .top.mesg -side right

frame .sep -height 2 -borderwidth 1 -relief sunken

frame .controls
button .controls.ok -text "OK" -command exit
button .controls.cancel -text "Cancel" -command exit
pack .controls.ok -side left -padx 4
pack .controls.cancel -side left -padx 4

pack .top -padx 8 -pady 8
pack .sep -fill x -pady 4
pack .controls -pady 4
```

The widgets are packed together as shown in Figure 2.8. We start by creating the top frame
and packing in the `questhead` icon and the message label. Next, we create the separator
line. This time we set the height, but we don't set the width. The packer will automatically
fix the width for us if we pack with `-fill x`, so setting a particular width is unnecessary.
Next, we create the control frame and pack in the OK and Cancel buttons. Finally, we pack
the top frame, the separator line, and the control frame from top to bottom in the main
window.

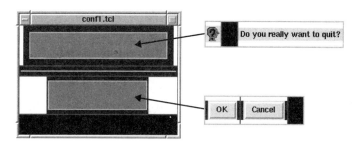

Figure 2.8. Using frames to build the confirmation dialog.

Notice that in the code for this last step, we didn't specify a `-side` option in the `pack` commands. The default side is `top`, and it is quite common to leave this out when packing things top to bottom.

2.1.5 Compressing windows

The packer gives each window a default size but does not fix the size of the window. The user can resize any top-level window by grabbing and moving part of its decorative border, and the packer will automatically adjust the internal layout for the new size. But what happens if a window is compressed smaller than its natural size?

Figure 2.9 shows what happens as our notice dialog is made smaller and smaller. Some of the widgets are compressed, and when there is no more room for them, they disappear entirely. Notice that the text message is squeezed out first, followed by the error icon, the separator, and finally the Dismiss button. This order is not arbitrary. It is exactly the opposite of the packing order for this window. The Dismiss button is packed first. It takes up a certain area, and the remaining widgets get whatever area is left over. The separator line is packed next, and the remaining widgets get whatever area is left over. By default, the packer gives a window its natural size, so there is just enough room for all of the widgets to fit inside it. But if the window is compressed to a smaller size, widgets later in the packing order lose out.

If a toplevel has frames within it, the size changes propagate from the toplevel to the frame and then to the widgets within it. You can see this in Figure 2.10, which shows what happens as our confirmation dialog is made smaller and smaller. In this example, there is a frame at the top with the icon and the text message, a separator line, and another frame at the bottom with the OK and Cancel buttons. When the width of the window is compressed, the top frame and the bottom frame are compressed as well. Within the top frame, the icon is packed first, so it takes up its normal area, and the label is crushed to a smaller width. Likewise, within the bottom frame, the OK button is packed first, so the Cancel button is

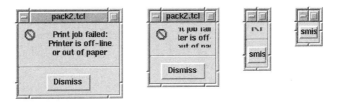

Figure 2.9. If a window is resized to be smaller, some widgets may disappear. Those packed early remain visible.

Figure 2.10. Widgets within a frame, such as the OK and Cancel buttons, gradually disappear. When there is no more room, the frame itself disappears.

crushed to a smaller width. As the height of the window is compressed, the bottom frame is crushed and eventually disappears. After that, the separator line disappears, followed by the top frame. Again, this is exactly the opposite of the packing order for these elements.

There is a lesson to learn from all this: When everything else is equal, you should pack the most important widgets first. That way, they will be visible even if the window is compressed to a smaller size. For example, we packed the confirmation dialog in Figure 2.10 from top to bottom. If instead we had packed it from bottom to top, the OK and Cancel buttons would stay visible as the window is compressed, giving the user a chance to dismiss the dialog. The OK and Cancel buttons are probably more important than the icon and the text message, so they should be packed first.

As another example, consider the listbox shown in Figure 2.11. We could pack the listbox first or the scrollbar first, and initially, they would look the same. But if we pack the scrollbar first, it won't disappear when the window is compressed. You can see this packing order in the following code:

```
scrollbar .sbar -command {.lbox yview}
pack .sbar -side right -fill y
listbox .lbox -width 15 -height 5 -yscrollcommand {.sbar set}
pack .lbox -side left
```

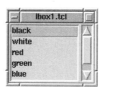

Figure 2.11. The scrollbar is packed before the listbox, so it does not disappear when the window is resized.

```
.lbox insert 0 "black" "white" "red" "green" "blue" "yellow"
.lbox selection set 0
```

Scrollbars should always be packed ahead of the widget they control. By the same token, the menu bar should always be the first thing packed into the main window of the application.

If you are sensitive to the packing order, you can create windows that are still usable even under the worst circumstances. But you can also prevent problems like this from happening in the first place. You can prevent a window from being resized at all, or you can give a window a minimum size, so that it can't be compressed too small. We will show you how to do this when we talk about top-level windows in Chapter 7.

2.1.6   Enlarging windows

In the previous section, we saw what happens when a window is compressed. But what happens when a window is enlarged? For example, suppose you want to see more of the listbox shown in Figure 2.11, so you enlarge the window. You get the result shown in Figure 2.12(a). Instead of getting larger, the listbox simply clings to the edge of the window, and a gap forms between the listbox and the scrollbar.

This may look strange, but if you think about how the packer works, it makes perfect sense. You could diagram the widget parcels as shown in Figure 2.12(b). As you recall, we packed the scrollbar on the right side and had it fill in the y-direction, so it would take up the entire right edge. Then we packed the listbox on the left side. When the window has its natural size, the listbox and the scrollbar fit snugly inside it. But when the window is enlarged, empty space appears around the listbox. For the moment, think about the empty space above and below the listbox. Since the listbox was packed with the default -fill none option, it remains centered in its parcel. We could fix this by packing the listbox with -fill y.

But there is another problem. There is also a gap between the listbox and the scrollbar. Packing the listbox with -fill x or -fill both won't fill in the gap. Remember, the -fill option affects only how the widget fills its parcel, which is the white area shown in

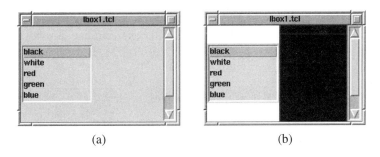

(a)   (b)

Figure 2.12. When the window is enlarged, the cavity appears. (a) Screen snapshot. (b) Diagram of the widget parcels.

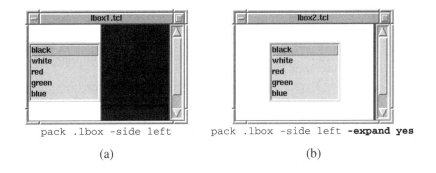

pack .lbox -side left   pack .lbox -side left **-expand yes**

(a)   (b)

Figure 2.13. The -expand option expands the parcel of space for the widget. (a) With -expand turned off, the parcel clings to the side where it was packed. (b) With -expand turned on, the parcel expands to cover any empty space in the cavity.

Figure 2.12(b). The parcel itself is packed tightly against the edge of the window. The empty space between the two parcels is the cavity, where other widgets could be packed.

We need a way to expand the parcel for the listbox so that it takes up the extra space. The `pack` command has a -expand option to handle this. We can pack the listbox so that its parcel expands into the cavity, like this:

```
pack .lbox -side left -expand yes
```

This gives us the result shown in Figure 2.13(b). This is almost what we wanted. The listbox is centered in a large parcel of space.

We could adjust its anchor point. Or, we could have it fill the entire parcel, like this:

```
pack .lbox -side left -expand yes -fill both
```

This creates the desired layout, which is shown in Figure 2.14(b). The lesson is this: If you want a widget to get larger when the window gets larger, you must use both `-expand` and `-fill`. The `-expand` option expands the space around the widget, and the `-fill` option fills that space.

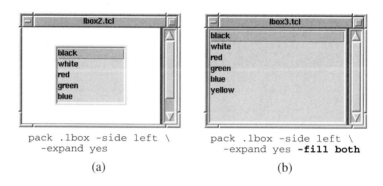

```
pack .lbox -side left \            pack .lbox -side left \
    -expand yes                        -expand yes -fill both
```

(a)   (b)

Figure 2.14. The `-fill` option causes a widget to fill up space in its parcel. (a) With `-fill` turned off, the widget sits at its anchor point in the center of the parcel. (b) With `-fill both`, the widget stretches in the *x*- and *y*-directions to cover its parcel.

You might think that all widgets should be packed to expand and fill, but this is rarely the case. When users resize a window, they are not trying to make the buttons or the scrollbars bigger. They are trying to see more of a listbox or a canvas or a text widget. The users want these types of widgets to get bigger, so you should pack them to expand and fill. But users want scrollbars to get only longer, so you should pack them only to fill.

Sometimes you'll want to pack a widget only to expand. This is useful, for example, when you want to create a row of evenly spaced buttons. You can pack them all to expand but not fill, and any extra space will be divided evenly as padding between them.

If a toplevel widget has frames within it, the size changes propagate from the toplevel to the frame and then to the widgets within it. Suppose we change the packing of our confirmation dialog to use `-expand` and `-fill` as follows:

```
frame .top
label .top.icon -bitmap questhead
label .top.mesg -text "Do you really want to quit?"
pack .top.icon -side left
pack .top.mesg -side right -expand yes

frame .sep -height 2 -borderwidth 1 -relief sunken
```

```
frame .controls
button .controls.ok -text "OK" -command exit
button .controls.cancel -text "Cancel" -command exit
pack .controls.ok -side left -padx 4 -expand yes
pack .controls.cancel -side left -padx 4 -expand yes


pack .top -padx 8 -pady 8 -expand yes -fill both
pack .sep -fill x -pady 4
pack .controls -pady 4 -fill x
```

The top frame is packed to expand and fill. So when the window is enlarged, the top frame gets bigger. This creates more area for the icon and the message within it. The icon is packed tightly against the left side, and the message is packed to expand but not to fill. This creates the effect shown in Figure 2.15. The icon sits on the left side of the window, but the message floats in the middle.

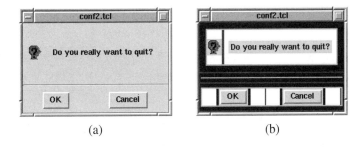

(a)   (b)

Figure 2.15. The confirmation dialog is packed so that the top frame expands, but the separator line and the bottom frame simply fill in the *x*-direction. (a) Screen snapshot. (b) Diagram of the widget parcels.

The separator line and the bottom frame are both packed to fill in the *x*-direction. Instead of getting bigger, these elements just get longer. When the bottom frame gets longer, it creates more room for the OK and Cancel buttons within it. These are both packed on the left side, so normally they would sit on the left side of the frame. But they are also packed to expand, so their parcels expand evenly to cover any empty space on the right. Since they are not packed to fill, they float in the middle of their parcels, giving them a nice spacing. Once again, you can see the difference between -expand and -fill. If you pack a widget to expand, the space around it expands. But if you pack it to fill, it will fill up that space and get bigger.

2.1.7   Unpacking widgets

If you create a widget but forget to pack it, it still exists. You can configure it or even invoke it from within the program. You just won't be able to see it anywhere on the screen. You might think that this is really more of a bug than a feature, but it turns out that you can use this to your advantage. You can make a widget come and go without destroying it, simply by packing it when it's needed and unpacking it when it's not.

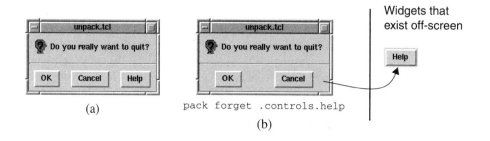

Figure 2.16. (a) A Help button is added to the confirmation dialog. (b) The Help button is unpacked. Although it is off the screen, it is still active and can be packed again later.

For example, suppose we add a Help button to our confirmation dialog, as shown in Figure 2.16(a). We might use the following code to create and pack the button:

```
button .controls.help -text "Help"
pack .controls.help -side left -expand yes -padx 4
```

Whenever we load a new question into this dialog, we could configure the Help button to bring up a viewer with some helpful documentation. But suppose that a particular question has no help information and that we want the Help button to go away. Instead of destroying it, we could simply hide it like this:

```
pack forget .controls.help
```

This command removes the button from the packing order, so it disappears from the screen. But it still exists. The button retains all of its configuration options and is ready when we need it again. We can make it reappear simply by packing it again:

```
pack .controls.help -side left -expand yes -padx 4
```

This appends it onto the packing order for the `.controls` frame, putting the button back on the end of the row of control buttons. This is fine for the current example. But if we wanted to change the position of the button, we could use the `-before` or `-after` options of the `pack` command to insert it elsewhere in the packing order. For example, we could put it between the OK and Cancel buttons, like this:

```
pack .controls.help -before .controls.cancel \
    -side left -expand yes -padx 4
```

We can use the idea of packing and unpacking widgets on a much larger scale to create the notebook shown in Figure 2.17. This notebook has three "pages" of widgets. Each page is an ordinary frame with many different widgets packed inside it. A radiobox above the notebook selects which page is active at any given time. When the Colors page is active, it is packed into the notebook. When another page is selected, the Colors page is unpacked, using `pack forget`, and the new page is packed into the notebook. One of the pages is always packed and visible, and the others sit off-screen. Using a notebook like this, you can organize the controls in your application so the user isn't faced with a barrage of dialogs or a brick wall of buttons.

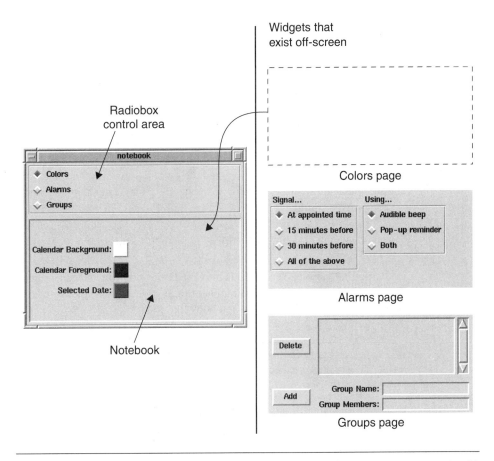

Figure 2.17. A notebook has a series of frames that sit off-screen. When you change pages, the old page is unpacked, and a new page is packed in its place.

We will design the notebook so that you can use it as follows. First, you create a note-book:

```
notebook_create .nb
pack .nb -side bottom -expand yes -fill both -padx 4 -pady 4
```

This creates a notebook called .nb and packs it into the main window. When you want to add a page to the notebook, you call another procedure:

```
set p1 [notebook_page .nb "Page #1"]
```

This creates an empty frame within the notebook and returns its window name. You create the widgets on this page as children of this frame. For example, you could add an icon and a message label to the page:

```
label $p1.icon -bitmap info
pack $p1.icon -side left -padx 8 -pady 8
label $p1.mesg -text "Something\non\nPage #1"
pack $p1.mesg -side left -expand yes -pady 8
```

You could create another page in a similar manner:

```
set p2 [notebook_page .nb "Page #2"]
label $p2.mesg -text "Something else on Page #2"
pack $p2.mesg -padx 8 -pady 8 -expand yes
```

Each page has a symbolic name that you can use to refer to it later on. We created the first page with the name "Page #1" and the second page with the name "Page #2". You can use these names when you want to display the pages. For example, you can display the first page with a command like this:

```
notebook_display .nb "Page #1"
```

You can display the second page with a command like this:

```
notebook_display .nb "Page #2"
```

By putting these two commands into a radiobox control, you can let the user select the page. We'll develop a radiobox component in Section 8.2.1, but let's make use of it here. You can create a radiobox for the notebook like this:

```
radiobox_create .controls
pack .controls -side top -fill x -padx 4 -pady 4
radiobox_add .controls "Show Page #1" {
    notebook_display .nb "Page #1"
}
radiobox_add .controls "Show Page #2" {
    notebook_display .nb "Page #2"
}
```

The radiobox lets us display the two simple pages that we created for the notebook, as shown in Figure 2.18.

Now that we understand how the notebook should work, we can see how it is imple-mented. First, we'll look at the notebook_create procedure, which creates a notebook:

```
proc notebook_create {win} {
    global nbInfo
```

(a)   (b)

Figure 2.18. A radiobox controls a simple notebook with two pages.

```
frame $win -class Notebook
pack propagate $win 0
set nbInfo($win-count) 0
set nbInfo($win-pages) ""
set nbInfo($win-current) ""
return $win
}
```

We start by creating the hull frame for the notebook. We give this frame the class name `Notebook` so you can specify resources for the notebook in the option database. For example, we include the following resources with the notebook code so that by default, all notebooks have a sunken border:

```
option add *Notebook.borderWidth 2 widgetDefault
option add *Notebook.relief sunken widgetDefault
```

The `pack propagate` command helps us control the size of the notebook window. We'll ignore this for now and explain it in detail later.

When we create each notebook, we save some information in the global `nbInfo` array. Each notebook has three fields in this array: a count of pages, a list of pages, and the name of the current page. Each of these fields will be updated later, when pages are added or displayed in the notebook. Finally, we return the name of the new notebook as the result of this operation.

Now we'll look at the `notebook_page` procedure, which adds a new page to an existing notebook. You pass in the name of a notebook created by `notebook_create` and a name identifying the new page:

```
proc notebook_page {win name} {
    global nbInfo
    set page "$win.page[incr nbInfo($win-count)]"
    lappend nbInfo($win-pages) $page
    set nbInfo($win-page-$name) $page
```

```
frame $page
if {$nbInfo($win-count) == 1} {
    after idle [list notebook_display $win $name]
}
return $page
}
```

We start by generating a unique name for the frame that contains the page. We'll call this frame the *page window*. We use the current page count in nbInfo($win-count) to generate unique names. If the notebook is named .nb, the page windows will be named .nb.page1, .nb.page2, .nb.page3, and so on. Whatever name we generate, we save it in the page variable, and we append it onto the list of pages for this notebook.

We associate the page window with a page name, such as "Page #1", which is passed in to this procedure. We do this by storing the page window in the array element nbInfo($win-page-$name). Later on, if we have the notebook name $win and the page name $name, we can look in this array and find the corresponding page window.

Finally, we create the frame for the page window, and we return its name as the result of this command. You can capture this result and use it to create child widgets on the page, as we showed earlier.

If this is the first page in the notebook, we arrange for it to be displayed when the application is idle. By then, the rest of the pages in the notebook should be in place, so we will be able to size the notebook properly. Notice that we're careful to wrap the notebook_display command with [list ...] when passing it to the after command, for the reasons described in Section 3.1.5.

Now we'll look at the notebook_display procedure, which brings up a particular page in the notebook. You pass in the name of a notebook and the name of the page that you want to display:

```
proc notebook_display {win name} {
    global nbInfo

    set page ""
    if {[info exists nbInfo($win-page-$name)]} {
        set page $nbInfo($win-page-$name)
    } elseif {[winfo exists $win.page$name]} {
        set page $win.page$name
    }
    if {$page == ""} {
        error "bad notebook page \"$name\""
    }

    notebook_fix_size $win

    if {$nbInfo($win-current) != ""} {
        pack forget $nbInfo($win-current)
    }
    pack $page -expand yes -fill both
```

```
            set nbInfo($win-current) $page
     }
```

If the page name is a symbolic name, such as "Page #1", we can find the corresponding page window in the slot `nbInfo($win-page-$name)` that we created earlier. We use
`info exists` to see whether this slot exists, and then we look up its value. To add some
flexibility, we also allow the page name to be a number, such as 0, 1, 2, and so on. In that
case, we look for a page window with the corresponding number. If for some reason we
can't find a page window by using either of these schemes, we use the `error` command to
signal the error.

Finally, we are ready to display the page. We get the name of the current page window
from `nbInfo($win-current)`, and we use `pack forget` to hide this page. Then we
pack the new page into the notebook frame and save it as the current page window. The
next time we call `notebook_display`, we will unpack this page and pack another in its
place, making it the current page.

Each page will probably be a different size. After all, the packer shrink-wraps each
frame around its contents. The Colors page in Figure 2.17, for instance, could be shrink-
wrapped much smaller than the Groups page. The notebook frame will also shrink-wrap
itself around the current page. When we switch between two pages like Colors and
Groups, the notebook window will abruptly change size unless we take some extra steps to
prevent this.

The `pack propagate` command, which we ignored earlier, prevents the notebook
from changing size:

```
.proc notebook_create {win} {
     global nbInfo
     frame $win -class Notebook
     pack propagate $win 0
     . . .
     }
```

Giving a zero value disables size propagation for the notebook window `$win`. This means
that the packer will not shrink-wrap the notebook around its current page. But we could set
the size of a notebook frame, such as `.nb`, like this:

```
.nb configure -width 3i -height 2i
```

Now, the notebook will be that size no matter what page is packed into it. The trick is to
choose a size that is just big enough for the largest page.

We use the procedure `notebook_fix_size` to scan through all of the pages and to
set the notebook size accordingly. We call this procedure from `notebook_display`
whenever we display a page. The procedure is implemented like this:

```
proc notebook_fix_size {win} {
     global nbInfo

     update idletasks
```

```
        set maxw 0
        set maxh 0
        foreach page $nbInfo($win-pages) {
            set w [winfo reqwidth $page]
            if {$w > $maxw} {
                set maxw $w
            }
            set h [winfo reqheight $page]
            if {$h > $maxh} {
                set maxh $h
            }
        }
        set bd [$win cget -borderwidth]
        set maxw [expr $maxw+2*$bd]
        set maxh [expr $maxh+2*$bd]
        $win configure -width $maxw -height $maxh
    }
```

We start with an `update idletasks` command. This forces the packer to finish
packing each of the pages, so we can figure out how big each page wants to be. The packer
normally waits until the application is idle before carrying out `pack` commands. This
improves its efficiency, since it applies all of the size changes at once. But in this case, we
cannot make our own size calculations until the packer has done its job, so we use
`update idletasks` to force it into action. If we had forgotten this, the
`winfo reqwidth` and `winfo reqheight` commands might report the wrong size (a
zero size or a partially packed size) for the notebook pages. We'll take a closer look at the
`update` command in Section 3.1.2.

After the sizes have been updated, we scan through the list of pages in
`nbInfo($win-pages)` and determine the maximum width and height for any page. We
use `winfo reqwidth` and `winfo reqheight` to get the requested size for each page.
The requested size is how big a widget wants to be. For a simple widget, such as a button,
this depends on the size of the text message it displays. For a frame, it depends on the size
and placement of the widgets packed within it; in other words, it depends on its shrink-
wrapped size. Although we used `pack propagate` to disable shrink-wrapping on the
notebook frame, we did not disable it on each of the individual pages. Therefore each page
will report its shrink-wrapped size, which is just big enough to display its contents.

We want the notebook to be big enough to display the largest page. But the notebook
window also has a border around it. Once we have determined the maximum size, we
compensate for the border and then configure the notebook frame to be that size. When we
pack each page in `notebook_display`, we turn on the `-expand` and `-fill` options, so
the smaller pages will stretch to cover the extra area.

How we pack the notebook itself will determine its overall size. We disabled its own
automatic sizing and explicitly set its width and height. So the requested size for the
overall notebook will be the width and height that we set. When the notebook is packed
into its parent window, it will ask to be at least this big. Of course, if its parent window is

compressed, the notebook may also be compressed, depending on where it appears in its parent's packing order. If the parent window is expanded, the notebook may also be expanded, again, depending on how it was packed. If we pack the notebook as we did earlier, the notebook will stretch to cover any extra space:

```
notebook_create .nb
pack .nb -side bottom -expand yes -fill both -padx 4 -pady 4
```

Since each of its pages is packed to expand and fill, they will stretch as well.

2.2   Using the `grid` command

Instead of packing widgets into a cavity, you can lay them out on a virtual grid of rows and columns. This model is much simpler than the cavity-based model of the packer but is just as powerful.

2.2.1   Grid-based model

A grid can have any number of rows and columns, and each row/column can have a different size. The combination of a row number and a column number identifies the space where a widget can reside. We'll refer to this space as a *parcel*.

The grid is good at aligning widgets with one another. Suppose, for example, that we create a canvas and its scrollbars, like this:

```
canvas .display -width 3i -height 2i -background black \
    -xscrollcommand {.xsbar set} -yscrollcommand {.ysbar set}
scrollbar .xsbar -orient horizontal -command {.display xview}
scrollbar .ysbar -orient vertical -command {.display yview}

.display create line 98.0 298.0 98.0 83.0 -fill green -width 2
.display create line 98.0 83.0 101.0 69.0 -fill green -width 2
.display create line 101.0 69.0 108.0 56.0 -fill green -width 2
...
```

We want the scrollbar for the *y*-direction aligned with the right side of the canvas and the scrollbar for the *x*-direction aligned with the bottom. These widgets naturally fall onto a grid, so we can use the following `grid` commands to position them:

```
grid .display .ysbar
grid .xsbar      x
```

If you mention several widgets in the same `grid` command, they are placed in different columns on the same row. So the first `grid` command represents the first row of our grid.

The canvas sits in the first column and the *y*-scrollbar in the second column, as shown in Figure 2.19(a). The next `grid` command is treated as another row definition. This time, the *x*-scrollbar sits in the first column. The x character represents an empty parcel, so nothing sits in the second column. In this case, we could have left the x out. But if we had more widgets in a third column or fourth column, we could use the x as a placeholder to skip over a parcel that we want to remain empty.

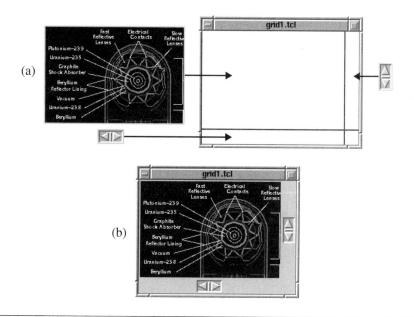

Figure 2.19. The `grid` facility aligns widgets on rows and columns. (a) Widgets are added to the grid. (b) Screen snapshot of the result.

Just like the packer, the gridder does a final "shrink-wrap" step before a window is displayed. The gridder sets the size of each row and column so that all of the widgets fit snugly within it. As you can see in Figure 2.19, the first column is dominated by the width of the canvas and the second column by the width of the y-scrollbar. Likewise, the first row is dominated by the height of the canvas and the second row by the height of the x-scrollbar. The dominant widgets fit snugly in their parcels, and the others are centered in the extra space.

Figure 2.19(b) shows the final result, which is not quite right. The scrollbars are aligned with the canvas, but they're too short. We'll see how to correct this by adding some grid options.

2.2.2 Gridding options

In the previous section, we saw how you can write `grid` commands that look like the arrangement you're trying to build. This is convenient in many cases, but it does make the order of your grid commands important, as it was for the packer. You can avoid this issue by using the -row and -column options to assign specific row and column coordinates to each widget as it is added to the grid. For example, we could rewrite the grid commands for our canvas example like this:

```
grid .display -row 0 -column 0
grid .ysbar -row 0 -column 1
grid .xsbar -row 1 -column 0
```

With explicit coordinates, we can put these commands in any order, and the effect would be the same. This form requires a little more typing, but it makes it easier to rearrange the widgets on the grid if the need arises.

Now let's get back to the scrollbars in Figure 2.19. As we pointed out earlier, they are in the right positions but are too short. Each scrollbar is smaller than its parcel and by default it is centered in the extra space. We need something like the -fill option on the packer to make each one stretch to cover its parcel.

The gridder has a -sticky option that controls how a widget fits within its parcel. You simply give it the sides of the parcel that you want a widget to stick to. You use n for the north side, s for south, e for east, and w for west. For example, we could fix our scrollbars like this:

```
grid .display -row 0 -column 0 -sticky nsew
grid .ysbar -row 0 -column 1 -sticky ns
grid .xsbar -row 1 -column 0 -sticky ew
```

We made the *y*-scrollbar stick to the north and south sides of its parcel, causing it to stretch along the right side of the canvas. We made the *x*-scrollbar stick to the east and west sides of its parcel, causing it to stretch along the bottom. This is illustrated in Figure 2.20.

The -sticky option takes the place of the packer's -anchor and -fill. Making a widget stick to one side is like setting the -anchor option of the packer. Making a widget stick to two opposite sides is like setting the -fill option. Notice that we gridded the .display canvas with -sticky nsew. We made it stick to all sides so that it will completely cover its parcel. This is the equivalent of -fill both for the packer.

The gridder has a few other options, which we will see in another example. Suppose we want to build a desktop calculator like the one shown in Figure 2.21. This is basically a collection of buttons, all neatly arranged on a grid. As we'll see in Section 7.5.3, this calculator handles numbers that are arbitrarily large, so we've added a scrollbar to adjust the readout.

We could create the widgets like this:

```
button .quit -text "Off" -command exit
entry .readout -state disabled -textvariable current \
    -xscrollcommand {.sbar set}
scrollbar .sbar -orient horizontal \
    -command {.readout xview}

button .key0  -text "0" -width 3 -command {keypress "0"}
```

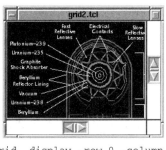

```
grid .display -row 0 -column 0          grid .display -row 0 -column 0 -sticky nsew
grid .ysbar   -row 0 -column 1          grid .ysbar   -row 0 -column 1 -sticky ns
grid .xsbar   -row 1 -column 0          grid .xsbar   -row 1 -column 0 -sticky ew
```

(a)   (b)

Figure 2.20. (a) By default, each widget is centered in its parcel. (b) The -sticky option attaches a widget to the various sides of its parcel.

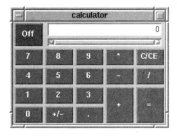

Figure 2.21. The gridder aligns the keys for a desktop calculator. Some of the widgets span more than one row or column.

```
button .key1   -text "1" -width 3 -command {keypress "1"}
button .key2   -text "2" -width 3 -command {keypress "2"}
button .key3   -text "3" -width 3 -command {keypress "3"}
button .key4   -text "4" -width 3 -command {keypress "4"}
button .key5   -text "5" -width 3 -command {keypress "5"}
button .key6   -text "6" -width 3 -command {keypress "6"}
button .key7   -text "7" -width 3 -command {keypress "7"}
button .key8   -text "8" -width 3 -command {keypress "8"}
button .key9   -text "9" -width 3 -command {keypress "9"}
button .point  -text "." -width 3 -command {keypress "."}
```

```
button .plus  -text "+" -width 3 -command {keypress "+"}
button .minus -text "-" -width 3 -command {keypress "-"}
button .times -text "*" -width 3 -command {keypress "*"}
button .div   -text "/" -width 3 -command {keypress "/"}
button .equal -text "=" -width 3 -command {keypress "="}
button .sign  -text "+/-" -width 3 -command {keypress "+/-"}
button .clear -text "C/CE" -width 3 -command {keypress "C/CE"}
```

We use the gridder to arrange these widgets:

```
grid .quit .readout -sticky nsew
grid .sbar -column 1 -sticky nsew
grid .key7 .key8 .key9 .times .clear -sticky nsew
grid .key4 .key5 .key6 .minus .div   -sticky nsew
grid .key1 .key2 .key3 .plus  .equal -sticky nsew
grid .key0 .sign .point -sticky nsew

grid configure .quit -rowspan 2
grid configure .sbar -columnspan 4 -padx 4
grid configure .readout -columnspan 4 -padx 4
grid configure .plus -rowspan 2
grid configure .equal -rowspan 2
```

The first set of `grid` commands adds the widgets to the grid in their respective rows and columns. But notice how both the `.readout` entry and its scrollbar stretch from the Off button to the right side of the window, across four columns in the grid. Similarly, the Off button spans the two rows containing the readout and the scrollbar. The + and = buttons also span two rows in the lower-right corner. You can adjust the span of a widget like this by setting its `-rowspan` or `-columnspan` option. In this case, we had the `.readout` entry and its scrollbar span four columns. The Off, +, and = buttons span two rows.

When you change the span of a widget, its parcel expands to cover the extra rows toward the bottom or extra columns toward the right. How the widget fills that extra space depends on the `-sticky` option. In this case, we set `-sticky nsew` for all of the widgets, so no matter how the parcels expand, the widgets will stretch to cover them.

Just like the packer, the gridder supports padding by means of the `-padx` and `-pady` options. In this example, we added a little padding around the readout, to give it some breathing room.

You can set any of these options when a widget is first added to the grid, or you can do it later on with a `grid configure` command. In this case, we used the `grid configure` command to set the spans and the padding. We could have included these options in the first `grid` command, like this:

```
grid .quit .readout -sticky nsew -columnspan 4 -padx 4 -pady 4
```

In that case, they would have applied to both `.quit` and `.readout`, which is not what we intended. Sometimes it is easier to put all of the widgets into the grid first and to configure a few of them later. Sometimes it is easier to put the widgets into the grid one at a time and to configure them as they go in. You may use either method depending on the problem at hand.

2.2.3 Resizing windows

Like the packer, the gridder has a recipe for laying out your window. So if the window changes size, the gridder can adjust the layout to compensate. As you can see in Figure 2.22, the gridder does a fairly poor job of this by default. The gridder fixes all of the rows and columns at their shrink-wrapped size. When the window is compressed, the outermost rows and columns disappear, and you see whatever is in the middle of the grid. When the window is enlarged, the grid keeps its size and floats in the center.

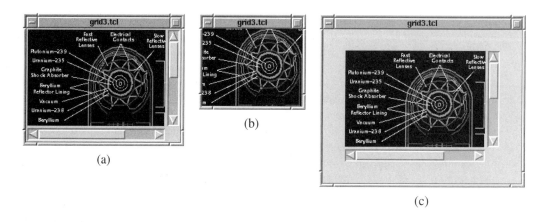

Figure 2.22. By default, the gridder handles size changes poorly. (a) Normal size. (b) Window is compressed. (c) Window is enlarged.

You can fix this by configuring certain rows and columns to change size. For example, think about the grid in Figure 2.22. It belongs to the main window ".", since the widgets `.display`, `.xsbar`, and `.ysbar` are children of the main window. When we resize the window, we want the width of the canvas to change, but we want the width of the y-scroll-bar to stay the same. This means that we want only the first column to change size. We can configure it like this:

```
grid columnconfigure . 0 -weight 1
```

This says that we are configuring column 0 of a grid in the main window ".". Remember, all rows and columns are indexed starting from 0.

By default, all rows and columns have a weight 0, so they don't change size. We make the column resizable by setting its `-weight` option to an integer greater than 0. When the window changes size, the area is divided up among the rows and columns according to their weight. If one column has a weight 2 and another has a weight 1, the first will get twice the extra area, or it will lose twice the area, compared to the second.

Similarly, we want the height of the canvas to change but want the height of the *x*-scrollbar to stay the same. This means that we want only the first row to change size. We can configure it like this:

```
grid rowconfigure . 0 -weight 1
```

Once these weights are set, the grid resizes properly, as shown in Figure 2.23.

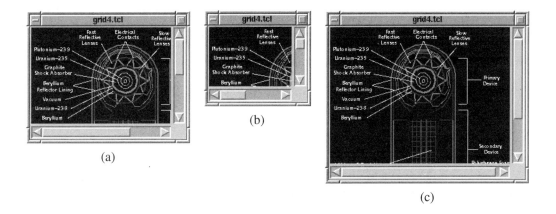

(a)

(b)

(c)

Figure 2.23. Assigning weights to specific rows and columns makes them resizable. (a) Normal size. (b) Window is compressed. (c) Window is enlarged.

If you want all of your rows or columns to change size uniformly, you should give them all the same weight. For example, we can fix the calculator shown in Figure 2.21 so that it resizes properly. We want all of the columns to change size uniformly, so we configure their weights like this:

```
set max [lindex [grid size .] 0]
for {set i 0} {$i < $max} {incr i} {
    grid columnconfigure . $i -weight 1
}
```

The command `grid size` returns a list with the number of columns and rows in a grid. We pick out the number of columns and save this in a variable `max`. Then we loop through the columns and set the weight of each one to 1.

We can use the same technique to configure the rows:

```
set max [lindex [grid size .] 1]
```

```
for {set i 2} {$i < $max} {incr i} {
    grid rowconfigure . $i -weight 1
}
```

This time, we call `grid size` and pick out the number of rows. We don't want the first row to change size. There isn't much use for a giant Off button or a giant readout with small numbers. So we skip over rows 0 and 1 and set the weight of the others to `1`. With all of these weights set, the calculator resizes properly.

2.2.4 Mixing `grid` and `pack`

The packer and the gridder are both quite powerful. But they are even more powerful when combined in an application. For example, suppose we want to build the electronic mail program shown in Figure 2.24. You can use this program to compose an e-mail message. When you click on the Send Message button, the message in the text area is sent to the address on the To: line.

The top part of this application is a form with labels and their corresponding entry fields. We create these widgets like this:

```
frame .controls
label .controls.tolab -text "To:"
entry .controls.to
label .controls.cclab -text "Cc:"
entry .controls.cc
label .controls.sublab -text "Subject:"
entry .controls.subject
button .controls.send -text "Send\nMessage" -command send_message
```

Using the gridder will help us align these things neatly into rows and columns. We use the `grid` command to arrange them like this:

```
grid .controls.tolab -row 0 -column 0 -sticky e
grid .controls.to -row 0 -column 1 -sticky ew
grid .controls.send -row 0 -column 2 -rowspan 3 -sticky nsew
grid .controls.cclab -row 1 -column 0 -sticky e
grid .controls.cc -row 1 -column 1 -sticky ew
grid .controls.sublab -row 2 -column 0 -sticky e
grid .controls.subject -row 2 -column 1 -sticky ew
grid columnconfigure .controls 1 -weight 1
```

We want the labels to be right-justified, so we grid them with `-sticky e` to align them on the east side of their column. However, we want the entries to stretch all the way across their column, so we grid them with `-sticky ew`. We put the Send Message button in the third column and have it span across all three rows. Finally, we unlock the column of entries so that it can be resized. That way, if the window is expanded, the user will have more room to type.

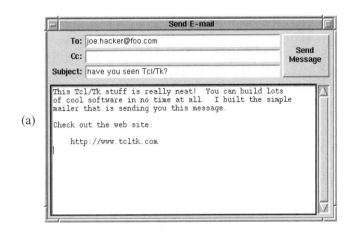

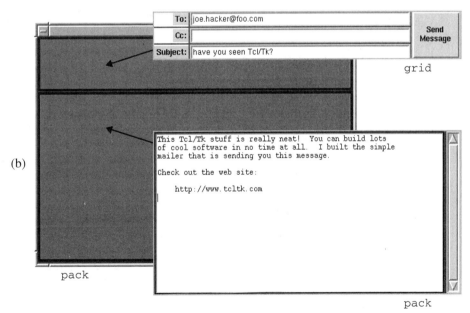

Figure 2.24. An electronic mail application. (a) Screen snapshot. (b) Widgets in the upper frame are laid out with `grid`. Widgets in the lower frame are laid out with `pack`. Then the two frames are packed into the main window.

The bottom part is a text widget and a scrollbar, which aren't really aligned with the widgets at the top—only with each other. We simply pack them together in a frame, like this:

```
frame .message
scrollbar .message.sbar -command {.message.text yview}
text .message.text -yscrollcommand {.message.sbar set}


pack .message.sbar -side right -fill y
pack .message.text -side left -expand yes -fill both
```

We pack the scrollbar on the right and the text widget on the left. We pack the scrollbar in first, so it won't get squeezed out if the window is compressed. We have it fill in the *y*-direction, so it will stretch to the same height as the text area. We pack the text area to expand and fill, so that it will get any extra area in the frame.

Now we have an upper frame built with the `grid` command and a lower frame built with the `pack` command. You can use `grid` and `pack` together in the same application, so long as you use them in different frames. If you grid one widget in a frame, you must grid the rest of the widgets in that frame. Likewise, if you pack one widget in a frame, you must pack the others in that frame. If you accidentally grid some widgets and pack others, the two geometry managers will fight for control, and the resulting struggle may crash your machine!

You can also use `grid` and `pack` at different levels of the widget hierarchy. Now that we have these two frames, for example, we need to position them in the main window. We could use the `grid` command to align them into a column, or we could use the `pack` command and simply pack them in. In this case, it is simpler to use the packer. The gridder would require extra commands to set the row and column weights so that the window would resize properly. The following `pack` commands will do the trick:

```
pack .controls -fill x -padx 4 -pady 4
pack .message -expand yes -fill both -padx 4 -pady 4
```

We pack the `.controls` frame on top and have it fill across the width. If the window gets bigger, the controls area will simply get wider, so you will have more room to type inside the entry fields. On the other hand, we pack the `.message` frame to expand and fill. If the window gets bigger, the text area will get wider *and* longer.

We cannot say that the packer or the gridder is better in all cases. Each has its strengths. You should break each window into groups of widgets and ask yourself whether each group should be packed or gridded. Also, ask yourself whether the groups themselves should be packed or gridded into their top-level window. You might find that you pack some widgets together in a frame and then put that frame on a grid. Or, you might find that you grid some widgets together and then pack the frame. Use both of these models, along with your good judgment.

2.3　Using the `place` command

Most of the time, you'll use `pack` or `grid` to position the widgets in your application. But Tk also has a `place` command, which lets you position widgets at absolute pixel coordinates or at relative positions within a window.

2.3.1　Coordinate-based model

Suppose we create an Exit button as follows:

```
button .exit -text "Exit" -command exit
```

We can use the placer to position the button, like this:

```
place .exit -x 0 -y 0 -anchor nw
```

This puts the button in its parent window at the pixel coordinate (0,0), which is the upper-left corner of the main window. The *x*-coordinates increase going toward the right, and the *y*-coordinates increase going down. We include the option `-anchor nw` so that the button is anchored with its north-west corner at the (0,0) coordinate, as shown in Figure 2.25(a).

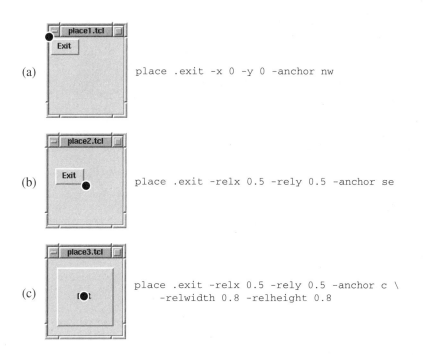

(a)　　`place .exit -x 0 -y 0 -anchor nw`

(b)　　`place .exit -relx 0.5 -rely 0.5 -anchor se`

(c)　　`place .exit -relx 0.5 -rely 0.5 -anchor c \`
　　　　`    -relwidth 0.8 -relheight 0.8`

Figure 2.25. The `place` facility puts widgets at absolute or relative coordinates.

You can also use coordinates that are relative to the overall size of the window. For example, you choose a point in the center of the window like this:

```
place .exit -relx 0.5 -rely 0.5 -anchor se
```

This time, we used the option -anchor se, so the button is anchored with its southeast corner on the point in the center of the window. This puts the button off-center, as shown in Figure 2.25(b). If we want the button centered in the window, we could anchor it on its center point with the option -anchor c.

The placer can set not only the position of the window but also its size. We can center the button and have it stretch to cover the window, like this:

```
place .exit -relx 0.5 -rely 0.5 -anchor c \
    -relwidth 0.8 -relheight 0.8
```

This gives the button a relative width and height that is 0.8 the size of its container, as shown in Figure 2.25(c). If you want an absolute size, you can use the -width and -height options to give the widget a size in pixels.

Unlike the packer or the gridder, the placer does *not* shrink-wrap the window around its contents. The placer treats the window like a bulletin board and places widgets at specific coordinates in the available space. If widgets overlap, the stacking order determines which will sit on top. Normally, widgets created later are higher in the stacking order. But you can use the raise and lower commands to change the stacking.

If you use relative coordinates and relative sizes, the window acts like a rubber sheet. When you stretch the window, the widgets within it move and stretch proportionately.

When you first start using Tk, you may be tempted to use the placer instead of the packer or the gridder. Don't fall into this trap! The packer and the gridder both handle size changes intelligently, but the placer does not. Suppose you create the perfect layout by placing widgets precisely where you want them. Now suppose that the user changes the font for the application. Remember, widgets have lots of resources that change their appearance and their overall size, and the user can change the default values for any of these resources. The packer and the gridder respond by adjusting the layout, but the placer doesn't. The placer puts the widgets at the coordinates you specify. If the user selects a larger font, the widgets will get bigger, and they will probably overlap.

2.3.2 Custom geometry managers

The placer is too simple-minded for most of your layout tasks, but it does provide all of the functionality that you need to build your own geometry managers. If you have a different model for laying out widgets—maybe with springs or glue between them—you can build it with a few Tcl procedures. Whenever a window changes size, you simply recompute the sizes and positions of its widgets according to your model and use the place command to carry out your changes.

For example, suppose that we want to build a paned window like the one shown in Figure 2.26. The window has a top area and a bottom area called *panes* and a line called the *sash* between them. In this case, the top pane has a list of directories, and the bottom pane has a list of files, so this window acts like a file browser. But in general, the top and bottom panes are just frames, and you can put anything in them.

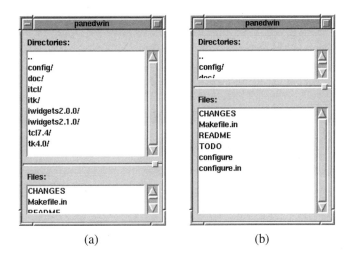

(a)   (b)

Figure 2.26. A paned window has a top area and a bottom area with a sash between them. You can (a) move the sash down to see more of the top or (b) move the sash up to see more of the bottom.

The little square on the sash is called a *grip*. You can click on it and drag the sash to a new position. You can move the sash down to get more area for directories, but you'll get less area for files. Likewise, you can move the sash up to get more area for files, but you'll get less area for directories.

We can create a few Tcl procedures to support the paned window, using the placer to position all of the widgets. When we're done, it will work like this: You create a new paned window by calling `panedwindow_create`, giving it a name for the paned window and its overall width and height:

```
panedwindow_create .pw 3i 4i
pack .pw -expand yes -fill both
```

This creates a frame named `.pw` to contain the paned window. Overall, it will be 3 inches wide and 4 inches high. Inside is a frame for the top pane, named `.pw.pane1`, and another frame for the bottom pane, named `.pw.pane2`, along with the dividing sash and its grip.

You fill up the top pane just by packing in some widgets, like this:

```
frame .pw.pane1.dirs
pack .pw.pane1.dirs -expand yes -fill both -padx 4 -pady 10
label .pw.pane1.dirs.lab -text "Directories:"
pack .pw.pane1.dirs.lab -anchor w
```

```
scrollbar .pw.pane1.dirs.sbar \
    -command {.pw.pane1.dirs.list yview}
pack .pw.pane1.dirs.sbar -side right -fill y
listbox .pw.pane1.dirs.list -selectmode single \
    -yscrollcommand {.pw.pane1.dirs.sbar set}
pack .pw.pane1.dirs.list -side left -expand yes -fill both
```

You do something similar for the bottom pane by packing widgets into .pw.pane2. When the paned window first appears, the sash will be halfway down, and the top and bottom panes will have equal area. After that, you can move the sash, as shown in Figure 2.26, to adjust the top and bottom areas.

Now let's see how a paned window is implemented. Here's the procedure that you use to create the paned window:

```
proc panedwindow_create {win width height} {
    global pwInfo

    frame $win -class Panedwindow -width $width -height $height
    frame $win.pane1
    place $win.pane1 -relx 0.5 -rely 0 -anchor n \
        -relwidth 1.0 -relheight 0.5
    frame $win.pane2
    place $win.pane2 -relx 0.5 -rely 1.0 -anchor s \
        -relwidth 1.0 -relheight 0.5

    frame $win.sash -height 4 -borderwidth 2 -relief sunken
    place $win.sash -relx 0.5 -rely 0.5 -relwidth 1.0 -anchor c

    frame $win.grip -width 10 -height 10 \
        -borderwidth 2 -relief raised
    place $win.grip -relx 0.95 -rely 0.5 -anchor c

    bind $win.grip <ButtonPress-1>   "panedwindow_grab $win"
    bind $win.grip <B1-Motion>       "panedwindow_drag $win %Y"
    bind $win.grip <ButtonRelease-1> "panedwindow_drop $win %Y"

    return $win
}
```

We start by creating a frame to contain the paned window. You pass in the name of this frame, along with its overall width and height. We give it the class name Panedwindow, so you can add resources for paned windows to the option database. For example, we include the following resource with the paned window code:

```
option add *Panedwindow.grip.cursor sb_v_double_arrow widgetDefault
```

This gives the grip a special up/down arrow cursor, letting the user know that it can be moved.

Next, we create the two frames representing the top and bottom panes. We place the top pane at a coordinate halfway across the top edge of the paned window, and we anchor it on its north side, so it hangs down from this point. We give it the full width of the paned window but only half the height. We place the bottom pane at a coordinate halfway along the bottom edge and anchor it on its south side, so it pushes up from this point. Again, we give it the full width of the paned window but only half the height. Together, the top and bottom panes make up the full height of the window.

Next, we create a frame for the sash line and another frame for the grip. We set the height of the sash frame to twice the border width, so all you see is the frame's sunken border looking like a grooved line. We place this frame on the boundary between the top and bottom panes and give it the full width of the paned window. We make the grip a small 10×10 pixel square with a raised border, and we place it on the sash toward the right-hand side of the paned window.

All of the widgets are now in position, and everything looks right. But you won't be able to move the sash unless we do something more. After all, the grip is just a frame. If you click on it, it does nothing. If you want to move the grip, we have to bind some new behaviors to it.

When you click on the grip, it will get a `<ButtonPress-1>` event. As you hold down the mouse button and drag the grip, it will get a series of `<B1-Motion>` events. And finally, when you release the grip at its new position, it will get a `<ButtonRelease-1>` event. We bind to each of these events so that we can handle them with special procedures.

When you click on the grip, the following procedure gets called:

```
proc panedwindow_grab {win} {
    $win.grip configure -relief sunken
}
```

This makes the grip look as if it's been pushed in, so you know that you've got hold of it.

As you drag the grip up and down, the following procedure gets called at each new position:

```
proc panedwindow_drag {win y} {
    set realY [expr $y-[winfo rooty $win]]
    set Ymax  [winfo height $win]
    set frac [expr double($realY)/$Ymax]
    if {$frac < 0.05} {
        set frac 0.05
    }
    if {$frac > 0.95} {
        set frac 0.95
    }
    place $win.sash -rely $frac
    place $win.grip -rely $frac
    return $frac
}
```

We compute the relative position of the mouse in the paned window and then place the sash and the grip at that new position. You can see the two `place` commands near the bottom of this procedure.

The y-coordinate that comes in tells us the position of the mouse on the screen. Remember, we set the binding like this:

```
bind $win.grip <B1-Motion> "panedwindow_drag $win %Y"
```

The `bind` facility replaces `%Y` with the so-called *root y-coordinate*, which is an absolute position. It is 0 at the top of the screen and a large number at the bottom.

What we really want is the y-coordinate relative to the upper-left corner of the paned window. So we use `winfo rooty` to get the position of the paned window on the screen, and we subtract the two coordinates. When you drag the grip to the top of the paned window, the value in `realY` will be 0; as you drag the grip downward, the value in `realY` will increase.

We can convert this from an absolute distance in pixels to a relative position within the paned window. We simply divide by the height of the paned window, which we get from `winfo height`. Notice that we use the `double` function to convert `realY` to a double-precision value before doing the division. This is important. If the `expr` command sees two integers, it will do integer division. So `252/375` will be 0, not `0.672`. Whenever you catch yourself typing the "/" for division, make sure that at least one of the operands is a floating-point value, or you will get strange results.

If you drag the grip up above the paned window, you will get a negative value in `frac`. Likewise, if you drag it down below the paned window, you will get a value larger than `1`. If we place the sash at either of these extremes, it will disappear, and you won't be able to grab it again to fix it. To prevent this, we cap the value in `frac` so that it is no smaller than `0.05` and no larger than `0.95`. If you try to drag the sash too far in either direction, it will stop moving near the ends.

When you release the grip, the following procedure gets called:

```
proc panedwindow_drop {win y} {
    set frac [panedwindow_drag $win $y]
    panedwindow_divide $win $frac
    $win.grip configure -relief raised
}
```

This moves the sash and the grip to their final positions by calling `panedwindow_drag`. Notice that we can get the relative position of the sash as the return value from this procedure. We were clever enough to return it when we defined the procedure earlier. We use another procedure, `panedwindow_divide`, to adjust the top and bottom areas to their final sizes, and we give the grip back its normal, raised appearance.

The `panedwindow_divide` procedure looks like this:

```
proc panedwindow_divide {win frac} {
    place $win.sash -rely $frac
    place $win.grip -rely $frac
```

```
place $win.pane1 -relheight $frac
place $win.pane2 -relheight [expr 1-$frac]
}
```

This procedure moves the sash and the grip to their relative positions and then sets the relative height of the top and bottom frames, as shown in Figure 2.27. Notice that in all of these `place` commands, we didn't include such options as `-relx`, `-relwidth`, or `-anchor`. We set these options once, when we first place the widgets. Any subsequent `place` commands update the options that we include and leave the others alone.

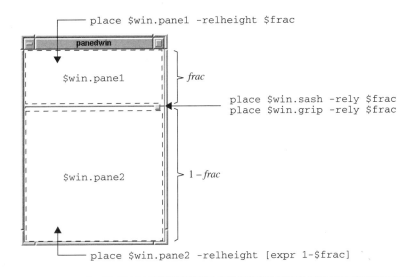

Figure 2.27. Whenever the sash is moved, the size and the placement of components in the paned window are updated.

We could have included `panedwindow_divide` as part of `panedwindow_drop`. But it is nice to have it broken out, so you can call it separately. When you first create a paned window, you may want to have, say, 30 percent of the area on top and 70 percent on the bottom. You can set this through `panedwindow_divide`, like this:

```
panedwindow_create .pw 3i 4i
panedwindow_divide .pw 0.3
pack .pw -expand yes -fill both
```

With the `place` command and a few Tcl procedures, we now have a new, albeit limited, geometry manager for Tk. We provide only two panes, and they are stacked vertically. But you can generalize this idea to create a more powerful paned window, and you can use the same concept to create many other facilities in Tk.

Chapter 3
Handling Events

You move the mouse pointer onto a button and click. As a user, you've probably done this a thousand times. As a programmer, you know that this action invokes the code stored in the `-command` option of the button. This seems simple enough. But when you start to use buttons in real applications, some subtle issues arise.

- How do you prevent the program from locking up while the button is executing its command?

- How do you prevent the user from interacting with the program while it is busy?

- How do you get the button to be invoked automatically whenever the user presses Return in an entry field? Normally, pressing Return does nothing.

   To understand these problems, we need to learn more about how Tk works. In this chapter, we'll take a closer look at the Tk widgets and use the `bind` command to customize their behavior. We'll use the `bindtags` command to handle groups of related bindings and the `after` command to make things happen as a function of time. But before we get too far into the details of these commands, let's take a closer look at how the `wish` program operates.

3.1 The event loop

Take a look at this Hello, World! script:

```
button .b -text "Hello, World!" -command exit
pack .b
```

It creates a button and packs the button into the main window—that much you can see. But what's interesting is the part that you can't see—the part that handles all of the interactions with the user.

When `wish` has finished executing this script, it pops up the main window and waits for something to happen. Suppose the user clicks on the Hello, World! button. The button receives a notification called an *event*—in this case, a `ButtonPress` event. The button reacts by changing to a sunken relief. Now suppose the user releases the mouse button. The Hello, World! button receives another event—this time, a `ButtonRelease` event. The button reacts by invoking its command and then reverting to its raised relief.

As the events stream into the program, they're held in a queue called the *event queue*. They're processed one at a time in an infinite loop called the *event loop*. The flowchart in Figure 3.1 presents an overview of this process.

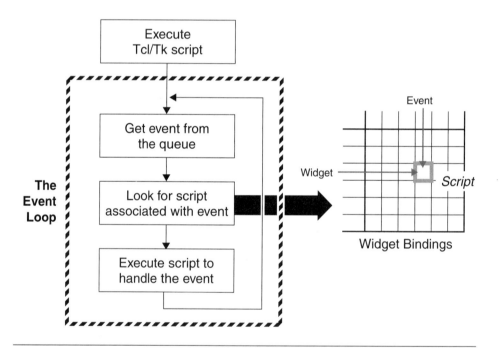

Figure 3.1. Tk programs spend most of their time in the event loop.

In the event loop, the program takes an event from the queue and looks for a script to handle that event. This script is called a *binding*. The Tk widgets come with default bindings to handle their normal behavior. A button widget automatically handles the click and release events, an entry widget automatically handles key presses, and so on.

If you want to override the default behavior or add a new behavior to a widget, you can use the `bind` command. This command has a rather complicated syntax, which we'll describe fully in Section 3.3. For now, let's look at a simple example to see how bindings are used in the event loop.

Suppose we add the following code to our Hello, World! script:

```
entry .field
pack .field
bind .field <KeyPress-Return> {
    .b flash
    .b invoke
}
```

The `bind` command stores a script in the table of widget bindings shown in Figure 3.1. In this case, it associates the following script with the `<KeyPress-Return>` event on the entry `.field`:

```
.b flash
.b invoke
```

Now suppose you type something into the entry and press Return. Each of the key strokes will generate a `<KeyPress>` event. When the entry receives the `<KeyPress>` event for the Return key, the entry will execute the script shown earlier. This will cause the Hello, World! button to flash and to invoke its command, as if you'd clicked on it. So instead of typing into the entry and reaching for the mouse to click on the button, you can type into the entry and press Return.

So far, we've limited our discussion to widget events, but other events can occur as well. The `after` command generates a timer event, which causes a script to be executed after a certain delay; we'll use this facility in Section 3.7 to make a bouncing ball move as a function of time. When a file descriptor becomes readable or writable, it generates a file event. We'll use this in Chapter 7 to handle communication with other programs.

All of the various kinds of events are handled in the event loop. They all indicate that something has happened within the program, and they invoke scripts to take the appropriate action.

3.1.1   Keyboard focus

When you click on an entry widget, you get an active cursor. On UNIX systems, the entry also becomes outlined, usually in black. This indicates that the entry has *focus*, which means that it will receive all of the keyboard-related events for the application.

In each top-level window, only one widget can have focus at a particular time. You may have several entry widgets in a dialog, and they would all listen for `KeyPress` events. But only one of them—the one that has focus—would receive the events.

For example, suppose we have the following code, which creates the entry form shown in Figure 3.2:

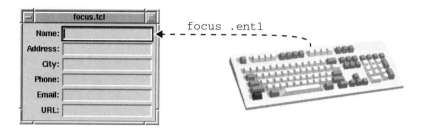

Figure 3.2. The `focus` command is used to establish the keyboard focus for a top-level window.

```
set x 1
foreach t {Name Address City Phone Email URL} {
    label .lab$x -text "$t:"
    entry .ent$x
    grid .lab$x -row $x -column 0 -sticky e
    grid .ent$x -row $x -column 1 -sticky ew
    incr x
}
```

We may want to assign focus to the first entry so that when the form appears on the screen, the user can start typing immediately. We can use the `focus` command to set the focus, like this:

```
focus .ent1
```

This assigns focus to `.ent1`, which is the first entry. After that, the user can click on another entry or can press the Tab key to shift the focus down to the next entry in the form. Tk has built-in bindings that handle these events and change the focus accordingly.

3.1.2 Forcing updates

When `wish` has handled all of the events in the event queue and has nothing better to do, it will update the widgets on the screen. This strategy lets Tk batch a series of changes, so they can be applied in a highly efficient manner. For example, suppose you create a label:

```
label .x
pack .x
.x configure -text "Hello, World!"
.x configure -borderwidth 2 -relief groove
```

You won't see the effect from each line of code—you won't see the label appear, then display the `Hello, World!` message, then get a grooved border. Instead, you'll see the label appear at once, in its final state.

This is normally what you want. But sometimes, when you change a widget, you want to see that change immediately. For example, consider the following script:

```
label .countdown -text "Ready"
pack .countdown -padx 4 -pady 4

button .launch -text "Launch" -command {
    for {set i 10} {$i >= 0} {incr i -1} {
        .countdown configure -text $i
        after 1000
    }
}
pack .launch -padx 4 -pady 4
```

This creates a Launch button and a Ready label. When you click on the button, the program enters a loop that counts down from 10 to 0. At each step, the label is modified to display the countdown. The `after` command suspends execution for 1,000 ms on each pass through the loop, so the countdown will change at 1-second intervals.

You might think that you'd see the label count down from 10 to 0. But if you run this, you'll see the program pause for 11 seconds, then display 0, as shown in Figure 3.3(a).

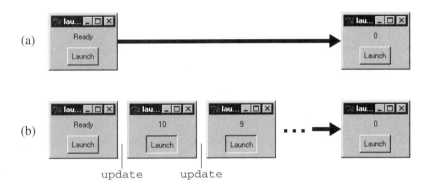

Figure 3.3. (a) When a label is configured again and again, only the last change is seen. (b) Adding an `update` command after each `configure` operation makes the change visible.

While the program is busy executing the command code for the button, it won't keep the widgets up to date. As far as Tk is concerned, it looks as though we've put 11 configure operations back to back. When the `for` loop terminates, the program returns to the event loop, and all of the remaining events are processed. Finally, when the program has nothing better to do, it brings the label up to date. Thus the label changes only once, displaying the final value, 0.

We can fix this example by putting an `update` command after each `configure` operation, like this:

```
button .launch -text "Launch" -command {
    for {set i 10} {$i >= 0} {incr i -1} {
        .countdown configure -text $i
        update
        after 1000
    }
}
```

The update command forces the program back into the event loop, where it processes events until the queue is empty. Then the command brings all of the widgets up to date, making the change to the label visible on the screen.

The second part—bringing the widgets up to date—is all that we need for this example. So instead of doing a full-blown update, we can do a partial update, like this:

```
button .launch -text "Launch" -command {
    for {set i 10} {$i >= 0} {incr i -1} {
        .countdown configure -text $i
        update idletasks
        after 1000
    }
}
```

The idletasks keyword tells the update command to ignore the event queue and to handle the second part—the widget updates that are normally deferred until the program is idle. So the label changes to display each value in the countdown.

3.1.3   Handling long-running bindings

Tk programs spend most of their time in the event loop, waiting for the next event. When it arrives, its binding is executed, and the program quickly returns to the event loop, waiting again for the next event. As long as each binding executes quickly, the program always appears to be responsive and up to date.

But what if a binding takes a minute or so to execute? As an example, consider the fractal generator shown in Figure 3.4. When you click on the Compute button, its command calls a Tcl procedure to generate a fractal image. For the image shown in Figure 3.4, this procedure takes 2.5 minutes to execute. (With the byte-code compiler in Tcl/Tk 8.0, this drops to 12 seconds, making the program much more fun to play with!)

While the program is busy generating the image, it won't process events. If you try to adjust the scale widgets, nothing happens. If you cover the program with another window and then expose it again, it won't update properly. At this point, most users would think that the program had mysteriously locked up. They would probably kill the program and file a bug report.

We can avoid this problem by calling update from time to time while the fractal is being generated:

```
proc fractal_draw {color maxiters size} {
    global fractal
    ...
```

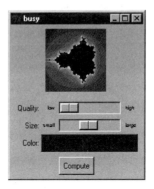

Figure 3.4. A fractal generator program.

```
$fractal(image) blank
for {set x 0} {$x < $size} {incr x} {
    set cr [expr double($x*$dr)/$size+$fractal(x0)]
    for {set y 0} {$y < $size} {incr y} {
        set ci [expr double($y*$di)/$size+$fractal(y0)]
        set zr 0.0; set zi 0.0
        for {set iter 0} {$iter < $maxiters} {incr iter} {
            set rsq [expr $zr*$zr]
            set isq [expr $zi*$zi]
            set zi [expr 2*$zr*$zi + $ci]
            set zr [expr $rsq - $isq + $cr]
            if {$rsq + $isq >= 4.0} {
                break
            }
        }
        $fractal(image) put $cmap($iter) -to $x $y
    }
    update
    }
}
```

This procedure generates the fractal image. We've left out a few details so that we could focus on the role of the update command. You'll find the rest of the code for this program in the file efftcl/lib/demos/busy.tcl, which can be obtained from the Web site mentioned on page xiv.

We start by using the blank operation to clear the image stored in the variable fractal(image). Then we scan the x and y variables through all of the pixels in the image. At each pixel, we apply the fractal formula to compute the color for that pixel. (For a simple explanation of this formula, see http://www.cygnus-software.com/theory/ theory.htm.) Then we use the `put` operation to store the pixel in the image.

As we're doing this, we call `update` from time to time to keep the program up to date. We could call it during each iteration through the fractal formula. Or, we could call it after generating each pixel. But either of these solutions would add a lot of event processing to the inner loops of the procedure, slowing it down tremendously. So instead, we call `update` after computing an entire column of pixels. That way, it gets called often enough that the program stays up to date but not so often that we sacrifice performance.

Each update will flush the current fractal image out to the screen, as shown in Figure 3.5. This lets the user see the image as it is being generated. Also, the image acts as a built-in progress gauge, letting the user know how close the task is to completion. Any long-running task should have a progress gauge of some sort. We'll show you how to build a simple gauge in Section 4.3.

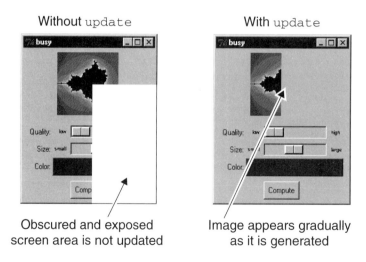

Figure 3.5. The `update` command keeps the fractal program from locking up.

You may be wondering why we didn't use `update idletasks` instead of `update`. As we explained in the previous section, `update idletasks` does a partial update—it forces only the most recent changes to the screen. If we used `update idletasks` in this example, it would flush out each column of pixels in the fractal image, but it wouldn't update anything else. Suppose the program were obscured by another window and then later exposed, as shown in Figure 3.5. The program would be notified by a series of `Expose` events. But unless we perform a full-blown update, the program won't process these events, and the damage won't be repaired. So you should always use `update` to keep the program up to date during a long-running task.

There is one caveat about `update`. It processes *all* of the events in the queue—not only the `Expose` events but also such events as `ButtonPress` and `KeyPress`. So while the fractal is being generated, for example, the user can adjust the scales, change the color, and even click on the Compute button. This last "feature" is a cause for concern. Suppose the user is halfway through the fractal calculation and changes the size and clicks on Compute again. The program will immediately begin to generate the new fractal, and when it is finished, it will continue generating the old one!

While a program is handling a long-running task, it is usually a good idea to lock out some of the interactions with the user. In the fractal program, for example, we could disable the Compute button while the fractal is being generated. We could modify the command for this button as follows:

```
button .compute -text "Compute" -command {
    set size [.controls.size get]
    .display configure -width $size -height $size
    set color [.controls.color cget -background]
    set maxiters [.controls.qual get]

    .compute configure -state disabled
    fractal_draw $color $maxiters $size
    .compute configure -state normal
}
```

Larger applications may have many widgets that need to be disabled during a long-running task. Instead of disabling them one by one, it is usually better to put the entire application in a "busy" state. In this state, the cursor changes to a watch or an hourglass, letting the user know that the program is busy. All of the windows remain up to date when they're obscured and exposed, but the user can't interact with any of the widgets.

To achieve the "busy" state, we must lock out all mouse-related and keyboard-related events. We'll do this by intercepting these events and delivering them to a widget that ignores them, as shown in Figure 3.6. We'll create a frame called `.busylock` and place it off-screen, so it's invisible to the user. Then we'll use the `grab` command to direct all mouse-related events to this frame, and we'll use the `focus` command to focus keyboard input on this frame.

We can write a procedure called `busy_eval` that makes it easy to handle the "busy" state. We could use this procedure in the Compute button of our fractal program as follows:

```
button .compute -text "Compute" -command {
    set size [.controls.size get]
    .display configure -width $size -height $size
    set color [.controls.color cget -background]
    set maxiters [.controls.qual get]
```

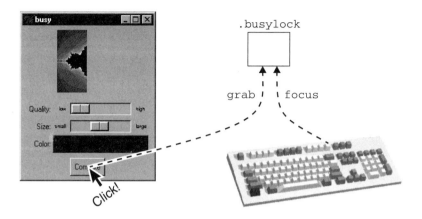

Figure 3.6. In the "busy" state, mouse and keyboard events are delivered to a widget that ignores them.

```
busy_eval {
    fractal_draw $color $maxiters $size
}
}
```

The busy_eval procedure puts the program into the "busy" state and then executes a script. In this case, it calls fractal_draw to generate the fractal image. When this is finished, the program returns to normal.

The busy_eval procedure is implemented as follows:

```
frame .busylock
bind .busylock <KeyPress> break
place .busylock -x -2 -y -2

proc busy_eval {script} {
    set fwin [focus]
    focus .busylock
    grab set .busylock

    set cursor [. cget -cursor]
    . configure -cursor watch
    update

    set status [catch {uplevel $script} result]

    . configure -cursor $cursor
    grab release .busylock
    focus $fwin
```

```
        return -code $status $result
    }
```

Outside of the procedure, we create the `.busylock` frame. We add a special binding so that the frame will ignore all KeyPress events. We'll see how the `break` command affects bindings in Section 3.5.2. But in simple terms, it overrides the built-in behaviors that Tk supplies. So keys that are handled automatically by Tk, such as Tab and Alt, will be ignored by `.busylock`.

In order for `grab` to work correctly on all platforms, the grab window must be packed, gridded, or placed somewhere in the application. If it's not, you'll get a "grab window not visible" error. So in this example, we use the `place` command to position `.busylock` just outside the main window, beyond its upper-left corner.

Inside the `busy_eval` procedure, we set up the "busy" state. We save the name of the widget that has keyboard focus in the variable `fwin`, so we can restore the focus later. Then we set the keyboard focus on `.busylock` and set the grab on `.busylock`. Finally, we change the cursor for the main window to the watch cursor, and we use the `update` command to flush this change out to the screen. Most of the widgets in the application inherit their cursor from the main window. So by setting the cursor for the main window, we've set the cursor for the entire application. (This isn't true for entry widgets, text widgets, or any widget that has the `-cursor` option set to something other than a null string. To get a watch cursor everywhere, you'd have to traverse the entire widget hierarchy and change each `-cursor` option. That can be slow and is not important for most applications.) Of course, we save the current cursor in the `cursor` variable, so that later we can change the cursor back to its normal appearance.

Once we've established the "busy" state, we execute the script argument. If we had used the `eval` command, the script would run in the context of the `busy_eval` procedure. Instead, we're careful to use the `uplevel` command, so the script will run in the calling context. This is an important difference. If the script uses any variables, they should be resolved in the calling context. For example, take another look at the code for our Compute button:

```
button .compute -text "Compute" -command {
    set size [.controls.size get]
    .display configure -width $size -height $size
    set color [.controls.color cget -background]
    set maxiters [.controls.qual get]

    busy_eval {
        fractal_draw $color $maxiters $size
    }
}
```

The script uses $color, $maxiters, and $size. These variables are not defined within `busy_eval`. They make sense only in the context of the code that calls `busy_eval`, which is one level up in the call stack.

Returning to the body of `busy_eval`, you'll notice that we're careful to catch any errors from the `uplevel` command. If the script generates an error, we don't want to leave the program in the "busy" state by accident. So we catch the status code and the result and then release the "busy" state. Finally, we return the result of the script as the result from `busy_eval`. We include the `-code` option on the `return` command so that we can return the status code too. That way, if the script generates an error, `busy_eval` will return an error as well.

3.1.4 Execution scope

Any code that is invoked from the event loop is executed at global scope. This means that bindings, for example, can access only global variables. Watch out for code like this:

```
proc wait_for_click {win} {      ;# BUG ALERT!
    set x 0
    bind $win <ButtonPress-1> {set x 1}
    bind $win <ButtonPress-2> {set x 2}
    vwait x
    return $x
}
```

It looks as though we're setting the variable x to 0, setting up some bindings to change it, waiting for it to change, and returning the result. But in fact there are two different x variables in this example. When we say `set x 0` and `return $x`, we're dealing with the local variable x that resides in the scope of the procedure. But we're dealing with a different variable when we say:

```
bind $win <ButtonPress-1> {set x 1}
bind $win <ButtonPress-2> {set x 2}
vwait x
```

These commands are associated with the event loop, so they operate in the global context on a global variable that also happens to be named x.

If you try this procedure, it will appear to work. It will indeed wait for a mouse click and will return a value. But it will return the value of the local variable x, which is always 0. For this procedure to work properly, x must be declared within the procedure as a global variable. Needless to say, such bugs can be extremely difficult to track down.

The same caution applies to any script that is invoked from the event loop. This includes the scripts given to `after` and `fileevent`, as well as the `-command` scripts assigned to a widget.

3.1.5 Quoting and the event loop

Sometimes you need to substitute values into a script before you pass it along to the `bind` or `after` commands. When you do, you must be careful how you handle quoting for the script.

Let's look at the "reminder" program shown in Figure 3.7. The user enters a message and clicks on the Remind Me button. After a brief delay, a notice dialog appears, displaying the message. In this example, we'll hard-code the delay to 5 seconds, so this implementation is useful only for people with short attention spans. But we could certainly generalize the program to handle arbitrary delays.

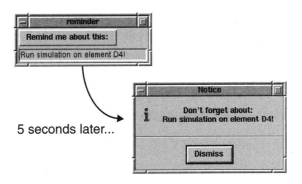

Figure 3.7. A reminder program pops up a notice dialog after a brief delay.

The widgets in the main window are created as follows:

```
button .remind -text "Remind me about this:" -command {
    reminder "Don't forget:\n[.mesg get]"
    .mesg delete 0 end
}
pack .remind -anchor w
entry .mesg
pack .mesg -fill x
```

When you click on the Remind Me button, it creates a `"Don't forget..."` message, using the contents of the entry widget, and passes that message to a procedure called `reminder`, which creates an `after` event that pops up a notice after a brief delay. In Section 6.4, we'll write a procedure called `notice_show` that creates a notice dialog. We'll use that procedure in this example so we can focus on the quoting issues.

You might be tempted to implement the `reminder` procedure as follows:

```
proc reminder {mesg} {
    after 5000 {notice_show $mesg}
}
```

If you do, you'll get an error. The braces prevent substitution of `$mesg`, so after a 5-second delay, Tk will execute the following command from the event loop:

```
notice_show $mesg
```

There is no `mesg` variable at the global scope, so this command will fail.

You need to substitute the value for `$mesg` before passing the command to `after`. You might be tempted to use double quotes, like this:

```
proc reminder {mesg} {
    after 5000 "notice_show $mesg"
}
```

or no quotes, like this:

```
proc reminder {mesg} {
    after 5000 notice_show $mesg
}
```

In either case, you'll get another error. After a 5-second delay, Tk will execute the following command from the event loop:

```
notice_show Don't forget:
Dentist appointment at 4:00pm
```

The `notice_show` procedure is expecting a single message string. But with this script, it looks as though you're passing two arguments (`Don't` and `forget:`) and then executing a command called `Dentist`. You've lost the fact that `$mesg` was a single argument on the command line.

You can fix this problem by adding explicit quotes around the message:

```
proc reminder {mesg} {
    after 5000 "notice_show \"$mesg\""
}
```

But what if the message also contains double quotes? Again, this strategy will fail.

Instead of adding the quotes by hand, it is better to use the `list` command, like this:

```
proc reminder {mesg} {
    after 5000 [list notice_show $mesg]
}
```

The `list` command formats each argument properly. The command will add backslashes or braces as needed, for example, to keep `$mesg` together as a single string value. This may seem like a trick, but it is really a well-known feature of the Tcl language. You can think of [`list ...`] as a set of quoting characters that works particularly well for Tcl commands.

3.2   Simple examples using `bind`

You can use the `bind` command to change the behavior for a single widget or for a whole class of widgets. Before we get too deep into the syntax of this command, let's look at some simple examples of how it is used.

3.2.1 Selecting an item from a listbox

In many programs, you can select an item from a listbox by double-clicking on the item. If you look at the listbox manual page, however, you won't find an option to control this behavior. You need to add this separately, using `bind`. To illustrate this, we'll create a listbox and populate it with a few elements. Then we'll use `bind` to add a new behavior for the double-click operation:

```
listbox .lb
label .choice
pack .lb .choice

foreach i {Blessed be the ties that bind} {
    .lb insert end $i
}
bind .lb <Double-ButtonPress-1> {
    .choice configure -text "selection: [.lb get active]"
}
```

The argument `<Double-ButtonPress-1>` describes a double-click event with mouse button 1. Whenever the listbox `.lb` receives this event, it uses the `get` operation to query the active element, and then it configures the label to display that element, as shown in Figure 3.8.

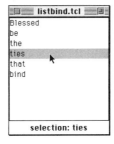

Figure 3.8. Double-clicking an entry in the listbox displays the selected entry.

3.2.2 Automatic button help

In many systems, moving the mouse pointer over a button will display a help message at the bottom of the window, describing the function that the button performs. It's easy to add this same behavior in Tk. Just bind to the `Enter` and `Leave` events, which occur when the mouse pointer enters or leaves the region of the screen occupied by the widget.

The following code shows an example of this:

```
frame .cmd
button .cmd.back \
    -bitmap [file join @$env(EFFTCL_LIBRARY) images back.xbm]
button .cmd.fwd \
    -bitmap [file join @$env(EFFTCL_LIBRARY) images fwd.xbm]
canvas .c
label .help -relief sunken -borderwidth 2 -anchor w
pack .cmd .c .help -side top -fill x
pack .cmd.back .cmd.fwd -side left

bind .cmd.back <Enter> {.help configure -text "Page backward"}
bind .cmd.back <Leave> {.help configure -text ""}
bind .cmd.fwd <Enter> {.help configure -text "Page forward"}
bind .cmd.fwd <Leave> {.help configure -text ""}
```

We create two buttons with arrow icons and a label for the help information. Then we bind to the Enter and Leave events on each button. When either button receives an Enter event, it displays its help message as shown in Figure 3.9. Likewise, when it receives a Leave event, it clears the help text.

Figure 3.9. Moving the mouse pointer over the button displays the help string.

Think about the power behind this mechanism. By specifying a few bindings when a window is created, we've set up a help-display system that will run without any further coding on our part. We don't need to worry about how this affects other aspects of our program, since the mechanism is automatic and self-contained.

In Section 6.7.2, we'll take this same concept one step further. We'll use the bind mechanism in conjunction with toplevel widgets to create a balloon help facility with pop-up messages.

3.2.3 Class bindings

We've seen how you can add bindings to an individual widget. You can also add bindings to an entire class of widgets, using the widget class name as the bind target. A widget's class name is the same as its creation command but starts with a capital letter. The class name for entry widgets is `Entry`, the class name for radiobutton widgets is `Radiobutton`, and so on.

Let's return to the entry form in Figure 3.2. Suppose we want each entry to light up when it receives keyboard focus, as shown in Figure 3.10.

Figure 3.10. A class binding on `FocusIn`/`FocusOut` affects all of the entry widgets in this form.

When each entry receives focus, it will get a `FocusIn` event. When the entry loses focus, it will get a `FocusOut` event. We can bind to these two events so that an entry will change color when it has focus. But instead of binding to each entry individually, we can bind to all of the entries at once by binding to class `Entry`, like this:

```
bind Entry <FocusIn>  {%W configure -background white}
bind Entry <FocusOut> {%W configure -background gray}
```

When a particular entry widget receives focus, Tk will substitute the name of that widget in place of `%W` and will execute the command. Tk can perform other substitutions too, as we'll see in Section 3.3.2. In this case, if an entry widget named `.ent1` receives focus, Tk will execute the following command:

```
.ent1 configure -background white
```

Similarly, when that entry loses focus, it will receive a `FocusOut` event, and Tk will execute the following command, making the widget go dim:

```
.ent1 configure -background gray
```

3.3 Syntax of the `bind` command

Now that we've seen how bindings are used, let's take a closer look at how they're specified. Figure 3.11 presents a summary of the `bind` command.

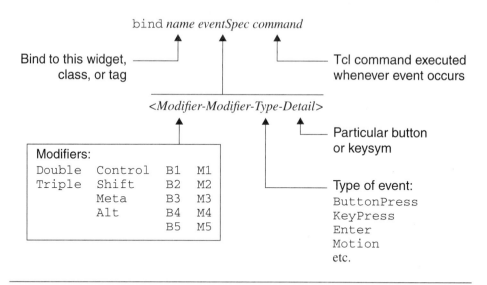

Figure 3.11. Syntax of the bind command.

The first argument is the widget or class of widgets that will receive the event. The second argument is the event that we're interested in, and the third argument is the script that is executed whenever the event occurs. The event specification and the script are optional. If they're left off, bind returns information about the bindings that are already defined. We'll use this feature in Section 3.6.1 to examine a widget's current binding state.

3.3.1 The event specification

Writing out the event specification is probably the trickiest part of creating bindings. However, you can follow a recipe to get it right every time. First, let's look at the ingredients. Then we'll present the recipe, in Section 3.3.1.4.

As you can see in Figure 3.11, an event specification has several fields:

Modifier: The modifier field is optional. It specifies a mouse button or a keyboard modifier that's being held down as the event occurs. For example, you might hold down the Shift key while you generate an event by clicking the mouse button. Modifiers can also specify a repeated event, such as a double-click or triple-click operation. Some events require a combination of modifiers. For example, you might hold down Control and Shift and double-click with the mouse. So a single event specification may have multiple modifiers.

Type: The most important field is the type field, which specifies the kind of event— mouse motion, key press, entering a widget, and so on.

Detail: The detail field is optional. If the type field is related to the mouse buttons, the detail indicates a particular mouse button that must be clicked. If the type field is related to a key press, the detail indicates a particular key that must be pressed.

We'll review the details of each of these fields and then see how they're combined.

3.3.1.1 Event types

The only required field in the event specification is the event type. This field tells what kind of event is being received.

There are 22 event types. Many windowing toolkits require intimate knowledge of these events to write even simple application programs. It is a testimony to how well Tk was designed and implemented that you need to know only about a dozen of these event types to write most programs (see Table 3.1). The events not covered here are useful mostly for low-level widget coding and are well documented in the reference manual, which you'll need to study anyway if you're writing low-level code.

Event Type	Description
`ButtonPress (Button)` `ButtonRelease`	Triggered when a mouse button is clicked or released.
`KeyPress (Key)` `KeyRelease`	Triggered when a key is pressed or released.
`Motion`	Triggered when there is mouse motion over the widget. This is often used for interactions on the canvas widget, as we'll see in Chapter 4.
`Enter` `Leave`	Triggered when the mouse pointer enters or leaves the boundary of a widget.
`FocusIn` `FocusOut`	Triggered when a widget gains or loses the keyboard focus. If you need to validate user input, you might handle it on `FocusOut`.
`Map` `Unmap`	Triggered when a widget appears (`Map`) or disappears (`Unmap`) from the screen. These will occur, for example, when a window is iconified/deiconified. If your program is a game or a system status screen, you may want to suspend processing when the program is not being viewed. These events provide a hook for doing that.

Table 3.1. Common event types for the `bind` command. Abbreviations are in parentheses.

Event Type	Description
Configure	Triggered when a window is reconfigured—usually because it has changed size. If you've been looking for a "resize" event, this is it. This is commonly used on the canvas widget to redraw the items whenever the canvas changes size. We'll see an example of this in Section 4.6.1.

Table 3.1. (continued) Common event types for the bind command. Abbreviations are in parentheses.

3.3.1.2 Modifiers

Modifiers are used to further specify mouse and keyboard events. For example, suppose you bind to the Motion event, like this:

```
bind .x <Motion> {puts "moving" }
```

The command will trigger whenever the mouse pointer moves over the widget. Now suppose you add a modifier, like this:

```
bind .x <Button1-Motion> {puts "moving, B1 pressed" }
```

The command will trigger only when you hold down the first mouse button and move the pointer. If you use the Shift modifier, the command will trigger only when you hold down the Shift key and move the pointer:

```
bind .x <Shift-Motion> {puts "moving, shift key pressed" }
```

If you want to be even more specific, you can combine modifiers, like this:

```
bind .x <Shift-Button1-Motion> {puts "moving, B1 pressed, Shifted" }
```

This command will trigger only when you hold down both the Shift key and the first mouse button and move the pointer.

If you add all of these bindings to the widget, only one of them will be triggered by a particular movement of the pointer. For example, if you start moving the mouse, you'll see:

```
moving
moving
moving
```

If you hold down Shift and continue moving the pointer, you'll see:

```
moving, shift key pressed
moving, shift key pressed
moving, shift key pressed
```

For each event, Tk finds the most specific binding for the widget and executes its associated command.

You can also use modifiers to specify a repeating action. Adding the modifier `Double` or `Triple` indicates that the specified event has to be repeated two or three times and that the following conditions must be true.

- The events must occur within a certain (short) amount of time. This ensures that two single clicks several minutes apart are not interpreted as a double-click.
- The events must occur without moving the mouse significantly.

These two restrictions ensure that double and triple mouse clicks are interpreted as people have come to expect. All of the available binding modifiers are summarized in Table 3.2.

Modifier	Description

`Control`
`Shift`
`Meta`
`Alt`
	Indicates that the given control key must be already pressed when the event occurs.

`Button1` `(B1)`
`Button2` `(B2)`
`Button3` `(B3)`
`Button4` `(B4)`
`Button5` `(B5)`
	Indicates that the given mouse button must be already pressed when the event occurs. Tk provides support for a five-button mouse, but most users will have only one, two, or three buttons.

`Double` `Triple`	Usually used for `ButtonPress` events. These modifiers specify that the event must be repeated either two or three times in close succession, without significant mouse movement. For example, `<Double-Button-1>` is the same as `<Button-1><Button-1>` but is constrained by the motion and time requirements.

`Mod1` `(M1)`
`Mod2` `(M2)`
`Mod3` `(M3)`
`Mod4` `(M4)`
`Mod5` `(M5)`
	Indicates that the given modification key must be already pressed when the event occurs. This is a carryover of old X terminology. Avoid these, and use one of the more descriptive modifiers (such as `Alt` or `Meta`) listed previously.

Table 3.2. Event modifiers for the `bind` command.

3.3.1.3 Details

The final field in the event specification is the detail field. Like the modifier field, it is used to further specify mouse and keyboard related events, as explained in Table 3.3.

Event Details	Description
Button Number (1-5)	If the event type is `ButtonPress` or `ButtonRelease`, you can add the button number (1–5) as a detail.
Key Symbol	If the event type is `KeyPress` or `KeyRelease`, the detail may be specified in the form of an X Window keysym.

Table 3.3. Event details for the `bind` command.

The keysym for most alphanumeric ASCII characters is the character. So you can bind to the c key like this:

```
bind .x <KeyPress-c> {puts "pressed c"}
```

You can bind to the capital C key like this:

```
bind .x <KeyPress-C> {puts "pressed C"}
```

or like this:

```
bind .x <Shift-KeyPress-c> {puts "pressed C"}
```

Having a capital letter in the detail field is like having a Shift modifier up front. You should avoid using capital letters unless you intend for the Shift key to be held down. For example, if you take a cursory look at the following code, you might think that it handles the Control-C event:

```
bind .x <Control-KeyPress-C> {puts "pressed ^C"}
```

But since we've used a capital letter, this code will handle only the Shift-Control-C event.

Some of the keys are represented by a textual keysym. This includes the symbol keys, such as +, -, <, >; the function keys; and other keys, such as the space bar or the Return key. Sometimes you'll find discrepancies between the physical keyboard labels and the logical names the windowing system has assigned the keys. For example, a key may be labeled Help but may be assigned the logical name F23.

If you don't know how to spell the keysym for a particular key, run the following program:

```
label .msg -width 30 -text "Press any key"
pack .msg

bind .msg <Key> {.msg configure -text "keysym = %K"}
focus .msg
```

Just put your mouse pointer on the window and press a key. In Figure 3.12, for example, we've pressed the * key and found that its corresponding keysym is `asterisk`.

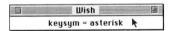

Figure 3.12. A simple program to inspect keysyms.

3.3.1.4 Constructing a sequence

Now that we've seen the various parts of the event specifier, let's take a look at the recipe to construct one.

1. First, determine the event type. If it's not a `ButtonPress`/`ButtonRelease` or `KeyPress`/`KeyRelease` event, you're done. The modifier and detail fields apply only to buttons and keys.

2. Next, fill in the detail field. If you've chosen a `KeyPress`/`KeyRelease` event, this will be the symbolic name of the desired key. Likewise, if this is a `ButtonPress`/ `ButtonRelease` event, this will be the number of the desired button. If you want the event to apply to all keystrokes or to all buttons, leave off the detail field.

3. Finally, fill in any modifier fields as needed.

Figure 3.13 shows some sample event specifications being constructed.

3.3.1.5 The difference between a mouse modifier and mouse detail

When examining the last example in Figure 3.13, you might ask why button motion must be specified as `<Button1-Motion>` and not as `<Motion-1>`. If fact, if you use the latter, it gives an error, saying "specified button '1' for non-button event."

Remember, the detail field applies only to `ButtonPress`/`ButtonRelease` and `KeyPress`/`KeyRelease` events—not to `Motion` events. Specifying `Button1` in the modifier means that button 1 was *already* pressed when the event occurred.

3.3.1.6 Sequence abbreviations

Several binding sequences are so commonly used that abbreviations have been provided for them. These sequences include `<ButtonPress-1>` through `<ButtonPress-5>`, which may be abbreviated as `<1>` - `<5>`. Also, `KeyPress` events may be abbreviated to the detail field. For example, `<KeyPress-a>` may be specified as either `<a>` or a.

We've found that it's better to avoid using abbreviations, however. They tend to confuse people, and if you're typing in a reasonable program, the savings in keystrokes is negligible. But we make an exception for `KeyPress` events with such modifiers as `Control` or `Alt`. Obviously, `<Control-c>` is a key press, and it is a bit more readable than `<Control-KeyPress-c>`.

- **Clicking button 1:**

  `<ButtonPress>` ⟶ `<ButtonPress-1>`

  Start with a   ...Which button?
  button press...   button 1.

- **Double-clicking button 2:**

  `<ButtonPress>` ⟶ `<ButtonPress-2>` ⟶ `<Double-ButtonPress-2>`

  Start with a   ...Which button?   ...add a modifier
  button press...   button 2...   for double-clicking.

- **Pressing any key:**

  `<KeyPress>`

  No modifiers needed.

- **Pressing the Return key:**

  `<KeyPress>` ⟶ `<KeyPress-Return>`

  Start with a   ...Which key?
  key press...   Return key.

- **Button 1 motion, with the Shift key held down:**

  `<Motion>` ⟶ `<Button1-Motion>` ⟶ `<Shift-Button1-Motion>`

  Start with a   ...add a modifier for   ...and a modifier for
  motion event...   holding down button 1...   holding down the Shift key.

Figure 3.13. Constructing event specifications.

3.3.1.7   Combining events

It's possible to bind a command to a multievent sequence. The command will be executed when the entire sequence of events occurs within the program. This is most useful for `KeyPress` events.

For example, many programs have keyboard shortcuts for items on the pull-down menus. This lets you access program functions without having to use the menus, so you can keep your hands on the keyboard. A shortcut may require one keystroke or a sequence of keystrokes. In the popular emacs editor, for example, you can type Control-x Control-f to load a file or Control-x Control-s to save a file. If you wanted to add these shortcuts to a Tcl/Tk application, you could use the following bindings:

```
bind . <Control-x><Control-f> {load_file}
bind . <Control-x><Control-s> {saveFile}
```

Notice that we added these bindings to the main window ".". As we'll see in Section 3.5, this means that they will work no matter where you type in the main window.

Multievent sequences also provide a handy way to add a back door to your program. A *back door* is an undocumented feature that lets you type in a password or click on a special spot to get special privileges in the program. For example, you could add a secret "power mode" to a game program with this binding sequence:

```
bind . <KeyPress-d><n><k><r><o><z> {set power_mode on}
```

The binding would be invoked whenever you type the secret password—no special processing is needed on the part of your application.

3.3.2 Percent substitutions

Before Tk executes the command for a particular binding, it substitutes information about the event into `%` fields in the command string. This allows you to parameterize your event-handling code with information about the current event.

There are many event parameters, but only a few of them are generally useful. These are summarized in Table 3.4. The rest are described on the `bind` manual page.

String	Replacement
`%%`	Replaced with a single percent.
`%W`	The name of the window receiving the event. Valid for all event types.
`%b`	The number of the mouse button that was clicked or released. Valid only for `ButtonPress` and `ButtonRelease` events.
`%A` `%K`	The key that was pressed or released. `%A` is the ASCII character corresponding to the key or to the empty string if the key is not an ASCII character. `%K` is the key's symbolic name. Valid only for `KeyPress` and `KeyRelease` events.
`%h` `%w`	The height and width of the widget. Valid only for `Configure` and `Expose` events.
`%x` `%y`	The x and y coordinates of the mouse pointer at the time of the event. Values are relative to the origin (0,0) at the upper-left corner of the widget receiving the event.

Table 3.4. Percent substitutions used to access event details in bindings.

String	Replacement
%X %Y	The *x* and *y* coordinates of the mouse pointer at the time of the event. Similar to %x and %y, but values are relative to the origin (0,0) at the upper-left corner of the desktop. Valid only for ButtonPress, ButtonRelease, KeyPress, KeyRelease, and Motion events.

Table 3.4. (continued) Percent substitutions used to access event details in bindings.

The following example shows how the % fields work:

```
canvas .c -background white
pack .c
array set colors {1 red 2 green 3 blue}
bind .c <ButtonPress> {
    .c create text %x %y -text "click!" -fill $colors(%b)
}
```

This creates a canvas widget and adds a binding for the ButtonPress event. Each time you click on the canvas, Tk substitutes the mouse coordinates into %x and %y and the button number into %b. So, whenever you click, it creates a click! message at the current mouse position. If you click with button 1, the message will be red; with button 2, it will be green; and with button 3, it will be blue.

Whenever a percent substitution is made, the replacement string is inserted as a properly formatted list element. For many commands, this produces the result that you would expect. For example, suppose you have the following binding for text widgets:

```
bind Text <KeyPress> {%W insert end %A}
```

If you have a text widget named .t and if the user types an X in that widget, Tk executes a command like this:

```
.t insert end X
```

If the user types a [in that widget, Tk executes a command like this:

```
.t insert end \[
```

This time, an extra \ character is added as part of the substitution, to ensure that [is treated as an ordinary character and not the start of an embedded command. So the replacement string has an intuitive behavior that works properly in many cases.

But suppose that for some reason, you added braces to the bind command, like this:

```
bind Text <KeyPress> {%W insert end {%A}}
```

Now if the user types a [in the widget, Tk executes a command like this:

```
.t insert end {\[}
```

So both \ and [are inserted into the widget.

In general, you should use the % fields as standalone arguments on a command line or as part of a double-quoted string. If you use the % fields within braces, you may get the wrong behavior for such characters as [,], {, }, ", and space.

3.4 More complex events

Now that we've seen some simple examples, let's look at some more complex examples. Here we'll combine several bindings to perform a task.

3.4.1 Click, drag, drop

A number of common operations involve combining mouse clicks with mouse motion.

- Highlighting text by selecting it with the mouse
- Dragging the bubble on a scrollbar
- Creating graphical items on a canvas
- Controlling a program by dragging and dropping screen elements around

Some of these operations—such as highlighting text or dragging the bubble on a scroll-bar—are already built into Tk. We'll see how to implement the others, using a series of bind commands.

Although the details of these operations differ, they all share a common event model.

1. You select an item or initiate an action by *clicking* the mouse button and holding it down. This triggers a script that selects an item to be dragged or creates a new object.

2. You move or modify the item by *dragging* the mouse around with the mouse button pressed. Usually the display is updated as you're doing this, so you get immediate feedback. If you're dragging an item, for instance, it will move with the mouse pointer. This action will be performed again and again as the mouse is moved from point to point.

3. You finalize the action by releasing the mouse button. You can also think of this as *dropping* the item. This commits a change or updates the program somehow. If you're dragging a selection rectangle, for instance, the items within it would become selected when you release the mouse button.

Figure 3.14 shows a state diagram for Click-Drag-Drop interaction. The program begins in the Start state. When you click on a button, it executes some code for that event and progresses to the Clicked state. If you release the button immediately, the program goes to the Dropped state. Or, if you move the mouse, the program goes into the Dragging state. From the Dragging state, only one transition is left. When you release the mouse button, the program moves to the final, Dropped state. Unless the bindings are explicitly changed, the program will return to the original Start state, waiting for you to start the cycle again.

You can see how this works in the following simple example:

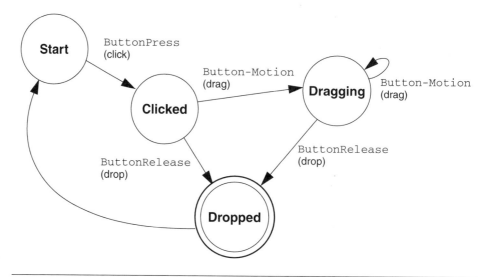

Figure 3.14. A state diagram for Click-Drag-Drop.

```
pack [canvas .c]

bind .c <ButtonPress-1> { puts "click %x %y" }
bind .c <B1-Motion> { puts "drag %x %y" }
bind .c <ButtonRelease-1> { puts "drop %x %y" }
```

The <ButtonPress-1> event handles the click, <B1-Motion> handles the drag, and
<ButtonRelease-1> handles the drop. When the canvas receives an event, Tk substi-
tutes the coordinates of the mouse pointer into the %x and %y fields and then executes
these commands. So running this program and clicking and dragging the mouse produce
the following output:

```
click 54 46
drag 56 48
drag 67 60
drag 97 86
drag 127 110
drag 154 122
drop 157 122
```

We see the button being clicked on, the mouse being moved, and the button being
released.

You should notice two important things about these events. First, the ButtonPress
and ButtonRelease events happen once, at the start and end of the sequence. The
Motion event occurs multiple times, at each motion point. The event does not occur at all
if the mouse is not moved, so be sure that your logic can handle a click-drop sequence.

When the mouse moves quickly, the windowing system will compress mouse events, so you may not get a motion event for every pixel. But you will get some sequence of points that represents the overall mouse motion.

Now let's put these bindings to work in an interactive drawing editor. We'll learn all about the canvas in Chapter 4, and we'll build a full-blown drawing editor in Section 4.7. For now, we'll concentrate on the bindings needed to draw an oval on a canvas. The code can be written as follows:

```
pack [canvas .c]

bind .c <ButtonPress-1>   {oval_create %W %x %y}
bind .c <B1-Motion>       {oval_move %W %x %y}
bind .c <ButtonRelease-1> {oval_end %W %x %y}

proc oval_create {win x y} {
    global oval
    set oval(x0) $x
    set oval(y0) $y
    set oval(id) [$win create oval $x $y $x $y]
}
proc oval_move {win x y} {
    global oval
    $win coords $oval(id) $oval(x0) $oval(y0) $x $y
}
proc oval_end {win x y} {
    global oval
    oval_move $win $x $y
    $win itemconfigure $oval(id) -fill lightblue
}
```

You can run this code and then click, drag, and drop to create ovals on the canvas, as shown in Figure 3.15. In this code, we bind the click, drag, and drop events to the following procedures.

Click: Invokes `oval_create` with the click coordinate. That procedure creates an oval item on the canvas at that coordinate. The procedure saves the item number and the starting coordinate in an array called `oval`, so we can access these values during the next two events.

Drag: Invokes `oval_move` with the drag coordinate. That procedure resizes the oval to fit between the starting coordinate and the current mouse coordinate.

Drop: Invokes `oval_end` with the drop coordinate. That procedure resizes the oval one last time, then changes its fill color to a final state. Since both the drag and the drop processing resize the item, it's a good idea to make a procedure that can be used during both events, such as `oval_move`.

We could have put the canvas commands directly in the bindings, but it's usually better to use procedures, for the following reasons.

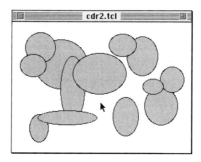

Figure 3.15. Using bind to draw ovals on a canvas. Remember the mantra: Click-Drag-Drop!

- The binding code is executed at the global scope, so any temporary variables that you use end up polluting the global namespace. For example, suppose we had a binding like this:

```
bind .c <ButtonPress-1> {
    set x0 [expr %x-4]
    set y0 [expr %y-4]
    %W create oval $x0 $y0 $x0 $y0
}
```

This sets the global variables x0 and y0 each time you click on the canvas. If you were thinking of these as temporary variables, you may have problems. You may accidentally clobber variables called x0 and y0 that are being used elsewhere in the program. This leads to subtle bugs that are often difficult to track down.

- If the binding code contains any format or scan statements, you may have problems with the % substitutions. For example, suppose we had a binding like this:

```
bind .c <ButtonPress-1> {
    set x0 %x
    set y0 %y
    %W create oval $x0 $y0 $x0 $y0
    puts [format "oval at: %d,%d" $x0 $y0]
}
```

Each time this code is executed, Tk substitutes the event information into the % fields. This changes %x and %y as you would expect, but it also changes the %d fields in the format command. The %d field gives you a low-level detail about a particular event. For a ButtonPress event, it gets replaced with ??, so if you were using the puts command for debugging, you would get some rather confusing output, like this:

```
oval at: ??,??
oval at: ??,??
...
```

You can get around this problem by replacing %d with %%d. That way, when Tk does the % substitutions for the binding, it will convert %% back to a single %. But you can avoid all of this in the first place by putting the code into a procedure and by passing parameters like %x and %y as arguments.

- You can use these same procedures to create ovals on many different canvas widgets. In fact, the bindings in this example are completely generic. You can copy them from one canvas widget to another, and they will work without any changes. The reason is that we used %W as the name of the canvas widget in each binding.

- If the code is more than a few lines long, it's easier to read as a procedure.

3.4.2 Customizing widget behavior

The bind command makes the Tk widgets extraordinarily versatile. You can add new behaviors to any kind of widget, so you can use a particular widget in many different ways. A label, for instance, is normally used to display an icon or a bit of text. But you can add some bindings to a label and make it act like a button or an entry widget. Normally, there is no reason to do this. If you need a button, you use a button widget. But sometimes you need something like a button, with a few modifications.

Suppose you need a toolbar like the one shown in Figure 3.16. Each toolbar has a number of tools represented by icons. When a particular tool is selected, its relief becomes sunken, and the other tools become raised. Only one tool can be selected at a time, so the tools in the toolbar act like radiobuttons. But they certainly don't look like radiobuttons. Instead of using radiobuttons directly, we'll build a toolbar, using labels and some special bindings.

Figure 3.16. Selecting a tool on the toolbar causes a command to be executed.

As usual, we'll write some procedures that make it easy to create a toolbar. You might use these procedures as follows to create the toolbar shown in Figure 3.16:

```
toolbar_create .tbar top {
    .show configure -text "MODE:\n%t"
}
pack .tbar -side left -fill y -padx 4 -pady 4
```

```
label .show -width 20 -background white
pack .show -side right -expand yes -fill both -padx 4 -pady 4

toolbar_add .tbar select [image create bitmap \
    -file [file join $env(EFFTCL_LIBRARY) images select.xbm]]
toolbar_add .tbar rect [image create bitmap \
    -file [file join $env(EFFTCL_LIBRARY) images rect.xbm]]
toolbar_add .tbar oval [image create bitmap \
    -file [file join $env(EFFTCL_LIBRARY) images oval.xbm]]
toolbar_add .tbar spline [image create bitmap \
    -file [file join $env(EFFTCL_LIBRARY) images spline.xbm]]
```

The `toolbar_create` procedure creates a new toolbar. You pass in the name of the toolbar, a value that controls the packing of the tools, and a callback command. In this example, the toolbar is called `.tbar`. Its tools will be packed in on side `top`, so they will flow from top to bottom. Whenever a tool is selected, the toolbar will substitute the tool name in place of `%t` and will execute the callback. If you select the `rect` tool, for example, the toolbar will execute the following command to display the name of the tool in the label named `.show`:

```
.show configure -text "MODE:\nrect"
```

The `toolbar_add` procedure adds new tools to the toolbar. You pass in the name of the toolbar, the name of the tool, and an image for the tool icon. The procedure creates a tool widget and packs it into the toolbar. In this example, we've added four tools: `select`, `rect`, `oval`, and `spline`, using a bitmap image for each tool.

Now let's see how these procedures are implemented. We define the `toolbar_create` procedure like this:

```
proc toolbar_create {win {origin "top"} {command ""}} {
    global tbInfo
    frame $win -class Toolbar
    set tbInfo($win-current) ""
    set tbInfo($win-origin) $origin
    set tbInfo($win-command) $command
    return $win
}
```

As usual, we create a hull frame in class `Toolbar` to contain the toolbar. Then we initialize the data structure for the toolbar: The `current` field contains the name of the tool that's currently selected; the `origin` field contains a value that affects the packing of the tools; and the `command` field contains a callback command.

At first, the toolbar is empty. We add a widget for each tool when you call `toolbar_add`, which is defined like this:

```
proc toolbar_add {win tool image} {
    global tbInfo
```

```
        set label "$win.tool-$tool"
        label $label -borderwidth 2 -relief raised -image $image
        pack $label -side $tbInfo($win-origin) -fill both

        bind $label <ButtonPress-1> [list toolbar_select $win $tool]

        if {[llength [pack slaves $win]] == 1} {
            after idle [list toolbar_select $win $tool]
        }
        return $label
    }
```

We create a label for each new tool and pack it on the side specified in the `origin` field. Each label must have a unique name, so we use the tool name as part of the widget name.

By default, each of the tool labels would be completely inactive. But we bind to the `<ButtonPress-1>` event, so clicking on a label invokes a procedure named `toolbar_select` to activate that particular tool. You can also call `toolbar_select` directly, to select a tool programmatically. We'll see how this procedure is implemented later.

Finally, we set things up so that the first tool will be selected by default. Each time we add a tool, we use `pack slaves` to get the list of labels that are packed into the toolbar. If we have one label, we've just added the first tool, and we select that tool.

But instead of calling `toolbar_select` directly, we arrange for it to be called later, when the application is idle. This is an important feature. When the tool is selected, the toolbar will execute its callback command. It is quite common for the callback to reference other widgets in the application. So it's better to select the default tool at the last possible moment, when the application is fully constructed.

We define the `toolbar_select` procedure like this:

```
    proc toolbar_select {win tool} {
        global tbInfo

        if {$tbInfo($win-current) != ""} {
            set label "$win.tool-$tbInfo($win-current)"
            $label configure -relief raised
        }
        set label "$win.tool-$tool"
        $label configure -relief sunken
        set tbInfo($win-current) $tool

        if {$tbInfo($win-command) != ""} {
            set cmd [percent_subst %t $tbInfo($win-command) $tool]
            uplevel #0 $cmd
        }
    }
```

We look for a tool name in the `current` field. If we find one, it represents the tool that is currently selected. We give this tool a raised border, indicating that it is no longer selected. Then we give the new tool a sunken border, and we save its name in the `current` field.

Finally, we substitute the tool name into the `%t` field of the callback command and then execute it. Instead of executing it in the current scope, we use `uplevel #0` to execute it at the global scope. That way, this component mimics the usual behavior for Tk callback commands discussed in Section 3.1.4. We use this pattern for handling the callback code in many of the components in this book. We'll describe it in detail in Section 8.2.3, when we provide some guidelines for library development.

At this point, the toolbar is complete. As you can see, we've taken ordinary labels and turned them into an interactive component through the power of the `bind` command.

3.5 Binding tags

A widget may respond to a single event with more than one behavior. For example, suppose you start up `wish` and create a label widget with two bindings for the same event:

```
$ wish
% pack [label .x -text "Target"]
% bind .x    <Enter> {puts "entering %W (via %W)"}
% bind Label <Enter> {puts "entering %W (via Label)"}
```

When the mouse pointer enters this widget, it may trigger one or the other or both of these bindings. You can determine how this widget will respond by using the `bindtags` command, like this:

```
% bindtags .x
⇒ .x Label . all
```

This command returns a list of all bindings that the widget will process, in the order that it will process them. In this case, the label will respond first to bindings on `.x`, then to bindings for class `Label`, then to bindings on the main window ".", and finally, to bindings on the keyword `all`. This process is illustrated in Figure 3.17.

So in this example, if you move the mouse pointer onto the label, the program will print the following messages:

```
⇒ entering .x (via .x)
  entering .x (via Label)
```

You can use the `bindtags` command to modify the list of binding tags. For example, suppose that we wanted these commands to be executed in a different order. We could rearrange the binding tags, like this:

```
% bindtags .x {Label .x . all}
```

Then the binding for class `Label` would be triggered first, like this:

```
⇒ entering .x (via Label)
  entering .x (via .x)
```

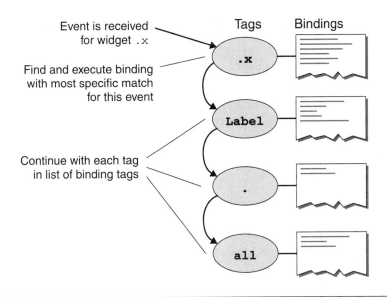

Figure 3.17. When it receives an event, a widget executes all of the bindings on its list of binding tags.

Suppose that for this particular label .x, we wanted to suppress the usual `Label` binding for labels. We could remove it from the list of binding tags, like this:

```
% bindtags .x {.x . all}
```

Then, if you moved the mouse pointer onto the label, the program would respond with only one of the messages:

⇒ *entering .x (via .x)*

Suppose that we wanted to disable all of the behaviors for this widget. We could give it an empty list of binding tags, like this:

```
% bindtags .x { }
```

Then, if you moved the mouse pointer onto the label, it wouldn't trigger any bindings. The label would completely ignore the bindings for .x and `Label`, since they're not on its list of binding tags.

Notice that in this last example, we were careful to include a space between the braces. This is important. If you set the binding tags to a null string, like this:

```
% bindtags .x {}
```

it will reset the binding tags back to their default state:

```
% bindtags .x
```

⇒ *.x Label . all*

So, if you want to clear the list of binding tags, you must set it to an empty list with at least one space character.

3.5.1   Default binding tags

When each widget is created, it is given a list of binding tags by default. Ordinary widgets get a list of four elements in the following order:

- Widget name (example: .x)
- Class name (example: Label)
- Toplevel widget containing this widget (example: .)
- Keyword all

This is just what we saw in the previous section. Bindings that are tied to the widget name are handled first. This allows you to override the default behavior of a widget with more specific bindings, as we'll see in the next section. The class bindings are handled next, followed by bindings for the toplevel widget that contains this widget and bindings for the keyword all.

The last two tags make it easy to add keyboard accelerators to your applications. For example, suppose that you bind to the main window, like this:

```
bind . <Control-z> do_undo
```

Now suppose that you create some entry widgets in the main window, like this:

```
pack [entry .e1]
pack [entry .e2]
pack [entry .e3]
```

Each of these widgets will have the name "." on its list of binding tags. So, you could type Control-z into any of these widgets, and they would respond by calling do_undo to perform an "undo" operation.

Binding to all works the same way, but it affects all of the widgets in the application—not just those in a particular window.

Toplevel widgets get a slightly different list of binding tags by default:

- Widget name (example: .t)
- Class name (example: Toplevel)
- Keyword all

This list is nearly identical to the previous list, with one exception. Toplevel widgets aren't contained in another toplevel, so the third element on the previous list is dropped.

3.5.2   Using **break** to interrupt event processing

As we saw in the previous section, the widget name appears first in the default list of binding tags. That way, you can bind directly to a widget and override the default behavior for its class.

For example, suppose we have an entry widget like the one shown in Figure 3.18. Normally, an entry widget will accept any characters that you type into it. But this entry will accept only numbers and dashes. If you type in other characters, a beep sounds. This kind of entry comes in handy when you're prompting for a phone number or a social security number.

Figure 3.18. An entry widget that accepts only numbers and dashes.

To get this behavior, we bind to the `<KeyPress>` event on the entry widget, like this:

```
label .prompt -text "Phone Number:"
pack .prompt -side left

entry .phone
pack .phone -side left

bind .phone <KeyPress> {
    if {![regexp "\[0-9\b-\]" "%A"]} {
        bell
        break
    }
}
```

We've done nothing to change the binding tags for the entry, so it follows the default list, as shown in Figure 3.19. First, it handles the binding for .phone, which checks for a valid character. Remember, Tk will automatically replace %A with the ASCII character for the key that was pressed. In the .phone binding, we use regexp to compare that character against the valid range, which includes the digits 0-9, the backspace character \b, and the dash. If the new character doesn't match one of these, we ring the bell and execute the break command.

Normally, the break command terminates a loop. But in the context of a binding, it stops any further processing of the binding tags. By executing the break command, we can prevent the usual Entry binding from inserting the character into the widget.

3.5.3   Inventing binding tags for groups of bindings

When we explore the canvas widget in Chapter 4, we'll create the interactive drawing editor shown in Figure 3.20. This editor has several drawing modes, controlled by the toolbar on the left side of the window. In this section, we'll see how you can use binding tags to switch between the various modes of the editor.

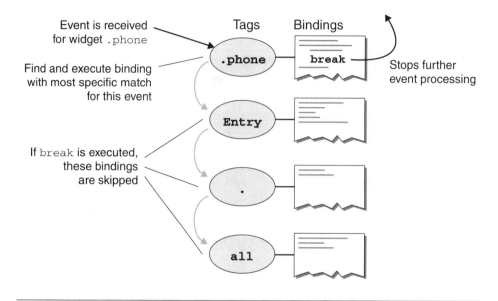

Figure 3.19. The break command interrupts the usual processing of binding tags.

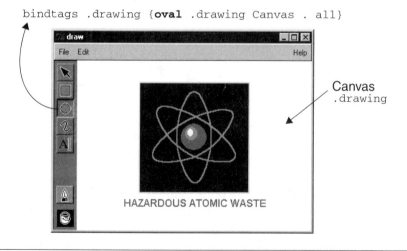

Figure 3.20. Setting the drawing mode by using binding tags.

Each drawing mode is implemented by a different set of bindings on the canvas. The "oval" mode, for example, has bindings for the click, drag, and drop events described in Section 3.4.1. The "text" mode has a binding for the click event, to select an existing text item or to create a new one. This mode also has bindings for KeyPress events that edit the text of the item.

When each tool is selected, its bindings must be added to the canvas. If the "oval" tool is selected, for example, we could add some bindings as follows:

```
bind .drawing <ButtonPress-1> {
    canvas_shape_create %W oval %x %y
}
bind .drawing <B1-Motion> {
    canvas_shape_drag %W %x %y
}
bind .drawing <ButtonRelease-1> {
    canvas_shape_end %W %x %y
}
```

These are just like the bindings that we saw earlier, in Section 3.4.1, but they use some library procedures that we'll describe in Section 4.7.1. Right now, we'll focus on the bindings and how they're added to the canvas.

When another tool is selected, we must be careful to remove these bindings. Otherwise, the user might accidentally trigger parts of the "oval" mode under the new tool. We could erase each binding by overwriting the binding code with a null string, like this:

```
bind .drawing <ButtonPress-1> {}
bind .drawing <B1-Motion> {}
bind .drawing <ButtonRelease-1> {}
```

This scheme works, but there is a much easier way to handle the drawing modes. Instead of adding/removing a series of bindings directly on the widget, we can use a single binding tag to control the drawing mode. For example, we can invent a new binding tag, called oval, and then bind all of the "oval" mode behaviors to it, like this:

```
bind oval <ButtonPress-1> {
    canvas_shape_create %W oval %x %y
}
bind oval <B1-Motion> {
    canvas_shape_drag %W %x %y
}
bind oval <ButtonRelease-1> {
    canvas_shape_end %W %x %y
}
```

Now we can activate this behavior by adding oval to the binding tags for the canvas widget, like this:

```
bindtags .drawing {oval .drawing Canvas . all}
```

When the canvas receives an event, it will handle the oval bindings first and will then look for bindings on .drawing, Canvas, ., and all. If the canvas receives a

`<ButtonPress-1>` event, for example, it will find the `<ButtonPress-1>` binding on `oval` and will call `canvas_shape_create` to create an oval item.

We can deactivate the "oval" tool by removing `oval` from the binding tags:

```
bindtags .drawing {.drawing Canvas . all}
```

When the canvas receives a `<ButtonPress-1>` event, it will completely ignore the `oval` bindings. It will look for bindings only on `.drawing`, `Canvas`, `.`, and `all`.

We could create another binding tag, called `text`, for all of the "text" mode behaviors:

```
bind text <ButtonPress-1> {
    canvas_text_select %W %x %y
}
bind text <KeyPress> {
    canvas_text_edit_add %W %A
}
bind text <KeyPress-Return> {
    canvas_text_edit_add %W "\n"
}
bind text <KeyPress-BackSpace> {
    canvas_text_edit_backsp %W
}
bind text <KeyPress-Delete> {
    canvas_text_edit_backsp %W
}
```

And again, we could activate the "text" mode by adding `text` to the binding tags:

```
bindtags .drawing {text .drawing Canvas . all}
```

All of the other modes in the drawing editor can be handled in the same manner.

In general, you can think of the binding tags as labels for the various behaviors of a widget. Certain tags are predefined, such as the widget name and the class name, but you are free to invent your own tags for new behaviors. You can activate any behavior by adding its tag to the list of binding tags. Likewise, you can deactivate a behavior by removing its tag from the list.

3.5.4   Binding to a top-level window

You can add keyboard accelerators to your application by binding directly to a top-level window, as we saw in Section 3.5.1. But you should think twice before binding to a top-level window for any other reason. All of the widgets inside the toplevel will inherit the behavior as well. This is what you want for keyboard accelerators, but it can cause problems in many other contexts.

For example, suppose that you have an application like the one shown in Figure 3.21. The canvas in the middle of the main window displays a drawing. When you resize the window, it automatically resizes the drawing.

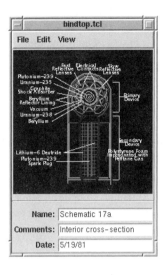
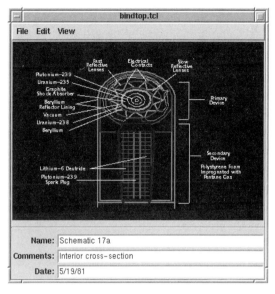

Figure 3.21. In this application, the canvas resizes its drawing automatically.

You can handle the automatic resizing by binding to the `Configure` event. Suppose you add a binding to the main window, like this:

```
bind . <Configure> {
    resize_drawing .display
}
```

At first glance, this appears to make sense. Whenever the main window changes size, the procedure `resize_drawing` is called to update the drawing on the canvas.

But because we've added the binding to the main window, it is inherited by all of the widgets within it. So the procedure `resize_drawing` would be called many times for a single resize operation. When the program starts up, for example, there is a noticeable delay. If you inserted a `puts` command into the binding, you would see the cause immediately: All of the widgets receive a `Configure` event when they appear on the screen, so `resize_drawing` is called 15 times during start-up!

You can solve this problem one of two ways. You could move the binding from the main window to the canvas, like this:

```
bind .display <Configure> {
    resize_drawing .display
}
```

That way, `resize_drawing` would be called once, each time the canvas changes size.

But suppose that for some reason, you really wanted to know about size changes for the main window. In that case, you could use a separate binding tag to add the behavior. You could create a tag called `resizeDrawing` and then add that tag to the main window, like this:

```
bind resizeDrawing <Configure> {
    resize_drawing .display
}
set tags [bindtags .]
bindtags . [linsert $tags 0 resizeDrawing]
```

None of the other widgets would have this tag by default. If you resized the application, many widgets would get `Configure` events, but only the main window would trigger a call to `resize_drawing`.

If you find yourself binding to a toplevel to handle something other than a keyboard accelerator, stop and think. Chances are, you should be using an alternative.

3.6 Debugging bindings

When you're debugging an application, you may wonder what bindings a widget has or what events it receives. In this section, we'll look at two procedures that can help you with debugging.

3.6.1 Displaying bindings

If a widget isn't behaving as you expected, you can use the following procedure to print out a summary of the widget's bindings:

```
proc bind_show {w {mode "-quiet"}} {
    puts "$w"
    foreach tag [bindtags $w] {
        puts "\t$tag"
        foreach spec [bind $tag] {
            puts "\t\t$spec"
            if {$mode == "-verbose"} {
                set cmd [bind $tag $spec]
                set cmd [string trim $cmd "\n"]
                regsub -all "\n" $cmd "\n\t\t\t" cmd
                puts "\t\t\t$cmd"
            }
        }
    }
}
```

We use the `bindtags` command to query the list of binding tags for the widget that's passed in as an argument. Then we iterate through the tags and print out a summary of the bindings for each tag. We use the `bind` command to query information about the bindings

that are already defined. When we give it a tag name, the `bind` command returns a list of
all events that are bound to that tag. When we give it a tag name and an event specification,
the command returns the binding code for that event. We always print out the event specification, and if you set the optional `mode` argument to `-verbose`, we print out the binding
code as well.

You could use this procedure to query the bindings for a button, as follows:

```
    % button .b
⇒   .b
    % bind .b <Enter> { puts "now entering %W" }
    % bind_show .b
⇒   .b
              .b
                     <Enter>
              Button
                     <Key-space>
                     <ButtonRelease-1>
                     <Button-1>
                     <Leave>
                     <Enter>

              .
              all
                     <Shift-Key-Tab>
                     <Key-Tab>
                     <Key-F10>
                     <Alt-Key>
```

We added one binding for the `<Enter>` event, but this button has many other bindings
listed under `Button` and `all`, which are predefined by Tk.

3.6.2 Monitoring events

At some point, you may be curious about the event stream. You may wonder what happens if you click on a widget, drag the mouse outside, and release the mouse button. Do
you get a `Leave` event, followed by a `ButtonRelease` event? Or is it the other way
around? Here's your chance to find out.

The following procedure creates special bindings that monitor all of the events in a
particular window:

```
proc bind_debug {w on} {
    set events {
        {ButtonPress      {W=%W #=%# x=%x y=%y b=%b s=%s }}
        {ButtonRelease    {W=%W #=%# x=%x y=%y b=%b s=%s }}
        ...
        {Visibility       {W=%W #=%# x=%x y=%y s=%s }}
    }

    foreach e $events {
        set type [lindex $e 0]
        set fmt [lindex $e 1]
```

```
        bind BindDebugger <$type> "puts \"<$type> $fmt\""
    }

    set allwin [bind_debug_allwindows $w]
    foreach w $allwin {
        set tags [bindtags $w]
        set i [lsearch $tags BindDebugger]
        if {$on} {
            if {$i < 0} {
                set tags [linsert $tags 0 BindDebugger]
                bindtags $w $tags
            }
        } else {
            if {$i >= 0} {
                set tags [lreplace $tags $i $i]
                bindtags $w $tags
            }
        }
    }
}
```

This procedure creates a binding tag named BindDebugger and binds a series of puts commands to all possible events on that tag. Each event has its own message string that displays the important details for that event. The bindings are generated in a loop, but if they were written out by hand, they would look like this:

```
bind BindDebugger <ButtonPress> \
    "puts \"<ButtonPress> {W=%W #=%# x=%x y=%y b=%b s=%s }\""
bind BindDebugger <ButtonRelease> \
    "puts \"<ButtonRelease> {W=%W #=%# x=%x y=%y b=%b s=%s }\""
...
```

Once these are in place, the bind_debug procedure turns the bindings on or off. If the on argument is positive and if the tag is missing from the list, the tag is added. Notice that the tag is inserted at the beginning of the list, so it will be executed even if another binding uses the break command.

If the on argument is negative and if the tag appears on the list, the tag is removed. This removes the extra bindings and turns off debugging information.

Let's use this procedure to resolve the question that we posed earlier: What happens if you click on a widget, drag the mouse outside, and release the mouse button? We can turn on debugging in the canonical Hello, World! program as follows:

```
package require Efftcl

button .b -text "Hello, World!" -command exit
pack .b

bind_debug . on
```

If we click on the button, drag the mouse outside, and release the button, we get the stream of events shown in Figure 3.22. As you can see, we get two `Leave` events: one that occurs *before* the `ButtonRelease` event and one that occurs *after*. Also, notice that we get `Motion` events on the widget `.b` even after the first `Leave` event. This highlights a feature that you might never have noticed about the windowing system. When you click on a widget, it sets an implicit grab on that widget. As you drag the mouse, the widget may get a `Leave` event, but it will continue to receive the `Motion` events. Finally, when you release the mouse button, the implicit grab is released, and the widget gets another `Leave` event, indicating that the mouse pointer has left that widget context completely.

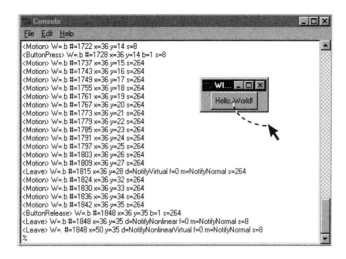

Figure 3.22. Using `bind_debug` to explore the events received from the windowing system.

3.7 Animation

The `after` command generates a timer event, which causes a script to be executed after a certain delay. For example, the following command causes the message `Hello, World!` to be printed on standard output after a delay of 1,000 ms:

```
after 1000 {puts "Hello, World!"}
```

By chaining `after` events, you can make things happen as a function of time, apparently executing in the background. The basic recipe looks like this:

```
proc animate {} {
    ...                       ;# do something
    after 100 animate         ;# and reschedule action
}
animate                       ;# start the animation
```

The procedure `animate` does some work and then finishes by rescheduling itself to be called again after a short delay. It's not enough to merely define this procedure—you have to call it once to start the animation. After that, it will reschedule itself each time it gets called.

Notice that `animate` is not a recursive procedure—it doesn't call itself. Instead, it calls `after`, which schedules an event and returns immediately. Then the `animate` procedure ends, and execution returns to the event loop. At some point in the future, the timer expires, and the `animate` procedure is called again. It does some work and reschedules itself to be called yet again. The process repeats as shown in Figure 3.23.

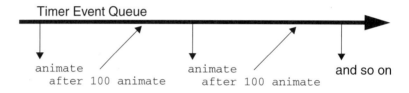

Figure 3.23. Time marches on. Each invocation of `animate` schedules the next invocation and returns to the event loop.

In this example, we gave the `after` command a delay of 100 ms, so this procedure will be called at intervals of at least 100 ms. But the delay may be longer than that if the program is busy performing other work. If you're trying to perform animation during a long-running calculation, you must call the `update` command from time to time, as we discussed earlier, in Section 3.1.3.

3.7.1 Animating items on a canvas

Let's use our basic animation recipe to move items on a canvas. We'll bounce a ball back and forth between two walls, as shown in Figure 3.24. Each time the ball hits a wall, we'll display the `Boing!` message.

We can implement this example as follows:

```
pack [canvas .c -width 200 -height 140 -background white]

.c create rectangle 10 10 20 130 -fill black
.c create rectangle 180 10 190 130 -fill black
```

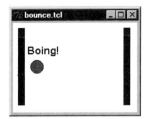

Figure 3.24. Using `after` to animate a bouncing ball on a canvas.

```
proc new_ball {xpos ypos speed color} {
    set x0 [expr $xpos-10]
    set x1 [expr $xpos+10]
    set y1 [expr $ypos+20]
    .c create oval $x0 $ypos $x1 $y1 \
        -fill $color -tag "ball-$ypos"
    bounce $xpos $ypos $speed
}

proc bounce {xpos ypos speed} {
    .c move "ball-$ypos" $speed 0
    set xpos [expr $xpos+$speed]
    if {$speed > 0 && $xpos >= 170} {
        set speed [expr -$speed]
        .c create text 175 [expr $ypos-5] -text "Boing!" \
            -anchor se -tag "boing-$ypos"
        after 300 [list .c delete boing-$ypos]
    } elseif {$speed < 0 && $xpos <= 30} {
        set speed [expr -$speed]
        .c create text 25 [expr $ypos-5] -text "Boing!" \
            -anchor sw -tag "boing-$ypos"
        after 300 [list .c delete boing-$ypos]
    }
    after 50 [list bounce $xpos $ypos $speed]
}

new_ball 100 60 10 red
```

We begin by creating a canvas and adding rectangles for the two walls. We'll study
the canvas in Chapter 4; for now, we'll skip over many of the canvas details and concentrate on the animation recipe.

The procedure `new_ball` adds a bouncing ball to the canvas. This procedure takes
four parameters: the *x*- and *y*-coordinates for the ball, the speed in the *x*-direction, and the

color of the ball. The procedure creates an oval on the canvas to represent the ball and then calls `bounce` to start the animation sequence that will make the ball bounce back and forth.

The procedure `bounce` takes three parameters: the *x*- and *y*-coordinates for the ball and the speed. The speed represents how many pixels the ball will move in 50 ms. If the speed is positive, the ball will move toward the right; if it's negative, the ball will move toward the left.

Inside the `bounce` procedure, we update the ball's position and adjust its speed. If the ball hits either wall, we reverse its direction and put up a `Boing!` message. We want this message to disappear after a brief delay, so we arrange for it to be deleted automatically after 300 ms.

At the end of the `bounce` procedure, we use the `after` command to schedule another call. Notice that as we're building the command for the next call, we substitute new values for the ball's position and speed. Thus each time `bounce` is called, it will have current information about the ball.

3.7.2   Debugging `after` events

In the previous section, we created a single bouncing ball on the canvas. Suppose that instead of calling `new_ball` once, we called it three times, like this:

```
new_ball 100 60 10 red
new_ball 100 90 5 blue
new_ball 100 30 -3 green
```

This would create three separate bouncing balls, each controlled by its own chain of `after` events. The first call to `new_ball` would call `bounce` with the coordinates for the red ball. After that, `bounce` would schedule itself to be called again and again, each time operating on the coordinates of the red ball. The second call to `new_ball` would call `bounce` with the coordinates for the green ball. That would create another chain of calls to `bounce`, each one operating on the coordinates of the green ball, and so on.

If you're debugging a program with many different `after` chains, you'll need a way to keep tabs on the `after` events. The `after` command itself can help. If you call `after info` with no arguments, it will return a list of tokens for pending `after` events. If you call `after info` with one of these tokens, it will return information about that event, including its command script.

We can use this to make a watch window for `after` events:

```
proc after_debug {} {
    toplevel .afterdb
    wm title .afterdb "After: Debug Info"
    text .afterdb.t -width 50 -height 10 -wrap none
    pack .afterdb.t -fill both -expand yes
    after_debug_update
}
```

```
proc after_debug_update {} {
    if {[winfo exists .afterdb.t]} {
        .afterdb.t delete 1.0 end
        foreach t [after info] {
            .afterdb.t insert end "$t\t[after info $t]\n"
        }
        after 100 after_debug_update
    }
}
```

You can use `after_debug` to activate a debugging mode in your programs. This creates a top-level window with a text widget that will display a summary of pending `after` events. Then the procedure calls `after_debug_update` to start a chain of calls that keep watch on the `after` events.

Each time the `after_debug_update` procedure is called, it clears out the text widget and inserts a summary of pending `after` events. Then it schedules itself to be called again in 100 ms. At any point, you could destroy the display window, so the procedure always checks to see whether the window still exists. If it doesn't, the procedure does nothing, and the chain of calls to `after_debug_update` stops.

If we add the `after_debug` call to our bouncing-ball example, we get a display like the one shown in Figure 3.25. This display changes continually, but over time, we can see the three chains of calls for the three bouncing balls, with occasional commands to delete the `Boing!` messages.

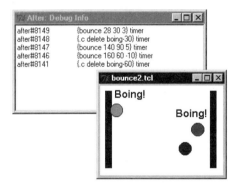

Figure 3.25. Using `after_debug` to monitor `after` events.

3.7.3   Library procedures for animation

Animation tasks are common enough that it's worthwhile making some library procedures to handle them. We'll write two procedures to control animation: `animate_start` and `animate_stop`.

Let's see how these procedures are used in a simple example. We'll create a label that displays a sequence of images, forming the animated logo shown in Figure 3.26. For now, we'll put the label together with Start and Stop buttons, so we can test it out. Later, in Section 8.1.3, we'll integrate this logo into an animated placard.

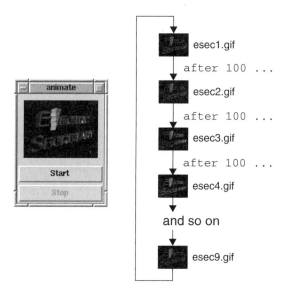

Figure 3.26. Using `after` to animate a series of images.

First, we'll load the sequence of images, like this:

```
set images {}
set counter 0
for {set i 1} {$i <= 9} {incr i} {
    set file [file join $env(EFFTCL_LIBRARY) images esec$i.gif]
    set imh [image create photo -file $file]
    label .l$i -image $imh
    lappend images $imh
}
```

The images are stored in a series of files named `esec1.gif`, `esec2.gif`, ..., `esec9.gif`. Therefore we can use a `for` loop to generate the file names and to load the images. When this loop is finished, the variable `images` will contain a list of image names for the animation sequence.

Notice that as we load each image, we create a dummy label that references the image. These labels are never packed, so they don't show up in the program. But they ensure that each image is ready to use, so it can be loaded quickly onto the screen. Without these labels, extra processing occurs each time an image is displayed, limiting the top speed of the animation.

Next, we create a label to display the images:

```
label .show -image [lindex $images 0]
pack .show -padx 8 -pady 8
```

This label starts by displaying the first frame of the animation. Then, when you click on the Start button, the label displays each of the frames in the sequence.

The Start button is created like this:

```
button .start -text "Start" -state normal -command {
    set pending [animate_start 100 $images {
        .show configure -image %v
    }]
    .stop configure -state normal
    .start configure -state disabled
}
pack .start -fill x
```

When you click on this button, it triggers a call to the `animate_start` procedure. It works as follows. You pass in a time delay, a list of values, and a code fragment. In this example, we specified a 100-ms delay, a list of image names, and the following command:

```
.show configure -image %v
```

Our animation library will execute this command at 100-ms intervals, each time substituting a different value from the image list in place of `%v`. Thus the label will change every 100 ms to display the next frame in the animation.

The `animate_start` procedure returns a token that identifies our animation sequence. When you want to stop the sequence, you can pass this token to the procedure `animate_stop`. In this example, we've saved the token in the variable `pending`, so we can use it in the Stop button, like this:

```
button .stop -text "Stop" -state disabled -command {
    animate_stop $pending
    .start configure -state normal
    .stop configure -state disabled
}
pack .stop -fill x
```

Now let's see how these library procedures are implemented. We can define the `animate_start` procedure like this:

```
set anInfo(counter) 0
proc animate_start {delay vlist command} {
    global anInfo

    set id "animate[incr anInfo(counter)]"
    set anInfo($id-delay) $delay
    set anInfo($id-vlist) $vlist
    set anInfo($id-command) $command
    set anInfo($id-pos) 0
    set anInfo($id-pending) [after $delay "animate_handle $id"]
    return $id
}
```

We begin by creating a token to identify the animation sequence. We glue the string
animate together with a unique counter value, so the first sequence has the name
animate1; the next, animate2; and so on. Then we create a data structure with the following fields for the sequence: the delay field contains the time delay; the vlist field
contains the value list; the pos field is an index for the current position in the value list; the
command field contains the code that is executed at each time step; and the pending field
contains a token for the pending after event.

The following procedure is called at each time step:

```
proc animate_handle {id} {
    global anInfo

    if {[info exists anInfo($id-pending)]} {
        set pos $anInfo($id-pos)
        set val [lindex $anInfo($id-vlist) $pos]
        set cmd [percent_subst %v $anInfo($id-command) $val]
        uplevel #0 $cmd

        if {[incr pos] >= [llength $anInfo($id-vlist)]} {
            set pos 0
        }
        set anInfo($id-pos) $pos
        set anInfo($id-pending) [after $anInfo($id-delay) \
            "animate_handle $id"]
    }
}
```

In this procedure, we find the value at the current position in the value list. Then we substitute the value in place of the %v fields in the command string, using the percent_subst
procedure that we'll describe in Section 7.6.7.3. With this in place, we evaluate the command at the global scope, using uplevel #0. That way, if the command references any
variables, they'll be treated as global variables in this procedure, not as local variables.

Finally, we set things up for the next call. We bump the position in the value list; if it
falls off the end, we start over at index 0. Then we use the after command to schedule
another call to animate_handle at the next time step. The after command returns an

identifier for the pending call, which we save in the `pending` field. We can use this identifier in `animate_stop` to cancel the call and to stop the animation sequence.

The `animate_stop` procedure is implemented as follows:

```
proc animate_stop {id} {
    global anInfo

    if {[info exists anInfo($id-pending)]} {
        after cancel $anInfo($id-pending)
        unset anInfo($id-delay)
        unset anInfo($id-vlist)
        unset anInfo($id-command)
        unset anInfo($id-pos)
        unset anInfo($id-pending)
    }
}
```

This procedure cancels the next call to `animate_handle`. The next time step won't take place, so it won't schedule any other calls to `animate_handle` for this sequence. Since the sequence is no longer active, we delete its data structure from the `anInfo` array.

We've taken our basic animation recipe and, with a little extra code, made it into a library that's easy to use. You'll notice it popping up in other examples throughout the book. In Section 4.7, we'll use it to create a shimmering selection rectangle for a drawing editor. In Section 5.1.3, we'll use it to create blinking words in a text widget. And in Section 8.1.3, we'll use it to create an animated placard for the Electric Secretary program.

Chapter 4
Using the Canvas Widget

You can turn an ordinary program into an extraordinary application by using graphics to convey information. After all, a picture is worth a thousand words. And in the realm of graphical user interfaces, an interactive picture is worth a thousand buttons!

Imagine an application that monitors a factory floor for problems on the production line. Suppose that the application displays a diagram of the factory floor and marks problem areas with a flashing red square. That kind of interface lets you see the status of the entire factory at a glance and is much more intuitive than a listbox full of status messages.

The Tk *canvas* widget makes it easy to build such things. You can create a canvas and add the lines, rectangles, and polygons that make up a drawing. You can even make the drawing come to life by binding actions to certain events on the canvas. When you click on a problem area on the factory floor, for example, the program could display the status for that area. When you drop a wrench icon onto the problem area, the program could send a message to dispatch a maintenance crew.

In this chapter, we'll see how you can use the canvas to build interactive displays. We'll start by explaining how the canvas works with some simple examples. Then we'll look at a series of case studies to see how the various features work together.

- We'll build a progress gauge showing the status of a task from 0 percent to 100 percent complete.

- We'll build a color-selection wheel.

- We'll add some tabs to the notebook we created in Section 2.1.7, to create a tabbed notebook.

- We'll build a calendar that lets you page through the months and click to select individual days.

- We'll build a simple drawing program that supports rectangles, ovals, lines and text. We'll add bindings so that you can select these items, resize them, move them, and change their color.

You can use the same techniques to build other displays, such as the factory floor monitor, a seat-assignment chart for airline reservations, or whatever else your application requires.

4.1   Understanding the canvas widget

You can create an empty canvas—just a blank area with no default behavior—like this:

```
canvas .c -width 2i -height 1i
```

In this example, the canvas is 2 inches wide and 1 inch high. You create a drawing on the canvas by adding drawing elements called *items*. For example, we can draw a line by creating a line item, like this:

```
.c create line 0 15  15 25  35 5  50 15  -width 2 -fill blue
```

Each pair of numbers represents an (x,y) coordinate for the line. Our line goes from $(0,15)$ to $(15,25)$ to $(35,5)$ to $(50,15)$. All of these coordinates are relative to the origin at $(0,0)$, which is in the upper-left corner of the window. Thus x-coordinates increase toward the right, and y-coordinates increase going down. In this example, the numbers are plain integers, so they are treated as pixel coordinates. But you can add a letter after each number to indicate its units. For example, the value 1.5i is 1.5 inches, and 10c is 10 centimeters.

Each item has configuration options that control its appearance. By default, lines are black. But this particular line is blue and has a width of 2 pixels.

You can create many kinds of items on the canvas. Figure 4.1 shows examples of the various types. If you are looking for a detailed description of each item and its configuration options, you can find it on the manual page for the canvas widget. But we'll mention each type briefly to give you a feeling for the things that you can create on a canvas.

- **line**
  A line has two or more coordinates. You can add arrowheads at the ends. If you turn on smoothing, the line is drawn as a set of Bézier splines.

- **rectangle**
  A rectangle has two coordinates representing two opposite corners. You can set a color and a line width for its outline, and you can set a separate color to fill its interior.

- **polygon**
  A polygon has three or more coordinates. As for a rectangle, you can set its outline color and its line width, and you can use a separate color to fill its interior. As for a line, you can turn on smoothing, and its outline will be drawn as a set of Bézier splines.

- **oval**
  An oval has two coordinates representing the rectangle that contains it. As for a rectan-

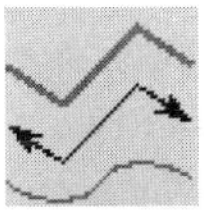

```
.c create line 0 15 15 25 35  5 50 15 -width 2 -fill blue
.c create line 0 30 15 40 35 20 50 30 -arrow both
.c create line 0 45 15 55 35 35 50 45 -smooth yes -fill red

.c create rectangle  5 10 35 35 -width 4
.c create rectangle 15 20 45 45 -fill red -stipple gray50

.c create polygon 5 5 30 20 45 10 \
    40 45 20 35 10 40 -fill green

.c create oval 10 10 30 30 -fill blue
.c create oval 15 15 45 45 -outline green -width 3

.c create arc 10 10 30 30 -extent 240 -fill blue
.c create arc 15 15 45 45 -start 45 -extent -180 \
    -style arc -width 3 -outline green

.c create bitmap 25 25 -anchor se -bitmap questhead
.c create bitmap 25 25 -anchor nw -bitmap error \
    -background red -foreground white

set imh [image create photo -file boom.gif]
.c create image 25 25 -anchor c -image $imh

.c create text 30 25 -anchor se -text "Hello"
.c create text 30 25 -anchor n -text "World!" \
    -font -*-times-medium-i-normal--14-140-*

.c create oval 5 5 45 45 -fill blue
entry .c.e -width 5
.c create window 25 25 -anchor c -window .c.e
```

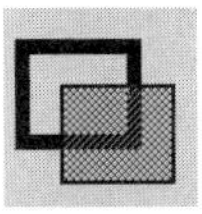

Figure 4.1. The various items that you can create on a canvas.

gle, you can set its outline color and its line width, and you can use a separate color to fill its interior.

- **arc**

  An arc is like an oval but has a starting angle and an extent that control how much of the oval is drawn. An arc can be drawn as a line or as a pie wedge or with a chord connecting the end points; you can control the style by using the -style option.

- **bitmap**

  A bitmap has one coordinate representing its anchor point. The bitmap is aligned with this point according to its -anchor option. Each bitmap has only two colors: a foreground color, which is normally black, and a background color, which is normally the same as the canvas widget.

- **image**

  An image has one coordinate representing its anchor point. But unlike a bitmap, an image can have any number of colors and will be dithered automatically when it is displayed on a monochromatic screen.

- **text**

  A text item has one coordinate representing its anchor point. A single text item can have multiple lines, and you can control their justification. You can also set the color and the font for the text.

- **window**

  A window item has one coordinate representing its anchor point. The item acts as a placeholder for a widget embedded in the canvas. Thus you can mix buttons and entries with the other graphics on the canvas. In Figure 4.1, for example, we put an entry widget on top of a blue oval.

Many of these items also have an option for their *stipple pattern*, which controls how they are filled in. By default, items are drawn with a solid color. But if you use a bitmap screen like gray50 as a stipple pattern, you will get a stenciled effect. Where the bitmap is black, the item will be drawn with its fill color, and where it is not, the item will be transparent. One of the rectangles in Figure 4.1, for example, has the stipple pattern gray50. Its interior is a red screen that lets the rectangle underneath it show through.

4.1.1 Scrolling

Each canvas has an unlimited drawing area, but the canvas widget itself has a certain size on the screen. By default, the canvas will display as much as it can starting from the (0,0) coordinate in the upper-left corner of the drawing area, as shown in Figure 4.2. The visible area of the canvas is called the *viewport*. You can add items outside of the viewport, but you won't see them unless you tell the canvas to change its view.

If your drawing extends beyond the viewport, you can attach scrollbars to control the view. For example, we used the following code to create the display in Figure 4.2:

```
canvas .display -width 3i -height 2i -background black \
    -xscrollcommand {.xsbar set} -yscrollcommand {.ysbar set}
scrollbar .xsbar -orient horizontal -command {.display xview}
scrollbar .ysbar -orient vertical -command {.display yview}

.display create line 98.0 298.0 98.0 83.0 -fill green -width 2
.display create line 98.0 83.0 101.0 69.0 -fill green -width 2
```

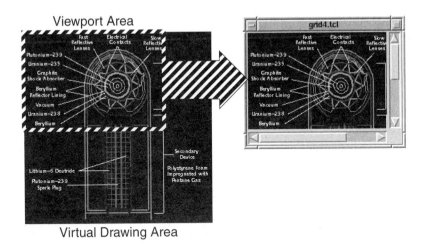

Viewport Area

Virtual Drawing Area

Figure 4.2. The canvas widget acts as a viewport, displaying part of the virtual drawing area that is available. You can add scrollbars to change the view.

```
.display create line 101.0 69.0 108.0 56.0 -fill green -width 2
...
```

This is the same code that we saw in Section 2.2.1. But at that point, we were concerned only with how scrollbars are positioned next to a canvas. Here we will explain how scrollbars are attached to control a canvas.

Each scrollbar has a `-command` option with a command to control the canvas view. In this example, when you adjust the horizontal scrollbar, it executes the command `.display xview`, with a few extra arguments to shift the viewport left or right. When you use the vertical scrollbar, it executes the command `.display yview`, again with suitable arguments, to shift the viewport up or down. The canvas has similar `-xscrollcommand` and `-yscrollcommand` options to control the scrollbars. In this example, whenever its view changes, the canvas executes the commands `.xsbar set` or `.ysbar set` with suitable arguments, to reposition the bubble in the middle of the each scrollbar.

These command options allow the canvas and the scrollbars to communicate with one another and stay in sync, but they aren't enough to make the canvas scroll properly. The canvas also has a `-scrollregion` option that sets the boundaries of the scrolling region. By default, the scrolling region corresponds to the viewport area. So even if your drawing is much larger than the viewport, the canvas will think that there is no room for scrolling. To make the canvas scroll properly, you must tell it the size of your drawing by giving it some coordinates, like this:

```
.display configure -scrollregion {0 0 250 375}
```

This says that the upper-left corner of the scrolling region is (0,0) and that the lower-right corner is (250,375). The canvas will let the viewport move within this region.

Quite often, you won't know the overall size of your drawing, and guessing at the size is prone to errors. If you make the scrolling region too small, you won't be able to see part of the drawing; if you make it too big, you will see a lot of empty area. Instead, you should use the following trick to set the scrolling region:

```
.display configure -scrollregion [.display bbox all] \
    -xscrollincrement 0.1i -yscrollincrement 0.1i
```

The command .display bbox all automatically computes a bounding box around all of the items currently on the canvas. We use this result to set the area for the scrolling region. You must do this *after* you've created all of the items for your drawing. If you add more items to the drawing, you should recompute the bounding box and set the scrolling region accordingly.

The canvas also has -xscrollincrement and -yscrollincrement options. You can set these to indicate how much the canvas should move when you press the arrows on either end of a scrollbar. In this example, we have the drawing shift in increments of 0.1 inch.

4.1.2 Display list model

The canvas remembers each item that you create. At any point, you can move, resize, or change the attributes of an item, and the drawing will be updated automatically. For example, suppose we create a canvas with the following code:

```
canvas .c -width 100 -height 110
pack .c


.c create oval 10 10 90 90 -fill yellow -width 2
.c create arc 15 15 85 85 -start 60 -extent 60 -fill black
.c create arc 15 15 85 85 -start 180 -extent 60 -fill black
.c create arc 15 15 85 85 -start 300 -extent 60 -fill black
.c create oval 40 40 60 60 -outline "" -fill yellow
.c create oval 44 44 56 56 -outline "" -fill black
.c create text 50 95 -anchor n -text "Warning"
```

As each item is created on this canvas, it is added to an internal list called the *display list*. When the canvas needs to display itself, it simply draws each item on the display list. It starts at the bottom and works its way toward the top, as shown in Figure 4.3.

Now suppose we want to change one of the items. Suppose our nuclear reactor goes critical, and we want to change the message from Warning to RED ALERT. We need a way of referring to the text item within the canvas.

When each item is created, the canvas assigns it a unique number, called an *item identifier*. You can capture the identifier whenever you create an item, like this:

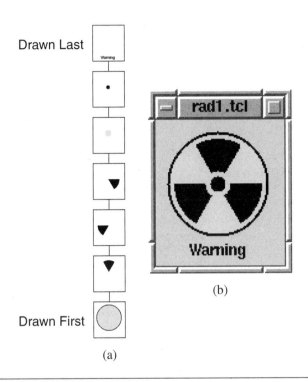

Figure 4.3. (a) The canvas keeps a display list of all its internal items. (b) The resulting picture.

```
    set id [.c create text 50 95 -anchor n -text "Warning"]
```
Here the variable id will contain an item number, such as 7. We can use this later on to configure the item:
```
    .c itemconfigure $id -text "RED ALERT"
```
This tells the canvas to find item number $id and change its -text option to RED ALERT.

When any item changes, the canvas figures out what portion of the drawing is affected and redraws that part of the display in a highly efficient manner, so the changes appear to be instantaneous. In this example, the area near the text item is regenerated, and the text changes immediately from Warning to RED ALERT.

The canvas also has search operations that help you find certain items in the display list. For example, its find enclosed operation will search for items that are contained within a bounding box.
```
    .c find enclosed 20 20 80 110
```

This command will find all items in the rectangle from (20,20) to (80,110) and return a list of item identifiers. We could use this in conjunction with the `itemconfigure` operation to highlight these items in red:

```
foreach id [.c find enclosed 20 20 80 110] {
    .c itemconfigure $id -fill red
}
```

This gives the result shown in Figure 4.4.

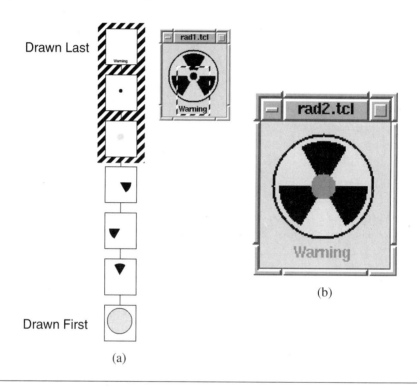

(a)

(b)

Figure **4.4.** (a) The canvas can search its display list for certain items. (b) Items can be configured to change their appearance.

The canvas has a few more search operations. You can find an explanation of each one on the canvas manual page. We mentioned the `find enclosed` operation here simply to show how canvas operations build on one another and how the item identifiers come into play. Later in this chapter, we'll see some examples that show the search operations in action.

4.1.3 Using tags

Item identifiers are useful, but since they are just numbers, they are not very meaningful. Your canvas programs will be much easier to understand if you tag important items with symbolic names. An easy way to do this is to set the `-tags` option as each item is created. For example, we could rewrite our code to tag some of the items in our radiation symbol, like this:

```
canvas .c -width 100 -height 110
pack .c


.c create oval 10 10 90 90 -fill yellow -width 2
.c create arc 15 15 85 85 -start 60 -extent 60 \
    -fill black -tags sign
.c create arc 15 15 85 85 -start 180 -extent 60 \
    -fill black -tags sign
.c create arc 15 15 85 85 -start 300 -extent 60 \
    -fill black -tags sign
.c create oval 40 40 60 60 -outline "" -fill yellow
.c create oval 44 44 56 56 -outline "" \
    -fill black -tags sign
.c create text 50 95 -anchor n -text "Warning" -tags message
```

We tagged the `Warning` message with the symbolic name `message`. When we need to change the message later on, we can use the tag name `message` as an item identifier:

```
.c itemconfigure message -text "RED ALERT" -fill red
```

That way, we don't have to create extra variables to store item identifiers, and the code is easier to follow.

You can also use tag names to identify a group of related items. For example, we tagged all of the black parts of the radiation sign with the symbolic name `sign`. Having done that, we can change the color of all four items at once with a single command:

```
.c itemconfigure sign -fill red
```

The canvas finds all items tagged with the name `sign` and changes their fill color to red, as shown in Figure 4.5. We could have accomplished the same thing by looping through a list of item identifiers and configuring each item individually. But using the tag is more convenient and much more efficient. Remember, the canvas operations are handled in compiled code, so they run much faster than a block of Tcl statements, which are all interpreted.

Each item can have many different tag names associated with it, so you can put the same item in different groups. For example, suppose we want to create a group of items called `hilite` that will all light up red at some point. We might include the `message` item and the `sign` items in this group so that we could configure them all with a single command, like this:

```
.c itemconfigure hilite -fill red
```

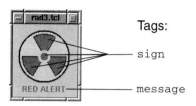

Figure 4.5. Tag names are used to identify items on the canvas.

We need to add the tag name `hilite` to all the items that we want to have in this group. One way to accomplish this is to add the tag when each item is created, like this:

```
.c create text 50 95 -anchor n -text "Warning" \
    -tags {message hilite}
```

As you can see, the `-tags` option accepts a list of tag names. In this example, the elements `message` and `hilite` are treated as separate names that both refer to the text item.

Another way is to add the tag name after the item has been created. The canvas `addtag` operation supports many different ways of finding and tagging items. For example, the following command finds all of the items with the tag name `sign` and adds the tag `hilite` to them:

```
.c addtag "hilite" withtag "sign"
```

At this point, we can use the name `message` to refer to the text item, the name `sign` to refer to the four parts of the radiation sign, or the name `hilite` to refer to all of these items.

4.1.4   Canvas bindings

You can add new behaviors to a canvas by using the `bind` command, just as you would for any other Tk widget. For example, suppose we want the radiation symbol to light up red whenever the mouse pointer enters the window, as shown in Figure 4.6. We can bind to the `<Enter>` and `<Leave>` events on the canvas, like this:

```
bind .c <Enter> {
    .c itemconfigure hilite -fill red
}
bind .c <Leave> {
    .c itemconfigure hilite -fill black
}
```

Here we are leveraging the tag names described in the previous section. When the mouse pointer enters or leaves the canvas, we change the fill color for all items tagged with the name `hilite`.

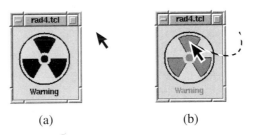

(a)   (b)

Figure 4.6. Binding to the canvas as a whole. (a) The pointer is outside the canvas. (b) The pointer moves inside the canvas, and the items tagged as hilite change color.

But unlike the other widgets, the canvas also lets you bind to events on the items within it. For example, suppose that we want the radiation sign to light up only when the mouse pointer is touching one of the hilite items. Instead of detecting <Enter> and <Leave> events on the canvas as a whole, we want to detect <Enter> and <Leave> events on the individual hilite items, as shown in Figure 4.7. So instead of using the usual bind command, which applies to an entire widget, we must use a special bind operation on the canvas, which provides access to items within the canvas. That operation looks like this:

```
.c bind hilite <Enter> {
    .c itemconfigure hilite -fill red
}
.c bind hilite <Leave> {
    .c itemconfigure hilite -fill black
}
```

These look like ordinary bind commands, but the .c prefix indicates that they apply only to items within the canvas, .c. These bindings are processed separately from the regular widget bindings on the canvas. So they aren't affected by the binding-tag mechanism that we discussed in Section 3.5. If they include the break command, they won't prevent the regular widget bindings from being executed.

Bindings can be applied to individual items through their item identifier or to groups of items through their tag names. In this case, we added bindings to all items with the tag name hilite.

Suppose we add another binding for the message item. When you click on this item, the text will toggle between Warning and RED ALERT:

```
.c bind message <ButtonPress-1> {
    if {[.c itemcget message -text] == "Warning"} {
        .c itemconfigure message -text "RED ALERT"
```

(a)   (b)

Figure 4.7. Binding to canvas items. (a) The pointer is on the canvas. (b) The pointer moves onto an item tagged `hilite`, and all items with this name change color.

```
    } else {
        .c itemconfigure message -text "Warning"
    }
}
```

Again, if we had added this binding to the canvas as a whole, the text would change no matter where you clicked on the canvas. But instead, we added the binding only to the `message` item, so you must click directly on the item for the text to change.

The canvas has one other feature that comes in handy for bindings. Whenever the mouse pointer touches an item, it is temporarily tagged with the name `current`. This makes it easy to figure out which item is active. For example, suppose that we want parts of the radiation sign to light up individually as the mouse pointer touches them, as shown in Figure 4.8. This technique is called *brushing*, and it helps the user realize what parts of your diagram are active.

As before, we bind this behavior to all of the items tagged with the name `hilite`:

```
.c bind hilite <Enter> {
    .c itemconfigure current -fill red
}
.c bind hilite <Leave> {
    .c itemconfigure current -fill black
}
```

But this time, only one item tagged with the name `current` will change color. In effect, we have added the same binding to a group of items named `hilite`, but we set up each item to react individually.

In the examples that follow, we'll see tags, bindings, and other canvas techniques in action. Throughout, there is one underlying philosophy for using the canvas: You must focus on the items within it. Decide how to tag items so that you can refer to them later. Tag related items with the same name so you can handle them as a group. In some cases, you may bind to events on the canvas as a whole. But more often than not, you will bind to individual items or groups of items, creating active areas on your display. If you have

(a)   (b)

Figure 4.8. Detecting the current item. (a) The pointer is on the canvas. (b) The pointer moves onto an item with the tag name `hilite`, but this time only the current item changes color.

worked with other graphical toolkits, this may seem like a paradigm shift, and it may take some getting used to. But once you have mastered tags, you have mastered the canvas.

4.2 Scrollable form

When the canvas is too small to display an entire drawing, you see only a small portion of it, and you can use scrollbars to adjust the view. We saw how this works in Section 4.1.1. But what if the canvas has widget items on it? As long as the canvas knows the size of its scrolling region, you can scroll the widgets in and out of the view.

You can mix widgets and graphics on the canvas to create some fancy displays. But in this example, we'll do something much simpler. We'll use the canvas to scroll through a long form like the one shown in Figure 4.9. This technique is handy when you have a lot of entries that won't fit on the screen all at once.

To build a scrollable form, we pack or grid a large collection of widgets together in a frame and then position the frame on the canvas. We use the frame's overall size to set the limits on the scrolling region for the canvas. Once the scrollbars are attached, the canvas handles the scrolling, and the scrollable form is complete.

The following procedure makes it easy to create a scrollable form. The procedure creates a canvas and attaches a vertical scrollbar and then positions an empty frame in the drawing area. You simply pass in a widget name for the whole assembly:

```
proc scrollform_create {win} {
    frame $win -class Scrollform

    scrollbar $win.sbar -command "$win.vport yview"
    pack $win.sbar -side right -fill y

    canvas $win.vport -yscrollcommand "$win.sbar set"
    pack $win.vport -side left -fill both -expand true
```

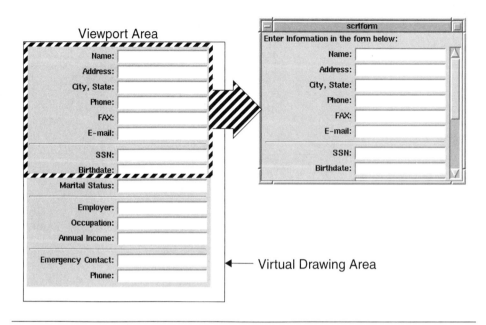

Figure 4.9. You can use the canvas to scroll over a large collection of widgets, in effect creating a scrollable form.

```
frame $win.vport.form
$win.vport create window 0 0 -anchor nw -window $win.vport.form

bind $win.vport.form <Configure> "scrollform_resize $win"
return $win
}
```

We start by creating a frame to wrap up the canvas and its scrollbar. Inside this frame, we create a canvas and a scrollbar, and we connect them as discussed in Section 4.1.1.

Next, we create an empty frame that will eventually contain all of the widgets for the form. Notice that the name of this frame—$win.vport.form—includes the canvas name—$win.vport—as a prefix. This is very important. It makes the frame sit inside the canvas, so that only part of it is visible in the viewport. If instead you use a name like $win.form, the frame will sit on top of the canvas. The frame will hang over the edges of the canvas and may even obscure the scrollbar.

We position the empty frame on the canvas by creating a window item. We anchor the northwest corner of the frame at the origin (0,0), which is the upper-left corner of the drawing area.

For the form to scroll properly, we need to set the size of the scrolling region. But there is one problem: We haven't added anything in the form frame yet, and we're not sure how big it will eventually be. Instead of setting the scrolling region directly, we bind to the `<Configure>` event on the form frame. The following procedure will be called automatically to set the scrolling region whenever the form frame changes size:

```
proc scrollform_resize {win} {
    set bbox [$win.vport bbox all]
    set wid [winfo width $win.vport.form]
    $win.vport configure -width $wid \
        -scrollregion $bbox -yscrollincrement 0.1i
}
```

This procedure uses the canvas `bbox` operation to compute the overall size of the drawing. This automatically takes into account the overall size of the frame. We set the scrolling region to cover this area, and we set the `-yscrollincrement` option to scroll in increments of 0.1 inch.

You may have noticed that this scrollable form doesn't have a horizontal scrollbar. We could have added one, but instead we assumed that the entire width of the form would be visible. After all, the user will probably want to see both the label and the entry when entering data into the form. We want to make sure that the canvas is just wide enough to display the entire form. So we use the `winfo width` command to determine the overall width of the form, and we use this result to set the `-width` option for the canvas.

At this point, the scrollable form is ready to use. We just need to pack some widgets into the form frame `$win.vport.form`. But instead of documenting this name as part of our scrollform library, we should wrap it up in a procedure. That way, we can make changes to the library later on, without breaking any code that uses the library.

Thus when you create a scrollable form, you can use the following procedure to get the name of the form frame:

```
proc scrollform_interior {win} {
    return "$win.vport.form"
}
```

We can use our new scrollform procedures to create the example shown in Figure 4.9. First, we create a title with a scrollable form beneath it:

```
label .title -text "Enter Information in the form below:"
pack .title -anchor w

scrollform_create .sform
pack .sform -expand yes -fill both
```

Next, we get the name of the form frame:

```
set form [scrollform_interior .sform]
```

Finally, we pack some widgets into the form frame. We could use a long series of commands to create the entries and their labels and pack them all together. But for a long form, it is much easier create the widgets in a loop, like this:

```
set counter 0
foreach field {
    "Name:"          "Address:"          "City, State:"
    "Phone:"         "FAX:"              "E-mail:"
    "-"

    "SSN:"           "Birthdate:"        "Marital Status:"
    "-"

    "Employer:"      "Occupation:"       "Annual Income:"
    "-"

    "Emergency Contact:"  "Phone:"
} {
    set line "$form.line[incr counter]"
    if {$field == "-"} {
        frame $line -height 2 -borderwidth 1 -relief sunken
        pack $line -fill x -padx 4 -pady 4
    } else {
        frame $line
        label $line.label -text $field -width 20 -anchor e
        pack $line.label -side left
        entry $line.info
        pack $line.info -fill x
        pack $line -side top -fill x
    }
}
```

The foreach command iterates through a list of names. Each name represents one line in the form. Normally, each line has an entry widget and its associated label. But if the name is "-", we create a separator line instead.

In either case, we need a unique widget name for each line. We want these widgets to sit inside the form frame, so the names must start with $form, which in this example expands to .sform.vport.form. We use the counter variable to generate a unique number for each line. During each pass through the loop, therefore, the line variable will have such values as .sform.vport.form.line1, .sform.vport.form.line2, and so on. We use these names to create a frame for a separator line or a frame containing a label and an entry.

When all of the widgets are packed in position, the form frame will shrink-wrap itself around its contents. Its size change will trigger a <Configure> event, and the scrollform_resize procedure will be called to adjust the scrolling region. If at some point we add some more lines, the form frame will change size again, triggering another <Configure> event and another call to scrollform_resize. Thus we can change the size of the form on the fly, and the scrollbars will adjust automatically.

At this point, our scrollable form is complete. As you adjust the scrollbars, the canvas will shift its view up and down, and the form will scroll.

4.3 Progress gauge

You can use the canvas to display the status of something like the factory floor we mentioned earlier. But what if something changes? You don't have to erase the drawing and start over. You can change certain items on the canvas and leave the rest of the drawing intact. We'll see how this works in the following example.

Suppose you need to read a large data file, download a Web page, or change the contrast of an image. Each of these tasks may take a while to perform, and while they are running, the user will want to know how much progress has been made. Many applications handle this by displaying a progress gauge like the one shown in Figure 4.10. The progress gauge displays the status of a task from 0 percent to 100 percent complete. As the numbers change in the foreground, a bar creeps from left to right in the background, giving a pictorial view of the progress.

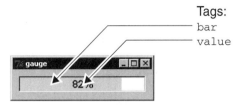

Figure 4.10. A progress gauge built by using the canvas.

Tk doesn't have a progress gauge widget, but it is easy to build something like this with the canvas. We can create a small canvas with two items: a text item for the percentage value and a rectangle for the bar in the background. We'll tag the text item with the name `value` and the rectangle with the name `bar`. That will make it easy to refer to these items later on. Whenever our progress changes, we'll update the percentage value in the `value` item and the coordinates for the `bar` item.

The following procedure makes it easy to create a progress gauge. You give it a widget name for the whole assembly and an optional color for the bar:

```
proc gauge_create {win {color ""}} {
    frame $win -class Gauge

    set len [option get $win length Length]
    canvas $win.display -borderwidth 0 -background white \
        -highlightthickness 0 -width $len -height 20
    pack $win.display -expand yes
```

```
if {$color == ""} {
    set color [option get $win color Color]
}
$win.display create rectangle 0 0 0 20 \
    -outline "" -fill $color -tags bar
$win.display create text [expr 0.5*$len] 10 \
    -anchor c -text "0%" -tags value
return $win
}
```

We begin by creating a frame for the whole assembly; we'll call this frame the *hull*. We give the hull the class name Gauge, so that you can add settings to the resource database to customize the gauges in your application. For example, we include the following resources with the gauge code:

```
option add *Gauge.borderWidth 2 widgetDefault
option add *Gauge.relief sunken widgetDefault
option add *Gauge.length 200 widgetDefault
option add *Gauge.color gray widgetDefault
```

By default, all gauges will have a gray bar and an overall sunken appearance. We were careful to give these settings a low priority, so you can override them in applications that use the gauge, as we'll see in Section 8.1.1.

The borderWidth and relief settings apply directly to the hull frame. All frames recognize these resources and handle them automatically. But we invented the resources length and color expressly for the gauge. These settings will not have any effect unless we query their values and handle them explicitly.

Returning to the gauge_create procedure, you can see that we query the length resource for the hull frame with an option get command. We use the result to set the width of the canvas, and we hard-code the height of the canvas to a reasonable size. This gives us some control over the initial size of a gauge. (To keep things simple, we will ignore any size changes that might occur, say, when the user expands a window and stretches out a progress gauge. In Section 4.6, we'll see how to make a canvas react to size changes.) Also, if the optional bar color was not passed in to this procedure, we use the default color resource, again determined from the option get command.

Finally, we create the two items on the canvas. The rectangle for the bar belongs in the background, so we create it first. Rectangles have a black outline by default, but we disable this by setting the outline color to the null string. We set the fill color to the bar color that we just determined. And of course, we tag the rectangle with the name bar, so we can refer to it later.

We place the text item in the middle of the canvas and have it display 0% as an initial value. We tag it with the name value, so we can refer to it later.

As your program works its way through a task, you can call the following procedure to update the gauge:

```
proc gauge_value {win val} {
    if {$val < 0 || $val > 100} {
        error "bad value \"$val\": should be 0-100"
    }
    set msg [format "%3.0f%%" $val]
    $win.display itemconfigure value -text $msg

    set w [expr 0.01*$val*[winfo width $win.display]]
    set h [winfo height $win.display]
    $win.display coords bar 0 0 $w $h

    update
}
```

You pass in the name of the gauge and the percentage value for the gauge to display. If the value is out of range, we immediately flag an error. Otherwise, we use the format command to neatly format the value, and we display the result in the value item.

The %3.0f part of the format string prints the floating-point value as an integer, rounding it if necessary. The 3 says that the number should take up three spaces, and the 0 says that there should be no digits after the decimal point. The extra %% at the end of the format string becomes a literal % in the display string. Thus the value 82.41 would be displayed as " 82%". (Notice that this string has a leading space, since our field width is three digits.)

Next, we adjust the length of the bar so that it reflects the new value. We use winfo width and winfo height to get the overall size of the canvas, and we scale the width down according to the percentage value. Once we have computed the size, we use the canvas coords operation to change the coordinates of the bar rectangle.

Finally, we use the update command to flush changes out to the display. The update command is very important. The canvas will avoid redrawing itself until the application is idle and has nothing better to do. You won't see the bar move or the text change unless we use update and force the canvas to redraw itself for each new value.

We can use our new gauge library to create the display shown in Figure 4.10. First, we create a gauge and pack it into the main window:

```
gauge_create .g PaleGreen
pack .g -expand yes -fill both -padx 10 -pady 10
```

Instead of relying on the default bar color, we used the value PaleGreen in this example. Now we perform our long-running task:

```
for {set i 0} {$i <= 100} {incr i} {
    after 100
    gauge_value .g $i
}
```

On each pass through the loop, we simply wait 100 ms, then call gauge_value with the current status and continue on through the loop. But in real-life applications, you would replace the after command with some real code. You might read in a file, handle some input on a socket, or process part of a list. As long as you call `gauge_value` from time to time with a progress value, you'll see your progress in the gauge.

4.4 HSB color editor

You can use the canvas to build interactive control panels. Certain items can act as knobs, or handles, that the user can drag around on the screen. We'll see how the canvas `bind` operation supports this in the following example.

Many drawing programs let you dial up your own colors, using a color wheel like the one shown in Figure 4.11. You position the dot on the wheel to select a particular color, and you adjust the bar on the right-hand side to make it lighter or darker. In the center of the wheel, the colors are said to be *unsaturated*—they are some shade of gray. As you move outward toward the edge of the wheel, they become *saturated*, or full of color. As you move around the edge of the wheel, the color changes from red to green to blue and back to red. The position around the rim determines the overall *hue* of the color. As you adjust the bar on the right-hand side, you control the *brightness* of the color. So as you move all of these controls, you are in fact adjusting the three components that determine a color: its hue, its saturation, and its brightness. This kind of color selector is referred to as a hue-saturation-brightness (HSB) color editor.

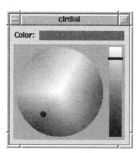

Figure 4.11. An HSB color editor built by using the canvas.

An HSB color editor is not included as part of Tk, but it is easy to build one, using the canvas. We could draw the various parts of the editor by adding items to the canvas. We could add a text item for the Color: label, a rectangle for the current color sample, some arcs for the color wheel, and so on. But for this example, we will use a few tricks to simplify things.

First, we will use the canvas only for the color wheel and the brightness controls. We'll create a separate label widget for the Color: label and a separate frame widget for the color sample, as shown in Figure 4.12. That way, we won't need any tricky canvas code to compute the size of the label and align it with the color sample. We'll see how to align things in the next section. For now, we'll simply use the `pack` command to align the three major elements.

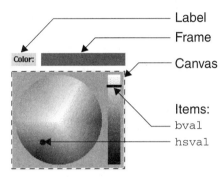

Figure 4.12. The HSB color editor has a label, a frame, and a canvas. Two items on the canvas act as markers for the current hue-saturation and brightness values.

Also, we'll use the predefined image shown in Figure 4.13 as the background of the color wheel and brightness controls. We could draw something similar by creating arc and rectangle items, but the result would look chunky. If we created lots of small arcs and rectangles, the picture would look better, but the controls might be sluggish. The canvas performs quite well with tens or hundreds of items, but as the number of items increases, the performance degrades. Quite often, you can use predefined images like this to add detail to a drawing without incurring a performance penalty.

The color editor boils down to a canvas with three items: an image for the background, an oval tagged with the name `hsval` to mark the current hue-saturation value, and a line tagged with the name `bval` to mark the current brightness value. We'll add bindings to the `hsval` and `bval` items so that you can move them around to adjust the color value.

The following procedure creates a color editor. You simply give it a widget name for the whole assembly:

```
proc colordial_create {win} {
    global env cdInfo
    frame $win -class Colordial

    canvas $win.dial
    pack $win.dial -side bottom
```

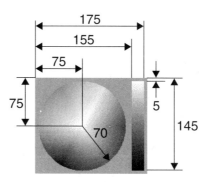

Figure 4.13. The background of the HSB color editor is a color image with fixed dimensions.

```
label $win.label -text "Color:"
pack $win.label -side left

frame $win.sample -width 15 -height 15
pack $win.sample -expand yes -fill both -padx 4 -pady 4

set fname [file join $env(EFFTCL_LIBRARY) images colors.gif]
set imh [image create photo -file $fname]
$win.dial create image 0 0 -anchor nw -image $imh
$win.dial create oval 0 0 0 0 -fill black -tags hsval
$win.dial create line 0 0 0 0 -width 4 -fill black -tags bval

$win.dial configure -width [image width $imh] \
    -height [image height $imh]

$win.dial bind hsval <B1-Motion> \
    "colordial_set_hs $win %x %y"
$win.dial bind bval <B1-Motion> \
    "colordial_set_b $win %y"

set cdInfo($win-hue) 0
set cdInfo($win-saturation) 0
set cdInfo($win-brightness) 1

colordial_refresh $win
return $win
}
```

As usual, we start by creating the hull frame, which contains the other components. We give it the class name `Colordial`, so you can add resources to the option database to customize all of the colordials in your application.

Next, we create the separate canvas, label, and frame widgets and pack them into the hull. By default, an empty frame has a width and height of 0 pixels, so we must do something to fix its size. We set its requested size to 15×15 pixels (so the frame will ask to be at least this big), and we pack it to expand and fill. Since it is packed after the other two widgets, it fills the area to the right of the label, in the upper-right corner of the hull.

Next, we create the three items on the canvas. The image is positioned with its northwest corner at the origin of the canvas. The `hsval` and `bval` items are created with dummy coordinates. We update them later, using the `colordial_refresh` command so that they have the right coordinates for the initial color value.

We use the `image create photo` command to load the color wheel image from a file called `colors.gif`. This file must be distributed along with the script file containing the code for our colordial. These files will be installed in a directory, such as `/usr/local/efftcl`. But instead of hard-coding the directory name, we use an environment variable—`EFFTCL_LIBRARY`—to point to the proper directory. We can write an installation program that sets up this variable when a program is installed, as we'll see in Chapter 8.

The canvas should be just big enough to display the color wheel image. We use the `image width` and `image height` commands to query the overall size of the image, and we configure the canvas to this size.

Next, we add the bindings that allow the `hsval` and `bval` items to be moved around on the canvas. We use the event specification `<B1-Motion>`, which triggers when you hold down mouse button 1 and drag the pointer around. We added the bindings to the individual `hsval` and `bval` items—not to the canvas as a whole. Thus you will get these events only when you click directly on one of the two items and then drag the mouse. Notice that we are careful to enclose the commands for the bindings in `" "` so that the value of `$win` is substituted in this context, while it is known. In effect, we are building custom bindings for each colordial we create.

Next, we set the initial color value. The global `cdInfo` array acts as a data structure. Each colordial has three slots in this array for the hue, saturation, and brightness components of its current color. The slots are parameterized by the name `$win`, so each colordial has its own set of slots. Once the color is set, we call `colordial_refresh` to update the display. This sets the background of the color sample and moves the `hsval` and `bval` items into the appropriate position. We'll see how this is implemented later.

Finally, we return the name of the new colordial as the result of this procedure.

When you click and drag on `bval`, it will trigger a series of calls to `colordial_set_b`, with the y-coordinate for each motion point. This procedure is implemented as follows:

```
proc colordial_set_b {win y} {
    global cdInfo
```

```
set bright [expr (145-$y)/140.0]
if {$bright < 0} {
    set bright 0
} elseif {$bright > 1} {
    set bright 1
}
set cdInfo($win-brightness) $bright
colordial_refresh $win
}
```

First, we convert the *y*-coordinate to the appropriate brightness level. The *y*-coordinates in the brightness area range from 5 to 145, as you can see in Figure 4.13. We scale the *y*-coordinate and then limit the brightness value so that it falls in the range 0 to 1. Finally, we update the brightness component of the data structure for this colordial and then use `colordial_refresh` to update the display.

Likewise, when you click and drag on `hsval`, it will trigger a series of calls to `colordial_set_hs` with the *x*- and *y*-coordinates for each motion point. This procedure is implemented as follows:

```
proc colordial_set_hs {win x y} {
    global cdInfo

    set hs [colordial_xy2hs $x $y]
    set hue [lindex $hs 0]
    set sat [lindex $hs 1]

    if {$sat > 1} {
        set sat 1
    }
    set cdInfo($win-hue) $hue
    set cdInfo($win-saturation) $sat
    colordial_refresh $win
}
```

Again, we convert the (*x*,*y*) coordinate to the appropriate hue and saturation values on the color wheel. This is straightforward, though a bit messy, so we have encapsulated the details in a procedure called `colordial_xy2hs`. It takes an (*x*,*y*) coordinate and returns a list containing the corresponding hue and saturation values. We won't show this procedure here, but you can find it in the file `efftcl/lib/scripts/clrdial.tcl`, which can be obtained from the Web site mentioned on page xiv.

Again, we limit the saturation to the range 0 to 1, so that it cannot be pulled beyond the color wheel. We update the hue and saturation components of the data structure and then use `colordial_refresh` to update the display.

The `colordial_refresh` procedure is implemented like this:

```
proc colordial_refresh {win} {
    global cdInfo
```

```
        set angle $cdInfo($win-hue)
        set length $cdInfo($win-saturation)
        set x0 [expr 75 + cos($angle)*$length*70]
        set y0 [expr 75 - sin($angle)*$length*70]
        $win.dial coords hsval \
            [expr $x0-4] [expr $y0-4] \
            [expr $x0+4] [expr $y0+4]

        set bright $cdInfo($win-brightness)
        set y0 [expr 145-$bright*140]
        $win.dial coords bval 154 $y0 176 $y0

        $win.sample configure -background [colordial_get $win]
    }
```

We save the current hue and saturation values in the angle and length variables. This makes the two lines of code that follow a bit easier to read. They are the formula for converting a polar coordinate, such as (*length,angle*), to a rectangular coordinate, such as (*x,y*). An angle of 0° and a length of 1 corresponds to the canvas coordinate (145,75). As you can see in Figure 4.13, this is the position for pure red, on the right-hand side of the wheel. An angle of 90° and a length of 1 corresponds to (75,5), which is the yellow-green color at the top of the wheel.

Once we have computed the coordinate (x0,y0), we change the coordinates for the hsval marker to center it on this point. Remember, an oval is characterized by the two corners of its bounding box. We set one corner 4 pixels to the left and 4 pixels above the coordinate, and we set the other corner 4 pixels to the right and 4 pixels down. This makes the hsval marker a circle 8×8 pixels in size.

In a similar manner, we scale the brightness value back to a *y*-coordinate in the range 5 to 145, and we update the coordinates of the bval line. The brightness scale extends from 155 to 175 along the *x*-axis, but we have stretched the line from 154 to 176. This makes it overhang by 1 pixel on each end, so it stands out from the background.

Finally, we change the background of the color sample frame to display the current color. We use the procedure colordial_get to convert the current color to a string that Tk can understand.

When you use a colordial in your own applications, you can use the same colordial_get procedure to query the current color on the dial. The procedure is implemented like this:

```
    proc colordial_get {win} {
        global cdInfo

        set h $cdInfo($win-hue)
        set s $cdInfo($win-saturation)
        set v $cdInfo($win-brightness)
        return [colordial_hsb2rgb $h $s $v]
    }
```

We pass the current hue, saturation, and brightness components to a procedure called colordial_hsb2rgb. This converts the color to equivalent red-green-blue (RGB) components. Exactly how this procedure works is outside the scope of this discussion.* However, we will include the procedure's implementation here so that we can show one important trick:

```
proc colordial_hsb2rgb {h s v} {
    if {$s == 0} {
        set v [expr round(65535*$v)]
        set r $v
        set g $v
        set b $v
    } else {
        if {$h >= 6.28318} {set h [expr $h-6.28318]}
        set h [expr $h/1.0472]
        set f [expr $h-floor($h)]
        set p [expr round(65535*$v*(1.0-$s))]
        set q [expr round(65535*$v*(1.0-$s*$f))]
        set t [expr round(65535*$v*(1.0-$s*(1.0-$f)))]
        set v [expr round(65535*$v)]

        switch [expr int($h)] {
            0 {set r $v; set g $t; set b $p}
            1 {set r $q; set g $v; set b $p}
            2 {set r $p; set g $v; set b $t}
            3 {set r $p; set g $q; set b $v}
            4 {set r $t; set g $p; set b $v}
            5 {set r $v; set g $p; set b $q}
        }
    }
    return [format "#%.4x%.4x%.4x" $r $g $b]
}
```

Once we have computed the proper r, g, and b values, we use the format command to convert them to a hexadecimal representation. The "#" sign appears literally in the final string. Each "%.4x" tells how to print the $r, $g, and $b components. The "x" says that they should be printed as hexadecimal numbers, and the ".4" says that they should be 4 digits wide, with leading zeros if need be. So overall, this handy statement will produce color values such as "#ffff00000000" for red, "#0000ffff0000" for green, and so on.

Now that you have these procedures, it is easy to add colordials to your applications. You can create a colordial like this:

---

* For more details, see J. D. Foley and A. Van Dam, *Fundamentals of Interactive Computer Graphics*, Addison-Wesley, 1982.

```
colordial_create .cd
pack .cd
```

You can spend some time adjusting the color. At any point, you can get the current color choice, like this:

```
set cval [colordial_get .cd]
```

You can then use that value to configure other widgets in your application.

4.5 Tabbed notebook

The coordinates in a drawing are not always fixed. Sometimes the size of one item depends on another. If you're drawing a bit of text, for instance, you may want to fit a rectangle around it. In this example, we'll see how you can build a display that adjusts its layout according to its contents.

In Section 2.1.7, we built a simple notebook that lets you browse through various pages of widgets. At the time, we used a radiobox to dial up a particular page. Now we'll use a canvas to decorate the top of each page with a tab, as shown in Figure 4.14. The result looks like the kind of notebook that you might find in an office supply store. We'll call this assembly a *tabnotebook*.

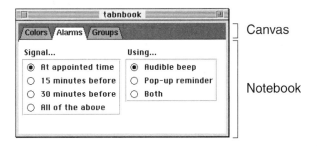

Figure 4.14. The tabs in a tabnotebook are drawn on a canvas.

We'll design the tabnotebook so that you can use it like the notebook described in Section 2.1.7. You create a tabnotebook as follows:

```
tabnotebook_create .tn
pack .tn
```

You use the tabnotebook_page procedure to create a new page:

```
set p1 [tabnotebook_page .tn "Colors"]
```

This creates an empty frame within the notebook and returns its window name. You can put widgets on this page by creating them as children of the frame. For example:

```
label $p1.mesg -text "Something on Colors page"
pack $p1.mesg -side left -expand yes -pady 8
```

You can select a particular page in the notebook by clicking on its tab or by calling the `tabnotebook_display` procedure, like this:

```
tabnotebook_display .tn "Colors"
```

Now that we understand how the tabnotebook works, let's see how it is implemented. The `tabnotebook_create` procedure looks like this:

```
proc tabnotebook_create {win} {
    global tnInfo

    frame $win -class Tabnotebook
    canvas $win.tabs -highlightthickness 0
    pack $win.tabs -fill x

    notebook_create $win.notebook
    pack $win.notebook -expand yes -fill both

    set tnInfo($win-tabs) ""
    set tnInfo($win-current) ""
    set tnInfo($win-pending) ""
    return $win
}
```

As usual, we start by creating the hull frame, which contains the other components. Inside the hull, we create a canvas and a notebook, and we pack them into position. We pack the canvas to fill across the top, so it will get wider as the window gets bigger. We pack the notebook to expand and fill, so it will get wider and taller as the window gets bigger.

We set the `-highlightthickness` option on the canvas to 0. This removes the focus highlight ring that normally appears around the canvas. The focus highlight ring changes color whenever you type onto the canvas. Since we won't be letting the user type directly onto the tabs, we don't need this ring, and we don't want the extra padding.

We give the hull the class name `Tabnotebook`, so you can add resources to the option database to customize all of the tabnotebooks in your application. For example, we include the following resources as defaults for the tabnotebook:

```
option add *Tabnotebook.tabs.background #666666 widgetDefault
option add *Tabnotebook.margin 6 widgetDefault
option add *Tabnotebook.tabColor #a6a6a6 widgetDefault
option add *Tabnotebook.activeTabColor #d9d9d9 widgetDefault
option add *Tabnotebook.tabFont \
    -*-helvetica-bold-r-normal--*-120-* widgetDefault
```

The first resource sets the background color for the canvas (named `tabs`) within our tabnotebook (class `Tabnotebook`). This is a standard option for the canvas, so Tk will handle it automatically. However, the other resources are names that we invented for the tabnotebook. We'll use the `option get` command to query their values as we draw the tabs.

We use the global `tnInfo` array as a data structure. Each tabnotebook has three slots in this array, parameterized by `$win`, the name of the tabnotebook. The slot `$win-tabs` stores the list of tab names. The slot `$win-current` stores the tab name for the page being displayed. And we'll see later how the `$win-pending` slot is used.

Once a tabnotebook has been created, you can add pages by calling the `tabnotebook_page` procedure:

```
proc tabnotebook_page {win name} {
    global tnInfo

    set page [notebook_page $win.notebook $name]
    lappend tnInfo($win-tabs) $name

    if {$tnInfo($win-pending) == ""} {
        set id [after idle [list tabnotebook_refresh $win]]
        set tnInfo($win-pending) $id
    }
    return $page
}
```

You pass in the name of the tabnotebook and the name of the new page. We call the `notebook_page` procedure defined in Section 2.1.7 to create the page, and we return this as the result of the procedure.

We also add the page name to the list of tabs, and we set things up so that the new tab will appear on the canvas. We will use a procedure called `tabnotebook_refresh` to clear the canvas and draw a new set of tabs. But if we call this procedure directly in `tabnotebook_page`, the canvas will be redrawn again and again as each new tab is added. In this case, it doesn't take long to generate the tabs, so calling the procedure directly is probably okay. But you may encounter performance problems when you build other canvas applications, so we'll show you how to optimize the drawing in this example.

Instead of calling `tabnotebook_refresh` immediately, we use the `after idle` command to defer the call. When the application is idle and has nothing better to do, it will draw the set of tabs. Each call to `after idle` returns a unique identifier, such as `after#12`. We save this identifier in the `$win-pending` slot for the tabnotebook. So the next time we add a page, we will know that one refresh call is pending, and we won't generate another.

All of the interesting canvas code appears in the `tabnotebook_refresh` procedure, which draws the tab set. The procedure looks like this:

```
proc tabnotebook_refresh {win} {
    global tnInfo

    $win.tabs delete all
```

```
set margin [option get $win margin Margin]
set color [option get $win tabColor Color]
set font [option get $win tabFont Font]
set x 2
set maxh 0

foreach name $tnInfo($win-tabs) {
    set id [$win.tabs create text \
        [expr $x+$margin+2] [expr -0.5*$margin] \
        -anchor sw -text $name -font $font -tags [list $name]]

    set bbox [$win.tabs bbox $id]
    set wd [expr [lindex $bbox 2]-[lindex $bbox 0]]
    set ht [expr [lindex $bbox 3]-[lindex $bbox 1]]
    if {$ht > $maxh} {
        set maxh $ht
    }

    $win.tabs create polygon 0 0  $x 0 \
        [expr $x+$margin] [expr -$ht-$margin] \
        [expr $x+$margin+$wd] [expr -$ht-$margin] \
        [expr $x+$wd+2*$margin] 0 \
        2000 0  2000 10  0 10 \
        -outline black -fill $color \
        -tags [list $name tab tab-$name]

    $win.tabs raise $id

    $win.tabs bind $name <ButtonPress-1> \
        [list tabnotebook_display $win $name]

    set x [expr $x+$wd+2*$margin]
}
set height [expr $maxh+2*$margin]
$win.tabs move all 0 $height

$win.tabs configure -width $x -height [expr $height+4]

if {$tnInfo($win-current) != ""} {
    tabnotebook_display $win $tnInfo($win-current)
} else {
    tabnotebook_display $win [lindex $tnInfo($win-tabs) 0]
}
set tnInfo($win-pending) ""
}
```

There's a lot of code here, but the end result is quite simple: The code clears the canvas and draws a tab for each page in the notebook. The position of each tab depends on the tabs before it, so we have to draw the tabs in order from left to right. We know what each tab should look like—it's just a polygon item for the tab and a text item for the label. But we don't know the exact coordinates for the polygon until we've drawn the text. After all, the tab name can be any length, and the text font can be any size. So we create the text item, draw a polygon around it, create the next text item, draw a polygon around it, and so on.

Let's go through the procedure step by step. Keep in mind that the `win` parameter refers to the entire tabnotebook assembly, so the canvas widget inside is `$win.tabs`.

We start by telling the canvas to delete all of its items. This clears any tabs that we may have drawn the previous time the tabs were refreshed.

Next, we initialize some variables that control the drawing process. We use the variable `x` to keep track of our position from left to right as we draw each tab. We use the variable `maxh` to store the height of the tallest tab.

The variable `margin` controls the padding around the label on each tab. The variable `color` controls the background color for each tab. The variable `font` controls the font used for the label. Instead of hard-wiring these values into the script, we query them from the option database. That way, you can customize the look of the tabnotebook for different applications.

Next, we iterate through the list of tab names and draw each tab, as shown in Figure 4.15. We can simplify the coordinates a bit if we draw each tab with its baseline at $y = 0$. Of course, if we left the tabs at this position, they would be outside the normal viewing area. So before we finish, we'll move them back down where they belong. But for now, we'll think of (0,0) as the lower-left corner of the tab set.

As we said earlier, we create the text item for each tab first. We position its south-west corner a little to the right of `$x` and a little above the baseline, as shown in Figure 4.15(a). Remember, the canvas returns a unique number for each item we create. We'll need this number to refer to the text item, so we save it in a variable called `id`.

We use the canvas `bbox` operation to query the bounding box for the text. This operation returns a list of four numbers representing the (x,y) coordinate for the upper-left corner and the (x,y) coordinate for the lower-right corner. We subtract the two x-coordinates to compute the overall width, and we subtract the two y-coordinates for the overall height.

Next, we create a polygon for the tab, as shown in Figure 4.15(b). This requires a long list of coordinates. The first point is (0,0), the next point is (`$x`,0), and so on. We extend the tab's baseline out to `2000` along the x-axis, which for all practical purposes is infinity. We draw the bottom of the tab down 10 pixels below the x-axis. When we shift all of the tabs down, this will be low enough that it will disappear off the bottom of the canvas.

As we create each polygon, we tag it with three names. The name `tab` applies to all of the tab polygons. We'll use this later to reset the background color for the tabs that are not selected. The name `tab-$name` applies to the polygon for a particular tab. We'll use this to set the background of the selected tab. The name `$name` applies to both the text and the polygon for each tab. We'll use this whenever we want to refer to the tab as a whole.

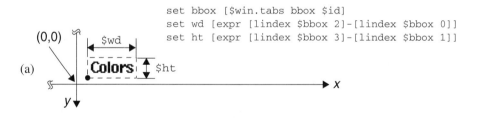

```
set bbox [$win.tabs bbox $id]
set wd [expr [lindex $bbox 2]-[lindex $bbox 0]]
set ht [expr [lindex $bbox 3]-[lindex $bbox 1]]
```

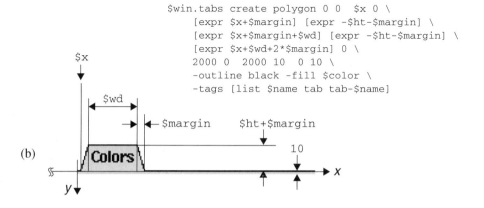

```
$win.tabs create polygon 0 0  $x 0 \
    [expr $x+$margin] [expr -$ht-$margin] \
    [expr $x+$margin+$wd] [expr -$ht-$margin] \
    [expr $x+$wd+2*$margin] 0 \
    2000 0  2000 10  0 10 \
    -outline black -fill $color \
    -tags [list $name tab tab-$name]
```

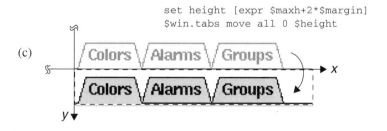

```
set height [expr $maxh+2*$margin]
$win.tabs move all 0 $height
```

Figure 4.15. A series of commands builds the tab display on the canvas.

Since the polygon is created after the text item, it would normally obscure the text. We fix this by using the canvas `raise` operation to raise the text item back to the top.

Finally, we bind to the `<ButtonPress-1>` event so that clicking on a tab will invoke `tabnotebook_display` and display its associated page. Notice that we bind to the tag name $name, which applies to both the text and the polygon. Thus you can click anywhere on a tab, and it will respond. Had we added the binding to only the polygon, you would have to click directly on the polygon to actuate the tab. If you clicked on the text by accident, it would do nothing.

Also, notice that we use the `list` command to wrap up the call to `tabnotebook_display`. This keeps $name together as a single argument, even if it has spaces embedded within it. Had we used `" "` instead, the page name "Employment History" would generate an error, for the reasons described in Section 3.1.5.

We repeat this process for each tab in the display, shifting the position $x toward the right as we go. When all of the tabs are drawn, we compute the overall height of the tab set and move the tabs down into position, as shown in Figure 4.15(c).

The canvas should be just big enough to display the final tab set, so we configure its width and height accordingly. We expose a few pixels below the baseline, but not the bottom of the tab polygon. This adds a little margin but still makes it look as though the tab is connected to the notebook below it.

If a page has already been selected, it is displayed again. As we'll see later, this raises the tab for that page and changes its color. If there is no current page, we select the first tab as the current page.

At long last, the refresh operation is done. We must be careful to reset the $win-pending slot in the tabnotebook data structure. If we add another page later on, this will allow us to start the cycle all over. Another call to `tabnotebook_refresh` will be pending, and when the application is idle, the tab set will be regenerated.

We need one more procedure for the tabnotebook. Clicking on a tab invokes `tabnotebook_display`, which is implemented like this:

```
proc tabnotebook_display {win name} {
    global tnInfo

    notebook_display $win.notebook $name

    set normal [option get $win tabColor Color]
    $win.tabs itemconfigure tab -fill $normal

    set active [option get $win activeTabColor Color]
    $win.tabs itemconfigure tab-$name -fill $active
    $win.tabs raise $name

    set tnInfo($win-current) $name
}
```

This procedure uses `notebook_display` to bring up the notebook page and then highlights the current tab and raises it to the foreground.

Having good tag names makes this easy. We can use the name `tab` to refer to all of the tab polygons, so we can reset them all back to their normal color with a single command. We can use the name `tab-$name` to refer to a particular tab polygon, so we can highlight that tab with the active color. And we can use the name $name to refer to both the text and the polygon for the tab, so we can raise both items to the foreground as a group.

4.6 Calendar

The drawing on a canvas has a fixed size. So when you resize a canvas, you'll see more or less of its drawing, and you can use scrollbars to adjust the view. But you may want a drawing to scale with the size of a canvas. For example, suppose the drawing shows the status of the factory floor mentioned earlier. When you expand the window, you should see a larger view of the factory—not a larger window with lots of empty space. In this example, we'll see how you can make a drawing react to size changes in the canvas. We'll also see some new techniques for handling selections and for updating complex displays.

Many business applications require a calendar like the one shown in Figure 4.16. Tk doesn't have a calendar widget, but as you probably know by now, it is easy to build one, using the canvas. We'll draw each day as a rectangle item with a text item for the day number. We'll even add an image item in the lower-right corner of each day so that we can add decorations for holidays. We'll use a text item at the top to display the current month, and we'll use window items to position some buttons on either side, so you can move back and forth through the months.

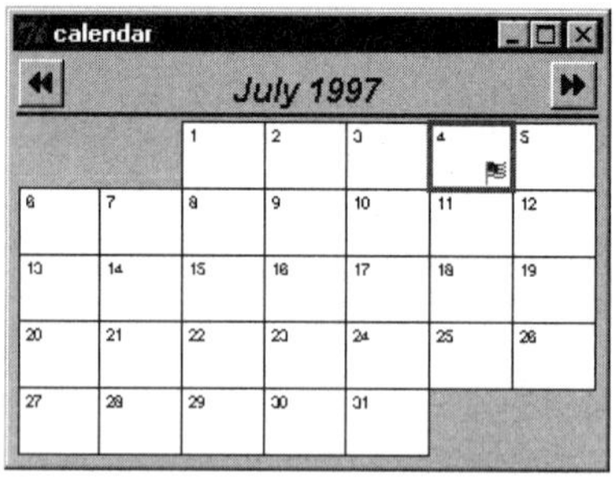

Figure 4.16. The canvas is used to create an interactive calendar.

4.6.1 Handling size changes

As usual, we'll write a procedure, called `calendar_create`, to create the calendar. You can call the procedure like this:

```
calendar_create .cal 7/4/97
pack .cal -expand yes -fill both
```

This creates a calendar named `.cal` and packs it into the main window. When the calendar appears, it will display July 1997, but you'll be able to change the month by clicking on the arrow buttons.

Notice that we packed the calendar to expand and fill. So if you expand the window, the canvas will expand too. Whenever the canvas changes size like this, we'll redraw the calendar to cover the new size.

You can see the basic size-handling code in the `calendar_create` procedure, which is implemented like this:

```
proc calendar_create {win {date "now"}} {
    global calInfo env

    if {$date == "now"} {
        set time [clock seconds]
    } else {
        set time [clock scan $date]
    }
    set calInfo($win-time) $time
    set calInfo($win-selected) ""
    set calInfo($win-selectCmd) ""
    set calInfo($win-decorateVar) ""

    frame $win -class Calendar
    canvas $win.cal -width 3i -height 2i
    pack $win.cal -expand yes -fill both

    button $win.cal.back \
        -bitmap @[file join $env(EFFTCL_LIBRARY) images back.xbm] \
        -command "calendar_change $win -1"

    button $win.cal.fwd \
        -bitmap @[file join $env(EFFTCL_LIBRARY) images fwd.xbm] \
        -command "calendar_change $win +1"

    bind $win.cal <Configure> "calendar_redraw $win"

    return $win
}
```

Much of this code follows the recipe that we use for creating an assembly of widgets. We use the global variable `calInfo` as a data structure for all calendars. Each calendar has four slots in this array, parameterized by the calendar name $win. We'll explain the slots $win-selected, $win-selectCmd, and $win-decorateVar later, when we need them. For now, we initialize them to the null string.

The slot $win-time stores an integer value from the system clock, measuring time as the number of seconds that have elapsed since January 1, 1970. When you call `calendar_create` with a date, such as 7/4/97, we use the `clock scan` command to convert this to a time value, and we store it in the array. But the date is optional; if you don't specify a value, it gets the default value now, and we use the `clock seconds` command to query the current system time. One way or the other, we get a time value, and we store it away so that when we draw the calendar later on, we'll display the month that contains that time.

We create a hull frame with the class name `Calendar` to act as a container for the assembly. That way, we can add resource settings to the options database to customize all of the calendars in an application. We create a canvas for the calendar and pack it to expand and fill in the hull. And we create the two buttons that let you page forward and backward through the months. Both of these buttons have bitmap labels with names of the form @*fileName*, so the bitmaps are loaded from files. But notice that neither of these buttons is packed into the hull. Instead, we'll position them on the canvas by creating window items when we draw the calendar.

All of the size-handling code boils down to a single `bind` command. Whenever a widget changes size, it receives a <Configure> event. So we bind to this event on the canvas. Whenever the canvas changes size, we call `calendar_redraw` to erase the canvas and to draw the calendar at the new size.

Notice that we don't have to call `calendar_redraw` explicitly to draw the first month. Instead, when the canvas window appears on the desktop, it will get a finite size, so it will get a <Configure> event, and `calendar_redraw` will be called automatically to handle the size change.

Having a "redraw" procedure like this is useful for other reasons, too. Suppose you click on one of the arrow buttons to change the month. We can adjust the calendar's $win-time slot forward or backward by a month and then call `calendar_redraw` to display the new month. Thus the `calendar_change` procedure is implemented like this:

```
proc calendar_change {win delta} {
    global calInfo

    set dir [expr ($delta > 0) ? 1 : -1]
    set month [clock format $calInfo($win-time) -format "%m"]
    set month [string trimleft $month 0]
    set year [clock format $calInfo($win-time) -format "%Y"]

    for {set i 0} {$i < abs($delta)} {incr i} {
        incr month $dir
        if {$month < 1} {
            set month 12
            incr year -1
        } elseif {$month > 12} {
            set month 1
            incr year 1
        }
    }
```

```
        set calInfo($win-time) [clock scan "$month/1/$year"]

        calendar_redraw $win
    }
```

We use the `clock format` command to extract the month and the year from the time
value. The `%m` field is replaced with the month number. We use `string trimleft` to
remove any leading `0`s from this number, so it is not misinterpreted as an octal value when
we change it later on. The `%Y` field is replaced with a year, such as `1997`. It won't have
leading `0`s, so it doesn't require the `string trimleft` step.

   You would normally call this procedure with a `delta` value of ±1 to move forward or
backward by one month. But you can use a larger `delta` value to skip over several months
at a time. We step forward or backward one month at a time, looking for changes to the
year. When the month is decremented below January, we wrap around to December of the
previous year. When the month is incremented beyond December, we wrap around to January of the next year. When we have arrived at a new month and year, we use the
`clock scan` command to convert that date back into a time value for the calendar. We
store that value in the `$win-time` slot for the calendar and then use `calendar_redraw`
to display the month containing that time.

   The `calendar_redraw` procedure erases the canvas and then creates the items to
draw a particular month. This procedure is fairly long, so we have simplified it here by
removing some code. We'll show the missing code later, as we continue to develop
the example, and you can find a complete listing in the file `efftcl/lib/scripts/`
`calendar.tcl`, which can be obtained from the Web site mentioned on page xiv. The
simplified version looks like this:

```
    proc calendar_redraw {win} {
        global calInfo
        ...

        $win.cal delete all

        set time $calInfo($win-time)
        set wmax [winfo width $win.cal]
        set hmax [winfo height $win.cal]

        $win.cal create window 3 3 -anchor nw \
            -window $win.cal.back
        $win.cal create window [expr $wmax-3] 3 -anchor ne \
            -window $win.cal.fwd
        set bottom [lindex [$win.cal bbox all] 3]

        set font [option get $win titleFont Font]
        set title [clock format $time -format "%B %Y"]
        $win.cal create text [expr $wmax/2] $bottom -anchor s \
            -text $title -font $font
```

```
incr bottom 3
$win.cal create line 0 $bottom $wmax $bottom -width 2
incr bottom 3

set font [option get $win dateFont Font]
set bg [option get $win dateBackground Background]
set fg [option get $win dateForeground Foreground]
...

set layout [calendar_layout $time]
set weeks [expr [lindex $layout end]+1]

foreach {day date dcol wrow} $layout {
    set x0 [expr $dcol*($wmax-7)/7+3]
    set y0 [expr $wrow*($hmax-$bottom-4)/$weeks+$bottom]
    set x1 [expr ($dcol+1)*($wmax-7)/7+3]
    set y1 [expr ($wrow+1)*($hmax-$bottom-4)/$weeks+$bottom]
    ...
    $win.cal create rectangle $x0 $y0 $x1 $y1 \
        -outline $fg -fill $bg

    $win.cal create text [expr $x0+4] [expr $y0+2] \
        -anchor nw -text "$day" -fill $fg -font $font

    $win.cal create image [expr $x1-2] [expr $y1-2] \
        -anchor se -tags [list $date-image]
    ...
}
...
}
```

We start by deleting all items on the canvas. That will erase any drawing that might exist from the previous time we called this procedure. We use `winfo width` and `winfo height` to determine the overall size of the canvas. Our *x*-coordinates will run from 0 to `$wmax`, *y*-coordinates from 0 to `$hmax`.

We position the arrow buttons by creating window items on the canvas, as shown in Figure 4.17(a). We place one button anchored on its northwest corner in the upper-left corner of the canvas, the other on its northeast corner in the upper-right corner of the canvas. These window items are merely placeholders for the buttons that we created in `calendar_create`. Thus we can delete the window items and make the buttons disappear without destroying the buttons themselves. Deleting a window item is analogous to the `pack forget` operation described in Section 2.1.7.

Next, we use the canvas `bbox` operation to get the *y*-coordinate for the bottom of the buttons. We use this as a baseline for the title that displays the current month, as shown in

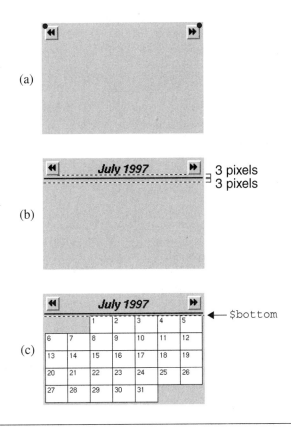

Figure 4.17. A calendar is drawn by creating items on the canvas.

Figure 4.17(b). We use the `clock format` command to extract the title from the calendar's time value. The `%B` field gets replaced with a full month name, such as `July`, and the `%Y` field gets replaced with the full year, such as `1997`. We create a text item centered on the width, anchored with its south side on the baseline.

Instead of hard-coding the title font, we query the `titleFont` resource from the option database. We query some other resources, too, including `dateBackground`, `dateForeground`, and `dateFont`. That way, you can customize the look of the calendar for different applications. For example, we include the following resources as defaults for the calendar:

```
option add *Calendar.dateBackground white widgetDefault
option add *Calendar.dateForeground black widgetDefault
option add *Calendar.selectColor red widgetDefault
```

```
option add *Calendar.selectThickness 3 widgetDefault
option add *Calendar.titleFont \
    -*-helvetica-bold-o-normal--*-180-* widgetDefault
option add *Calendar.dateFont \
    -*-helvetica-medium-r-normal--*-100-* widgetDefault
```

Once we have created the title, we move down 3 pixels, add a line item, and move down another 3 pixels. The variable `bottom` contains our final position. We'll fit the date squares into the remaining height.

We use another procedure, called `calendar_layout`, to determine where the date squares fall on the calendar. We won't show you how this is implemented. If you're curious, you can look at the file `efftcl/lib/scripts/calendar.tcl`. The procedure returns a list of values that looks like this:

```
1 07/01/1997 2 0   2 07/02/1997 3 0   3 07/03/1997 4 0 ...
```

The first four elements represent the first day on the calendar; the next four elements, the next day; and so on. Of the four elements, the first is the number of the day; the second is the date, including the month and the year; the third is the column for the day of the week; and the last element is the row for the week. The last group of four elements represents the last day on the calendar. So the very last element in the list is the index for the very last row of weeks. We use this to determine the total number of weeks, so we can divide up the remaining space on the canvas.

Normally, you use a simple `foreach` command to iterate through the values in a list. But what do you do when the values have a sequence that repeats itself like this? You give the `foreach` command a list of variables that represents your sequence. For example, we can iterate through our list with the following command:

```
set layout [calendar_layout $time]
foreach {day date dcol wrow} $layout {
    ...
}
```

The `foreach` command extracts the first four values from the list `$layout`; assigns them to the variables `day`, `date`, `dcol`, and `wrow`; and then executes the body of the loop. On the next pass, it extracts the next four values and again executes the body of the loop. So you can use the `foreach` command to not only iterate through a list, but also dissect it.

As we iterate through our list of layout information, we create the items to represent each date square, as shown in Figure 4.17(c). We use the row and column numbers for each date to compute the coordinates (x0,y0) and (x1,y1) for its background rectangle. We create the rectangle and add a text item in its upper-left corner to display the day number. We also add a blank image in the lower-right corner. We'll use this later to add decorations for important holidays.

At this point, the calendar is complete. When it appears on the desktop, the canvas will get a `<Configure>` event, triggering a call to `calendar_redraw` to draw the calendar. If you expand the window, the canvas will get another `<Configure>` event, triggering another call to `calendar_redraw`. All items from the previous calendar will be deleted, and new items will be created to fill the canvas at its new size.

4.6.2 Sensors and callbacks

Suppose you use this calendar as part of an application for handling appointments. When you click on a particular day, we could highlight that day and bring up a list of appointments. Many canvas drawings have "hot spots," or items within them that can be selected. In this section, we'll see how you can support selections in a generic way. We'll add support for a selection callback that lets you customize how the calendar will react in different applications.

If we want an item to respond when you click on it, we could bind to its `<ButtonPress-1>` event. Each date square on the calendar is composed of three items: the background rectangle, the day number, and an image that might be used for decorations. If we want the date square to respond when you click on it, we could bind to `<ButtonPress-1>` on all three items. Or, we could tag all three items with the same group name and bind to the group as a whole. This is how we handled the tabs in the tabnotebook described in Section 4.5.

But another technique for handling selections is sometimes easier to use. Instead of binding to all three items in each date square, we cover each square with an invisible rectangle and bind to that rectangle. The canvas will let you use `""` as a color name, so you have a way of suppressing the outline color or the fill color of an item. If you suppress both colors, you will get an invisible item. But the item will still react to events on the canvas as if it were filled with a solid color. We'll call this kind of item a *sensor*.

We can add some code to `calendar_redraw` to create a sensor over each date square, like this:

```
proc calendar_redraw {win} {
    ...

    foreach {day date dcol wrow} $layout {
        ...
        $win.cal create rectangle $x0 $y0 $x1 $y1 \
            -outline $fg -fill $bg

        $win.cal create text [expr $x0+4] [expr $y0+2] \
            -anchor nw -text "$day" -fill $fg -font $font

        $win.cal create image [expr $x1-2] [expr $y1-2] \
            -anchor se -tags [list $date-image]

        ...
```

```
            $win.cal create rectangle $x0 $y0 $x1 $y1 \
                -outline "" -fill "" \
                -tags [list $date-sensor all-sensor]

            $win.cal bind $date-sensor <ButtonPress-1> \
                [list calendar_select $win $date]
        }
        ...
    }
```

Again, we've left out some code to avoid repeating what was shown in the previous section.

Notice that we create the sensor after the other three items, so it will cover them on the canvas. Had we done it the other way around, the sensor would be covered and would not get any events. If for some reason we had to create the sensor earlier in the procedure, we could fix this problem by using the canvas raise or lower operations to achieve the proper stacking order.

We tag each sensor with the name $date-sensor, so the sensor for July 1, 1997, has the tag 07/01/1997-sensor. Also, we tag all sensors with the name all-sensor so we can handle them as a group.

Finally, we bind to the <ButtonPress-1> event on each sensor, so clicking on it triggers a call to calendar_select to select that date. We use list to format the binding, as we discussed in Section 3.1.5. The values for $win and $date are substituted as the binding is created, so each sensor has its own custom binding that tells the calendar to select its date.

The calendar_select procedure highlights a particular date on the calendar and is implemented like this:

```
proc calendar_select {win date} {
    global calInfo
    set time [clock scan $date]
    set date [clock format $time -format "%m/%d/%Y"]

    set calInfo($win-selected) $date

    set current [clock format $calInfo($win-time) \
        -format "%m %Y"]
    set selected [clock format $time -format "%m %Y"]

    if {$current == $selected} {
        set fg [option get $win dateForeground Foreground]
        $win.cal itemconfigure all-sensor \
            -outline "" -width 1

        set color [option get $win selectColor Foreground]
        set width [option get $win selectThickness Thickness]
```

```
                    $win.cal itemconfigure $date-sensor \
                        -outline $color -width $width
                    $win.cal raise $date-sensor
                } else {
                    set calInfo($win-time) $time
                    calendar_redraw $win
                }

                if {[string trim $calInfo($win-selectCmd)] != ""} {
                    set cmd $calInfo($win-selectCmd)
                    set cmd [percent_subst %d $cmd $date]
                    uplevel #0 $cmd
                }
            }
```

The first two `set` commands look a bit strange, but they do something important. They
normalize the `date` argument to a standard format by converting the date to a system time
value and then back again. For example, suppose that you use a command like the following:

```
        calendar_select .cal "July 1, 1997"
```

Then the `date` argument will be normalized to `07/01/1997`. As long as the date is in this
format, we can access the sensor by using the tag name `$date-sensor`.

Next, we save the selected date in the `$win-selected` slot of the calendar data structure. Later on, if you need to know what date is currently selected, you can call the following procedure:

```
        proc calendar_get {win} {
            global calInfo
            return $calInfo($win-selected)
        }
```

This procedure looks into the data structure and returns the selected date.

Getting back to the `calendar_select` procedure, we need to determine whether the
selected date is displayed on the current calendar. Normally, we will enter this procedure
when you click on a date. So normally, the selected date is indeed displayed. But you
could call this procedure from elsewhere in an application, and in that case, you could
select any date. To check for this, we use the `clock format` command to build two
strings. One represents the month and year currently displayed on the calendar. The other
represents the month and year of the selected date. If the two are different, we redraw the
calendar to display the selected date.

Otherwise, we highlight the selected date by changing the outline of the sensor rectangle, making it visible. We also raise the sensor so that its outline is not obscured by any
other items on the canvas. Instead of hard-coding the color and thickness of the selection
highlight, we query them from the option database, using the `option get` command.

Notice how our tag names simplify this operation. We remove the highlight from all sensors, using the tag name `all-sensor`. Then we add the highlight to the selected date, using the tag name `$date-sensor`.

Finally, we want the canvas to react to the date selection by bringing up a list of appointments, inserting the date in an entry widget, or something like that. Instead of hard-coding the behavior in this procedure, we set things up so you can customize the calendar with your own callback command. Just as you would configure the `-command` option of each button, you can add a command to each calendar. You can add this same feature to other libraries that you create, if you follow the recipe shown here.

We use the `$win-selectCmd` slot of the calendar data structure to store the selection callback for each calendar. If this slot contains a string, we invoke it as a command. First, we substitute the selected date into any `%d` field in the command, using the `percent_subst` procedure described in Section 7.6.7.3. Thus you can have a callback command like this:

```
puts "selected: %d"
.entry delete 0 end
.entry insert 0 "%d"
```

When you select the date `07/01/1997`, it would execute this:

```
puts "selected: 07/01/1997"
.entry delete 0 end
.entry insert 0 "07/01/1997"
```

This mimics the way the `bind` command works.

When all the substitutions are in place, we invoke the callback command, using `uplevel #0`. This forces the command to execute outside our procedure, in the global scope. If the callback sets any variables, they will be treated as global variables.

You can use the following procedure to set the callback command for a calendar:

```
proc calendar_select_cmd {win cmd} {
    global calInfo


    if {![info exists calInfo($win-selectCmd)]} {
        error "bad calendar name \"$win\""
    }
    set calInfo($win-selectCmd) $cmd
}
```

The procedure checks to make sure that the slot `$win-selectCmd` exists and then assigns a code fragment to it.

Putting all of this together, we can create the application shown in Figure 4.18. When you select any date on the calendar, that date is automatically typed into the entry widget below the calendar. You might use this as part of a dialog box for selecting dates. That way, the user can either browse through the calendar or enter a date by hand.

This requires just a few lines of code:

```
calendar_create .cal 7/4/1997
pack .cal -expand yes -fill both
```

Figure 4.18. Selecting a date on the calendar fills in the entry below it.

```
entry .entry
pack .entry -fill x -padx 4 -pady 4

calendar_select_cmd .cal {
    puts "selected: %d"
    .entry delete 0 end
    .entry insert 0 "%d"
}
```

By adding a selection callback, we've added a great deal of power to our simple calendar library. It now provides a convenient way of selecting dates for many different applications.

4.6.3 Monitoring variables

Suppose we use the canvas to display the status of something, such as our factory floor. We might use global variables to keep track of the output of the production line, the inventory at each station, and so on. But we need to know when something changes, so we can update the canvas. In this example, we'll see how you can monitor global variables in your application. When a variable changes, you can have the canvas update itself automatically to display the change.

Returning to our calendar example, we want to mark holidays and other important dates with an image in the lower-right corner, like the flag shown in Figure 4.16. Each date already has a blank image in the lower-right corner, so we can configure the image item on a certain date to display a particular image.

But how do we know which dates to decorate and what images to use? We can use an array variable to store all of the important dates for the calendar. We might initialize the array like this:

```
set holidays(07/04/1997) [image create photo -file flag.gif]
set holidays(12/25/1997) [image create photo -file bell.gif]
...
```

The image in the file `flag.gif` is associated with the Fourth of July holiday; the image in `bell.gif` is associated with Christmas; and so on.

We need to make sure that the calendar will consult the array as it draws each month. Suppose you call the following procedure:

```
calendar_decorate_with .cal holidays
```

It will tell a calendar named `.cal` to use an array named `holidays` for decorations. This procedure is implemented as follows:

```
proc calendar_decorate_with {win decorateVar} {
    global calInfo

    if {![info exists calInfo($win-decorateVar)]} {
        error "bad calendar name \"$win\""
    }
    set calInfo($win-decorateVar) $decorateVar
    calendar_redraw $win

    global $decorateVar
    trace variable $decorateVar wu "calendar_decorate $win"
}
```

First, we check to make sure that `$win` refers to a calendar. We look for the `$win-decorateVar` slot in the calendar data structure; if it doesn't exist, we report an error. Otherwise, we store the array name, such as `holidays`, in the `$win-decorateVar` slot, so we can refer to it later. With the new information in place, we call `calendar_redraw` to update the calendar. As it draws each date, it will look for an entry in the array of decorations and will display the appropriate image.

We add the following code to `calendar_redraw` to handle the decorations:

```
proc calendar_redraw {win} {
    global calInfo

    if {$calInfo($win-decorateVar) != ""} {
        upvar #0 $calInfo($win-decorateVar) decorate
    }
    ...
    foreach {day date dcol wrow} $layout {
        ...
        $win.cal create image [expr $x1-2] [expr $y1-2] \
            -anchor se -tags [list $date-image]

        if {[info exists decorate($date)]} {
            $win.cal itemconfigure $date-image \
                -image $decorate($date)
        }
```

```
          . . .
      }
          . . .
  }
```

Again, we've left out some code to avoid repeating what was shown in previous sections.

The slot `calInfo($win-decorateVar)` contains a name, such as `holidays`, which is the variable we will consult for decorations. So we have one variable acting like a pointer to another variable. We can access the other variable quite easily if we connect to it by using `upvar`. The `upvar` command says that we have a variable named `$calInfo($win-decorateVar)` (for example, `holidays`) in another context but that in this procedure, we'll call it `decorate`. Normally, `upvar` looks up to the calling procedure for the variable you're trying to access. But in this case, we included the `#0` argument, telling `upvar` to look for a global variable (at level #0 in the call stack). From this point on, the name `decorate` is an alias for the variable we're trying to access. When we query `decorate`, for example, we are really querying `holidays`. If we set `decorate`, we are really setting `holidays`.

As we draw each day on the calendar, we create a blank image tagged with the name `$date-image`. This will make it easy to refer to the image later on. The image item for the date July 20, 1997, will have the name `07/20/1997-image`. After we create each image, we use `info exists` to look for an entry in the decorations array. If we find one, we modify the image item to display the image for that date.

Now suppose that sometime later in the application, we add an entry to the `holidays` array. For example, we might let the user enter birthdays in a dialog. If one of those birthdays falls on the current calendar, its image should change immediately. A birthday cake icon should appear in the lower-right corner to mark the holiday.

We could say that whenever you update the `holidays` array like this, you must call `calendar_redraw` to see the changes. But we might need to modify the `holidays` array in many places in the application. If we forget to redraw after any one of them, users will report it as a bug.

There is a better way to handle this. We can monitor changes to any variable by putting a trace on it. In the last two lines of the `calendar_decorate_with` procedure, we put a trace on the decorations array. First, we declare it as a global variable. Otherwise, it would be treated as a local variable, and the trace would be forgotten when we exit the procedure. Next, we use the `trace variable` command to add the trace. The argument `wu` says that we want to be notified when the variable is written to (w) or unset (u). When this happens, it will trigger a call to `calendar_decorate` to update the calendar.

Notice that in these two lines of code, we refer to the decorations array as `$decorateVar`. If we had used the name `decorateVar`, we would have attached the trace to the `decorateVar` variable in this procedure. Again, the variable `decorateVar` contains a name of another variable, such as `holidays`, which is the variable that we want to trace. So `decorateVar` is acting like a pointer to another variable. When we use `$decorateVar` as a variable name, it is like dereferencing the pointer.

When we add a holiday, like this:

```
set holidays(07/20/1997) [image create photo -file birthday.gif]
```

or remove a holiday, like this:

```
unset holidays(07/20/1997)
```

it will trigger a call to the trace procedure, `calendar_decorate`. It is implemented as
follows:

```
proc calendar_decorate {win name1 name2 op} {
    upvar #0 $name1 decorate

    if {[info exists decorate($name2)]} {
        set imh $decorate($name2)
    } else {
        set imh ""
    }
    $win.cal itemconfigure $name2-image -image $imh
}
```

Notice that the procedure takes four arguments. We included the `win` argument when
we added the trace in `calendar_decorate_with`. The other three arguments are added
automatically on each call by the trace facility. The variable `name1` contains the name of
the variable being traced. In our case, `name1` will contain the name `holidays`. If this variable is an array, the variable `name2` indicates what slot is being modified. In our case, it
will have the value `07/20/1997`. The variable `op` contains the operation (`w` or `u`) that is
currently being traced.

Once again, the variable `name1` is acting like a pointer to another variable. So once
again, we use `upvar #0` to connect to it. We'll refer to the global variable called `$name1`
by using a local variable called `decorate`.

We use the `info exists` command to look for a decoration in the slot
`decorate($name2)`. If it exists, the trace is telling us that it was just modified, so we
look up the new image value. If it doesn't, the trace is saying that it was just deleted,
so we clear out the image. In either case, we tell the canvas to look for an item
named `$name2-image` and to change its image. When you modify the slot
`holidays(07/20/1997)`, the canvas will look for an item called `07/20/1997-image`.
If it finds that item, it updates the image. Otherwise, it ignores the request.

You can see the power of the trace facility in the following simple example:

```
image create photo flag \
    -file [file join $env(EFFTCL_LIBRARY) images flag.gif]

calendar_create .cal
calendar_decorate_with .cal flags
calendar_select_cmd .cal {set flags(%d) flag}

pack .cal -expand yes -fill both
```

We create a calendar and tell it to use an array called `flags` for decorations. Then we tell it to set the `flags` array whenever you select a date. If you click on the date December 22, 1992, it will store the name `flag` in the slot `flags(12/22/92)`. This will trigger a call to `calendar_decorate`, and a flag will appear on that day. In fact, a flag will appear on each day you select. Another part of the application may be using `flags` as a data structure. But as application programmers, we never worry about redrawing the calendar. When we add dates to the `flags` array, the calendar reacts automatically.

4.7 Simple drawing package

The canvas lets you create items, change their colors, raise them, lower them, move them, resize them, and so on. This may seem familiar. Many commercial drawing packages work in almost the same way. In fact, you can use the canvas to build a commercial drawing package. In this section, we'll build the simple drawing program shown in Figure 4.19. Along the way, we'll see some new techniques, such as editing text on the canvas, saving the contents of a canvas, and generating PostScript output for a printer.

Figure 4.19. The canvas is used to create an interactive drawing program.

We can create most of the drawing program by using components that we developed in other chapters. Figure 4.20 shows the interface broken down into its major components.

• Along the top, we have a menu bar named `.mbar`. This is a frame with a few menubuttons packed inside it.

• Along the side, we have a toolbar named `.tools.tbar`. This is created with the toolbar library that we developed in Section 3.4.2. The toolbar includes the following,

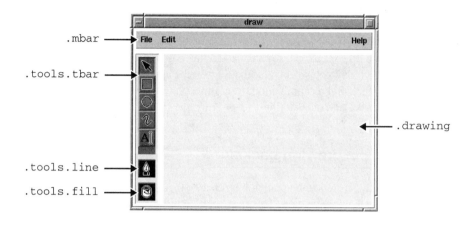

Figure 4.20. Major components in the drawing program.

shown in order from top to bottom: the selection tool, the rectangle tool, the oval tool, the spline tool, and the text tool. Selecting a tool activates the appropriate set of bindings for the canvas. For example, if you select the rectangle tool, the canvas has a set of bindings for the click, drag, and drop operations used to create a rectangle. We use binding tags to switch between the different bindings for each tool, as described in Section 3.5.3.

- Under the toolbar, we have the color selectors `.tools.line` and `.tools.fill`. They set the outline color and the fill color for new items. When you click on the color selectors, you get a short menu of color choices.

- Most of the window is covered by the drawing canvas named `.drawing`. It is packed to expand and fill, so if you stretch out the window, the canvas will get bigger.

The code that creates these components is not particularly interesting. Similar code appears in the chapters just mentioned. If you would like to see the details, you'll find the code in the file `efftcl/apps/draw`, which can be obtained from the Web site mentioned on page xiv. In the rest of this section, we'll assume that all of these components exist, and we'll focus on the canvas and its drawing operations.

4.7.1 Drawing items

In Section 3.4.1, we saw how you can bind to the click, drag, and drop events to create ovals on a canvas. We'll repeat this briefly here, so we can emphasize the role of the canvas.

When you select the rectangle tool, the following bindings are activated on the canvas:

```
bind rect <ButtonPress-1> {
    canvas_shape_create %W rectangle %x %y
}
bind rect <B1-Motion> {
    canvas_shape_drag %W %x %y
}
bind rect <ButtonRelease-1> {
    canvas_shape_end %W %x %y
}
```

Remember, the `bind` command automatically substitutes values into the % fields. The `%W` field will contain the name of the canvas, which in our program is `.drawing`. The `%x` and `%y` fields will contain the coordinates of the mouse pointer relative to the upper-left corner of the canvas at the time of the event.

When you click on the canvas, the `canvas_shape_create` procedure creates a new rectangle item with both corners at the click point. The procedure is implemented like this:

```
proc canvas_shape_create {win shape x y} {
    $win create $shape \
        $x $y $x $y -outline black -width 2 \
        -tags "rubbershape"
}
```

We create an item of type `$shape`, which in this case is `rectangle`, and we tag it with the name `rubbershape`. This makes it easy to change the item in the following steps.

As you hold down the mouse button and drag the pointer, the `canvas_shape_drag` procedure moves the lower-right corner of the rectangle. The procedure is implemented like this:

```
proc canvas_shape_drag {win x y} {
    set coords [$win coords "rubbershape"]
    set coords [lreplace $coords 2 3 $x $y]
    eval $win coords "rubbershape" $coords
}
```

We use the canvas `coords` operation to get the coordinates of the item called `rubbershape`. This returns a list of four numbers, representing the upper-left and lower-right corners of the rectangle. We substitute the current drag point into the list, using `lreplace`, then assign the new coordinates back to the item. Notice that we use the `eval` command in this last step. The canvas `coords` operation requires individual coordinate numbers, like this:

```
$win coords "rubbershape" 12 42 36 54
```

If we give it a list of coordinates like this:

```
$win coords "rubbershape" $coords     ;# error!
```

it will see only one argument, which it will interpret as a rather strange-looking number, and it will report an error. The `eval` command joins its arguments together and then interprets the result. In doing so, it strips off the quotes that normally delimit arguments, like this:

```
eval .drawing coords "rubbershape" {12 42 36 54}
.drawing coords rubbershape 12 42 36 54
```

So the `eval` command causes the numbers in `$coords` to be treated as separate arguments on the command line.

When you release the mouse button, `canvas_shape_end` drops the rectangle and applies the colors from `.tools.line` and `.tools.fill`. The procedure is implemented like this:

```
proc canvas_shape_end {win x y} {
    global canvInfo

    canvas_shape_drag $win $x $y

    $win itemconfigure "rubbershape" \
        -outline $canvInfo($win-penColor) \
        -fill $canvInfo($win-fillColor)

    $win dtag "rubbershape"
}
```

We call `canvas_shape_drag` to update the coordinates for this last point and then set the proper outline and fill colors. The colormenus store their values in the `$win-penColor` and `$win-fillColor` slots of the canvas data structure. We'll see how that happens later in this section. At this point, we "drop" the rectangle by using the canvas `dtag` operation to delete the `rubbershape` tag. The rectangle will remain, but we won't be able to use the name `rubbershape` to refer to it. So the next time we create an item called `rubbershape` and drag its corner around, this rectangle won't be affected.

4.7.2 Selecting items

When the selection tool is active, you can select items and change their characteristics. First, you drag out a *selection rectangle*, as shown in Figure 4.21(a). When you release the mouse button, the selection rectangle disappears, and the selected items are enclosed in a dashed rectangle that we'll call the *marker rectangle*, as shown in Figure 4.21(b). We'll animate the dashes on this rectangle so that they move, or *shimmer*, as a function of time. This makes it obvious that the marker rectangle is part of the selection process, not a new item in the drawing.

When you enter the selection mode, we add the following bindings to the canvas:

```
bind select <ButtonPress-1> {
    canvas_shape_create %W rectangle %x %y
}
```

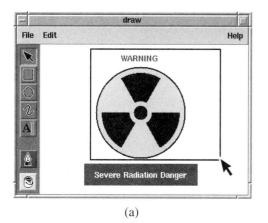
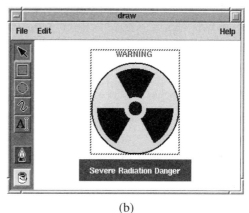

(a)   (b)

Figure 4.21. (a) You select items by dragging out a selection rectangle. (b) Selected items are highlighted by a marker rectangle with a shimmering pattern.

```
bind select <B1-Motion> {
    canvas_shape_drag %W %x %y
}
bind select <ButtonRelease-1> {
    canvas_select_end %W %x %y
}
bind select <Shift-ButtonRelease-1> {
    canvas_select_end %W %x %y add
}
```

We handle the click and drag events just as we described in the previous section. So when you click on the canvas, we create a rectangle, and as you drag the mouse pointer, we stretch out the rectangle. But we handle the release event differently. Instead of leaving the rectangle as a new item on the canvas, we call `canvas_select_end` to handle the selection process. We look for items within the rectangle, mark them as "selected," and then delete the selection rectangle.

There are two flavors of the release event. Normally, the items within the selection rectangle become selected, and any items that were previously selected are forgotten. But if you hold down the Shift key while making the selection, the items in the selection rectangle are *added* to the items that were previously selected. So you can build up a selection by holding down the Shift key as you select more and more items.

The `canvas_select_end` procedure is implemented like this:

```
proc canvas_select_end {win x y {op "clear"}} {
    global env canvInfo
```

```
canvas_shape_drag $win $x $y

set coords [$win coords "rubbershape"]
foreach {x0 y0 x1 y1} $coords {}
$win delete "rubbershape"

canvas_select_done $win $op

if {abs($x1-$x0) < 2 && abs($y1-$y0) < 2} {
    set items [$win find overlapping $x0 $y0 $x0 $y0]
    $win addtag "selected" withtag [lindex $items end]
} else {
    eval $win addtag "selected" enclosed $coords
}

set coords [$win bbox "selected"]
if {$coords != ""} {
    foreach {x0 y0 x1 y1} $coords {}

    $win create line \
        $x0 $y0 $x1 $y0 $x1 $y1 $x0 $y1 $x0 $y0 \
        -fill black -width 2 -tags "marker"

    set images {
        stripes.xbm stripes2.xbm stripes3.xbm stripes4.xbm
    }
    set file [file join $env(EFFTCL_LIBRARY) images %v]
    set cmd [list $win itemconfigure marker -stipple @$file]
    set canvInfo($win-shimmer) [animate_start 200 $images $cmd]
}
}
```

We start by calling `canvas_shape_drag` to stretch the rectangle to its final position, and we use the canvas `coords` operation to query its final coordinates. This returns a list of four numbers defining the upper-left and lower-right corners of the selection rectangle. We could use the `lindex` command to pick apart the list, like this:

```
set x0 [lindex $coords 0]
set y0 [lindex $coords 1]
set x1 [lindex $coords 2]
set y1 [lindex $coords 3]
```

But we can accomplish the same thing more compactly with a `foreach` command, like this:

```
foreach {x0 y0 x1 y1} $coords {}
```

This picks out the first four elements of the `$coords` list, assigns them to the four variables, and then executes the body, which does nothing. Since only four elements are in the `$coords` list, the loop terminates immediately. As you can see, the `foreach` command provides a handy way of dissecting lists.

At this point, we know the coordinates of the selection rectangle, and we are done with the rectangle itself, so we delete it. We are about to find the items within the selection rectangle and to select them somehow. But what do we do with the items that are currently selected? If the `op` argument has the default value `clear`, we'll clear the current selection. But if it has the value `add`, we'll add the items to the current selection. In either case, we need to delete the marker rectangle that marks the current selection. We handle all of this by calling `canvas_select_done`. We'll see how this is implemented later.

First, we'll finish discussing `canvas_select_end`. We can keep track of selected items by tagging them with the name `selected`. The following command adds this tag to all of the items within the current selection rectangle:

```
eval $win addtag "selected" enclosed $coords
```

The `enclosed $coords` part says that the tag should be added only to the items that are completely enclosed in the rectangle defined by `$coords`. Once again, the four numbers within `$coords` must appear as separate arguments on the command line, so we use the `eval` command to break them out.

If you click and release on the same point, it will look as though you've drawn a tiny selection rectangle. We can detect this by checking for a small difference in the *x*- and *y*-coordinates. When we see this, we'll assume that you were clicking on a particular item, and we'll select that one item. We can use the following command to get a list of all items under the click point:

```
set items [$win find overlapping $x0 $y0 $x0 $y0]
```

This tells the canvas to find all of the items that touch a tiny rectangle from ($x0,$y0$) to ($x0,$y0$). The item number for the topmost item will be at the end of this list. We can tag that one item with the name `selected`, like this:

```
$win addtag "selected" withtag [lindex $items end]
```

Near the bottom of `canvas_select_end`, we create the marker rectangle that surrounds the selected items. We use the canvas `bbox` operation to get the coordinates of a bounding box that contains the selected items. If we get back a null string, no items are selected, and we don't need the marker. This would occur, for example, when you select a blank area of the canvas.

Otherwise, we use the `foreach` command to pick apart the coordinate list, and we create a line item tagged with the name `marker` to represent the marker rectangle. We use a line item instead of a rectangle item so that we can add the dash pattern to the boundary. We set the dash pattern like this:

```
$win itemconfigure marker -stipple @$file
```

This tells the canvas to draw the line, using a bitmap pattern in the file named `$file`, which will be a pattern of diagonal stripes. Where the bits are set, the line will be drawn in black; where they are not, the line will be invisible.

We add the shimmering effect by changing the pattern as a function of time. The four files in the `images` list form a sequence of stripe patterns, each shifted by 1 pixel from the one before it. We use the `animate_start` procedure developed in Section 3.7.3 to cycle through the patterns. Every 200 ms, a new pattern name is substituted into the %v field inside the cmd string, and the command is executed, assigning a new stipple pattern to the marker. We save the result from animate_start in the $win-shimmer slot of the canvas data structure, so that we can stop the animation later on, when we delete the marker rectangle.

At this point, the selection operation is complete. The selected items are tagged with the name selected, and we can manipulate them with such commands as:

```
.drawing raise "selected"
```

and

```
.drawing lower "selected"
```

These commands handle the Bring to Front and Send to Back operations found in many commercial drawing packages. We can add them to the Edit menu with some code, like this:

```
.mbar.edit.m add command -label "Bring to Front" -command {
    .drawing raise "selected"
}
.mbar.edit.m add command -label "Send to Back" -command {
    .drawing lower "selected"
}
```

In the remaining sections, we'll see how to implement other operations, such as move, delete, resize, and so on.

But what happens when you choose a new tool from the toolbar? The selection mode ends, so we need to forget about the selected items. The toolbar takes care of this by calling canvas_select_done, which is implemented as follows:

```
proc canvas_select_done {win {op clear}} {
    global canvInfo

    $win delete "marker"
    if {[info exists canvInfo($win-shimmer)]} {
        animate_stop $canvInfo($win-shimmer)
        unset canvInfo($win-shimmer)
    }
    if {$op == "clear"} {
        $win dtag "selected"
    }
}
```

First, we delete the shimmering marker rectangle. We delete the rectangle itself with a canvas delete operation, but we must do something more to stop the shimmering. If we find a $win-shimmer slot in the canvas data structure, it contains an identifier for the shimmer animation. We call animate_stop to stop the animation cycle, and we delete the $win-shimmer slot from the data structure.

Next, we remove the `selected` tag, using the canvas `dtag` operation. This removes the tag from all items on the canvas but leaves the items intact. In effect, this clears the current selection.

Notice that we remove the tag only when the `op` argument has the value `clear`, which it gets by default. If we pass in the value `add`, the selected items will remain selected. So we can use this procedure in `canvas_select_end` to clear the previous selection before defining a new one. When you hold down the Shift key, you'll get the `add` argument, and the new items will be added to the previous selection.

4.7.3   Moving and deleting items

Once you've selected some items, it is trivial to move them and delete them. We can add the following keyboard bindings to handle these operations:

```
bind select <KeyPress-BackSpace> {
    canvas_select_delete %W
}
bind select <KeyPress-Delete> {
    canvas_select_delete %W
}
bind select <KeyPress-Up> {
    canvas_select_move %W 0 -2
}
bind select <KeyPress-Down> {
    canvas_select_move %W 0 2
}
bind select <KeyPress-Left> {
    canvas_select_move %W -2 0
}
bind select <KeyPress-Right> {
    canvas_select_move %W 2 0
}
```

These bindings belong to the `select` binding tag. So like the bindings in the previous section, they are active when the selection tool is active.

You can delete the selected items by pressing the backspace or Delete keys. This triggers a call to `canvas_select_delete`, which is implemented like this:

```
proc canvas_select_delete {win} {
    $win delete "selected"
    canvas_select_done $win
}
```

We delete all items tagged with the name `selected` and then clear the marker rectangle by calling `canvas_select_done`.

You can move the selected items by pressing the arrow keys on the keyboard. Many drawing packages call this the *nudge* operation. Each key press triggers a call to `canvas_select_move` with a 2-pixel offset in either the *x*- or the *y*-direction. The move operation is handled like this:

```
proc canvas_select_move {win dx dy} {
    $win move "selected" $dx $dy
    $win move "marker" $dx $dy
}
```

We move all of the items tagged as `selected` by an amount `$dx` in the *x*-direction and an amount `$dy` in the *y*-direction. Of course, we update the marker rectangle by the same amount, so that it follows the selected items.

4.7.4 Configuring items

At any point, you can change the drawing colors by using the `.tools.line` and `.tools.fill` colormenus. We can detect the color change by assigning a callback to each menu, like this:

```
colormenu_action .tools.line {canvas_pen .drawing "%c"}
colormenu_action .tools.fill {canvas_fill .drawing "%c"}
```

Whenever you choose a new color, the colormenu substitutes the color name in the `%c` field and executes its command. If you choose red as the line color, for example, it will trigger the following command:

```
canvas_pen .drawing "red"
```

We'll see how colormenus are implemented in Section 8.2.3.

The `canvas_pen` procedure changes the line color of any items currently selected and then makes note of the new line color. The procedure is implemented like this:

```
proc canvas_pen {win color} {
    global canvInfo

    foreach item [$win find withtag "selected"] {
        switch [$win type $item] {
            rectangle - polygon - oval - arc {
                $win itemconfigure $item -outline $color
            }
            line - text {
                $win itemconfigure $item -fill $color
            }
            bitmap {
                $win itemconfigure $item -foreground $color
            }
        }
    }
    set canvInfo($win-penColor) $color
}
```

The canvas `itemconfigure` operation lets you change the characteristics of one or more items. If the selected items were all rectangles, for example, we could change their line color with a single command, like this:

```
$win itemconfigure $item -outline $color
```

But not all items have a `-outline` option. For example, the color of a line item or a text item is determined by its `-fill` option.

Thus we need to scan through the list of selected items and handle each one according to its type. We use the `foreach` command to iterate through a list of items tagged with the name `selected`, and we use the canvas `type` operation to determine the type of each item. The - character between labels in the `switch` statement acts as an "or" operator. If an item is a rectangle, a polygon, an oval, or an arc, we set its `-outline` color. If it's a line or a text item, we set its `-fill` color. If it's a bitmap, we set its `-foreground` color.

Finally, we save the new line color in the slot `$win-penColor` in the canvas data structure. We use this color whenever we create an item, as we saw in Section 4.7.1.

A similar thing happens when you choose a new fill color. If you choose green as the fill color, for example, it will trigger this command:

```
canvas_fill .drawing "green"
```

The `canvas_fill` procedure looks a lot like the `canvas_pen` procedure but sets the fill color instead of the line color. The procedure is implemented like this:

```
proc canvas_fill {win color} {
    global canvInfo

    foreach item [$win find withtag "selected"] {
        switch [$win type $item] {
            rectangle - polygon - oval - arc {
                $win itemconfigure $item -fill $color
            }
            bitmap {
                $win itemconfigure $item -background $color
            }
        }
    }
    set canvInfo($win-fillColor) $color
}
```

Again, we use `foreach` to scan through the items tagged with the name `selected`, and we check the type of each item. If an item is a rectangle, a polygon, an oval, or an arc, we sets its `-fill` color. If it's a bitmap, we set its `-background` color. Otherwise, it has no fill color, and we ignore it.

And again, we save the new fill color in the slot `$win-fillColor` in the canvas data structure. Any new items will automatically be filled with this color.

4.7.5 Resizing items

Many drawing packages add little black squares called *handles* around the edges of the
marker rectangle. You can click and drag on the handles to adjust the size of the item. We
could add handles to our drawing program as well, but it would complicate the code quite
a bit. Instead, we'll provide a simple-minded way to resize items so we can illustrate the
core of the resize operation.

We'll add two items to the Edit menu, like this:

```
.mbar.edit.m add command -label "Enlarge" -command {
    canvas_select_scale .drawing 1.1 1.1
}
.mbar.edit.m add command -label "Reduce" -command {
    canvas_select_scale .drawing 0.9 0.9
}
```

When you select Enlarge, the selected items will enlarge by 10 percent, making them 1.1
times their current size. When you select Reduce, they will reduce by 10 percent, making
them 0.9 times their current size.

In either case, we call `canvas_select_scale`, which is implemented as follows:

```
proc canvas_select_scale {win sx sy} {
    foreach {x0 y0 x1 y1} [$win bbox "selected"] {}

    set xm [expr 0.5*($x0+$x1)]
    set ym [expr 0.5*($y0+$y1)]
    $win scale "selected" $xm $ym $sx $sy
    $win scale "marker" $xm $ym $sx $sy
}
```

The canvas `scale` operation scales the coordinates of one or more items by a certain
amount in the *x*- and *y*-directions. For example, you can scale all of the items on a canvas
to 1.5 times their current size, like this:

```
.drawing scale "all" 0 0 1.5 1.5
```

The 0 0 arguments give an (*x*,*y*) coordinate for the center of the scaling operation. In this
case, we enlarged the items around the origin in the upper-left corner of the canvas. All of
the items spread out toward the right and toward the bottom, making the overall drawing
larger.

In the `canvas_select_scale` procedure, we don't want the items to move as they
spread out, so we scale them around their midpoint. That way, they get larger, but they stay
in the same place on the drawing. We use the canvas `bbox` operation to get a bounding box
for the selected items. We need to do some arithmetic on these coordinates, so we use the
`foreach` command to break up the list. This command assigns the values to the variables
x0, y0, x1, and y1 and then does nothing in the body of the loop. This is a handy trick. It
is more compact and convenient than an equivalent series of `lindex` commands.

Once we have the coordinates, we compute the midpoint by averaging the *x* and *y* values. We use the `scale` operation to scale the selected items by $sx in the *x*-direction and

by $sy in the *y*-direction. Of course, we scale the marker rectangle by the same amount, so that it follows the selected items.

4.7.6   Entering text

The canvas will support text entry just like an entry widget or a text widget, but it is not automatically turned on. You have to add the right bindings to the canvas to enable this feature. In this section, we'll see how to do this in the context of our drawing program.

The text tool lets you add text annotations to the drawing. You can click on the canvas to get a text-insertion cursor and type in the appropriate text. If you click on an existing text item, you'll edit that item. Otherwise, you'll get a new text item.

We can handle the click event with a binding, like this:

```
bind text <ButtonPress-1> {
    canvas_text_select %W %x %y
}
```

Since this binding belongs to the text bind tag, the toolbar adds it to the canvas whenever the text tool is active.

When you click on the canvas, it triggers a call to canvas_text_select with the name of the canvas and the coordinates of the click point. This procedure is implemented as follows:

```
proc canvas_text_select {win x y} {
    global canvInfo

    canvas_text_done $win

    if {[$win type current] == "text"} {
        $win addtag "editText" withtag current
    } else {
        $win create text $x $y \
            -fill $canvInfo($win-penColor) \
            -anchor w -justify left -tags "editText"
    }

    focus $win
    $win focus "editText"
    $win icursor "editText" @$x,$y
}
```

First, we call canvas_text_done to close the editing mode for any other text item that we might be editing. We'll see how this procedure is implemented later.

Next, we look for an existing text item at the click point. Remember, the canvas recognizes the name current as the item under the mouse pointer. So we can look for a text item by querying the type of the current item. If we find a text item, we tag it with the name editText. Otherwise, we create a new text item at the click point ($x,$y) and tag it with the name editText. As you type characters at the keyboard, we'll simply add them to the item called editText.

Now that we've selected a text item, we must direct the keyboard input to it. We do this by setting the keyboard focus, as described in Section 3.2.3. We use one command to set the widget focus for the program:

```
focus $win
```

This command directs all keyboard events to the canvas widget $win, so they will trigger any <KeyPress> bindings that we have on the canvas. We use another command to set the focus to a particular item within the canvas widget:

```
$win focus "editText"
```

This command directs all keyboard events on the canvas to the item called editText, so they will trigger any additional <KeyPress> bindings that we have added to that item. This also enables the insertion cursor for the editText item, so we can edit the text interactively.

The insertion cursor appears as a blinking line on the canvas. Exactly where it appears depends on its current position. We set its position by using the command:

```
$win icursor "editText" @$x,$y
```

This command tells the canvas to put the cursor for the editText item near the click point ($x,$y) on the canvas. So if you click in the middle of a text item, the insertion cursor will appear at that point.

Now that the text is selected, we need some bindings to handle key press events. We could use the bind command to add these bindings to the canvas as a whole. Or, we could use the canvas bind operation to add the bindings to individual items within the canvas. Or, we could use a mixture of bindings. In this example, we can handle all key press events in exactly the same way—by applying them to the item called editText. So in this example, we will bind to the canvas as a whole.

We add the following bindings to handle key press events:

```
bind text <KeyPress> {
    canvas_text_edit_add %W %A
}
bind text <KeyPress-Return> {
    canvas_text_edit_add %W "\n"
}
bind text <KeyPress-BackSpace> {
    canvas_text_edit_backsp %W
}
bind text <KeyPress-Delete> {
    canvas_text_edit_backsp %W
}
```

Most of the keys that you type are handled by the generic <KeyPress> binding. After each key stroke, the bind facility replaces %W with the name of the canvas and %A with the

ASCII code for the key and then calls `canvas_text_edit_add`. This procedure adds the
new character at the position of the insertion cursor, like this:

```
proc canvas_text_edit_add {win str} {
    $win insert "editText" insert $str
}
```

The first `insert` keyword tells the canvas to insert some text into one or more text items.
The next word, `editText`, is the tag name indicating what text items to modify. The next
word tells the canvas what character position to use when inserting the text. In this case,
the keyword `insert` says that the text should be added just before the insertion cursor.
Finally, we give the canvas the character `$str` to insert. When the character is added, the
insertion cursor shifts over automatically to make room for it.

The more specific key press bindings handle some special cases. We bind to
`<KeyPress-Return>` to handle the Return key properly. The ASCII code for the Return
key is the carriage-return character, `\r`. But we want the Return key to add a newline character, `\n`, so that we can force text entry onto another line.

We bind to both `<KeyPress-BackSpace>` and `<KeyPress-Delete>`, so pressing
either of these keys triggers a call to `canvas_text_edit_backsp` to erase a character.
This is implemented as follows:

```
proc canvas_text_edit_backsp {win} {
    set pos [expr [$win index "editText" insert] - 1]
    if {$pos >= 0} {
        $win dchars "editText" $pos
    }
}
```

We use the canvas `dchars` operation to delete a character in the text item called
`editText`. But we have to tell it which character to delete. The insertion cursor identifies
the character to the right of it. Thus if we told `dchar` to delete at the insertion cursor, like
this:

```
$win dchars "editText" insert
```

it would delete the character after the insertion cursor, not the one before it.

Instead, we use the canvas `index` operation to find the position of the insertion cursor
in the `editText` item. This returns a number representing the character position. Characters are numbered from 0, so 5 refers to the sixth character in the string. We subtract 1 to
get the character before the insertion cursor, and then we delete that character.

If you change tools or if you select another text item, we need to end the current editing operation. We handle this in `canvas_text_done`:

```
proc canvas_text_done {win} {
    set mesg [$win itemcget "editText" -text]
    if {[string length [string trim $mesg]] == 0} {
        $win delete "editText"
    }
```

```
$win dtag "editText"
$win focus ""
}
```

The first part eliminates any blank items. This might happen, for example, if you erase all of the text in an item or if you click to create a text item and then change your mind and select another tool. We use the `itemcget` operation to get the contents of the `editText` item; if it is blank, we delete it.

Next, we remove the `editText` tag from the current text item. If we didn't do this, you would notice a problem when you edited another text item—both items would be tagged with the name `editText`, so each keystroke would apply to both items! (In fact, this could be a bug or a feature, depending on how you write the user's guide.)

Finally, we reset the focus within the canvas so that no specific item has the focus. This hides the text-insertion cursor, indicating that the editing operation is done.

4.7.7 Printing a drawing

Adding a print feature to our drawing program is remarkably simple. The canvas has a `postscript` operation that you can use to generate PostScript output for the current drawing. For example, the canvas in our drawing program is named `.drawing`, so the following command returns a very long string containing a PostScript representation of the canvas:

```
.drawing postscript
```

By default, the canvas will generate PostScript for only the visible portion of the drawing. Normally, the entire drawing is visible in our drawing program. But suppose that we compress the window to a smaller size and then try to print. Or, suppose that at some point, we add scrollbars to the drawing program. In either case, we want to print the entire drawing—not just the part that is showing on the screen.

We need to pass the overall size of the drawing to the `postscript` operation, so we write a procedure to handle this:

```
proc draw_print {} {
    set x0 0
    set y0 0
    set x1 [winfo width .drawing]
    set y1 [winfo height .drawing]

    foreach {x0 y0 x1 y1} [.drawing bbox all] {}
    set w [expr $x1-$x0]
    set h [expr $y1-$y0]

    return [.drawing postscript -x $x0 -y $y0 -width $w -height $h]
}
```

We use the canvas `bbox` operation to get a bounding box that surrounds all of the items, and we pick out the coordinate numbers x0, y0, x1, and y1. Then we compute the overall width by subtracting the *x*-coordinates and the overall height by subtracting the *y*-coordinates. If the canvas is empty, the `bbox` operation will return the null string, and the `foreach` command won't assign values to any of the variables. So we're careful to initialize these variables to the size of the canvas at the start of the procedure.

Once we've computed the size of the drawing, we tell the canvas to generate Post-Script for a region of width `$w` and height `$h`, with its upper-left corner at the coordinate (`$x0,$y0`). We return the PostScript as the result of `draw_print`.

On Windows platforms, we can save the PostScript in a file, and the user could print the file by dragging it onto a printer icon. On UNIX platforms, we can use the `lpr` program to route output to a printer, like this:

```
exec lpr << [draw_print]
```

The `exec` command executes `lpr` as another process, feeding the PostScript output to its standard input. This queues up a print request, and a moment later, the printer produces the drawing.

Of course, that simple `lpr` command sends output to a default printer. In a real application, you should be able to send output to different printers or perhaps save it in a file. We'll develop a printer dialog to handle all of this in Section 6.6.3. Let's assume that we've done the work and use it here.

First, we can create a printer dialog, like this:

```
printer_create .print
```

Then we can add a Print... entry to the File menu to handle printing:

```
.mbar.file.m add command -label "Print..." -command {
    printer_print .print draw_print
}
```

When you select the Print... option, the printer dialog will appear, as shown in Figure 4.22. You can change the printer command to send output to a specific printer, or you can specify a file name for the output. When you click on the Print button, the dialog uses the command argument `draw_print` to generate output and then routes the output accordingly.

4.7.8 Saving a drawing

Our drawing program should be able to save a drawing in a file so you can load it again later to make changes. To accomplish this, we ask the canvas for a list of its items and then examine each item and write a description of it out to a file.

There are many ways to format the output file. Depending on what format you choose, your job of loading the file can be easy or difficult. For example, suppose we use one line to represent each item on the canvas. The first thing on the line could be a number representing the item type—1 for rectangle, 2 for oval, and so on. The next thing could be a list of coordinates. The rest of the line might depend on the type of the item. The description of a rectangle would have its outline color, its fill color, and its line width, whereas the description of a text item would have the text message, its fill color, and its anchor point.

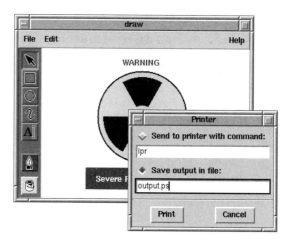

Figure 4.22. The printer dialog routes PostScript output to a printer.

After we settle a few more details, we might end up with a drawing file that looks something like this:

```
1 {79.0 24.0 256.0 196.0} #da18d6efdd41 black 2
3 {78.0 212.0} {HAZARDOUS ATOMIC WASTE} #23b397c5291d w
2 {145.4 87.45 188.6 129.75} black #23b397c5291d 2
2 {152.6 92.85 171.5 112.65} "" green 2
```

There are a few problems with this format. For one thing, we need to write a lot of code to load this data back into our application. Handling the various item types and their specialized argument lists is rather tedious and error prone. Also, it's not obvious what the various fields in this format represent. Which is first, the outline color or the fill color? What exactly is item type 3? What does the w represent at the end of that line? If you try to maintain this code over a period of several months, you may find yourself asking these same questions again and again.

Instead, let's write out the same information but format it to look like a series of Tcl commands. For example:

```
.drawing create rectangle 79.0 24.0 256.0 196.0 \
    -outline #da18d6efdd41 -fill black -width 2
.drawing create text 78.0 212.0 \
    -text {HAZARDOUS ATOMIC WASTE} -fill #23b397c5291d -anchor w
.drawing create oval 145.4 87.45 188.6 129.75 \
    -outline black -fill #23b397c5291d -width 2
.drawing create oval 152.6 92.85 171.5 112.65 \
    -outline {} -fill green -width 2
```

This format is quite expressive—it is obvious which is the outline color and which is the fill color. And this format is already well documented. If you forget what a parameter such as -anchor means, you can always look it up in the manual page for the canvas command. But more important, this format is extremely easy to load. You can simply execute the drawing file by using something like the source command, as we'll see in the next section.

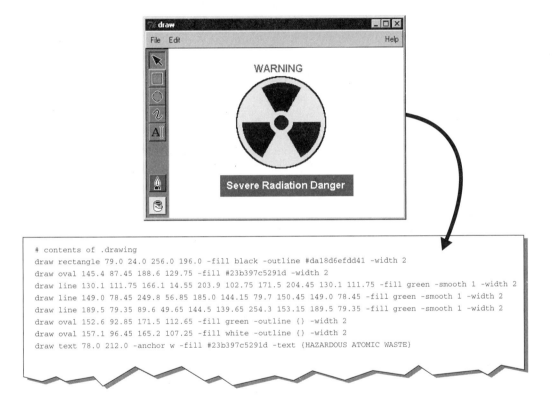

```
# contents of .drawing
draw rectangle 79.0 24.0 256.0 196.0 -fill black -outline #da18d6efdd41 -width 2
draw oval 145.4 87.45 188.6 129.75 -fill #23b397c5291d -width 2
draw line 130.1 111.75 166.1 14.55 203.9 102.75 171.5 204.45 130.1 111.75 -fill green -smooth 1 -width 2
draw line 149.0 78.45 249.8 56.85 185.0 144.15 79.7 150.45 149.0 78.45 -fill green -smooth 1 -width 2
draw line 189.5 79.35 89.6 49.65 144.5 139.65 254.3 153.15 189.5 79.35 -fill green -smooth 1 -width 2
draw oval 152.6 92.85 171.5 112.65 -fill green -outline {} -width 2
draw oval 157.1 96.45 165.2 107.25 -fill white -outline {} -width 2
draw text 78.0 212.0 -anchor w -fill #23b397c5291d -text {HAZARDOUS ATOMIC WASTE}
```

Figure 4.23. The contents of a drawing canvas can be saved as a series of Tcl commands.

We can improve this format a bit by removing the reference to a specific widget, such as .drawing. After all, if we ever decided to rename the .drawing widget, all of the drawing files would be useless. Let's replace .drawing create with a generic command called draw, as shown in Figure 4.23. This decouples the format from our current program, so we could use it for different applications.

Note: *This example teaches an important lesson: Tcl is not just a command language; it is also a data language.*

Whenever you find yourself inventing a text-based file format, think about saving the information as a series of Tcl commands. You can load the data by executing it in a Tcl interpreter where the commands are defined. In fact, this same idea has revolutionized the output format for most printers. Today, almost all documents are formatted as a series of commands in the PostScript language. A PostScript printer treats each job as a program and executes it to draw the pages in the document.

Now let's look at the code needed to save a canvas to a drawing file. First, we'll write a procedure called `canvas_save` to take the name of a canvas and return a script full of `draw` commands. This procedure might be useful for many different canvas applications. It is implemented like this:

```
proc canvas_save {win} {
    set script "# contents of $win\n"
    foreach item [$win find all] {
        set tags [$win gettags $item]
        if {[lsearch $tags "canvas_save_ignore"] < 0} {
            set type   [$win type $item]
            set coords [$win coords $item]
            set opts ""
            foreach desc [$win itemconfigure $item] {
                set name [lindex $desc 0]
                set init [lindex $desc 3]
                set val  [lindex $desc 4]
                if {$val != $init} {
                    lappend opts $name $val
                }
            }
            append script "draw $type $coords $opts\n"
        }
    }
    return $script
}
```

We start by initializing the `script` variable to contain a comment line, describing the lines that follow. Notice that this line, and every other line that we add to the script, is terminated by \n, the newline character.

We use the command `$win find all` to query a list of all items on the canvas. We build a description of each item, including its type, its coordinates, and its configuration options, and then append a `draw` command for it onto the script.

We query the information for each item directly from the canvas. The command `$win type $item` returns the item type—rectangle, oval, text, and so on. The command `$win coords $item` returns the coordinates for each item. Unfortunately, there is no simple command that returns the configuration options for each item in the for-

mat that we need, so we loop through the options and build our own. The command
`$win itemconfigure $item` returns a list of all configuration options. Each element in
this list has five values: the option name, two null strings (which we ignore), the initial
value, and the current value. We pick out the initial value and the current value and then
check to see whether they're the same. If they are not, we append the option name and its
current value onto a list of option settings in the `opts` variable. When we're done, this
variable will contain only the options that differ from their default value.

Notice that we skip any items tagged with the name `canvas_save_ignore`. This is
a handy feature. Suppose you have just selected some items in the drawing, so the canvas
contains a selection rectangle, as shown in Figure 4.21(b). This rectangle isn't really part
of the drawing, so we don't want it to be included in the output from `canvas_save`.
Before we call this procedure, we can tag such transient items with the name
`canvas_save_ignore`, and they won't be saved.

Now that we have the `canvas_save` procedure, we can use it to save a drawing in a
file. We'll add a **Save As...** option to the **File** menu, like this:

```
.mbar.file.m add command -label "Save As..." -command draw_save
```

When you select **Save As...**, it calls the following procedure to save the drawing:

```
proc draw_save {} {
    global env
    set file [tk_getSaveFile]
    if {$file != ""} {
        .drawing addtag "canvas_save_ignore" withtag "marker"
        set selected [.drawing find withtag "selected"]
        .drawing dtag "selected"

        set cmd {
            set fid [open $file w]
            puts $fid [canvas_save .drawing]
            close $fid
        }
        if {[catch $cmd err] != 0} {
            notice_show "Cannot save drawing:\n$err" error
        }

        .drawing dtag "canvas_save_ignore"
        foreach item $selected {
            .drawing addtag "selected" withtag $item
        }
    }
}
```

This procedure uses `tk_getSaveFile` to get the name of the output file. This pops
up a file selection dialog, letting you navigate the file system and select a file. If you click
on the **Cancel** button, `tk_getSaveFile` returns a null string, and the `draw_save` proce-

dure does nothing. Otherwise, `tk_getSaveFile` returns the name that you selected for the save file.

To save the drawing, we need to open the file, write out the script from `canvas_save`, and close the file. Any of these operations could fail, so we wrap them all up as a small script and execute that script by using the `catch` command. If we catch any error, we use the `notice_show` procedure developed in Section 6.4 to display the error message in a notice dialog.

Before we call `canvas_save`, we do two important things.

- We add the tag `canvas_save_ignore` to all of the items tagged with the name `marker`. This prevents the selection rectangle and other transient items from being included in the output.

- We remove the tag `selected` from any selected items. We do this by deleting the tag via the command `.drawing dtag "selected"`. If we didn't do this, the `selected` tag would appear in the drawing output. It would be listed in the `-tags` option for selected items, and this would lead to a subtle bug. The next time the drawing was loaded, these items would act as though they were selected—you could use the arrow keys to shift them about—but no selection rectangle would be visible.

After we call `canvas_save`, we put things back the way they were.

- We remove the tag `canvas_save_ignore` from the marker items by deleting the tag.

- We add the tag `selected` to all of the selected items.

4.7.9 Loading a drawing

In the previous section, we saved a drawing as a series of Tcl commands. We can load the drawing simply by executing it as a Tcl program. In our drawing program, for example, we might load a drawing by adding some code like this:

```
proc draw {args} {
    eval .drawing create $args
}
source $file
```

First, we define a `draw` procedure to handle all of the `draw` commands in the drawing file. Then we use the `source` command to execute a particular drawing file, the name of which is stored in the `file` variable. As this file is executed, each of the `draw` commands adds an item to a particular canvas called `.drawing`.

The `draw` procedure uses the special `args` argument, so it will take any number of arguments. It passes these arguments on to the `.drawing create` command, which creates the item on the canvas. For example, suppose the drawing file contains a command like this:

```
draw rectangle 79.0 24.0 256.0 196.0 -fill red
```

When it is executed, this command will pass its arguments to the canvas, like this:

```
.drawing create rectangle 79.0 24.0 256.0 196.0 -fill red
```

The `eval` command in the `draw` procedure is needed to make this work properly. It treats the elements within `$args` as separate words on the command line. Without the `eval` command, `$args` would be treated as a single word, like this:

```
.drawing create {rectangle 79.0 24.0 256.0 196.0 -fill red}
```

The canvas widget would think that we're trying to create an item with a strange type name `"rectangle 79.0 24.0 256.0 196.0 -fill red"`, and it would complain that this is an invalid type. Adding the `eval` command avoids this error.

There is a problem with the way that we have loaded this drawing. Suppose that some nefarious user gives you a drawing file that looks like this:

```
draw rectangle 79.0 24.0 256.0 196.0 -fill red
exec rm -rf .
```

When you source in this file, the first command will create a rectangle on the canvas, and the second will execute a program. All UNIX systems and some Windows systems have a program called `rm` that deletes files. So if you load this drawing, it will delete the current directory!

Note: *Using Tcl as a data language is extremely powerful, but it is also extremely dangerous.*

Fortunately, there is a simple solution for this problem. Whenever you want to execute commands from an untrusted source, you must do so in a protected context called a *safe interpreter*. We'll talk about safe interpreters and show you exactly how to use them when we look at client/server applications in Section 7.6.6.

Chapter 5
Using the Text Widget

Imagine that you're building a word processor that has an area where you can enter paragraphs of text. You can apply character styles to bits of text, underline them, strike them out, change their color, or change their font. You can define tab stops, so you can align words into columns. You can even display pictures within the text.

You can implement all of this with Tk's powerful text widget. Each text widget has its own buffer that will store an arbitrarily large amount of text. If the window is too small to display the entire buffer at once, you can attach vertical and horizontal scrollbars to shift the view.

By default, the text widget supports the kind of editing that you'd find in any commercial word processor—you can click to position the cursor, enter and delete characters, highlight and replace characters, and so on. The text widget even supports many of the editing commands for the popular emacs editor. Of course, you can also add bindings—or completely redefine the bindings—to support your own text editing operations.

Some of the features of the text widget are modeled after the canvas widget we studied in the previous chapter. So if you've mastered the canvas, learning to use the text widget is easy. Just as you can tag items on a canvas, you can tag a range of characters in a text widget. This lets you refer to the characters with a symbolic name so you can find them, delete them, or change their appearance. Just as you can bind to items on a canvas, you can bind to bits of text within the text widget. This lets you create active elements, such as hypertext links, that light up when you touch them or load a new page when you click on them.

In this chapter, we'll examine the text widget and see how it can be used to build text-based displays. We'll start by explaining its features with some simple examples. Then we'll look at a series of case studies to see how its features work together. We'll build

- A simple text editor that lets you compose electronic mail messages
- A read-only text display for viewing online help
- An editor that lets you enter appointments into a daily calendar
- A hierarchy viewer that lets you expand and collapse various levels of the hierarchy

Once you understand the text widget, you'll be able to use it in many ways in your Tcl/Tk applications.

5.1   Understanding the text widget

You can create a text widget as follows:

```
text .t -width 40 -height 7
pack .t
```

The `-width` and `-height` options set the size of the widget in characters and lines. In this case, the text widget will be 40 columns wide and 7 lines high.

Each text widget has its own internal buffer containing the text that it will display. You can add text to the buffer, like this:

```
.t insert end {Emergency Instructions
In case of a nuclear meltdown, engage
the Emergency Core Coolant System (ECCS)
and rotate the Flow Control knob fully
clockwise.}
```

The `insert` operation tells the text widget to insert some text. The `end` argument indicates where the text should be inserted—at the end of the buffer. The last argument is a long string of emergency instructions that is added to the buffer.

You can add more and more text to the buffer by using the `insert` operation, as we did here, or by typing directly into the widget. As long as your computer has memory available, the buffer will expand, and the text widget will store the text. But although the buffer can be arbitrarily large, the widget itself is not. So the widget acts as a viewport into its internal buffer, as shown in Figure 5.1. Later on, we'll see how to use scrollbars to adjust the view.

5.1.1   Indexing model

Each character within the buffer can be addressed according to its position, which is called an *index*. We've already seen one example of an index: The name `end` refers to the end of the buffer. Another way to express an index is using a line number and a character number, with a "." between them. Lines are numbered from 1, but characters are numbered from 0. So the first position within the buffer is the index `1.0`.

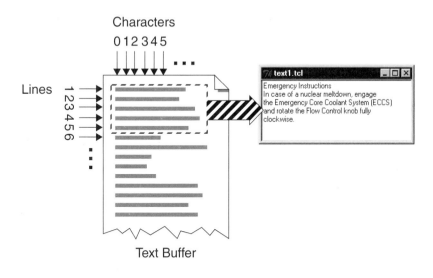

Figure 5.1. The text widget displays the contents of its internal text buffer, which can be arbitrarily large. Text within the buffer is addressed by its line number and character number.

You can use the `get` operation to extract text from the text widget. Just give it a starting index and an ending index, like this:

```
% .t get 2.21 2.29
```
⇒ *meltdown*

In this case, we asked for text on the second line, from the twenty-second character up to the thirtieth character. (Remember, characters are numbered from 0.) The result is the word `meltdown`.

You can use other operations to manipulate the text in the buffer. For example, instead of retrieving the word `meltdown`, you could replace it by deleting that range of characters and inserting some new text:

```
.t delete 2.21 2.29
.t insert 2.21 "accident"
```

Of course, you can also modify the text by clicking on the text widget and typing into it. The two commands we showed are equivalent to highlighting the word `meltdown`, pressing the backspace key, and typing the word `accident`.

At some point, when you're finished making changes, you may want to extract the final text from the widget. You can do this by getting all characters from the start to the end of the buffer, like this:

```
% .t get 1.0 end
```
⇒ *Emergency Instructions*
   In case of a nuclear accident, engage
   the Emergency Core Coolant System (ECCS)
   and rotate the Flow Control knob fully
   clockwise.

If you try this and look closely at the result, you'll see that the text widget adds an extra newline at the end of the text. The text widget always keeps a newline character at the end of the buffer. When you ask for everything, you accidentally get this extra newline.

This is a minor nuisance, but you can avoid it by being a bit more careful with the second index. Instead of asking for everything up to the end of the buffer, ask for everything up to one character before the end, like this:

```
.t get 1.0 "end - 1 char"
```

The quotes keep the string `end - 1 char` together, so it is treated as a single index. When the text widget interprets this index, it finds the `end` position and then moves back one character toward the start of the buffer.

You can add modifiers like this to move an index any number of characters in the + or - direction. You can also move an index any number of lines in the + or - direction. For example, if we wanted to go back five characters and two lines from the end, we could use an index like this:

```
.t get 1.0 "end - 5 chars - 2 lines"
```

The text widget has a few other symbolic names that often come in handy. The name `insert` refers to the position of the insertion cursor. Suppose that the insertion cursor is between the `m` and the `e`, as shown in Figure 5.2(a). If you ask for the character at the insertion cursor, you get the letter `e`:

```
% .t get insert
```
⇒ *e*

This is the letter that gets pushed aside when you type some text into the widget.

It is sometimes useful to find the word that contains the insertion cursor or the entire line that contains the cursor. You can use the `wordstart`/`wordend` and `linestart`/`lineend` modifiers to handle this, as shown in Figure 5.2(a). These modifiers work just like the +/- `char` and +/- `line` modifiers, shifting any index to the start/end of the nearest word or to the start/end of the line.

You can also use the name `sel` to refer to any characters that are currently selected. For example, in Figure 5.2(b), the word `nuclear` is selected. The first index of any selection is called `sel.first`; the last is called `sel.last`. (Don't confuse this notation with the *line.char* numbering scheme, however. In this case, `sel` is the name for a range of selected characters, not a line number.) So you can get the selected characters as shown in Figure 5.2(b). As always, you can combine an index name, such as `sel.first` or `sel.last`, with other modifiers to extract a different range of characters.

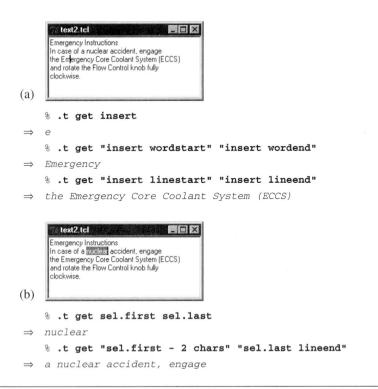

```
      %  .t get insert
  ⇒   e
      %  .t get "insert wordstart" "insert wordend"
  ⇒   Emergency
      %  .t get "insert linestart" "insert lineend"
  ⇒   the Emergency Core Coolant System (ECCS)
```

```
      %  .t get sel.first sel.last
  ⇒   nuclear
      %  .t get "sel.first - 2 chars" "sel.last lineend"
  ⇒   a nuclear accident, engage
```

Figure 5.2. Characters within the text widget can be referenced with symbolic names. (a) The position of the insertion cursor is called `insert`. (b) Selected characters fall in the range `sel.first` to `sel.last`.

When you combine symbolic names, such as `insert` or `end`, with modifiers, such as `- 5 chars`, you have a powerful way of accessing characters. But sometimes you need to map a symbolic name back to a numerical index so you can figure out where a character sits. For example, suppose you want to know how many lines are in the buffer. You can ask for the numerical index of the last character, like this:

```
      %  set index [.t index "end - 1 char"]
  ⇒   5.10
```

The `index` operation converts the symbolic index `end - 1 char` to its corresponding line/character position. In this case, the last character is on line 5, at character position 10. This is the implicit newline at the end of the buffer. Remember, when we ask for everything *up to* this character, we get everything but this newline.

If you want to know how many lines are in the buffer, you can extract the line number from this index. Just split the index at the period, and use `lindex` to extract the first number:

```
% set lines [lindex [split $index .] 0]
⇒ 5
```

In this case, the buffer has five lines of text, as you can see in Figure 5.2.

5.1.2 Scrolling

As we mentioned earlier, the text widget acts as a viewport for its internal buffer. If the widget has more text than it can display, you can use scrollbars to control its view.

You can use the following code to attach scrollbars to the text widget:

```
text .t -width 30 -height 5 -wrap none \
    -xscrollcommand {.xsbar set} \
    -yscrollcommand {.ysbar set}
scrollbar .xsbar -orient horizontal -command {.t xview}
scrollbar .ysbar -orient vertical -command {.t yview}

grid .t .ysbar -sticky nsew
grid .xsbar -sticky nsew
grid columnconfigure . 0 -weight 1
grid rowconfigure . 0 -weight 1
```

This code adds both horizontal and vertical scrollbars, as shown in Figure 5.3.

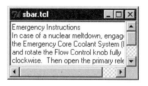

Figure 5.3. You can attach scrollbars to a text widget, to control the view.

Scrollbars work the same way whether you're attaching them to a text widget, a canvas, a listbox, or an entry. In Section 4.1.1, we saw how scrollbars work with the canvas, so we won't repeat the discussion here. But the recipe is this: You set the `-xscrollcommand` and `-yscrollcommand` options on the text widget to control the scrollbars, and you set the `-command` option on each of the scrollbars to control the view on the text widget.

The `grid` commands align the scrollbars with the text widget. We saw in Section 2.2.2 how these commands work, so we won't discuss them here.

Notice that we set the `-wrap` option on the text widget to `none`. With this setting, long lines will be clipped at the edge of the widget, and you can use the horizontal scrollbar to shift the view back and forth. Other wrap modes handle long lines differently, and we'll talk more about them later. But for the horizontal scrollbar to work properly, the `-wrap` option must be set to `none`.

5.1.3   Using tags

The text widget has a powerful way of grouping the characters within it. You can apply a symbolic name called a *tag* to a range of characters. This lets you

- Keep track of the characters as they move about during editing operations
- Associate styles with the characters
- Add bindings to the characters

You may be feeling an eerie sense of *déjà vu*. Tags in the text widget are just like the tags in the canvas widget that we studied in Section 4.1.3. But now we're working with characters instead of canvas items.

Suppose you want to dress up the text for the emergency instructions shown in Figure 5.1. You could tag different bits of text with different names and then change their character styles, as shown in Figure 5.4.

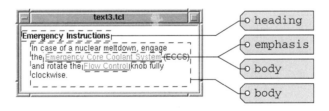

Figure 5.4. Tags are used to associate styles with groups of characters.

We've tagged the first line with the name `heading`, and we'll show you how this is done. But now, we can set the characteristics for `heading`, like this:

```
.t tag configure "heading" -spacing1 0.1i -spacing3 5 \
    -font -*-helvetica-bold-r-normal--*-120-*
```

We've given `heading` a bold Helvetica font. Also, we've set the spacing above this line to 0.1 inch and the spacing below the line to 5 pixels.

In Figure 5.4, we've tagged the rest of the text with the name `body`, which is configured like this:

```
.t tag configure "body" -lmargin1 0.2i
```

The `-lmargin1` option sets the indentation on the left-hand side of each line to 0.2 inch. Other options control the indentation on the right-hand side, the justification, and so on. You can refer to the text widget manual page for more details.

Returning to Figure 5.4, you'll notice that we've tagged a few phrases with the name `emphasis`, which is configured like this:

```
.t tag configure "emphasis" -foreground red \
    -underline yes
```

These characters are underlined and displayed in red, so they stand out from the rest of the text.

Notice that a particular range of characters can have more than one tag name. For example, the range `Emergency Core Coolant System` has two tags: `body` and `emphasis`. This range is displayed using characteristics from both of these tags.

Notice also that the same tag name can be applied to more than one range of characters. For example, the tag `emphasis` is applied to both `Emergency Core Coolant System` and `Flow Control`. Changing the character style for `emphasis` will affect both of these ranges. For example, we could make both of them blue, like this:

```
.t tag configure "emphasis" -foreground blue
```

Or, we could make both of them blink by changing their color from red to white to red to white, and so on, like this:

```
animate_start 500 {red white} {
    .t tag configure "emphasis" -foreground %v
}
```

As you'll recall, in Section 3.7.3, we developed the `animate_start` procedure, which sets up a chain of `after` events so that a command is executed at regular intervals. Each time the command is executed, a different value is substituted into the `%v` field. In this case, we're executing the `tag configure` operation again and again, alternating between the values `red` and `white`.

In order to use tags like this, we have to apply them to the text within the widget. You can use the `tag add` operation to add a tag to a range of characters. For example, we could create the text widget, insert some text, and apply the tags, like this:

```
text .t -width 40 -height 7 -background white \
    -font -*-helvetica-medium-r-normal--*-120-*
pack .t

.t insert end {Emergency Instructions
In case of a nuclear meltdown, engage
the Emergency Core Coolant System (ECCS)
and rotate the Flow Control knob fully
clockwise.}

.t tag add "heading" 1.0 {1.0 lineend}
.t tag add "body" 2.0 end
```

```
.t tag add "emphasis" 3.4 3.33
.t tag add "emphasis" 4.15 4.28
```

We add the tag `heading` to the first line by asking for characters from `1.0` to the end of the line containing `1.0`. We add the tag `body` to all of the characters from the start of line 2 to the end of the buffer. And we add the tag `emphasis` to two different ranges of characters on the third and fourth lines.

Tags accumulate as you apply them. Both `Emergency Core Coolant System` and `Flow Control` fall in the range `2.0` to end, so they both have the tag `body`. But they also have the tag `emphasis`, since we added that tag to them as well.

Tags move with the characters as you edit the buffer. For example, if you insert some text at the start of line 4, the `Flow Control` characters will shift toward the right, and the `emphasis` tag will move with them. If you insert some characters in the middle of `Flow Control`, the `emphasis` tag will stretch to cover the new characters.

Figuring out indices, such as `3.4` and `3.33`, for a particular range of characters can be quite tedious. Fortunately, there's another, much easier, way to add tags to the text. Instead of adding the tags after the fact, you can add them as the text is being inserted into the widget. For example:

```
.t insert end "Emergency Instructions\n" heading
.t insert end "In case of a nuclear meltdown, " body
.t insert end "engage\nthe " body
.t insert end "Emergency Core Coolant System" {body emphasis}
.t insert end " (ECCS)\nand rotate the " body
.t insert end "Flow Control" {body emphasis} " knob fully\n" body
.t insert end "clockwise." body
```

The `insert` operation accepts lots of arguments. The first argument is always the index where the text will be inserted. In this case, we used the `end` index, so each bit of text is appended onto the buffer. The remaining arguments take the form *string tags string tags*, and so on. If you leave off the last *tags* value, the text widget inserts the string without any tags. That is how we've been using the `insert` operation until now.

Normally, the *tags* argument is a tag name, such as `heading` or `body`. But if you want to add several tags to one string, you can wrap up the tags in a list. For example, when we inserted the text `Emergency Core Coolant System`, we included the tag list `{body emphasis}`. The braces here are important. If you leave them off, like this:

```
.t insert end "Emergency Core Coolant System" body emphasis
```

the text widget will think that `Emergency Core Coolant System` is a string tagged with `body` and that `emphasis` is another string but with no tag.

The `insert` operation is quite powerful, but its syntax is a bit cumbersome. If you're inserting a lot of text, you can simplify things by defining a few formatting procedures, like this:

```
proc heading {mesg} {
    .t insert end $mesg "heading"
}
```

```
proc body {mesg} {
    .t insert end $mesg "body"
}
proc emphasis {mesg} {
    .t insert end $mesg "body emphasis"
}
```

Each of these procedures takes a string and appends it into the text widget with the appropriate tags. With these procedures, the emergency instructions can be written like this:

```
heading "Emergency Instructions\n"
body "In case of a nuclear meltdown, engage\nthe "
emphasis "Emergency Core Coolant System"
body " (ECCS)\nand rotate the "
emphasis "Flow Control"
body " knob fully\nclockwise."
```

Now suppose that these commands were saved in a file. Then we could load the emergency instructions by executing that file. In effect, we have invented our own mark-up language, using Tcl as the basic syntax.[*]

5.1.4 Text bindings

Like the canvas, the text widget can be used to create interactive displays. For example, when you touch a word with the mouse pointer, the word might change color. When you click on a word, it might load another page of text. You can accomplish such things by adding bindings for specific events.

There are two ways to add bindings to the text widget.

- You can use the `bind` command to handle events on the text widget as a whole.
- You can use the `bind` operation on the text widget to handle events on a bit of text within the widget.

Let's look at the first method. Suppose you're displaying some emergency instructions, and you want each word to light up as you touch it with the mouse pointer. Figure 5.5 shows how this would look.

First, we'll create a tag called `hilite` that we can add to a word to make it light up. We'll set its foreground to red, like this:

```
.t tag configure "hilite" -foreground red
```

Now we'll track the mouse pointer by binding to the `<Motion>` event on the text widget, like this:

---

[*] For a more complete treatment of this idea, see Don Libes, "Writing CGI Scripts in Tcl," *Fourth Annual Tcl/Tk Workshop '96 Proceedings*, Monterey, CA, July 10–13, 1996.

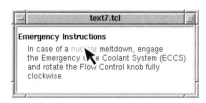

Figure 5.5. Binding to the overall text widget. At each motion event, the word beneath the mouse pointer is highlighted in red.

```
bind .t <Motion> {
    .t tag remove "hilite" 1.0 end
    .t tag add "hilite" "@%x,%y wordstart" "@%x,%y wordend"
}
```

At each motion point, we remove the `hilite` tag from the entire buffer and then add it to the word beneath the mouse pointer. We find the character under the mouse pointer by using the index name @x, y, where x and y are the pixel coordinates of the mouse. In the `bind` command, this is written as @%x, %y. Remember, `bind` automatically substitutes the mouse coordinates into the %x and %y fields of the command string each time it is executed. So if we move the mouse to the coordinate (17,49), we get the index @17, 49. Of course, we're looking for the entire word at that coordinate, so we add the `wordstart`/ `wordend` modifiers to get the range of characters that contains the word.

In this example, the entire widget is active. You can touch any word, and it will light up. But in some cases, you may want only certain parts of the text to be active. For example, suppose you're adding hypertext links to an online help facility. When you click on ordinary text, nothing happens. But when you click on a hypertext link, it loads another page of text, as shown in Figure 5.6. In a case like this, it's much easier to bind to events on the bit of text representing the link.

In the previous section, we defined the procedures `heading`, `body`, and `emphasis` to insert text into the widget. Now let's define a procedure called `link` that inserts a hypertext link. The procedure looks like this:

```
set linkNum 0
proc link {mesg linkCode} {
    global linkNum
    set tag "link[incr linkNum]"
    .t insert end $mesg [list body $tag]
    .t tag configure $tag -foreground red -underline 1
    .t tag bind $tag <Enter> \
        ".t tag configure $tag -foreground blue"
    .t tag bind $tag <Leave> \
        ".t tag configure $tag -foreground red"
```

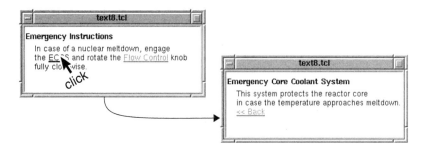

Figure 5.6. Binding to characters within the widget. When you touch a hypertext link, it changes color. When you click on it, another page of text appears.

```
.t tag bind $tag <ButtonPress> \
    ".t delete 1.0 end; $linkCode"
}
```

This procedure takes two arguments: the text representing the link and some code to exe-cute when you click on the link. We tag each link with a unique name, so we can bind dif-ferent actions to different links. We use the global variable linkNum to generate a unique number for each link. The first link will be tagged link1; the second, link2; and so on.

As we insert the text for the link into the buffer, we tag it with body and with its unique name. That way, the link will have the same characteristics as the rest of the para-graph, as well as some special characteristics that we add just for it. To make the link stand out, for example, we underline it and display it in red.

Then we set up three bindings on this bit of text. When you move the mouse pointer onto the link, it gets an <Enter> event, and the link turns blue. When you move the mouse pointer off the link, it gets a <Leave> event, and the link turns back to red. When you click on the link, it gets a <ButtonPress> event, and we traverse the link. We clear out all of the text in the buffer and then execute the code for the link to load a new page.

Each page of help text could be wrapped up as a procedure. That way, we can execute the procedure to load the page. For example, the page of emergency instructions could be written like this:

```
proc show_main {} {
    heading "Emergency Instructions\n"
    body "In case of a nuclear meltdown, engage\nthe "
    link "ECCS" show_eccs
    body " and rotate the "
    link "Flow Control" show_flow
    body " knob\nfully clockwise."
}
```

This includes two `link` commands: one for the link ECCS, which calls the procedure show_eccs, and another for the link Flow Control, which calls the procedure show_flow. The show_eccs procedure could be written like this:

```
proc show_eccs {} {
    heading "Emergency Core Coolant System\n"
    body "This system protects the reactor core\n"
    body "in case the temperature approaches meltdown.\n"
    link "<< Back" show_main
}
```

This procedure contains a link called Back, which restores the first page of instructions.

Since you can bind to both the text widget and the text within it, you may wonder what happens when you bind to the same event at both levels. The answer is that both bindings are triggered. When you click on a hypertext link, for example, it triggers the <ButtonPress> binding for the link text, which clears the buffer and loads another page. But it also triggers the normal <ButtonPress> binding for a text widget, which sets the position of the insertion cursor.

More than two bindings might be triggered. One event can trigger several bindings at both the text level and the widget level. For example, suppose that a word has three tags and that each tag has a binding for <ButtonPress>. Then a single <ButtonPress> event on that word would trigger all three bindings. A similar thing happens at the widget level. Suppose that the widget has two bindings for <ButtonPress>—one directly on the widget and another for the widget class Text. Again, the same <ButtonPress> event would also trigger these two bindings.

The text level and the widget level are treated as two different responses to the event. You can break out of either response by using a `break` command, as discussed in Section 3.5.2. For example, when you click on the hypertext link, we don't really want to position the insertion cursor. We can avoid this by breaking out of the event processing that occurs at the widget level:

```
bind .t <ButtonPress> break
```

Now when the widget receives a <ButtonPress> event, it will handle the binding at the text level, which loads a new page. Then it will handle the bindings at the widget level. The first binding stops any further processing, so the insertion cursor is left alone.

5.1.5 Using marks

The text widget has another feature that comes in handy from time to time. You can set a *mark*, which is an invisible position between two characters. As you edit the text, the mark will shift along with the characters, so you can follow a bit of text as it moves around within the buffer.

For example, suppose we've loaded the emergency instructions into a text widget, as shown in Figure 5.1. We could mark the start of these instructions with a symbolic name, like this:

```
.t mark set "emergency" 1.0
```
Next, we could insert some more text, like this:
```
.t insert 1.0 "Introduction\n" heading "blah\nblah\nblah\n" body
```
The instructions would shift down, and the mark would move with them.

Once we've defined a mark, we can use it as an index in any of the text operations. For example, we could get the heading for the emergency instructions, like this:
```
set heading [.t get emergency "emergency lineend"]
```
And we could insert more text just before the emergency instructions, like this:
```
.t insert emergency "More Stuff\n" heading "blah\nblah\n" body
```
Marks are not nearly as powerful as tags, but they do come in handy from time to time. We'll see an example that uses them in Section 5.5.

One mark, however, is extremely useful. Each text widget has a built-in mark called `insert`, which acts as the insertion cursor. Normally, you position the cursor by clicking on the text widget. But you can also position the cursor programmatically, by setting its mark, like this:
```
.t mark set insert 1.0
```
This moves the insertion cursor to the start of the buffer.

Like any other mark, you can query its position by using `insert` as an index. We saw several examples of this in Figure 5.2.

5.1.6   Wrap modes

Each line of text within a text widget can be arbitrarily long, but the widget itself has a finite size. So how does the text widget display a very long line? There are three different answers to this question, shown in Figure 5.7. The various display modes are controlled by the `-wrap` option, which can be set for the widget as a whole or for each tag individually.

If the `-wrap` option is set to `none`, each line is clipped at the edge of the widget. Each line of text corresponds to one physical line on the screen. You can enlarge the window to see more of the text. Or, as we saw in Section 5.1.2, you can attach a horizontal scrollbar to shift the view back and forth.

If the `-wrap` option is set to `char`, a single line of text may occupy several physical lines on the screen. The text widget draws as many characters as possible on one line. If need be, the widget drops down to the next line and draws more characters, then drops down to the next line, and so on. If you resize the window, the text widget automatically redraws all of its lines to take advantage of the new width.

If the `-wrap` option is set to `word`, again, a single line of text may occupy several physical lines on the screen. But in this case, the text widget breaks long lines at even word boundaries, so you get the behavior that you might expect from a word processor or a Web browser. In this mode, each line of text acts like a paragraph. Again, if you resize the window, the text widget automatically redraws all of its lines to take advantage of the new width.

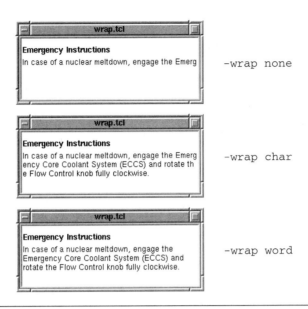

Figure 5.7. The -wrap option controls how a single line of text is displayed.

When you're dealing with indices, such as 1.0 or 4.12, line numbers, such as 1 and 4, refer to lines in the buffer, not the physical lines on the screen. Thus the indices are independent of the wrap mode. For example, suppose we query a character from the text in Figure 5.7, like this:

```
.t get 2.72
```

We'll always get the (character, regardless of the wrap mode.

5.1.7 Tab stops

The text widget handles tab stops in much the same way as any commercial word processor. You can set its -tabs option to a list of tab stops, like this:

```
text .t -tabs {1.5i 2i 2.5i}
```

In this case, there are three tab stops: one at 1.5 inches, another at 2 inches, and another at 2.5 inches. If you insert some words separated by the tab character (\t), each word will be aligned at a tab stop:

```
.t insert end "\tcolumn1\tcolumn2\tcolumn3"
```

You can also set the -tabs option for each tag, so you can control the tab stops separately on each line. For example, you could create a heading style and apply it to one line of text, like this:

```
.t tag configure "heading" -tabs {1.5i 2.5i}
.t insert end "\theading1\theading2" heading
```

The tab stops for this tag override the default tab stops that we assigned to the widget.

By default, text is aligned with its left-hand side at the tab stop. But text can also be aligned on its right-hand side or on its center point. You can control this by adding the keyword left, right, or center after each tab stop in the list. For example, suppose we set the tabs like this:

```
.t configure -tabs {1.5i right 2i center 2.5i left}
```

The first tab stop will be right-aligned, the second will be center-aligned, and the third will be left-aligned.

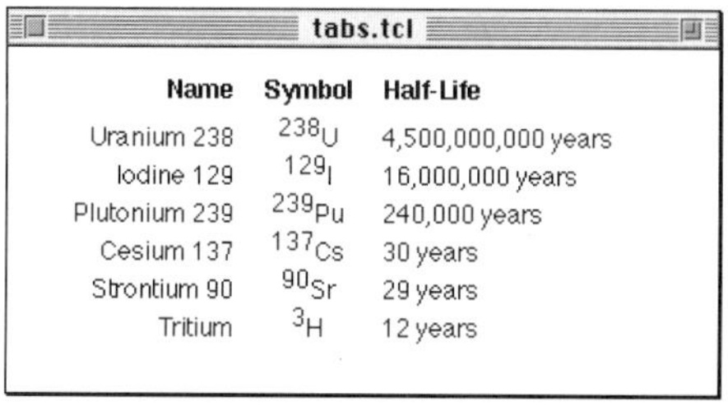

Figure 5.8. Tab stops are used to align words, producing a table format.

We can use all of this to construct the table shown in Figure 5.8. The table has three columns, showing the half-life for several radioactive elements. The code used to generate the table is as follows:

```
text .t -width 50 -height 10 -background white \
    -font -*-helvetica-medium-r-normal--*-120-* \
    -tabs {1.5i right 2i center 2.5i left}
pack .t

.t tag configure "heading" -spacing1 10 -spacing3 5 \
    -font -*-helvetica-bold-r-normal--*-120-*
.t tag configure "superscript" -offset 5 \
    -font -*-helvetica-medium-r-normal--*-80-*

.t insert end "\tName\tSymbol\tHalf-Life\n" heading

foreach {name num symbol hlife} {
    "Uranium 238" 238 U "4,500,000,000 years"
    "Iodine 129" 129 I "16,000,000 years"
    "Plutonium 239" 239 Pu "240,000 years"
```

```
                "Cesium 137" 137 Cs "30 years"
                "Strontium 90" 90 Sr "29 years"
                "Tritium" 3 H "12 years"
        } {
            .t insert end "\t$name"
            .t insert end "\t$num" superscript "$symbol"
            .t insert end "\t$hlife\n"
        }
```

In this case, we've set the tab stops for the entire widget. We've used tags only to control the fonts for the heading and superscript characters.

First, we insert the heading line. Then we use `foreach` to iterate through a list of half-life information, and we insert each entry into the table. Each entry starts with a tab (`\t`), and each line ends with a newline (`\n`).

5.2 Simple text editor

The default bindings on a text widget support interactive editing, so each text widget acts like a ready-made text editor. If your application needs an editor, it's easy to add one.

For example, the application shown in Figure 5.9 lets you compose electronic mail (e-mail) messages. The application has three entry widgets for address information and a text widget for editing the body of the message.

Figure 5.9. The text widget acts as an editor for an application that sends electronic mail.

We saw how these widgets were assembled in Section 2.2.4, but let's take another look at the text widget and its scrollbar. They're created like this:

```
frame .message
scrollbar .message.sbar -command {.message.text yview}
text .message.text -yscrollcommand {.message.sbar set}

pack .message.sbar -side right -fill y
pack .message.text -side left -expand yes -fill both
pack .message -expand yes -fill both -padx 4 -pady 4
```

Once they're packed into position, this simple editor is ready to use. You can click to position the cursor and enter some text for the message. If you highlight some text and press the backspace key, the text will be deleted. If you highlight some text and type something else, it will be replaced. You can even use the arrow keys to move the cursor.

When you've finished editing the message, you click on the Send Message button. Doing that invokes a procedure to gather the various entries and send the e-mail message. The procedure extracts the message body from the text widget, like this:

```
set text [.message.text get 1.0 end]
```

Then the procedure sends the message, using a procedure called email_send, like this:

```
email_send $to $from $cc $subject $text
```

We'll see how the email_send procedure is implemented in Section 7.3, as we learn about using pipes to communicate with other processes.

We can improve our simple text editor a bit by adding a pop-up menu, as shown in Figure 5.10. You can click with the third mouse button to bring up a menu with common editing operations. If you've highlighted some text, you can select Cut to remove it or Copy to capture it. After that, you can select Paste to insert the text at the cursor.

The menu is created like this:

```
menu .message.text.edit -tearoff 0
.message.text.edit add command -label "Cut" \
    -command {tk_textCut .message.text}
.message.text.edit add command -label "Copy" \
    -command {tk_textCopy .message.text}
.message.text.edit add command -label "Paste" \
    -command {tk_textPaste .message.text}
```

For the menu to work properly, it must be a child of the text widget. So its name is a combination of the text widget's path, .message.text, and the unique name edit.

Handling operations to cut, copy, and paste is easy. Tk comes with the library procedures tk_textCut, tk_textCopy, and tk_textPaste that perform these functions. We pass in the name of our text widget, and Tk handles the rest.

We want the menu to appear whenever you click the third mouse button on the text widget. This won't happen automatically, but we can add this behavior with the following code:

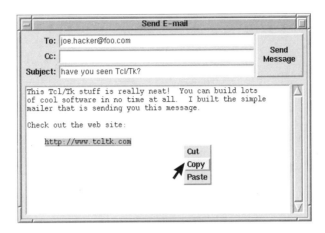

Figure 5.10. A pop-up menu can be added to the text widget to support editing operations.

```
bind .message.text <ButtonPress-3> {
    tk_popup .message.text.edit %X %Y
}
```

When the text widget receives a <ButtonPress-3> event, it will trigger a call to the Tk library procedure tk_popup, which posts the menu. We pass in the name of the menu and the location on the desktop where it should appear. The tk_popup procedure interprets the location as an absolute coordinate on the desktop, where (0,0) is the upper-left corner of the screen. In this case, we've used %X and %Y to get the location of the mouse pointer. Remember, the bind facility will replace these fields with the coordinate of the pointer at the time of the event. It is important to use the uppercase letters %X and %Y instead of the lowercase letters %x and %y, so we get an absolute coordinate on the desktop.

Once the menu is posted, the rest is handled automatically. If you select one of the menu entries, its function is invoked and the menu disappears.

5.3 Read-only text display

As we saw in the previous section, the text widget lets you edit its contents. But in some cases, you may want to disable this feature. Suppose you're using the text widget to display online help, as shown in Figure 5.11. You shouldn't be able to edit the help text interactively—it would be too easy to press the backspace key and erase important information!

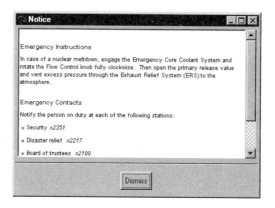

Figure 5.11. A read-only text display used for online help.

You can lock out changes to the text within a text widget by setting the `-state` option to `disabled`. For example, you can insert some text and lock out any further changes, like this:

```
text .t
pack .t
.t insert end "Read-only text"
.t configure -state disabled
```

If you click on the widget in this mode, you won't get an insertion cursor, but the widget isn't completely inactive. You can still use scrollbars to adjust the view, and you can click and drag to select a range of characters. But if you try to type into the widget, nothing will change.

Disabling the widget locks out *all* changes to the text—those that you make interactively and those that you make programmatically. For example, suppose that you try to change the text for the previous example:

```
.t delete 1.0 end
.t insert end "Some different read-only text"
```

These statements will have no effect. As long as the `-state` option is set to `disabled`, the text within the text widget won't change for any reason.

If you want to change the text, you must unlock the widget, make changes, and lock it up again, like this:

```
.t configure -state normal
.t delete 1.0 end
.t insert end "Some different read-only text"
.t configure -state disabled
```

We can use these ideas to create an online help dialog like the one shown in Figure 5.11. As always, we'll make some library procedures to create and control the dialog. We'll start with the procedure `textdisplay_create`, which creates a text dialog. The procedure is implemented like this:

```
proc textdisplay_create {{title "Text Display"}} {
    set top [dialog_create Textdisplay]
    wm title $top $title
    set info [dialog_info $top]
    scrollbar $info.sbar -command "$info.text yview"
    pack $info.sbar -side right -fill y
    text $info.text -wrap word -yscrollcommand "$info.sbar set"
    pack $info.text -side left -expand yes -fill both

    set cntls [dialog_controls $top]
    button $cntls.dismiss -text "Dismiss" -command "destroy $top"
    pack $cntls.dismiss -pady 4
    focus $cntls.dismiss

    $info.text configure -state disabled
    $info.text tag configure normal -spacing1 6p \
        -font -*-helvetica-medium-r-normal--*-120-*
    $info.text tag configure heading -spacing1 0.2i \
        -font -*-helvetica-bold-r-normal--*-120-*
    $info.text tag configure bold \
        -font -*-helvetica-bold-r-normal--*-120-*
    $info.text tag configure italic \
        -font -*-helvetica-medium-o-normal--*-120-*
    $info.text tag configure typewriter -wrap none \
        -font -*-courier-medium-r-normal--*-120-*
    return $top
}
```

We start by calling the `dialog_create` procedure, which creates a dialog and returns its automatically generated name. We'll see how this procedure is implemented in Section 6.4, when we look at dialogs in greater detail. But it works like this. The procedure creates a new toplevel widget with an automatically generated name. Inside the toplevel, the procedure creates an empty frame on top for information, a separator line, and an empty frame on the bottom for controls. We get the name of the top frame by calling `dialog_info`, and we pack a text widget and its scrollbar into this frame. We get the name of the bottom frame by calling `dialog_controls`, and we pack a Dismiss button into it. We set up the Dismiss button to destroy the toplevel widget, which will make the dialog disappear.

Before we return, we define a series of tags that we can use as character styles for the help text. Normal text should be tagged with the name `normal`, and it will be displayed in a medium Helvetica font. Headings should be tagged with the name heading, and they will be displayed in a bold Helvetica font. Other bits of text can be tagged as bold or italic to emphasize them or as typewriter to give them a constant-width font.

When we created the text widget, we set its -wrap option to word. In this mode, you should think of each newline character as a paragraph marker. The text widget will automatically wrap a very long line onto several lines in the widget. So each line acts like a paragraph; you should add a newline only to denote the end of that paragraph. With this in mind, we set the -spacing1 option to control the spacing above each paragraph. Any paragraph tagged as heading will have a 0.2-inch space above it, whereas any paragraph tagged as normal will have only 6/72-inch space above it.

For some lines, it may be better to have -wrap set to none, so the lines don't wrap. For example, suppose you want to show some program code in the text display. Newlines are important in program code. If the lines wrap, the code will be difficult to read. You can override the default wrap mode for the widget by creating a tag with its own wrap mode. For example, we defined the typewriter tag with -wrap set to none. If you apply this tag to each line of program code, it'll be displayed in a constant-width font, and the line won't wrap.

In the midst of creating this text display, we set the -state option on the text widget to disabled, making this a read-only display. Notice that we did this *before* configuring all of the tags. Disabling a widget locks out changes on its text buffer but doesn't prevent other changes. You can add tags and change their characteristics, but you can't add any text until the widget is back in the normal state.

Once you've created a text display, you can use this procedure to add some text to it:

```
proc textdisplay_append {top mesg {tag "normal"}} {
    set info [dialog_info $top]
    $info.text configure -state normal
    $info.text insert end $mesg $tag
    $info.text configure -state disabled
}
```

When you call this procedure, you pass in the name of the text display, which is returned from textdisplay_create. Also, you pass in a bit of text and a tag such as heading or normal. If the tag isn't specified, it defaults to normal.

In this procedure, we call dialog_info to get the frame that contains the text widget. Once we have this, we can use $info.text to refer to the text widget. We configure the widget to state normal, insert the new text, and configure it back to disabled so it remains in the read-only state.

You can use the following procedure to clear the text:

```
proc textdisplay_clear {top} {
    set info [dialog_info $top]
    $info.text configure -state normal
    $info.text delete 1.0 end
    $info.text configure -state disabled
}
```

The procedure works just like `textdisplay_append`. You pass in the name of the text display, and it unlocks the widget, clears the text, and locks it up again.

Here's another handy procedure. It loads a text display with the contents of a file:

```
proc textdisplay_file {top fname} {
    set info [dialog_info $top]
    set fid [open $fname r]
    set contents [read $fid]
    close $fid
    $info.text configure -state normal
    $info.text delete 1.0 end
    $info.text insert end $contents "typewriter"
    $info.text configure -state disabled
}
```

We use the `open`, `read`, and `close` commands to load the file into a variable called `contents`. Remember, there is no limit to what a variable can hold, so this code works whether the file is 10 bytes long or 10,000,000 bytes long. After the file has been loaded, this procedure works just like `textdisplay_append`. It unlocks the widget, adds the text with the `typewriter` tag, and locks the widget up again.

Now that we've defined these procedures, we might use them as follows:

```
set win [textdisplay_create "Notice"]
textdisplay_append $win "Emergency Instructions\n" heading
textdisplay_append $win "In case of a nuclear meltdown, ...\n"
textdisplay_append $win "Emergency Contacts\n" heading
textdisplay_append $win "Notify the person on duty at each ...\n"
textdisplay_append $win " \273 Security"
textdisplay_append $win " x2351\n" italic
textdisplay_append $win " \273 Disaster relief "
textdisplay_append $win " x2217\n" italic
textdisplay_append $win " \273 Board of trustees "
textdisplay_append $win " x2100\n" italic
```

This code creates the dialog shown in Figure 5.11. We've removed some of the text in the two long paragraphs, to shorten the example a bit. Each paragraph ends with a newline (\n) character. The two headings are tagged `heading`, the three phone numbers are tagged `italic`, and the rest of the text is tagged `normal`. The three phone numbers are formatted as a bullet list, with the octal character code \273 acting as a bullet symbol.

5.4 Appointment editor

We've already seen how the text widget can act as an editor or as a read-only display. But suppose you need a little of both. Suppose you're building a form with entries that can be edited and with labels that are read-only. For example, the text widget shown in Figure

5.12 acts as an appointment editor for a calendar program, displaying a list of time slots for any given day. Each time slot has an alarm bell and one or more comment lines. You can edit the comments (shown on the gray and white lines), but the rest of the text is read-only.

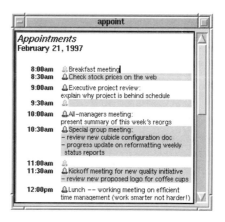

Figure 5.12. The text widget is used to build the appointment editor for an office calendar.

You might be tempted to build something like this with a bunch of separate widgets. You might use label widgets for the time strings and entry widgets for the comment lines. But if you use one text widget for the entire form, the result is much better. The text widget makes this appointment editor look like a page from a real calendar, keeping all of the text together as a single flow. If you're editing a comment and you press Return, the comment continues on another line, and the remaining appointments shift down to make room for it. If you press the backspace key to erase the line, it disappears, and the remaining appointments shift back up.

This example is a bit involved, so we'll attack it one piece at a time. First, we'll load the appointment text into the widget and add tags to control its appearance. Then we'll add special bindings that limit any editing to the comment fields. Finally, we'll see how images, such as the alarm bell, can be added to the text. When all of this is in place, we'll have a customized editor that shows off many different features of the text widget.

5.4.1 Using tags to apply styles

When you set out to build a text display, you should think about the various character styles that it will contain and invent a tag for each style. For example, we'll tag the text in our appointment editor as shown in Figure 5.13. The `title` tag controls the font for the

`Appointments` line at the top of the display. The `date` tag controls the date displayed just below that. The `hour` tag controls the font for all of the time strings, and the `comment` tag identifies the various comment lines.

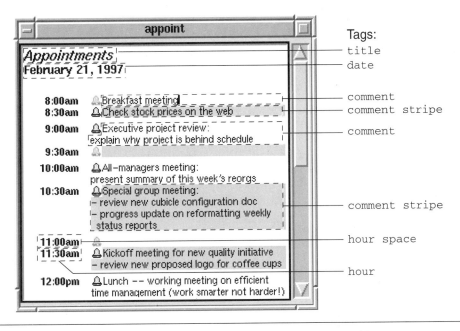

Figure 5.13. Tags are used to apply styles to the characters within the text widget.

We can add a few extra tags to handle minor variations on each style. For example, every other comment in Figure 5.12 has a gray background. Instead of alternating between two different comment styles, we can handle this variation by combining two tags. We define a single `comment` tag, and we add a `stripe` tag to every other line. The `stripe` tag overrides the background color, making it gray.

We can use the same trick to add some blank space above hour slots, such as `8:00am`, `9:00am`, `10:00am`, and so on. We define a tag called `space` that overrides the line spacing, and we add this tag to the time strings that represent whole hours.

Now let's make some library procedures to handle the appointment editor. The following procedure creates an appointment editor and initializes all of its styles. You simply pass in a widget name for the whole assembly:

```
proc appointment_create {win} {
    frame $win -class Appointment
    scrollbar $win.sbar -command "$win.text yview"
```

```
pack $win.sbar -side right -fill y
text $win.text -background white -wrap word \
    -cursor left_ptr -tabs {2c right 2.4c left} \
    -yscrollcommand "$win.sbar set"
pack $win.text -side left -expand yes -fill both

$win.text tag configure title \
    -font [option get $win titleFont Font]
$win.text tag configure date \
    -font [option get $win dateFont Font]
$win.text tag configure hour \
    -font [option get $win hourFont Font]
$win.text tag configure comment \
    -lmargin1 2.4c -lmargin2 2.4c \
    -font [option get $win commentFont Font]
$win.text tag configure stripe \
    -background [option get $win stripeBackground Background] \
    -foreground [option get $win stripeForeground Foreground]
$win.text tag configure space -spacing1 5
```

...set up special bindings to edit comments...

```
return $win
}
```

We start by creating a frame called the *hull* for the whole assembly. Then we create the
text widget and its scrollbar, and we pack them into the hull.

We set the class name for the hull to Appointment, so that you can add settings to
the resource database to customize all of the appointment editors in your application. For
example, we include the following resources with the appointment editor code:

```
option add *Appointment.stripeBackground LightGray widgetDefault
option add *Appointment.stripeForeground black widgetDefault
option add *Appointment.titleFont \
    -*-helvetica-bold-o-normal--*-140-* widgetDefault
option add *Appointment.dateFont \
    -*-helvetica-bold-r-normal--*-120-* widgetDefault
option add *Appointment.hourFont \
    -*-helvetica-bold-r-normal--*-100-* widgetDefault
option add *Appointment.commentFont \
    -*-helvetica-medium-r-normal--*-100-* widgetDefault
```

As always, we're careful to give these settings the lowest priority, widgetDefault, so
they're easy to override.

None of these resources are normal Tk options, so they don't automatically affect the
Tk widgets. But we can use the option get command to query these settings for each

appointment editor. For example, we can use the following command to query the title font:

```
option get $win titleFont Font
```

This command looks for a specific `titleFont` setting or a generic `Font` setting on the hull frame `$win`. It will return the `titleFont` setting as shown previously, unless that value has been overridden.

We use the values obtained from `option get` to configure the tags in the text widget. The `titleFont` resource sets the font for the `title` tag; the `dateFont` resource, for the `date` tag; and so on. Instead of hard-coding the gray color for striped comments, we use the `stripeBackground` resource to control it. We also use the `stripeForeground` resource, so you can change the foreground color for the striped comments as well.

We add resources for colors and fonts, things that are most likely to be customized in an application. For other options, we simply hard-code a value. In the `space` tag, for example, we use `-spacing1 5` to set the line spacing; this adds a 5-pixel spacing above any line that starts with this tag. This should be good enough for all applications.

Handling the comments properly is a little tricky. Each comment starts on one line, but you can continue the comment onto new lines. There are two ways of doing this.

- You can continue typing past the right-hand margin, and the comment will automatically wrap onto a new line. We set the `-wrap` option on the text widget to `word`, so the lines will wrap on even word boundaries. The left-hand margin for each of the wrapped lines is controlled by the `-lmargin2` option. We configured the `comment` tag with `-lmargin2 2.4c`, so these lines will start at 2.4 cm, which is the position of the bell.

- You can press Return to force a comment onto a new line. In this case, a newline character (`\n`) is added to the comment to force the line break, so the next comment line will be an entirely new line in the text buffer. The left-hand margin for the start of a line is controlled by the `-lmargin1` option. We configured the `comment` tag with `-lmargin1 2.4c`, so the new line will start at 2.4 cm. This takes effect only when the `comment` tag is applied to the first character on a line. So it affects any new comment lines, but it doesn't affect the line containing the alarm bell. Now if you type past the right-hand margin, this line will also wrap onto multiple lines, and each of these lines will be controlled by the `-lmargin2` option, as we already described.

Near the end of the `appointment_create` procedure, we set up the bindings that allow you to edit the comments. We've left out that code for now. We'll take a closer look at it later, in Section 5.4.3.

As always, we finish by returning the widget name from the procedure `appointment_create`. This mimics the Tk behavior for a widget-creation command.

Once you've created an appointment editor, you can load it with a particular set of appointments. We'll store the appointments for any given day in an array, as shown in Figure 5.14. Each time slot contains a list with two values: the alarm status (on or off) and a message string for the comment field.

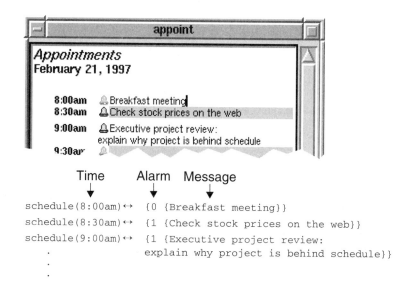

Figure 5.14. The appointments for a particular day are stored in an array. Each time slot contains a list with an alarm status and a message.

You can use the following procedure to load appointment data into an appointment editor. You pass in the name of the editor, the date, and the name of the array that contains the appointments.

```
proc appointment_load {win date scheduleVar} {
    upvar $scheduleVar schedule

    $win.text delete 1.0 end
    $win.text insert end "Appointments\n" title

    set time [clock scan $date]
    set day [clock format $time -format "%B %d, %Y"]
    $win.text insert end "$day\n\n" date

    set timeSlots [array names schedule]
    set timeSlots [lsort -command appointment_cmp $timeSlots]
    foreach slot $timeSlots {
        appointment_load_slot $win $slot $schedule($slot) $timeSlots
    }

    set range [$win.text tag nextrange comment 1.0]
```

```
if {$range != ""} {
    set index [lindex $range 0]
    $win.text mark set insert $index
}
focus $win.text
}
```

The arguments for a Tcl procedure are normally passed by value—each of the arguments contains a copy of the string that was passed in. In this case, we want to pass the array variable by reference so we can access its elements within the procedure. We handle that by passing in the *name* of the array and by using the upvar command to gain access to it. The upvar command says that there's a variable called $scheduleVar in the calling context but that in this procedure, we'll refer to it as schedule.

For example, we could set up an array and pass it into the appointment_load procedure, like this:

```
set appoint(8:00am) {0 {Breakfast meeting}}
set appoint(8:30am) {1 {Check stock prices on the web}}
set appoint(9:00am) {1 {Executive project review:
explain why project is behind schedule}}


appointment_create .page
appointment_load .page 02/21/1997 appoint
```

In this case, the schedule array within appointment_load refers to the appoint array shown here. We can reference an element like schedule(8:00am), and we'll get the corresponding element appoint(8:00am). We can change the schedule array by adding, deleting, or modifying its elements, and the same change will be applied to the appoint array.

Now, getting back to the appointment_load procedure, we start by using the delete operation to clear the text widget. Then we insert the Appointments line tagged with the name title. We insert the date below that, tagged with the name date. We want to make sure that the date string is properly formatted with the month, the day, and the year. So we use clock scan to convert the date string to an integer time value, and we use clock format to convert the time value back to a human-readable string. With these conversions, you can pass in a date as 02/21/1997, and the date line will read February 21, 1997.

Next, we use the array names command to get the list of time slots in the schedule array. Unfortunately, these slots are returned in a random order, so we use the lsort command to sort them. By default, lsort returns the items in alphabetical order, and it also has options to handle integers and real numbers. If you want to sort by any other criterion, you must supply your own comparison procedure through the -command option. In this case, we're using the appointment_cmp procedure to handle sorting based on time. We won't show that procedure here. You can find it in the file efftcl/lib/scripts/appoint.tcl, which can be obtained from the Web site men-

tioned on page xiv. It takes two times, such as 9:30am and 1:00pm, and returns -1 if the
first is less than the second, +1 if the first is greater than the second, and 0 if they are
equal. The lsort command calls this procedure again and again as it sorts the elements in
the list.

Once the time slots are in the proper order, we iterate through the list and add each
appointment to the display. We use a procedure called appointment_load_slot to handle this, making our code a bit easier to read. We'll see how this is implemented later.

Before we return, we move the insertion cursor to the start of the first comment. We
use the tag nextrange operation on the text widget to find the proper position. This
operation searches for the first occurrence of the comment tag after the position 1.0. If it
finds that tag, the operation returns a list with the starting index and the ending index. We
pick out the starting index and put the insertion cursor there. Finally, we assign focus to
the text widget, so you can begin entering comments immediately.

Now let's look at the appointment_load_slot procedure, which adds each of the
appointments to the text widget. The procedure is implemented like this:

```
proc appointment_load_slot {win slot appmt allSlots} {
    if {[string match "*:00*" $slot]} {
        set htags "hour space"
    } else {
        set htags "hour"
    }
    $win.text insert end "\t$slot\t" $htags

    appointment_load_bell $win $slot $appmt

    set pos [lsearch $allSlots $slot]
    if {$pos % 2 != 0} {
        set ctags "comment stripe"
    } else {
        set ctags "comment"
    }

    set mesg [lindex $appmt 1]
    $win.text insert end "$mesg\n" $ctags
}
```

First, we add the time string with the appropriate tags. We use the string match
command to find times containing :00, which represents the start of an hour. These slots
are tagged with both hour and space; the other time slots are simply tagged with hour.

Next, we call appointment_load_bell to add the alarm bell. We'll see how this is
implemented in the next section.

Finally, we add the comment string with its appropriate tags. We want to add the
stripe tag to every other comment. So we use the lsearch command to find the position of this slot in the list of all time slots. We use the *modulus operator* (%) to determine

whether the position is even or odd. The operator divides the position by 2 and returns the remainder. If the remainder is nonzero, the position is odd, and we add the `stripe` tag.

Notice that we added tab characters (`\t`) to align the time slots and the comments into columns. When we created the text widget in the `appointment_create` procedure, we set its default tab stops to {`2c right 2.4c left`}. Thus the time strings will be aligned on their right sides at 2.0 cm, and the comments will be aligned on their left sides at 2.4 cm. Notice also that we ended each appointment with a newline character (`\n`), so the next appointment will start on a new line.

5.4.2 Embedded windows

You can add any Tk widget to the flow of text within the text widget. If you insert some characters in front of it, the widget will shift down; if you delete the characters, the widget will shift back. This powerful feature lets you build sophisticated displays. If you were using the text widget to display a Web page, for example, you could use this feature to add form controls, such as checkbuttons, radiobuttons, and entries.

In this section, we'll do something much simpler. We'll add a label to the appointment editor to display the image of an alarm bell. This is the only way of adding an image into the flow of text, so it is important to learn this technique.

First, we'll load the two images for the alarm bell and will store them in a global array called `appInfo`:

```
set appInfo(alarm-on) [image create photo \
    -file [file join $env(EFFTCL_LIBRARY) images bell.gif]]
set appInfo(alarm-off) [image create photo \
    -file [file join $env(EFFTCL_LIBRARY) images bell2.gif]]
```

These images will be installed in a directory, such as `/usr/local/efftcl`, along with the library script for our appointment editor. Instead of hard-coding the directory name, we use an environment variable, `EFFTCL_LIBRARY`, to point to the proper directory. We can write an installation program that sets up this variable when a program is installed, as we'll see in Chapter 8.

Now each time we need to add an alarm bell to the text, we call the following procedure. We pass in the name of the appointment editor, the time slot, and the data for that time slot.

```
proc appointment_load_bell {win slot appmt} {
    global appInfo

    set name "$win.text.bell$slot"
    label $name -borderwidth 0
    bind $name <ButtonPress-1> \
        "appointment_toggle $win $name $slot"

    set alarm [lindex $appmt 0]
```

```
if {$alarm} {
    set appInfo($win-$slot) 1
    $name configure -image $appInfo(alarm-on)
} else {
    set appInfo($win-$slot) 0
    $name configure -image $appInfo(alarm-off)
}
$win.text window create end -window $name
}
```

When you embed a widget into the text widget, you must choose its name carefully.

- The embedded widget must be a child of the text widget. So in this case, the name must start with $win.text.

- The embedded widget must have a unique name. In this case, each time slot has a unique name, so we can use the name bell$slot for each widget. If the time slot is 10:30am, we'll get a widget named bell10:30am. This may seem a bit odd, but it is perfectly legal. If any of the time slots contained the . character, however, this trick would fail. Tk treats any . character as a separator between names in the widget hierarchy.

We use the label command to create a label, and we use the window create operation to insert the window at the end of the text buffer. In between, we decide which image to display. We look in the appointment record (shown in Figure 5.14). If the alarm is on, we use the image in appInfo(alarm-on); otherwise, we use appInfo(alarm-off).

We also add a binding so that you can click on the alarm bell to toggle its state. We save the current state for each alarm bell in an array element appInfo($win-$slot). Thus if the appointment editor is called .ap, the alarm status for 10:30am is stored in appInfo(.ap-10:30am). When you click on that bell, the following procedure is invoked to toggle that state:

```
proc appointment_toggle {win label slot} {
    global appInfo
    if {$appInfo($win-$slot)} {
        set appInfo($win-$slot) 0
        $label configure -image $appInfo(alarm-off)
    } else {
        set appInfo($win-$slot) 1
        $label configure -image $appInfo(alarm-on)
    }
}
```

We look at the current state. If it's on, we turn it off, and we change the label to display the "off" image. Otherwise, we turn it on, and we change the label to the "on" image.

5.4.3   Changing text bindings

By default, the text widget will let you edit any of the text within it. In this section, we'll change the bindings on the text widget to handle the customized editing that we need for appointments. We'll make the text in the comment fields editable, but we'll treat any other text as read-only.

Let's take another look at the `appointment_create` procedure, which creates an appointment editor. This time, we'll focus on the code that modifies the bindings:

```
proc appointment_create {win} {
    ...code shown earlier...
    set btags [bindtags $win.text]
    set i [lsearch $btags Text]
    if {$i >= 0} {
        set btags [lreplace $btags $i $i]
    }
    bindtags $win.text $btags

    bind $win.text <KeyPress> {appointment_insert %W %A}
    bind $win.text <Control-KeyPress-h> {appointment_backspace %W}
    bind $win.text <KeyPress-BackSpace> {appointment_backspace %W}
    bind $win.text <KeyPress-Delete> {appointment_backspace %W}
    bind $win.text <KeyPress-Tab> {appointment_next %W; break}

    $win.text tag bind comment <ButtonPress-1> {
        focus %W
        %W mark set insert @%x,%y
    }

    return $win
}
```

We want to suppress all of the usual editing capability that is built into a text widget. This comes from bindings defined in the Tk library for class `Text`. We can remove these bindings from a particular widget by changing its list of binding tags, as we discussed in Section 3.5. We query the binding tags, search for the name `Text`, and remove it. Notice that we use the `lreplace` command to delete the list element. This is not intuitive, but it is the only way to delete an element. We replace all the elements from `$i` to `$i` with nothing—in effect, deleting the element.

Next, we define the bindings to handle our own editing operations. We bind to the generic `<KeyPress>` event, so that most keystrokes are handled by calling `appointment_insert`, which we'll define later. Remember, the `bind` facility automatically replaces `%W` with the name of the text widget and `%A` with the ASCII code for the key that was pressed.

We can override the generic `<KeyPress>` binding with specialized bindings for various keys. When you press the backspace key, for example, we don't want to insert a character; we want to delete the character to the left of the cursor. So we bind to the specific `<KeyPress-BackSpace>` event and handle it by calling `appointment_backspace`. We handle Control-h and Delete the same way, since these are synonymous with backspace.

We handle the Tab key by calling `appointment_next`, which moves the cursor to the next time slot in the editor. So you can press Tab to move from comment to comment, down the list of appointments. Normally, pressing the Tab key shifts the keyboard focus to another widget in the display. This is handled by a binding to the `all` string, which Tk adds by default. So if we aren't careful, pressing the Tab key will not only move the cursor but also shift the focus over to another widget. We can avoid this by moving the cursor and executing the `break` command. When the `bind` facility sees the break, it will skip over the rest of the binding tags (including `all`) and will terminate the processing for that event.

Finally, we add a binding for `<ButtonPress-1>`, so you can click to position the cursor. We want to position the cursor only when you click on a comment field. So instead of binding to the widget as a whole, we bind directly to the `comment` tag. When you click on a comment, we use `mark set` to position the cursor at the click point. Remember, the `bind` facility replaces `%x` and `%y` with the coordinates for the click point, and the text widget interprets `@x, y` as a text index. We also assign focus to the text widget, in case it doesn't have it already.

Now that the bindings are all in place, let's look at the procedures used to handle them. Here is the `appointment_insert` procedure, which handles a normal keystroke:

```
proc appointment_insert {twin c} {
    set tags [$twin tag names insert]
    if {$c == "\r" || $c == "\n"} {
        $twin insert insert "\n" $tags
    } elseif {[scan $c {%[ -~]} dummy] == 1} {
        $twin insert insert $c $tags
    }
}
```

The procedure takes as arguments the name of the text widget and the character to be inserted. If the character is a carriage return (`\r`) or a newline (`\n`), we insert a newline. Otherwise, we use the `scan` command to determine whether it is a printable character. The `scan` command matches the character `$c` against the pattern `%[ -~]`, which represents all possible characters between the space and the tilde in the ASCII character set (that is, all printable characters). If scan can match the character, it stores the character in the `dummy` variable and returns `1`, and we insert the character into the text widget. Otherwise, we ignore the character.

If you insert a character in the middle of a tagged range, the tag will stretch to cover it. But if you insert a character at the start of a tagged range, the tag will shift down, leaving the character uncovered. To be safe, we tag each character as we insert it. We use the tag names operation to query the tags at the insert mark, and we apply the same tags when we insert the character.

The code we use to insert a character looks a bit strange, since we use the insert keyword twice. The first insert tells the text widget to do an insert operation. The second insert says to insert at the insertion cursor, which is represented by a built-in mark called insert.

Now let's look at the appointment_backspace procedure, which erases a single character:

```
proc appointment_backspace {twin} {
    set tags [$twin tag names insert-1char]
    if {[lsearch $tags "comment"] >= 0} {
        $twin delete insert-1char
    }
}
```

The insert mark refers to the character to the *right* of the insertion cursor, but we want to delete the character to the *left*. So we invoke the delete operation with the index insert-1char. There's one catch: We don't want to delete past the beginning of a comment. So before we delete a character, we use tag names to get its tags, and we make sure that the character is marked as a comment.

Here is the appointment_next procedure, which moves the cursor to the next comment:

```
proc appointment_next {twin} {
    set range [$twin tag nextrange hour insert]
    if {$range != ""} {
        set index [lindex $range 0]
        set range [$twin tag nextrange comment $index]
        set index [lindex $range 0]
        $twin mark set insert $index
    } else {
        set range [$twin tag nextrange comment 1.0]
        set index [lindex $range 0]
        $twin mark set insert $index
    }
    $twin see insert
}
```

We use the tag nextrange operation to search through the text in the appointment editor. We start by searching for the first occurrence of the tag hour after the insert mark. If we get something other than the null string, we've found the start of the next time slot. We use lindex to get the starting index for the time, and then we search for the first comment after that position. We get the starting index for the comment and set the insert mark at that position.

If we can't find another `hour` tag, the cursor must be somewhere in the last comment. So we start from the top, find the start of the very first comment, and set the `insert` mark at that position.

The `mark set` operation will place the cursor anywhere within the text buffer. The cursor's new position doesn't have to be showing on the screen. Suppose that the cursor is in the `12:00`pm slot in Figure 5.12. If you press Tab, the cursor will move down to the `12:30`pm slot, which is off the screen. When the cursor disappears like this, it's very disconcerting. So whenever you move the cursor, it's a good idea to adjust the view to its new position. In this example, we use the `see` operation, telling the text widget that we want to see the `insert` position. If this is already visible, the text widget does nothing. Otherwise, it adjusts its view accordingly.

5.4.4 Retrieving appointments

We have a way of loading appointments and making changes to them. Now we need a way of getting the appointments back out of the editor. We'll write a procedure called `appointment_get` to handle this. You pass in the name of an appointment editor and the name of an array, and it will take the appointments from the editor and store them in the array. The procedure is implemented as follows:

```
proc appointment_get {win scheduleVar} {
    global appInfo
    upvar $scheduleVar schedule

    set range [$win.text tag nextrange comment 1.0]
    while {$range != ""} {
        set pos [lindex $range 0]
        set nextpos [lindex $range 1]
        set comment [string trim [eval $win.text get $range]]
        set range [$win.text tag prevrange hour $pos]
        if {$range != ""} {
            set slot [string trim [eval $win.text get $range]]
            set schedule($slot) [list $appInfo($win-$slot) $comment]
        }
        set range [$win.text tag nextrange comment $nextpos+1char]
    }
}
```

We use `upvar` to pass the appointment array by reference, just as we did for the `appointment_load` procedure. That way, we can use it to return appointment data from the procedure.

Each of the comments is tagged with the name `comment`, so they are easy to find. We simply use the `tag nextrange` operation to search for them. This returns a list with two indices, indicating the range of characters for the next occurrence of a tag. If it cannot find the tag, the operation returns the null string. We search for the first comment, starting from position `1.0`. After that, we search for comments starting from `$nextpos+1char`, which is one character past the end of the previous comment.

We use the `get` operation to extract the text for each comment. Since both the starting index and the ending index are stored in the `range` variable, you might be tempted to use the `get` operation, like this:

```
$win.text get $range     ;# error!
```

If you do, you'll get an error. The text widget expects to see these indices as two separate arguments on the command line, so we must use the `eval` command to break them out. The `eval` command joins its arguments together and then interprets the result, breaking down the boundaries that normally delimit arguments, like this:

```
      eval $win.text get $range
  ➡   eval .ap.text get {1.8 2.21}
  ➡   .ap.text get 1.8 2.21
```

Once we have a comment, we need to figure out its time slot. We use `tag prevrange` to search backward from the start of the comment for the `hour` tag. If we can find this tag, we extract its text to get the name of the time slot.

Finally, we build an appointment record and store it in the `schedule` array. Each record is a list of two elements, as shown in Figure 5.14. One element is the current alarm status, which is stored in `appInfo($win-$slot)`; the other element is the comment message that we just extracted.

We scan down through the text in the text widget, handling each appointment in this manner until there are no more comments. Then we return, passing all of the information back via the `schedule` array.

The appointment editor is now complete. If we put this together with the calendar component that we developed in Section 4.6, we have the start of a powerful calendar application that we'll call the Electric Secretary. You can click on the calendar part to select a particular day, and the appointments for that day will be loaded into the editor. You can look at the appointments and can edit them interactively. If you make any changes, they are sent back to a centralized database for storage. We'll see how this part works in Section 7.8, when we look at client/server architectures.

5.5 Hierarchical browser

The text widget is very good at inserting and deleting text. You can harness its power to build many kinds of dynamic displays. For example, consider the hierarchical browser shown in Figure 5.15. This browser displays a tree of elements—in this case, the files in a directory called `tcl-tk`. You can click on the arrows to expand or collapse the various levels of the hierarchy. The `lib` directory, for example, is shown both collapsed and expanded in Figure 5.15.

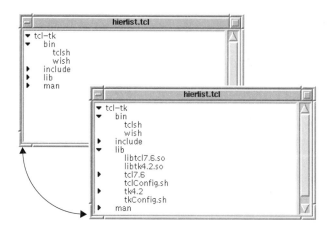

Figure 5.15. The text widget is used to build a hierarchical browser. Clicking on an arrow expands or collapses part of the hierarchy.

When a directory is expanded, we insert its elements into the text, and the text widget will shift the rest of the elements down to make space. When a directory is collapsed, we delete its elements, and the text widget will shift the other elements back up, to compensate. Since the text widget handles all of this in a highly optimized manner, the performance is snappy even if you view hierarchies with thousands of elements.

Now suppose that the `lib` directory is suddenly expanded and we need to insert its elements into the text. Where exactly should they be inserted? If the `bin` and `include` directories are collapsed, the `lib` element will be on line 4, but otherwise, it might be on line 6 or line 8. Keeping track of the position of each element is very difficult. Fortunately, the text widget can handle this for us. We'll use marks to track the elements. As an element moves about, its mark will follow. When we want to expand an element, we can use its mark to determine its position, and we can insert its contents in the space below it.

5.5.1 Hierarchical data

Before we start building the browser, let's think about the data it will use. Each element in the browser is a node in a tree. We can represent each node as a list with two elements: its label and its list of child nodes. Each child node also has a node label and its own list of child nodes. All of the data for an entire tree could be represented as one very long string containing a series of nested lists.

Figure 5.16 shows an exploded view of such a string. The main list has one element— a node labeled `tcl-tk`. Its list of children contains four elements—the nodes `bin`, `include`, `lib`, and `man`. The list of children for `bin` contains two elements—the nodes tclsh and wish. The list of children for each of these nodes is empty, so the tree stops here. Of course, the other branches—include, lib, and man—each have their own list of children, so the tree has other data that isn't shown in Figure 5.16.

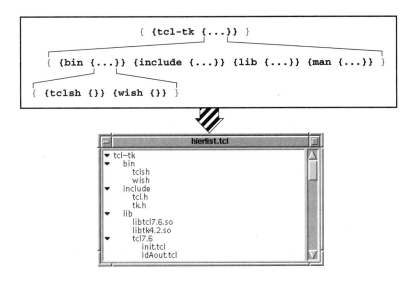

Figure 5.16. Hierarchical data is stored in nested lists, which form a tree. Each node has a label and a list of child nodes.

This tree representation is easy to generate, so it makes a natural interface for our hierarchical browser. For example, you could use the following procedure to generate a file tree. You pass in the name of a directory, and it returns a string containing all of the nodes for that file tree:

```
proc find_files {dir} {
    set flist ""
    set pattern [file join $dir *]
    foreach file [lsort [glob -nocomplain $pattern]] {
        if {[file isdirectory $file]} {
            set contents [find_files $file]
        } else {
            set contents ""
        }
        lappend flist [list [file tail $file] $contents]
    }
    return $flist
}
```

The `glob` command returns a list of files matching the pattern `$pattern`. Since this pattern has the file name `*`, it gives us all of the files in the specified directory. If no files match this pattern, the `glob` command normally returns an error. But we've included the `-nocomplain` option, so if the directory is empty, `glob` will return an empty list.

We use the `lsort` command to sort the files in alphabetical order, and then we run through the list. If a file name represents a directory, we call `find_files` recursively to determine its list of children. Otherwise, we set its contents to the null string. Once we have the contents, we append a node description onto the return list. Remember, each node is a list containing its label and its contents. In this case, we take the file name as the node label. But instead of using the complete file path, we use `file tail` to extract the simple name at the end of the path. After looping through all of the files, we return the file tree that we've built up in `flist`.

Using lists to represent a tree is a convenient interface. You can pass an entire tree as a single string, so you can take the output from a procedure such as `find_files` and hand it directly to a browser. But within the browser, the nested lists are awkward, to say the least. Suppose you click on the arrow to expand the `lib` directory. How do we find the list that represents this node? We would have to traverse the tree, following the branches that lead to this node.

The tree is much easier to manage if we use a different representation within the browser. Instead of storing the entire tree as a series of nested lists, we can assign each node a unique name and store the entire tree in an array. The node names could be anything, but we'll choose names like those shown in Figure 5.17. They indicate at a glance where each node sits in the hierarchy. The node `tcl-tk` is the first node from the root of the tree, so its name is `root-1`. The node `bin` is the first node under `tcl-tk`, so its name is `root-1-1`, and so on.

Now that we have a name for each node, we can store the entire tree in an array, like this:

```
set node "root-1"
set data($node-label) "tcl-tk"
set data($node-children) {root-1-1 root-1-2 root-1-3 root-1-4}
set node "root-1-1"
set data($node-label) "bin"
set data($node-children) {root-1-1-1 root-1-1-2}
...
```

Each node has two slots in the array: one called `$node-label`, which stores the node label, and another called `$node-children`, which stores the list of children. You can think of the entire array as a chunk of memory and of each pair of slots as a data structure. Each node name is a "pointer" that addresses the data for a particular node. Each list of children is a list of pointers to other nodes.

We can use the following procedure to convert a list-based representation of a tree to its corresponding array-based representation:

```
proc hierlist_data_add {var node label info} {
    upvar #0 $var data
```

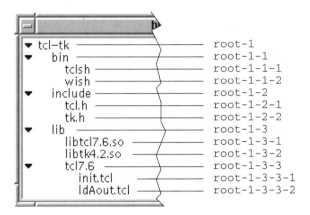

Figure 5.17. The name of each node indicates its position in the hierarchy.

```
set data($node-label) $label
set data($node-children) ""

set num 0
foreach rec $info {
    set subnode "$node-[incr num]"
    lappend data($node-children) $subnode
    set sublabel [lindex $rec 0]
    set subinfo [lindex $rec 1]
    hierlist_data_add $var $subnode $sublabel $subinfo
    }
}
```

This procedure adds one node into the array and then recursively adds all of its children into the array. You can start the entire conversion process by defining a root node, like this:

```
set treeList [find_files /usr/local]
hierlist_data_add treeArray root "" $treeList
```

In this case, we're adding a node called root to an array called treeArray. The label for this node is unimportant; it will never show up in the browser, so we pass in a null string. The content of this node is the list-based representation of a file tree returned from the find_files procedure.

Inside the hierlist_data_add procedure, we use upvar to gain access to the tree array. The #0 argument says that we're looking for a global variable. Its name at the global scope is $var, which is something like treeArray, but in this procedure, we'll call it data.

We create a node by adding two elements to the `data` array—one for the label and one for the list of children. We start with an empty list of children and gradually build up the list in the loop that follows.

Remember, the `info` variable contains a list-based representation for the nodes in a tree. We iterate through this list and create a node for each element. We use the `num` variable as a counter to give each of the child nodes a unique name. During the first call, the node name will be `root`, and the children will be named `root-1`, `root-2`, and so on. During the next (recursive) call, the node name will be `root-1`, and the children will be named `root-1-1`, `root-1-2`, and so on. This scheme generates all of the node names shown in Figure 5.17.

We add each child node to the list of children for the parent node. Then we extract its label and its list of children, and we call `hierlist_data_add` to add that node and its children to the array. When all of the dust has settled, we have a complete, array-based representation for the original tree.

Each browser will display one tree, and you may have many different browsers in a single application. Now suppose that all of the browsers use a global variable called `treeArray` to store their data. Clearly, this won't do. As one browser loads its data, it will overwrite the contents of another browser. Each browser must have its own global variable to store the array-based representation of its tree.

The following procedure solves that problem:

```
proc hierlist_data {win info} {
    global hierInfo

    if {[info exists hierInfo($win-data)]} {
        set var $hierInfo($win-data)
        upvar #0 $var data
        unset data
    } else {
        set counter 0
        while {1} {
            set var "hierData#[incr counter]"
            upvar #0 $var data
            if {![info exists data]} {
                break
            }
        }
        set hierInfo($win-data) $var
    }
    hierlist_data_add $var root "" $info
}
```

You pass in the name of a browser and the list-based representation of a tree, and it creates the array-based representation for that browser. It looks a bit complicated, but it does something quite simple. It creates a unique global variable for the browser and then calls `hierlist_data_add` to store the tree in that variable.

The `while` loop within the `else` clause finds a unique name for the global variable. We use the `counter` variable to generate a series of names. On the first pass through the loop, we get the name `hierData#1`; on the next pass, `hierData#2`; and so on. We use the `upvar` command to connect a global variable with each of these names to a local variable called `data`. If that variable doesn't exist, we've found a name that's not being used, and we break out of the loop.

We store the name of the global variable in an array called `hierInfo`. That way, if we call this procedure again for the same browser, we'll find a variable name sitting in the `hierInfo($win-data)` slot. Instead of creating another global variable, we'll simply use the existing variable. Of course, we'll want to discard the old tree data that's stored in the variable. So we use the `unset` command to delete the array, and then we rebuild the tree from scratch.

5.5.2 Creating the hierarchical browser

Now that we know how to handle hierarchical data, let's focus on the browser itself. The following procedure creates a browser. You simply pass in a widget name for the entire assembly:

```
proc hierlist_create {win} {
    frame $win -class Hierlist
    scrollbar $win.sbar -command "$win.hbox yview"
    pack $win.sbar -side right -fill y
    text $win.hbox -wrap none -takefocus 0 \
        -yscrollcommand "$win.sbar set"
    pack $win.hbox -side left -expand yes -fill both

    set tabsize [option get $win indent Indent]
    set tabsize [winfo pixels $win $tabsize]
    set tabs "15"
    for {set i 1} {$i < 20} {incr i} {
        lappend tabs [expr $i*$tabsize+15]
    }
    $win.hbox configure -tabs $tabs

    set btags [bindtags $win.hbox]
    set i [lsearch $btags Text]
    if {$i >= 0} {
        set btags [lreplace $btags $i $i]
    }
    bindtags $win.hbox $btags

    bind $win <Destroy> "hierlist_destroy $win"
    return $win
}
```

As always, we start by creating a hull frame, and we pack a text widget and a scrollbar within it.

We set the class name for the browser to `Hierlist`, so you can set resources to control its appearance. The following resources are included in the browser code:

```
option add *Hierlist.activeColor gray widgetDefault
option add *Hierlist.indent 15 widgetDefault
option add *Hierlist.hbox.background white widgetDefault
option add *Hierlist.hbox.width 40 widgetDefault
option add *Hierlist.hbox.height 10 widgetDefault
option add *Hierlist.hbox.cursor center_ptr widgetDefault
option add *Hierlist.hbox.font \
    -*-lucida-medium-r-normal-sans-*-120-* widgetDefault
```

All of the resources have the low-priority `widgetDefault`, so they are easy to override.

The `activeColor` and `indent` settings are not recognized by any of the Tk widgets. They are new resources that we invented specifically for the hierarchy browser. We'll see the code that uses them later, but they work as shown in Figure 5.18. The `indent` resource controls how much the various levels of hierarchy are indented. By default, each level is offset from the previous level by 15 pixels. The `activeColor` resource controls a special highlight color. As the mouse pointer touches each line in the text widget, we'll change its background color to the `activeColor` setting. This provides a visual cue that helps you see the arrow that controls an element.

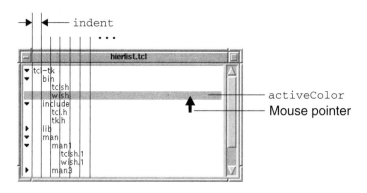

Figure 5.18. Resources control the appearance of the hierarchical browser.

The other resources are handled automatically by Tk. They're prefixed by the name `*Hierlist.hbox`. We'll talk more about the syntax of resource names in Section 8.1.1.1, but in this case, the name `*Hierlist.hbox` refers to the text widget (named `hbox`) within our browser (class `Hierlist`). These resources set the background color, the font, the cursor, and the initial size of the browser to reasonable default values.

Let's get back to `hierlist_create`. After we create the text widget, we initialize a series of tab stops that we can use to indent the various levels of the hierarchy. The first tab stop is set at 15 pixels, putting the first level just beyond the arrows. The rest of the tab stops are set according to the `indent` resource. We use the `option get` command to get the value of this resource, and we use `winfo pixels` to convert it to an integer number of pixels. That way, you can set the `indent` resource to a screen distance such as `0.1i` or `5m`, and we'll get a pixel value that we can multiply. Once we've built up the list of tab stops, we assign it to the `-tabs` option on the text widget.

Before we return, we remove the `Text` element from the list of binding tags. This defeats the interactive editing facilities for the text widget. After all, we want this browser to be read-only. You might wonder why we didn't configure the `-state` option to `disabled`, as we did earlier, in Section 5.3. This also defeats the editing capabilities, but it leaves some other text widget behaviors in place. For example, you can click and drag to select characters even when the text widget is disabled. This is normally quite handy, but in our browser, the selection would interfere with the highlight color for the active line. So we remove *all* of the normal text widget behaviors in one shot, by pruning them out of the binding tags.

When you use binding tags like this to disable a widget, you should be careful to do one other thing: You should set the `-takefocus` option to `0` so that the widget won't receive focus. That way, as you press the Tab key to shift the focus, the widget will be overlooked. If you forget to do this, you can tab the focus onto the widget, and you'll see its insertion cursor. Of course, in our browser, you won't be able to edit anything, since we've removed its editing capabilities. But the cursor will appear nevertheless.

You don't have to worry about this problem if you set the `-state` option to `disabled`. Any widget is automatically overlooked when it is disabled. But in this example, we didn't use the `-state` option, so we were careful to set the `-takefocus` option to `0` when we created the text widget.

In this example, we're careful to do one other thing. We bind to the `<Destroy>` event on the hull frame. Thus when the browser is destroyed, the following procedure is called automatically:

```
proc hierlist_destroy {win} {
    global hierInfo
    if {[info exists hierInfo($win-data)]} {
        set var $hierInfo($win-data)
        upvar #0 $var data
        unset data
        unset hierInfo($win-data)
    }
}
```

This procedure destroys the data associated with the browser. For this component, it is important to clean things up properly. The tree associated with each browser can be extremely large, and if we don't delete it, it can represent a significant memory leak. We get the name of the array that contains the tree from the slot `hierInfo($win-data)`. Then we delete the array and remove the slot from the `hierInfo` data structure.

5.5.3   Using tags and marks

When you expand a node, its child nodes will be inserted beneath it in the hierarchy. When you collapse a node, its child nodes will be deleted. In either case, we need to know exactly where to insert and delete the text. In this section, we'll see how to use tags and marks to track the position of text within the text widget.

As we're inserting each node into the browser, we'll add a mark on the line below it. Let's see what the marks would look like for the example in Figure 5.16. Normally, marks are invisible, but for this example, we've displayed each mark with a special M symbol in Figure 5.19. As you can see, the node `root-1` (`tcl-tk`) has a mark called `root-1:start` on the line below it. This mark indicates the position of its child nodes (`bin`, `include`, `lib`, and `man`). Similarly, the node `root-1-1` (`bin`) has a mark called `root-1-1:start` on the line below it, indicating the position of its child nodes (`tclsh` and `wish`). Every node has a "start" mark—even if it is not expanded. For example, the node `root-1-3` (`lib`) has a mark called `root-1-3:start` on the line below it. When this node is expanded, we'll insert its children at that position.

When a node is expanded, we'll also add an "end" mark at the end of its child nodes. For example, the node `root-1` (`tcl-tk`) has a mark called `root-1:end` that falls just after the "start" mark for its last child (`man`). Similarly, the node `root-1-1` (`bin`) has a mark called `root-1-1:end` that falls just after the "start" mark for its last child (`wish`). So we can collapse any node by deleting all of the text between its "start" and "end" marks.

These marks flow with the text, so they'll keep the proper place as text is inserted and deleted. For example, suppose that we expand the `lib` node by inserting its children at `root-1-3:start`. Then the `man` node will shift down, pushing its mark `root-1-4:start` along with it. If the `lib` node is collapsed, the `man` node will shift back up, pulling its mark along with it. No matter how many nodes have been expanded or collapsed, we can always insert the children of the `man` node at `root-1-4:start`, and they'll appear at the proper place in the list.

Inserting text at a mark can be tricky. For example, suppose we try to expand the `lib` node. We might insert some text for its first child, like this:

```
$win.hbox insert root-1-3:start "libtcl7.6.so\n"
```

We're assuming that the `win` variable contains the name of a browser created by `hierlist_create`, so `$win.hbox` refers to the text widget inside it. In this case, we're telling the text widget to insert the string `"libtcl7.6.so\n"` at the mark `root-1-3:start`. This seems simple enough, but if we're not careful, this command will have an unfortunate side effect. As it inserts the text, the command will shift the mark `root-1-3:start` over, so it will no longer mark the start of the children. Instead, it will

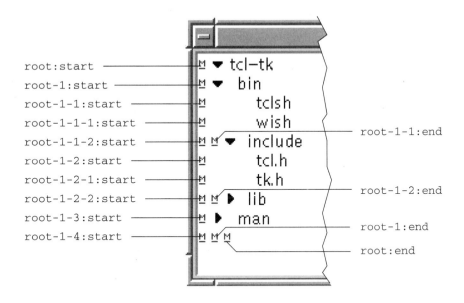

Figure 5.19. Marks (normally invisible but shown here as small Ms) are used to keep track of positions within the hierarchical browser.

mark the position after the first child. If we continue to insert text at this mark, the mark will continue to shift down.

By default, all marks act like the insertion cursor—as text is inserted, the mark shifts over toward the right, so that it follows the new text. This behavior is controlled by the *gravity* of the mark. By default, all marks gravitate toward the right, but you can make a mark gravitate toward the left, like this:

```
$win.hbox mark gravity root-1-3:start left
```

Now if we insert some text, the mark will float to the left of the new text, so it will keep its position. You should use `left` gravity when you want put text just *after* a mark; use `right` gravity when you want to put text just *before* a mark.

Using `left` gravity can produce surprising results. For example, suppose we insert some entries at the mark `root-1-3:start`, which we just configured with `left` gravity.

```
$win.hbox insert root-1-3:start "libtcl7.6.so\n"
$win.hbox insert root-1-3:start "libtk4.2.so\n"
$win.hbox insert root-1-3:start "tcl7.6\n"
```

You might think that these entries would appear in alphabetical order, just as they're listed here. In fact, they'll appear in the opposite order. As each entry is added, it pushes the rest of the text down. So `"libtcl7.6.so\n"` is added first; then `"libtk4.2.so\n"` is inserted in front of it, pushing it down; then `"tcl7.6\n"` is inserted in front of that, pushing that down. Marks with `left` gravity stay in place, but they reverse the effect of your `insert` operations.

Of course, we can solve this problem by reversing all of the `insert` operations. But there's a better way to handle this. We can create a mark with `right` gravity, position it on the mark with `left` gravity, and then use it to handle the insertions in a normal manner. For example, the following code creates a mark called `pos` at the same position as `root-1-3:start`:

```
$win.hbox mark set pos root-1-3:start
$win.hbox insert pos "libtcl7.6.so\n"
$win.hbox insert pos "libtk4.2.so\n"
$win.hbox insert pos "tcl7.6\n"
```

This mark will have `right` gravity by default. As we insert text at `pos`, it will shift over toward the right, so all three entries will be inserted in alphabetical order. However, the original mark, `root-1-3:start`, has `left` gravity, so it will stay put as the text is inserted.

Now let's see how all of this comes together to support the hierarchical browser. The following procedure expands a node by inserting its children at its "start" mark. You pass in the name of the browser and the name of the node that's being expanded.

```
proc hierlist_insert {win node} {
    global hierInfo
    set var $hierInfo($win-data)
    upvar #0 $var data

    set indent ""
    foreach digit [split $node "-"] {
        append indent "\t"
    }

    set activebg [option get $win activeColor Color]
    $win.hbox mark set pos "$node:start"

    foreach subnode $data($node-children) {
        if {$data($subnode-children) != ""} {
            set arrow "$win.hbox.arrow-$subnode"
            label $arrow -image $hierInfo(sideArrow) \
                -borderwidth 0
            bind $arrow <ButtonPress-1> \
                "hierlist_expand $win $subnode"
            $win.hbox window create pos -window $arrow
        }
        $win.hbox insert pos \
            "$indent$data($subnode-label)\n" $subnode
```

```
                    $win.hbox tag bind $subnode <Enter> \
                        "$win.hbox tag configure $subnode -background $activebg"
                    $win.hbox tag bind $subnode <Leave> \
                        "$win.hbox tag configure $subnode -background {}"


                    $win.hbox mark set "$subnode:start" pos
                    $win.hbox mark gravity "$subnode:start" left
                }
                $win.hbox mark set "$node:end" pos
            }
```

First, we use the `upvar` command to access the tree data for the browser. Remember, each browser has its own global variable that contains an array-based representation of the tree, as we described in Section 5.5.1. The `upvar` command establishes a link with the global variable so that within this procedure, we can refer to it as `data`.

Next, we build a string of tab characters. We'll use this string as we insert the child nodes, to indent them to the proper position (see Figure 5.18). When we expand the `root` node, we'll need one tab character for its children, putting them at the first tab stop, which is just past the arrows. When we expand the `root-1` node, we'll need two tab characters for its children. When we expand the `root-1-1` node, we'll need three tab characters, and so on. In general, we'll need one tab for each of the dash-separated parts of the node name that we're expanding. So we use the `split` command to break up the node name, and we add a tab character (`\t`) for each of its parts.

Next, we create a mark called `pos` at the "start" mark for the node. This mark has `right` gravity, so it works in an intuitive manner. We can use it to insert the child nodes in their normal order.

We iterate through the list of child nodes and insert each node into the browser. If a child node also has children, we add an arrow at the start of the line. We create a label widget to display the arrow image, and we use `window create` to insert it into the text at position `pos`.

The label widget's name, `$win.hbox.arrow-$subnode`, may look a bit strange, but it follows the rules described earlier, in Section 5.4.2. This name starts with `$win.hbox`, so it is a child of the text widget, and it ends with `$subnode` (which is something like `root-1` or `root-1-3-2`), so each name is unique.

Each label displays one of two arrow images, which are loaded like this:

```
        set hierInfo(sideArrow) [image create photo \
            -file [file join $env(EFFTCL_LIBRARY) images side.gif]]
        set hierInfo(downArrow) [image create photo \
            -file [file join $env(EFFTCL_LIBRARY) images down.gif]]
```

Both of these images must be distributed along with the code for the hierarchy browser. Instead of hard-coding the names for these files, we use the environment variable `EFFTCL_LIBRARY` to point to the library directory. We can write an installation program that sets this variable when the library is installed, as we'll see in Chapter 8.

We create each node in the collapsed state. So we create each arrow with the side arrow image, and we set up the `<ButtonPress-1>` binding to expand the node when you click on the arrow. We'll see how this is handled later.

Next, we insert the string `"$indent$data($subnode-label)\n"`, which represents the node label. Remember, the `indent` variable contains a series of tab characters that will put this node in the proper column on the browser. The `data` variable contains the entire tree data structure, and the slot `data($subnode-label)` contains the label for node `$subnode`. Of course, we terminate the entire string with a newline character (`\n`), so the next child will appear on a new line.

Notice that as we insert this string, we tag it with the unique name `$subnode`. This lets us handle the `<Enter>` and `<Leave>` events, so we can highlight each line as the mouse pointer touches it. When we get an `<Enter>` event on the line, we change its background to the active color. When we get a `<Leave>` event, we change its background back to the null string, so it defaults to the normal background color for the text widget. We use the `option get` command to query the `activeColor` resource. But instead of querying this again and again for each line, we query it once—outside of the loop—and save its value in the variable `activebg`.

Once we've inserted the text for each node, the `pos` mark will be sitting on the line below it. This is just the right place for its "start" mark. So before we move on to the next node, we create the "start" mark for this node. We set its gravity to `left`, so it will stay put when we expand the node later on.

After we've created all of the child nodes, we add the "end" mark for the parent node. Then we return.

Now that we have the `hierlist_insert` procedure, the rest of the browser is easy to implement. For example, the following procedure will load a new tree into the browser. You pass in the name of a browser and a list-based representation of the tree:

```
proc hierlist_display {win info} {
    hierlist_data $win $info
    $win.hbox delete 1.0 end
    $win.hbox mark set "root:start" 1.0
    $win.hbox mark gravity "root:start" left
    hierlist_insert $win "root"
}
```

First, we call `hierlist_data` to store the data for the tree. Then we clear out the text widget and insert the contents of the root node. But before we call `hierlist_insert`, we must create a "start" mark for the root node. We create this mark by hand at the position `1.0`. From that point on, the "start" marks are created automatically as each child node is added to the browser.

When you click on an arrow, the following procedure is called to expand the node:

```
proc hierlist_expand {win node} {
    global hierInfo
```

```
        set arrow "$win.hbox.arrow-$node"
        set image [$arrow cget -image]
        if {$image == $hierInfo(sideArrow)} {
            $arrow configure -image $hierInfo(downArrow)
            bind $arrow <ButtonPress-1> \
                "hierlist_collapse $win $node"
            hierlist_insert $win $node
        }
    }
```

We look at the arrow's image to see whether the node is already expanded. If the node has a side arrow, we convert it to a down arrow, and we call `hierlist_insert` to add its children. We also change the binding, so the next time you click on the arrow, it will collapse the node.

We use a similar approach to collapse a node:

```
    proc hierlist_collapse {win node} {
        global hierInfo

        set arrow "$win.hbox.arrow-$node"
        set image [$arrow cget -image]
        if {$image == $hierInfo(downArrow)} {
            $arrow configure -image $hierInfo(sideArrow)
            bind $arrow <ButtonPress-1> \
                "hierlist_expand $win $node"
            $win.hbox delete "$node:start" "$node:end"
        }
    }
```

Again, we look at the arrow's image to see whether the node is already collapsed. If the node has a down arrow, we convert it to a side arrow, and we delete the children between the "start" and "end" marks for the node. We also change the binding, so the next time you click on the arrow, it will expand the node.

As you can see, tags and marks provide powerful ways of handling the text within a text widget. Tags let you identify a range of text, so you can bind to it and control its style. In this example, we used tags to handle the active color, so each line lights up as you touch it with the mouse pointer. Marks track a relative position within the text, so you can find it later on. In this example, we used marks to track the start/end of child nodes in the hierarchy. When combined, tags and marks help you build sophisticated displays—like a hierarchical browser—with just a few pages of code.

Chapter 6
Top-level Windows

When the `wish` program starts up, it automatically creates the main window for the application. You create the other widgets and pack, grid, or place them inside the main window to create your program. But what if you want to pop up another window?

Tk has a special widget, called a *toplevel* widget, to handle this. You can create a toplevel widget like this:

```
toplevel .popup
```

You then fill it with other widgets to define its appearance.

In this chapter, we'll use toplevel widgets to build

- A notice dialog, sometimes called an *alert*
- A confirmation dialog, which asks a question and waits for a response
- A printer dialog, which saves output in a file or routes it to a printer
- A balloon help facility

Along the way, we'll explore various strategies for creating top-level windows and for making them come and go on the desktop. We'll see how to create modal dialogs, which ask the user a question and wait for the response. We'll also build a "sticky-notes" application that lets you tear off pages from a memo pad and post messages on the desktop.

6.1 Toplevel widgets

Suppose you want to let the user know about an error in your application. You might pop up a notice dialog with an error message like the one shown in Figure 6.1.

Figure 6.1. Simple notice dialog.

The code needed to create the dialog looks something like this:

```
toplevel .notice
frame .notice.info
pack .notice.info -expand yes -fill both -padx 2 -pady 2
label .notice.info.icon -bitmap error
pack .notice.info.icon -side left -padx 8 -pady 8
label .notice.info.mesg -text "File not found"
pack .notice.info.mesg -side right -expand yes -fill both \
    -padx 8 -pady 8
frame .notice.sep -height 2 -borderwidth 1 -relief sunken
pack .notice.sep -fill x -padx 4
button .notice.dismiss -text "Dismiss" -command {destroy .notice}
pack .notice.dismiss -pady 4
```

The `toplevel` command creates a new toplevel widget called `.notice`. By itself, this would be an empty window, much like the main window that appears when you start up a `wish` application. Other widgets are created and packed into the toplevel widget to make it look like a notice dialog. The names of these widgets must be prefixed by the name of the toplevel that contains them. In this case, all of the widgets in the notice dialog start with the name `.notice`. Without this prefix, the widgets would appear as components in the main application window.

Unlike the other widgets, the toplevel widget has no `pack` command. In fact, if you try to pack this widget, you'll get an error. All toplevel widgets reside on the desktop, and the window manager is responsible for their placement.

When the user clicks on the Dismiss button, the dialog should disappear. One way to accomplish this is to destroy the toplevel widget with the command `destroy .notice`. Destroying a toplevel widget also destroys the widgets within it, so the entire window disappears from the desktop.

6.2   Setting the widget class

When you create a toplevel, you can use the `-class` option to change its widget class, like this:

```
toplevel .notice -class Notice
```

After the widget has been created, you can query the `-class` option, but you can't change it. If you don't set it, the default class for a toplevel widget is `Toplevel`.

In this example, we changed the class of our notice dialog to `Notice`. This makes it easy to set resources that affect the notice dialog but not the rest of the application. A few `option add` commands cause the notice dialog to have a white foreground and a red background and to use a bold italic font for the primary message, like this:

```
option add *Notice*background red
option add *Notice*foreground white
option add *Notice*mesg.font -*-helvetica-bold-o-normal--*-140-*
```

We'll take a closer look at how these commands work in Section 8.1.1, when we study the option database.

Having a special `Notice` class also makes it easy to add bindings to a notice dialog. For example, suppose that you want to prevent a notice dialog from being lost on the desktop. If a user accidentally covers a notice with another window, the following code will cause the notice to spring up on the desktop:

```
bind Notice <Visibility> {raise %W}
```

This binding affects all widgets in class `Notice` and therefore applies to the `.notice` widget in our example. This binding would also apply to any other widget we created with class `Notice`. When a widget in this class is obscured by another window, it receives a `Visibility` event, and the `raise` command is invoked to bring it back into full view.

One word of caution: This binding is too simple-minded to be useful in real applications. If two notice windows overlap on the desktop, they'll both fight to be on top. We'll present a better solution for keeping important windows visible later in this chapter, when we discuss modal dialogs.

6.3   Communicating with the window manager

When you create a toplevel widget, it automatically pops up on the desktop. You're not responsible for packing, gridding, or placing the toplevel widget itself, only the widgets within it. The size and placement of each top-level window is determined by a special program called the *window manager,* which controls the look and feel of the desktop.

This last remark is very important: The window manager controls the look and feel of the desktop and therefore controls the size, placement, and visibility of top-level windows. The window manager also adds the title bar and the decorative border that surrounds a top-level window. If you want a window to pop up at a particular location, you must talk to the window manager. If you want to constrain the size of the window, talk to the window manager. If you want to change the title displayed in the title bar of a window, talk to the window manager.

Tk has a wm command for sending such requests to the window manager. Sending requests is a simple matter, but having them carried out may not be. Window managers treat all requests as suggestions, or *hints*. Most of these requests are honored, but some window managers may treat a request differently from others and may choose to ignore certain requests.

Note: *If you ever get weird bug reports involving a window's appearance that you can't explain from your code, double-check the window manager and windowing environment of the user. Odd things can happen as a result of quirky window managers and strange system default settings.*

Whenever you create a toplevel widget, it's a good idea to send the following hints to the window manager:

```
wm title .notice "Application: Notice"
wm group .notice .
```

The wm title command sets the title displayed above the window. This causes the notice dialog to have the title Application: Notice above it. A top-level window is usually labeled with both the application name and the function it represents. That way, when a window is sitting on a crowded desktop, the user can tell at a glance where it came from and what it does.

The wm group command tells the window manager that .notice is in a group of windows with the main application window "." as the leader. Some window managers use this, for example, to iconify all of the windows in a group when the leader is iconified.

6.3.1 Window placement

All window managers have a policy for placing new windows on the desktop. Whenever you create a toplevel widget, the window manager will decide where to put it. Some window managers tile windows, others stack them, and others ask the user to position them.

Suppose you want a toplevel widget to pop up at a certain location. For example, you want a notice dialog to pop up near the corner of the main application window, so it doesn't get lost on the desktop. You can use the wm geometry command to accomplish this:

```
set x [expr [winfo rootx .]+50]
set y [expr [winfo rooty .]+50]
wm geometry .notice "+$x+$y"
```

The winfo rootx and winfo rooty commands query the location of the main application window "." on the desktop. We offset its location by 50 pixels and ask the window manager to display the notice dialog at this coordinate. The syntax +x+y is used to represent the (x,y) coordinate for the upper-left corner of the window.

Suppose you want to center the window on the desktop. You can query the size of the desktop and the size of the window, compute the coordinate for its upper-left corner, and set its position, like this:

```
set xmax [winfo screenwidth .notice]
set ymax [winfo screenheight .notice]
set x [expr ($xmax-[winfo reqwidth .notice])/2]
set y [expr ($ymax-[winfo reqheight .notice])/2]
wm geometry .notice "+$x+$y"
```

We use `winfo reqwidth` and `winfo reqheight` to query the requested size, which is how big the window wants to be. Using these commands can be a little tricky. They may report the wrong size if the `pack` and `grid` commands have not had a chance to lay out the widgets inside the window. Layout calculations are usually put off until the last possible moment, when the application is idle. We can force these calculations to occur by adding an `update idletasks` command, as we explained in Section 3.1.2. Unfortunately, that will also force the window to appear on the screen. Setting the position after that will cause the window to suddenly jump to the center of the screen. All of that extra flashing is quite annoying to the user.

We can solve this problem by using a combination of `after idle` and `update idletasks`, like this:

```
after idle {
    update idletasks
    set xmax [winfo screenwidth .notice]
    set ymax [winfo screenheight .notice]
    set x [expr ($xmax-[winfo reqwidth .notice])/2]
    set y [expr ($ymax-[winfo reqheight .notice])/2]
    wm geometry .notice "+$x+$y"
}
```

This says that when the application is idle, it should center the window. We include an extra `update idletasks` command at the start of the script. This forces all of the other idle tasks, such as the packing and gridding calculations, to be completed first. With this scheme, the `winfo reqwidth` and `winfo reqheight` commands work properly, but the whole operation is deferred to the idle period. That way, the window pops up cleanly, with no extra flashing.

In some cases, controlling the placement of top-level windows is good. But whenever possible, let the window manager do its job. After all, the user probably selected the window manager because of the way it works or, at the very least, has grown accustomed to it over time. If you fix the placement for *all* of your top-level windows, you're putting the window manager out of business, and you're probably just irritating the user.

6.3.2 Window size

When a toplevel widget first appears on the desktop, it will have its natural (requested) size. The window manager adds a decorative border around the window to display the title of the window and to provide controls for moving, resizing, and iconifying it. Most window managers let the user grab a side or a corner of the decorative border and drag it around to adjust the window size.

Suppose the user grabs a corner of our notice dialog and compresses it to a smaller size. There won't be enough room to display all of its internal widgets. As we explained in Section 2.1.5, the widgets packed last will be squeezed the most, and if the window is made small enough, many of them will simply disappear. You can prevent this by asking the window manager not to allow resizing:

```
wm resizable .notice 0 0
```

The two 0 values are separate Boolean controls for the width and the height. Zero values prevent resizing, and nonzero values allow it. So it's possible to fix the width but make the height resizable, or vice versa.

You should prevent resizing only for the simplest windows. If a window contains a listbox, for example, the user will probably want to enlarge it to see more items on the list. Instead of fixing the size, it's better to give the window manager a minimum window size and to let the user expand the window as needed.

A good choice for the minimum size is the window's requested size. That way, the window is guaranteed to have enough room for all of its internal widgets. We can set the minimum size as follows:

```
after idle {
    update idletasks
    set w [winfo reqwidth .notice]
    set h [winfo reqheight .notice]
    wm minsize .notice $w $h
}
```

Again, since we're dealing with the `winfo reqwidth` and `winfo reqheight` operations, we use a combination of `after idle` and `update idletasks`, as discussed in the previous section.

6.4 Simple dialogs

After you've created a few dialogs, they all start to look the same. They all have an area on top for information, a separator line, and an area on the bottom for control buttons. They all need some `wm` commands to set the title, the group, and the minimum window size. Instead of writing this code again and again, you can encapsulate it in a procedure.

We can make a procedure that you can use, like this:

```
dialog_create Dialog .d
```

With these arguments, the procedure would create a toplevel widget in class `Dialog` named `.d` and then fill it with other widgets to create the empty dialog shown in Figure 6.2.

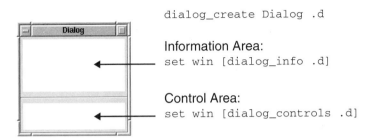

Figure 6.2. Generic dialog created by `dialog_create`.

This procedure is implemented as follows:

```
proc dialog_create {class {win "auto"}} {
    if {$win == "auto"} {
        set count 0
        set win ".dialog[incr count]"
        while {[winfo exists $win]} {
            set win ".dialog[incr count]"
        }
    }
    toplevel $win -class $class
    frame $win.info
    pack $win.info -expand yes -fill both -padx 2 -pady 2
    frame $win.sep -height 2 -borderwidth 1 -relief sunken
    pack $win.sep -fill x -pady 4
    frame $win.controls
    pack $win.controls -fill x -padx 4 -pady 4
    wm title $win $class
    wm group $win .
    after idle [format {
        update idletasks
        wm minsize %s [winfo reqwidth %s] [winfo reqheight %s]
    } $win $win $win]
    return $win
}
```

Notice that the second argument is optional. If it's not specified, it gets the default value, `auto`, and a widget name is selected automatically. Since no two widgets can have the same name, we're careful to select a widget name that's not already in use. We initialize a counter and generate names, such as `.dialog1`, `.dialog2`, until we find a name that's not recognized as an existing widget.

Once we have the window name, we create the toplevel widget and its internal components. We create empty frames to represent the areas for information and controls, and we pack a separator line in between them.

We complete the dialog by sending some information to the window manager. We use the class name as a default window title, and we group the dialog with the main application window. We also set the minimum size of the window to its requested size, using the `after idle` technique discussed in the previous section. In this case, however, the window name is not hard-coded into the command; it is contained in the `win` variable. We use the `format` command to build the necessary command string, substituting the window name in place of each `%s` field.

When the dialog is complete, we return its name as the result of this procedure. If the name is automatically generated, we can capture the result and store it in a variable, using it later on to identify the window. For example, we might create a dialog and change its title, like this:

```
set top [dialog_create Dialog]
wm title $top "Electric Secretary: Notice"
```

Of course, this dialog would be empty, like the one shown in Figure 6.2. We can customize its appearance by creating other widgets and packing them into the information and control frames. We can avoid having to remember the names of these frames if we define the following procedures:

```
proc dialog_info {win} {
    return "$win.info"
}
proc dialog_controls {win} {
    return "$win.controls"
}
```

The `dialog_info` procedure takes the name of a dialog created by `dialog_create` and returns the name of the information area frame at the top of the dialog. Similarly, the `dialog_controls` procedure returns the name of the control area frame at the bottom of the dialog. Having these procedures insulates our code from changes. If we decide to change the layout of the dialog, it may be necessary to change the widget hierarchy, which in turn may change the names of these internal frames. If that happens, we can update these procedures, and any code that uses them will remain unchanged.

We can use all of these dialog procedures to create various kinds of dialogs. For example, we can create another procedure to pop up a notice dialog like the one shown in Figure 6.1:

```
option add *Notice*dismiss.text "Dismiss" widgetDefault
proc notice_show {mesg {icon "info"}} {
    set top [dialog_create Notice]
    set x [expr [winfo rootx .]+50]
    set y [expr [winfo rooty .]+50]
    wm geometry $top "+$x+$y"
    set info [dialog_info $top]
```

```
label $info.icon -bitmap $icon
pack $info.icon -side left -padx 8 -pady 8
label $info.mesg -text $mesg -wraplength 4i
pack $info.mesg -side right -expand yes -fill both \
    -padx 8 -pady 8
set cntls [dialog_controls $top]
button $cntls.dismiss -command "destroy $top"
pack $cntls.dismiss -pady 4
return $top
}
```

This procedure takes two arguments: a text message and a bitmap name. These are displayed in the information area at the top of the dialog. In Figure 6.1, for example, the notice dialog displays the `error` bitmap along with the `File not found` message. In this case, we made the bitmap name an optional argument. If it's not specified, the `info` bitmap is assumed by default.

We use the `dialog_create` procedure to create a dialog in class `Notice`, and we save its automatically generated name in the variable `top`. We want to make sure that the user sees this notice, so we position it near the main application window, using the `wm geometry` command, as discussed in Section 6.3.1.

We use the `dialog_info` procedure to determine the name of the information frame at the top of the dialog. We create two labels—one for the bitmap and another for the text message—and we pack them in place.

The control area at the bottom has a single Dismiss button. We use the `dialog_controls` procedure to determine the name of the control frame, and we create the button and pack it in place.

We use the `focus` command to assign the default keyboard focus for this toplevel widget. When the dialog appears on the desktop, the Dismiss button will have a special ring around it, indicating that it's receiving input from the keyboard. Instead of using the mouse, the user can press the space bar to select the button and dismiss the dialog.

Notice that instead of hard-coding the label for the Dismiss button, we soft-coded it, using the `option add` command. We gave this resource the lowest priority, `widgetDefault`. If we decide later on that we want to use a different label, we can supply a different resource value. For example, we could use the label `OK` instead of `Dismiss` by adding the following command to our application script:

```
option add *Notice*dismiss.text "OK" startupFile
```

Since this setting has a higher priority of `startupFile`, it takes precedence over `Dismiss`.

We can use our `notice_show` procedure whenever we need to pop up a message. For example, if we encounter an error opening a file, we can report the error like this:

```
if {[catch {open $file r} result] != 0} {
    notice_show $result error
}
```

The catch command attempts to execute the open command to open a file for reading. If anything goes wrong, it returns a nonzero status code, along with an error message in the result variable. The call to notice_show creates a notice dialog with the error icon and the error message and immediately returns. The program execution continues with the next statement, and the notice remains on the desktop until the user dismisses it.

6.5 Modal dialogs

Many dialogs can pop up on the desktop, and the user can choose to look at them or to ignore them. But some dialogs demand an immediate response from the user. For example, suppose that the user has clicked on an Exit button and that you want to confirm this action. You might pop up a dialog like the one shown in Figure 6.3. As long as this dialog is present, the user cannot do anything else in the application but must select either OK to exit the application or Cancel to continue. Dialogs like this temporarily lock the application in a different mode and are therefore called *modal dialogs*.

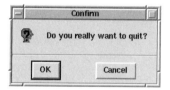

Figure 6.3. Confirmation dialog.

Many applications have lots of things that need to be confirmed. All of them can be handled quite easily if we create the following procedure:

```
option add *Confirm*icon.bitmap questhead widgetDefault
option add *Confirm*mesg.wrapLength 4i widgetDefault
proc confirm_ask {mesg {ok "OK"} {cancel "Cancel"}} {
    global confirmStatus
    set top [dialog_create Confirm]
    set info [dialog_info $top]
    label $info.icon
    pack $info.icon -side left -padx 8 -pady 8
    label $info.mesg -text $mesg
    pack $info.mesg -side right -expand yes -fill both \
        -padx 8 -pady 8
```

```
set cntls [dialog_controls $top]
button $cntls.ok -text $ok -command {set confirmStatus 1}
pack $cntls.ok -side left -expand yes
button $cntls.cancel -text $cancel -command {set confirmStatus 0}
pack $cntls.cancel -side left -expand yes
focus $cntls.ok
wm protocol $top WM_DELETE_WINDOW "$cntls.cancel invoke"
dialog_wait $top confirmStatus
destroy $top
return $confirmStatus
}
```

This procedure takes three arguments: the message presented to the user, the label for the OK button, and the label for the Cancel button. These last two arguments are optional. If they're not specified, the default labels are OK and Cancel.

Again, we use the dialog_create procedure to create a new dialog in class Confirm. In the information area at the top of the dialog, we display an icon and the message passed in to the procedure. We use dialog_info to determine the name of the information frame, and we create the two labels and pack them in place. Notice that we soft-code the -bitmap option for the icon, again by using an option add statement. That way, we can override the questhead bitmap with another bitmap to customize the look of an application. Notice also that we soft-code the wrap length for the message label to 4 inches. If the message is too long to fit on one line, the label will automatically wrap the text onto multiple lines so that the message width does not exceed 4 inches.

In the control area at the bottom of the dialog, we add the OK and Cancel buttons. Selecting the OK button sets confirmStatus to 1 (Boolean "yes"). Selecting Cancel sets it to 0 (Boolean "no"). So when the user has made a choice, confirmStatus will hold the result.

We assume that selecting OK is the likely response, so we assign keyboard focus to this button. If the user is wondering which option to pick, this sends a subtle hint that OK is the preferred choice. It also makes it easy for the user to choose OK simply by pressing the space bar.

The wm protocol command is extremely important for a modal dialog like this. Right now we'll explain what it does, and a little later in this section, we'll explain why it is so important. From time to time, the window manager communicates with an application by sending it protocol messages, and the wm protocol command says how this application should respond to a particular message. For example, many window managers provide a control menu in the title bar above a top-level window. The user can select the Close or Quit option from this menu to dismiss the window. When this happens, the window manager sends a WM_DELETE_WINDOW message to the application. Tk usually responds to this message by destroying the toplevel widget that received it.

Suppose that instead of clicking on our OK or Cancel buttons, the user selects Close or Quit from the control menu. The window will go away, but our confirmStatus variable will not be set. What choice did the user make? We can assume that if the user was afraid to answer the question, the intent was probably Cancel. We use the `wm protocol` command to intercept the `WM_DELETE_WINDOW` message and handle it by invoking the Cancel button. That way, the `confirmStatus` variable will be properly set.

The heart of the whole `confirm_ask` operation is the `dialog_wait` procedure. This procedure grabs the attention of the application and waits for the user to make a choice. The procedure will not return until the `confirmStatus` variable has been set. When this happens, the confirm dialog is no longer needed, so we destroy it and return a Boolean value representing the user's choice.

Returning to the example in Figure 6.3, we could use our `confirm_ask` procedure to confirm any attempt to exit an application. We replace the usual `exit` command with our own version. That way, we can use the `exit` command anywhere in the application, but the decision will always be confirmed:

```
rename exit tcl_exit
proc exit {{status 0}} {
    if {[confirm_ask "Do you really want to quit?"]} {
        tcl_exit $status
    }
}
```

We use the `rename` command to rename the usual `exit` command to `tcl_exit`, so we can still access it. Then we define our own `exit` command. Like the usual `exit` command, it takes an integer status code, which by default is 0. But our version uses `confirm_ask` to pop up a dialog and wait for the user's response. If the answer is "yes," we use the `tcl_exit` command to exit the application. Otherwise, we do nothing.

The *modal* part of our modal dialog is contained in the `dialog_wait` procedure:

```
proc dialog_wait {win varName} {
    dialog_safeguard $win

    set x [expr [winfo rootx .]+50]
    set y [expr [winfo rooty .]+50]
    wm geometry $win "+$x+$y"

    wm deiconify $win

    grab set $win

    vwait $varName

    grab release $win
    wm withdraw $win
}
```

This procedure takes two arguments: the toplevel widget for the dialog and the status variable that will be set when the user has made a choice. We want to make sure that the user sees this dialog, so we position it near the main application window, using the `wm geometry` command, as discussed in Section 6.3.1.

The dialog may be iconified or withdrawn from the desktop, so we use `wm deiconify` to make sure that it is visible. Then we set a grab. This forces all of the pointer events in the application to be directed to the toplevel widget, as we explained in Section 3.1.3. So it prevents the user from doing anything else before confirming the choice. The user may try to click on a button or bring up a menu on the main application window. But with the grab in place, it will look as though the user is clicking on an empty region of the dialog. By default, a grab affects only windows that are part of the same application, so the user can still interact with other applications on the desktop.

With the grab in place, we simply wait for the status variable to change, which means that the user has clicked on OK or Cancel. The vwait command will not return until the status variable has been set. While it is waiting, it sits in the event loop, processing events, so the user can still interact with the application. After all, we're waiting for the user to click on OK or Cancel! At some point, the user will click on a button, its command will be invoked, the status variable will be set, and the vwait command will return control.

At that point, we resume normal operation by releasing the grab. We use wm withdraw to hide the dialog without destroying it. In many cases, this is a better way to take down a dialog, and we'll explore this strategy more carefully in the next section.

Using grabs in an application is a little tricky and can sometimes lead to angry users reporting mysterious "bugs." Suppose the user sees the dialog shown in Figure 6.3. Instead of clicking on OK or Cancel, this user selects Close or Quit from the control menu in the title bar. Tk normally handles this by destroying the toplevel widget. This leaves us in the middle of an operation, stuck at the vwait command, waiting for the user to make a choice without any buttons left to choose! But we've already solved this problem. As you'll recall, we used the wm protocol command in the confirm_ask procedure. If the window is dismissed in this manner, the program will act as if the user had clicked on the Cancel button.

But suppose that instead of dismissing the window, the user iconifies it, or it simply gets lost under a pile of windows on the desktop. The user may not see the dialog, but the grab will remain in effect. The application won't respond, and many users will think that it has mysteriously locked up!

Whenever you introduce a grab, you must make sure that the grab window cannot get lost. In the dialog_wait procedure, we guard against this by calling the procedure dialog_safeguard to add a binding to the window:

```
bind modalDialog <ButtonPress> {
    wm deiconify %W
    raise %W
}
proc dialog_safeguard {win} {
    if {[lsearch [bindtags $win] modalDialog] < 0} {
        bindtags $win [linsert [bindtags $win] 0 modalDialog]
    }
}
```

We create a binding tag, modalDialog, and attach it to any toplevel widget acting as a modal dialog. Binding tags are used like this to add new behaviors to widgets, as we discussed in Section 3.5. Whenever the toplevel widget receives a ButtonPress event, it will automatically deiconify and raise itself up on the desktop. Normally, you would have to click on the background area of the modal dialog to trigger this binding. But remember, a grab is in place. When you click on any other window in the application, it is as if you're clicking on the modal dialog itself. So if the modal dialog gets lost or iconified, a button click on any other window will bring it back into view.

We use the `dialog_safeguard` procedure to add this binding tag to each modal dialog. The command `bindtags $win` returns the current list of binding tags for the window, and the `lsearch` command looks for `modalDialog` on the list. If it's not found, it is inserted at index 0 in the list. The `linsert` command builds a new list of binding tags, and this is assigned back to the window, using the `bindtags` command.

You may wonder why we used a separate binding tag instead of binding directly to the toplevel widget. Any behaviors added to the toplevel widget are automatically inherited by all of the widgets within it. So if we added this behavior directly to the toplevel widget, it would be triggered, for example, when the user clicked on the OK or Cancel button. In this case, the effect would be relatively harmless—the dialog would raise itself just before it's dismissed. But as a rule, it's better to avoid binding directly to a toplevel widget, unless you're adding menu accelerators.

6.6 Controlling access to dialogs

Dialogs come and go as needed in an application. Some, such as the notice dialog, appear only to display a message and are quickly dismissed. Others come and go many times, but each time they reappear, they retain the information they had when the user dismissed them. For example, the user may spend a few minutes finding a particular directory in a file-selection dialog and then dismiss the dialog. When the dialog reappears, it should display that same directory.

Although there are many kinds of dialogs, there are two strategies for controlling access to them. The difference between the two strategies boils down to whether a dialog retains its information between appearances.

6.6.1 Create/destroy strategy

When a dialog is created on the fly, it pops up on the desktop. When it is destroyed, it disappears from view. We can use this behavior to our advantage to control access to dialogs. We call this the *create/destroy strategy*. It may look familiar. We've already used it to handle the notice dialog described in Section 6.4. Here is another view of the notice dialog, with the important code in boldface type:

```
proc notice_show {mesg {icon "info"}} {
    set top [dialog_create Notice]
    ...
    set cntls [dialog_controls $top]
    button $cntls.dismiss -command "destroy $top"
    pack $cntls.dismiss -pady 4
```

```
      . . .
  }
```

The call to `dialog_create` creates a new toplevel widget and returns its name. We fill this toplevel with controls; when the program execution returns to the event loop and the application is brought up to date, the new dialog appears on the desktop. At some point, the user clicks on the Dismiss button, and the `destroy` command is executed, causing the toplevel to disappear from the desktop.

The create/destroy strategy works well when a dialog does not retain information between appearances. Each notice dialog, for example, appears only once. When it is dismissed, it is gone for good.

As another example, consider the "sticky-notes" application shown in Figure 6.4. When the user clicks on the notepad button, a new note dialog appears with the specified title. Many different notes can be posted like this, and messages can be added to the text area on each one. When a particular note is no longer needed, it can be discarded by clicking on its Delete button.

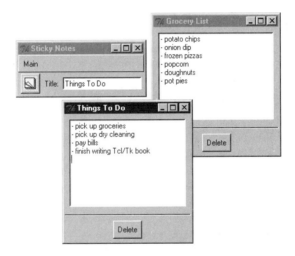

Figure 6.4. Sticky-notes application.

Each note dialog is created by the following procedure:

```
proc sticky_note {title} {
    set top [dialog_create Note]
    set info [dialog_info $top]
    text $info.text -width 30 -height 10
    pack $info.text -expand yes -fill both -padx 4 -pady 4
```

```
    focus $info.text
    set cntls [dialog_controls $top]
    button $cntls.delete -text "Delete" -command "destroy $top"
    pack $cntls.delete
    wm title $top $title
}
```

Again, you can see the create/destroy pattern: Each call to `dialog_create` creates a
new toplevel widget, and its built-in Delete button is set up to destroy it at some point. We
create a text widget to handle the note text, and we pack it into the information area.
Since this is a brand-new text widget, it will be empty. The user will probably want to
enter notes right away, so we assign the default keyboard focus to the text widget. We
finish the dialog by titling it with the argument passed in to this procedure.

All of the note dialogs are created the same way, but each one is independent of the
others. Many applications are designed to have separate but identical work areas like this.
For example, a drawing editor may let you bring up many different drawings, each in its
own editing window. A Web browser may let you load many different Web pages, each in
a separate viewing window. The create/destroy strategy works particularly well for managing identical work areas in applications like these.

6.6.2 Help from the window manager

Suppose the user becomes a "sticky-notes" fanatic, posting dozens of notes all over the
desktop. At some point, the user may feel that the desktop is too cluttered. The user may
want to hide the notes temporarily and bring them back only to get some needed information. But if the user deletes the notes, they're gone for good.

Instead of destroying a toplevel widget, we can ask the window manager to remove it
from the screen, or *withdraw* it. For example, the following procedure will hide all of the
notes in our sticky-notes application:

```
proc sticky_hide {} {
    global notepos
    foreach win [winfo children .] {
        if {[winfo class $win] == "Note"} {
            set notepos($win) [wm geometry $win]
            wm withdraw $win
        }
    }
}
```

This procedure uses `winfo children` to get a list of child widgets that belong to the
main window "." for this application. The list includes such widgets as `.mbar` and
`.title`, which are packed in the main window. The list also includes toplevel widgets,
such as `.dialog1`, `.dialog2`, ..., that were created by `dialog_create` to represent the
various notes. Since we set the class of each note dialog to `Note`, we can identify the notes
later on by looking for that class name. When we find a note, we use `wm geometry` to

query its current location on the desktop, and we save that information in the global `notepos` array. We'll need this later if we want the note to pop back up at the same location. Finally, we use `wm withdraw` to withdraw the note, thereby removing it from the desktop.

Even though a dialog is withdrawn, it still exists. All of its internal widgets also exist, and they retain their information. You can query their information, change their information, and even reconfigure widgets in the withdrawn state. The widgets continue to work as usual but without a visual representation.

When we want to bring the notes back to the desktop, we call the following procedure:

```
proc sticky_show {} {
    global notepos
    foreach win [winfo children .] {
        if {[winfo class $win] == "Note"} {
            if {[info exists notepos($win)]} {
                wm geometry $win $notepos($win)
            }
            wm deiconify $win
            raise $win
        }
    }
}
```

Again, we find the note dialogs by searching the main window for children in class `Note`. When we find a note, we make it visible by asking the window manager to *deiconify* it. This will restore the note from either a withdrawn state or an iconified state. We also raise the note, in case it's already on the desktop but buried under other windows.

Notice that we're careful to restore any geometry information that we stored earlier in the `notepos` array. This ensures that each note will pop back up at its previous location. Without this, some window managers will use their own policy to place each note as it reappears on the desktop.

6.6.3 Show/hide strategy

Instead of managing a dialog by creating it and destroying it, we can create it once and immediately withdraw it. When the user needs it, we can deiconify it; when the user is done with it, we can withdraw it again. We call this the *show/hide strategy* for managing dialogs. It is particularly useful when a dialog needs to retain information between appearances.

For example, suppose we add a Print... option to the main menu of our sticky-notes application. Selecting this option might bring up a printer dialog like the one shown in Figure 6.5. When the user clicks on the Print button, a summary of all existing notes is generated. The user can choose to route this output to a printer or to save it in a file.

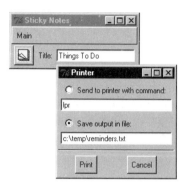

Figure 6.5. Sticky-notes application with a printer dialog.

Suppose the user has chosen to save output in a file and after spending a moment to enter the file name, is interrupted by a phone call. The user clicks on the Cancel button and creates another note during the phone conversation. Later, when trying to print the notes, the user will expect the printer dialog to reappear looking exactly as it had before. The user will be very irritated if the radiobutton must be adjusted or the file name entered again.

For things that have only one logical instance in the program, such as the printer dialog, it is best to use the show/hide strategy. That way, the dialog will naturally retain its state as it comes and goes on the desktop. With the show/hide strategy, a dialog is created only once, so it's usually convenient to give the dialog a name that is easy to remember. For example, if we want to create a printer dialog, we could call a procedure like this:

```
printer_create .print
```

This will create a new toplevel widget called .print and will fill it with other widgets so that it looks like the dialog shown in Figure 6.5. This procedure is implemented as follows:

```
proc printer_create {top} {
    global prInfo
    set top [dialog_create Printer $top]
    set info [dialog_info $top]
    radiobutton $info.printer \
        -text "Send to printer with command: " \
        -variable prInfo($top-where) -value "printer"
    entry $info.printerCmd
    radiobutton $info.file \
        -text "Save output in file: " \
        -variable prInfo($top-where) -value "file"
    entry $info.fileName
```

```
grid $info.printer -row 0 -sticky w
grid $info.printerCmd -row 1 -sticky ew
grid rowconfigure $info 2 -minsize 6
grid $info.file -row 3 -sticky w
grid $info.fileName -row 4 -sticky ew
$info.printerCmd insert 0 "lpr"
$info.fileName insert 0 "output.txt"
$info.printer invoke
bind $info.printerCmd <FocusIn> "$info.printer invoke"
bind $info.fileName <FocusIn> "$info.file invoke"
set cntls [dialog_controls $top]
button $cntls.ok -command "set prInfo($top-status) 1"
pack $cntls.ok -side left -expand yes
focus $cntls.ok
button $cntls.cancel -command "set prInfo($top-status) 0"
pack $cntls.cancel -side left -expand yes
wm protocol $top WM_DELETE_WINDOW "$cntls.cancel invoke"
wm withdraw $top
return $top
}
```

We call `dialog_create` to create a generic dialog in class `Printer`, using the name in the `top` argument. Then we find the information area at the top of the dialog and fill it with the radiobuttons and entries needed for the two printing options. We use the `grid` command to arrange these widgets. This makes it easy to add some padding between the two options by inserting an empty row with a fixed size.

The radiobuttons for each printer dialog need a status variable to wire them together. We have one global `prInfo` array for all of the variables related to printer dialogs, and we use a different slot `prInfo($top-where)` for each pair of radiobuttons. This slot is parameterized by the name `$top`, so it will be unique for each printer dialog. This guarantees that the radiobuttons in each printer dialog will be wired to each other but not to another printer dialog or to anything else in the application.

We fill the two entry widgets with their default values, and we invoke the `printer` radiobutton to make it the active choice. We also add bindings to the entry widgets so that whenever they receive focus and the user starts to edit their text, their corresponding radiobutton is selected automatically.

We find the control area at the bottom of the dialog, and we add the OK and Cancel buttons to it. We assign keyboard focus to the OK button, indicating that it is the more likely choice.

Notice that before we return, we withdraw the dialog, using `wm withdraw`. This ensures that even though the dialog has been created, it will remain hidden until it is needed. This statement can appear anywhere within the procedure or anywhere within the program, as long as it is executed before we return to the event loop and update the application. If it is left out, the printer dialog will accidentally appear when the application starts up, before the user has requested any printing.

Our printer dialog should be a modal dialog. Once it appears, the user should be prevented from doing anything else before confirming or canceling the Print... operation. To make this a modal dialog, we follow the pattern shown in Section 6.5 for the confirm dialog. As in the confirm dialog, the OK and Cancel buttons for our printer dialog set a status variable, indicating the user's choice. We use the variable prInfo($top-status) to represent this choice, so that each printer dialog has its own status variable. Also, as in the confirm dialog, we set the WM_DELETE_WINDOW protocol so that any attempt to dismiss the window is equivalent to clicking on the Cancel button.

We use the following procedure to pop up the printer dialog and handle the response:

```
proc printer_print {top cmd {ok "Print"} {cancel "Cancel"}} {
    global prInfo
    set cntls [dialog_controls $top]
    $cntls.ok configure -text $ok
    $cntls.cancel configure -text $cancel
    dialog_wait $top prInfo($top-status)
    if {$prInfo($top-status)} {
        switch $prInfo($top-where) {
            printer {
                ... execute cmd and send the result to the printer ...
            }
            file {
                ... execute cmd and save the result in a file ...
            }
        }
    }
}
```

This procedure requires two arguments: the name of the printer dialog and a command that generates the text to print. We also allow the labels for the OK and Cancel buttons to be supplied as optional arguments. If they're not specified, the default labels are Print and Cancel. The first order of business is to find these buttons and update their labels accordingly.

Next, we use the dialog_wait procedure to set a grab on the dialog and wait for the status variable prInfo($top-status) to change. Clicking on the OK button sets this variable to 1, and clicking on Cancel sets it to 0. When either of these buttons has been selected, the dialog_wait procedure returns control, and execution continues with the if statement.

If the user confirms the Print... operation, we evaluate the command string $cmd and route the result accordingly. The variable prInfo($top-where) contains the current selection from the radiobuttons. If it has the value printer, the result string is fed to the command in the printerCmd entry. If it has the value file, the result is saved in the file identified by the fileName entry.

The show/hide strategy is handled in the dialog_wait procedure described in Section 6.5. Here it is again, with the important parts in boldface type:

```
proc dialog_wait {win varName} {
    ...
    wm deiconify $win
    grab set $win
    vwait $varName
    grab release $win
    wm withdraw $win
}
```

We use the `wm deiconify` command to show the dialog on the desktop. The grab is set, and we wait for the user to choose one of the control buttons. Finally, we use the `wm withdraw` command to hide the dialog until the next time it is needed.

Having created these procedures, it takes just a few lines of code to add a printer dialog to an application. Returning to our sticky-notes application, for example, we can see how the printer dialog is managed. Following is an excerpt from the `efftcl/apps/sticky` script. It creates a printer dialog named `.print` and builds the main menu for the application:

```
...
printer_create .print
frame .mbar -borderwidth 1 -relief raised
pack .mbar -fill x
menubutton .mbar.main -text "Main" -menu .mbar.main.m
pack .mbar.main -side left
menu .mbar.main.m
.mbar.main.m add command -label "Show Notes" -command sticky_show
.mbar.main.m add command -label "Hide Notes" -command sticky_hide
.mbar.main.m add command -label "Print..." -command {
    printer_print .print sticky_print
}
.mbar.main.m add separator
.mbar.main.m add command -label "Exit" -command exit
...
```

When the user selects the Print... option, we use `printer_print` to activate the dialog and handle the response. If the user clicks on the Print button, the `sticky_print` command is executed to generate a summary of the notes. The command simply scans through all of the notes and builds a long string of information, as follows:

```
proc sticky_print {} {
    set all ""
    foreach win [winfo children .] {
        if {[winfo class $win] == "Note"} {
            set title [wm title $win]
            set info [dialog_info $win]
            set note [string trim [$info.text get 1.0 end]]
            append all "NOTE: $title\n$note\n\n"
```

```
            }
        }
        return $all
    }
```

We find all of the notes as we did in Section 6.6.2, by searching for children of the main window that have the class name `Note`. We append a summary of each note to the `all` variable, including the note title and its text. We use the `wm title` command to query the title back from the note window, and we use the `get` operation of the text widget to query its text. The note text may have blank lines at the top or bottom, so we use the `string trim` operation to trim these off.

The `all` string is limited only by the amount of memory available to store it. It could be a few lines of output or a few megabytes of output. Regardless, the `sticky_print` procedure returns this string, and the `printer_print` procedure captures the result and routes it either to a printer or to a file, using the option the user selected.

6.7 Unmanaged windows

In rare cases, you may create a top-level window that you don't want the user to move, resize, or iconify. You can tell the window manager to ignore a top-level window, leaving it *unmanaged* on the desktop. If you do this, the window manager won't wrap a decorative border around the window, so the user won't be able to resize it or reposition it. For ordinary dialogs, this would be a disaster. But if you're trying to pop up something, such as a balloon help window, for example, this behavior is quite useful. In this section, we explore two examples of unmanaged windows, showing how they are used in real-life applications.

6.7.1 Introductory placard

In Section 7.8, we'll talk about a calendar application called the Electric Secretary. When this application starts up, it takes a few seconds to connect to an appointment server. While the application is loading, the introductory placard shown in Figure 6.6 pops up on the middle of the screen. This lets the user know that the application has started but that it's busy initializing itself. When the application is finally ready, the placard is removed, and the main window appears as usual.

A simple placard can be displayed as follows. First, we withdraw the main window and create a separate toplevel to represent the placard:

```
wm withdraw .
toplevel .placard -borderwidth 4 -relief raised
wm overrideredirect .placard 1
```

Figure 6.6. Introductory placard for the Electric Secretary application.

We set the `overrideredirect` flag for the placard, causing the window manager to ignore this window. It won't get a decorative border, so it looks more like the splash screens that you see in Windows 95 applications.

Since the window manager is ignoring the window and the user can't reposition it, we must be careful to position it ourselves. We want the user to see it right away, so we center it on the screen, using the technique shown in Section 6.3.1:

```
after idle {
    update idletasks
    set xmax [winfo screenwidth .placard]
    set ymax [winfo screenheight .placard]
    set x0 [expr ($xmax-[winfo reqwidth .placard])/2]
    set y0 [expr ($ymax-[winfo reqheight .placard])/2]
    wm geometry .placard "+$x0+$y0"
}
```

We pack in a series of labels to display the necessary information:

```
label .placard.info \
    -text "http://www.awl.com/cp/efftcl/efftcl.html"
pack .placard.info -side bottom -fill x
catch {.placard.info configure \
    -font -*-helvetica-medium-r-normal--*-100-*}
set imh [image create photo \
    -file [file join $env(EFFTCL_LIBRARY) images esec6.gif]]
label .placard.icon -image $imh
pack .placard.icon -side left -padx 8 -pady 8
label .placard.title -text "Calendar and\nAppointment Manager"
pack .placard.title -fill x -padx 8 -pady 8
catch {.placard.title configure \
    -font -*-helvetica-bold-o-normal--*-140-*}
label .placard.status -text "Connecting to server..."
pack .placard.status -fill x -pady 8
catch {.placard.status configure \
    -font -*-helvetica-medium-r-normal--*-120-*}
```

We use special fonts for some of the labels. However, we cannot be sure that these fonts will be available on all displays. Some X terminals are notorious for having only the bare minimum fonts installed. If we configure the -font option directly when a widget is created and if a font isn't available, the command will fail and the program will abort. Instead, we configure the -font option with a separate statement, and we use the catch command to ignore any errors. If a font isn't available, we'll get the default font for the widget. If you're using the latest release of Tcl/Tk, there are other strategies for handling fonts, as we'll see in Section 9.1.4.

At this point, our placard is ready to be displayed on the screen. But if we simply go on setting up the rest of the program, the user won't see the placard. We must include an update command to flush our changes out to the screen:

```
update
...set up the rest of the application...
```

When we're done setting up the rest of the application, we take down the placard and pop up the main window:

```
update
destroy .placard
wm deiconify .
```

We use another update to force the main window to be packed and brought up to date. This will avoid any size changes or flashing when the main window appears on the screen. Then we take down the placard by destroying it, and we bring back the main window by deiconifying it. This is the last command in our script, so the program drops into the event loop and begins responding to the user.

6.7.2   Balloon help

Many applications have toolbars like the one we created in Section 3.4.2. Usually, the meaning of each tool icon is obvious only to the authors of the program. Everyone else needs a little more explanation, especially when they're first using the program.

In this section, we'll create a simple help facility that works with any Tk widget. If you rest the mouse pointer on a widget and wait for a few seconds, some help information will appear. In Figure 6.7, for example, a help message has appeared below the paint can icon in our draw application. We call this a *balloon help* facility because the message pops up in a small window near the widget, making it look like a cartoon balloon on a comic strip.

The balloon window is an ordinary toplevel widget, with one label for the arrow icon and another for the help text. However, we want this window to look like a part of the main program, not like a separate dialog, so we use the wm overrideredirect command to suppress the window manager's decorative border.

The code used to create the window looks like this:

Figure 6.7. Balloon help appears below the paint can.

```
option add *Balloonhelp*background white widgetDefault
option add *Balloonhelp*foreground black widgetDefault
option add *Balloonhelp.info.wrapLength 3i widgetDefault
option add *Balloonhelp.info.justify left widgetDefault
option add *Balloonhelp.info.font \
    -*-lucida-medium-r-normal-sans-*-120-* widgetDefault
toplevel .balloonhelp -class Balloonhelp \
    -background black -borderwidth 1 -relief flat
label .balloonhelp.arrow -anchor nw \
    -bitmap @[file join $env(EFFTCL_LIBRARY) images arrow.xbm]
pack .balloonhelp.arrow -side left -fill y
label .balloonhelp.info
pack .balloonhelp.info -side left -fill y
wm overrideredirect .balloonhelp 1
wm withdraw .balloonhelp
```

We start by soft-coding most of the configuration options for the balloon window. By default, the balloon will have black writing on a white background, and the `info` widget will display the help message in a Lucida font. If the message is longer than 3 inches, it will wrap onto multiple left-justified lines. Since we use the lowest priority—`widgetDefault`—for each of these settings, you can override them later on to customize the balloon help facility for different applications.

We create a toplevel widget named `.balloonhelp` and give it the class `Balloonhelp` so that our soft-coded resources will take effect. We want this window to stand out on the desktop, so we give it black border that is 1 pixel wide. We create a label for the arrow icon and another for the help message, and we pack both of them in on the left side of the balloon window.

Finally, we ask the window manager to ignore this window by setting its overrideredirect flag to 1, and we make it invisible by withdrawing it from the desktop. When we need it later on, we will fill in the help message, place it below a particular widget, and deiconify it to bring it up.

Now that we have a balloon window, we need to have some widgets that use it. If we look into our draw application, we can find the code that creates the two color selectors at the bottom of the toolbar:

```
...
colormenu_create .tools.fill -image [draw_bitmap paint]
pack .tools.fill -side bottom -padx 4 -pady 4
colormenu_create .tools.line -image [draw_bitmap pen]
pack .tools.line -side bottom -padx 4 -pady 4
...
```

Each call to colormenu_create creates a menubutton and a pop-up menu that can be used as a color selector. We'll see how this procedure is implemented in Section 8.2.3, but for now, we can treat .tools.fill and .tools.line like any other widget.

We can create a procedure called balloonhelp_for to attach balloon help to these widgets. We'll call this procedure with the name of each widget and its help message, as follows:

```
balloonhelp_for .tools.fill \
    "Fill color:\nClick to select a new color"
balloonhelp_for .tools.line
    "Pen color:\nClick to select a new color"
```

The help message can be as long as we want, but it should be brief and to the point. After all, if your users like to read, they will read the manual! If the help message is too long to fit on one line, it will automatically wrap onto multiple lines, as we described earlier. We can also force line breaks at any point by including the newline character (\n) in the message. In this example, we added newlines to make Fill color: and Pen color: look like headings above the help messages.

The procedure balloonhelp_for looks like this:

```
proc balloonhelp_for {win mesg} {
    global bhInfo
    set bhInfo($win) $mesg
    bind $win <Enter> {balloonhelp_pending %W}
    bind $win <Leave> {balloonhelp_cancel}
}
```

Here, we do two things. First, we save the help message in the bhInfo array. We'll need the help message later on when we pop up the balloon window for this widget. Next, we bind to the Enter and Leave events so that we'll know when the mouse pointer is touching this widget.

When the pointer moves onto the widget, we'll get an Enter event, and the bind facility will call balloonhelp_pending with the name of the widget in place of %W. If the pointer remains on the widget, the balloon window will appear shortly thereafter.

When the pointer moves off the widget, we'll get a Leave event, and the bind facility will call balloonhelp_cancel. This will either cancel the effect of balloonhelp_pending or take down the balloon window if it has already appeared.

The procedure balloonhelp_pending looks like this:

```
proc balloonhelp_pending {win} {
    global bhInfo
    balloonhelp_cancel
    set bhInfo(pending) [after 1500 [list balloonhelp_show $win]]
}
```

We simply cancel any pending balloon help and set things up so that balloonhelp_show will be called 1.5 seconds later to pop up the balloon window. We use list to format the command for after, as we discussed in Section 3.1.5. We save the result of the after command in the slot bhInfo(pending), so we can use this later in balloonhelp_cancel to cancel the request.

The procedure balloonhelp_cancel looks like this:

```
proc balloonhelp_cancel {} {
    global bhInfo
    if {[info exists bhInfo(pending)]} {
        after cancel $bhInfo(pending)
        unset bhInfo(pending)
    }
    wm withdraw .balloonhelp
}
```

If we can find the slot bhInfo(pending), it will contain an identifier for the pending balloonhelp_show command. We cancel this command and delete the slot. We also withdraw the balloon window in case it's already sitting on the desktop.

When the procedure balloonhelp_show is eventually called, it pops up the balloon window displaying the help message for a particular widget. It looks like this:

```
proc balloonhelp_show {win} {
    global bhInfo
    if {$bhInfo(active)} {
        .balloonhelp.info configure -text $bhInfo($win)
        set x [expr [winfo rootx $win]+10]
        set y [expr [winfo rooty $win]+[winfo height $win]]
        wm geometry .balloonhelp +$x+$y
        wm deiconify .balloonhelp
        raise .balloonhelp
    }
    unset bhInfo(pending)
}
```

We find the help message for the widget named $win in the array bhInfo, and we load it into the label in the balloon window. We find the position of the widget on the root window and offset it slightly so that the balloon window will appear below and a little to the right of the widget. The winfo rootx and winfo rooty commands return the coordinates for the upper-left corner of the widget, so we offset to the right by 10 pixels and down by the full height of the widget. We use wm geometry to place the balloon window at these coordinates, and we deiconify it. Since the window is unmanaged, we must explicitly raise the window to make sure that it sits on top of other windows on the desktop.

Once your users have mastered your program, they may want to disable the balloon help messages. We can use a Boolean variable, bhInfo(active), to control this. Initially, this variable is set to 1, and balloon help is active. If we set it to 0, the balloonhelp_show procedure will still be called, but it won't display the balloon window.

Instead of documenting this variable as a "feature" of the package, we create the following procedure to control balloon help:

```
set bhInfo(active) 1
proc balloonhelp_control {state} {
    global bhInfo
    if {$state} {
        set bhInfo(active) 1
    } else {
        balloonhelp_cancel
        set bhInfo(active) 0
    }
}
```

We can use this procedure in the Help menu of our draw application to turn balloon help on or off:

```
menubutton .mbar.help -text "Help" -menu .mbar.help.m
pack .mbar.help -side right

menu .mbar.help.m
.mbar.help.m add command -label "Hide Balloon Help" -command {
    set mesg [.mbar.help.m entrycget 1 -label]
    if {[string match "Hide*" $mesg]} {
        balloonhelp_control 0
        .mbar.help.m entryconfigure 1 -label "Show Balloon Help"
    } else {
        balloonhelp_control 1
        .mbar.help.m entryconfigure 1 -label "Hide Balloon Help"
    }
}
```

We create Hide Balloon Help as the first entry on the Help menu. When you select this entry, it calls `balloonhelp_control` to turn off balloon help and then changes its label to Show Balloon Help. When you select this entry again, it calls `balloonhelp_control` to turn on balloon help and then changes its label back to Hide Balloon Help.

Chapter 7
Interacting with Other Programs

So far, we have talked about writing individual programs. In this chapter, we'll show how Tcl/Tk can interact with other programs. External applications can be called to perform tasks, and applications can be split into cooperating front-end and back-end processes. These processes can run on the same computer or across a network.

If you're wondering why all of this is important, consider the tale of two GUI programmers, shown in Figure 7.1. The Sad GUI Programmer mixes his GUI code in with the rest of the application. When someone finds a bug in the program, he gets blamed for it; if the program crashes, the GUI is an immediate suspect. The Happy GUI Programmer, on the other hand, uses the ideas described in this chapter. He has a front-end GUI process controlling a separate back-end application. When someone finds a bug in the application program, he tells the back-end guys to fix it and goes to lunch.

7.1 Executing other programs

Let's start by looking at how Tcl/Tk can be used to drive other programs. Suppose your application has an extensive online help system. You might want to minimize the storage space needed for all of the help files by installing them in compressed form. On UNIX systems, you can compress the help files by using the `compress` program, and you can display a compressed file by using the `zcat` program, which prints the original file to standard output.

Now suppose that we want to display one of these help files in a Tcl/Tk application. We can use the `textdisplay` procedures developed in Chapter 5 to display the help text, but how do we decompress it and read it in? We can use the `exec` command to execute the

Figure 7.1. A tale of two GUI programmers.

Epilogue

❏ While the application guys were fixing their bugs, the Happy GUI Programmer wrote several profitable applications and was generously rewarded by his employer.

❏ The Happy GUI Programmer's manager won several prestigious quality awards and went on to lead a large division of the company.

❏ The Sad GUI Programmer learned to write two-process GUIs and eventually retired happily to a small cottage in the country.

❏ The application guys are still trying to figure out what's wrong.

Figure 7.1, continued.

zcat program from within our Tcl/Tk application. The exec command executes another program and returns its standard output as a Tcl result string. If the program exits with a nonzero status code, or fails, the exec command returns an error.

Implementing an online help system with compressed files boils down to a few lines of code:

```
set help [textdisplay_create "On-line Help"]
set info [exec zcat overview.Z]
textdisplay_append $help $info
```

First, we use the textdisplay_create procedure to create a text-display dialog with the title On-line Help. This procedure returns the name of the new dialog. We'll need this name when we want to refer to the dialog, so we store it in a variable called help. Next, we use the exec command to execute the zcat program for a help file called overview.Z. This returns the entire contents of that file, which we store in a variable called info. (This may be few lines or several megabytes of information. Tcl won't complain unless your computer runs out of memory to store the information.) Finally, we call the textdisplay_append procedure to load the information into the help dialog.

7.1.1 Execution pipelines

Many UNIX programs are designed to work together. The output from one program can be fed to the input of another. For example, suppose that our help files are not plain text but instead are in the nroff format used by UNIX manual pages. Furthermore, they are compressed. We can use the zcat program to decompress them and feed the output to the nroff program, which formats the text. The nroff program inserts some control characters to handle bold and italic text, but we can strip these out by feeding its output to the colcrt program. The result of all this will be a very long string of help information that we can display in our online help window.

The exec command supports the execution of several programs in a pipeline. Programs are separated in the exec command by the pipe "|" symbol, indicating that the output of one program feeds the input of the next. We could modify our help system to display compressed, nroff-format files, like this:

```
set help [textdisplay_create "On-line Help"]
set info [exec zcat eccsman.Z | nroff -man | colcrt]
textdisplay_append $help $info "typewriter"
```

Again, we use the textdisplay_create procedure to create a help window. This time, instead of executing the zcat program by itself, we put it in a pipeline along with nroff and colcrt. All three of these programs operate on the help file, producing the result that we store in the info variable. Finally, we call textdisplay_append to display the help text. We add the "typewriter" argument so that the text will be displayed in a constant-width font, as is customary for manual pages.

7.1.2 Building commands and handling errors

Now that you understand how the exec command works, let's use it in a more complicated example. Suppose that we have an application with a print function, as in Figure 7.2. We've already explained how the printer dialog box is constructed (Section 6.6.3), so we'll skip the details here and concentrate on the mechanism that is used to do the printing.

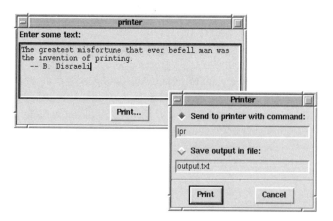

Figure 7.2. Printing a bit of text. We use the exec command on the lpr program to send the output to the printer.

We can execute a UNIX program such as `lpr` to handle the printing. For example, we can use the following command to print a simple message:

```
exec lpr << "The greatest misfortune that ever befell man was
the invention of printing.
-- B. Disraeli"
```

The `<<` characters redirect the string to the standard input of the `lpr` program, which then routes the string to a printer.

But for the program shown in Figure 7.2, we don't want to hard-code the `lpr` program or the message. Instead, we'll handle things in a generic way. Recall that we set up the `printer_print` procedure to take a command as one of its arguments. When you click on the Print button, the `printer_print` procedure executes this command to get some text and then routes the text to the printer. In this example, the command will return the text from the text widget in the main window. But you can pass any command in to the `printer_print` procedure, so you can use this dialog to print things from any application. And you can change the printer program in the dialog, so you can route your output to different printers.

In order to do all of this, we need to execute a command within `printer_print`, like this:

```
exec program << [command]
```

Here, *program* is the printing program from the entry widget on the printer dialog, and *command* is the command that you pass in to `printer_print`. For a particular printing task, we can substitute in the *program* and the *command* and build a printing command that looks just like the previous one. Our `printer_print` procedure uses the following code to build a printing command:

```
set print "exec [$info.printerCmd get] << \[$cmd\]"
```

If you look back at the `printer_create` procedure in Section 6.6.3, you'll see that the entry widget containing the print program is `$info.printerCmd`. So we use the command `[$info.printerCmd get]` to get the contents of this widget. Also, the `cmd` variable contains the command passed in to `printer_print`. We substitute these things into the `exec` command string, building a command and storing it in the `print` variable. We'll use this command to do the printing.

Notice that we escaped the brackets around `$cmd` with a backslash, so they will appear in the final `exec` command, as we showed earlier. That way, we will execute the *command* string and direct its output into the *program* for `exec`. Whenever you build up a code fragment like this, you run into the following problem: There are some things that you want to substitute when you build the command and others that you want to substitute later, when you execute the command. You can put backslashes in to handle this, as we did, but this can be quite confusing.

There is another way to build up the printing command, without the backslashes. We can use the `format` command to substitute parameters into the command string, like this:

```
set print [format {
    exec %s << [%s]
} [$info.printerCmd get] $cmd]
```

The first argument to the `format` command is a template for the string that we're building. Within this template, each `%s` marks the spot where a parameter will be substituted. The first `%s` will be replaced with the result from `[$info.printerCmd get]`; the second, with the value from `$cmd`.

Once we've built up the printing command, we can execute it to handle the actual printing. If anything goes wrong, the `exec` command will return an error. We can use the `catch` command to execute our printing command and catch any errors that might result. So the code within `printer_print` that does the printing looks like this:

```
if {[catch $print result] != 0} {
    notice_show $result error
} elseif {[string trim $result] != ""} {
    notice_show $result info
} else {
    notice_show "Document printed" info
}
```

The `catch` command executes our printing command, `$print`, and returns its status code. If the status code is nonzero, something went wrong. For example, the `lpr` program could return an "unknown printer" error. In that case, the `result` variable contains the error message `"unknown printer"`, and we use the `notice_show` procedure developed in Section 6.4 to display that message with the `error` bitmap.

Even if the printing program executes successfully, it could return some useful information. For example, the `lpr` program might return the message `"printer request is lp-210"`. In that case, the status code will be zero, and again, the `result` variable will contain the message. We pop up a notice dialog to display that message with the `info` bitmap. Of course, even if the program doesn't issue any diagnostic message, we'll display the message `"Document printed"` to indicate that the job has been printed.

Note that in addition to using `exec` as we have here, we can use the `open` command to execute other programs. We'll cover that approach in the sections that follow.

7.2 Collecting output from long-running programs

Using `exec` is fine for short-lived programs that produce a small amount of output, but for long-running programs, it suffers from two problems.

- Your program will block, resuming its execution only after the program running under `exec` has finished.

- When the program running under `exec` has finished, the output of the program will be returned to you in one chunk.

The first issue is very serious when writing a graphical user interface, since no event processing takes place while you are waiting for the subprocess to complete. In other words, your program won't be responsive to the mouse or the keyboard, and its windows won't refresh themselves properly when you cover and uncover them. This is both ugly and confusing to the user, who may conclude that your program has died.

The second problem is an issue with programs that run for a long time and produce periodic output. For example, the Point-to-Point Protocol (PPP) has become a popular way of establishing an Internet connection via dialup modems. On many Linux systems, the program pppstats is used to monitor the PPP connection and to print statistics about the throughput of the dialup link. When the program is running, it updates its status information every so often by printing a line of information containing statistics on the number of packets sent and received, the number of errors, and the input and output throughput in bits per second. Its output looks like this:

```
$ pppstats
      in   pack  comp uncomp    err |    out   pack  comp uncomp    ip
 1397955   1500   726    577      0 | 231377   1518   506    777   235
   15792     19    15      4      0 |  12151     17    11      6     0
   14376     20    15      5      0 |  15118     20    11      9     0
   14966     18    12      6      0 |  12134     16    10      6     0
   14273     17    14      3      0 |  10630     17    12      5     0
   15824     19    14      5      0 |  12243     20    12      8     0
   ...
```

This program is a good candidate for a graphical front end. We can read its output, filter out everything but the in and out columns, and display these values in a line chart.

The pppstats program runs forever, so we can't just use exec and wait for it to finish. And even if pppstats did terminate, we would get its output all at once instead of getting it a little at a time as it becomes available.

To handle the output properly, we must use the open command in place of exec. Normally, the open command opens a file and returns its file handle. But it can also execute a process and return a file handle for its input/output. So you can read from or write to the process as if it were an ordinary file. To do this, you simply replace the usual file name with an execution pipeline that starts with the pipe "|" symbol, like this:

```
open "|pppstats" "r"
```

The usual open command options apply to processes as well as to files. Thus we can open the process for reading ("r"), for writing ("w"), or for reading and writing ("r+"). In this case, we've opened the pppstats program for reading, so we can monitor its standard output.

Once we've started the subprocess, we need to know when it has output available. Remember, the pppstats program prints a line of information every so often. We can use the fileevent command to know when the output has arrived. The fileevent command is like the bind command in Tk, but it works with file handles. It registers a script with the event loop; when a file handle becomes readable or writable, it executes the script to handle that event.

For example, we can use the following command to handle each line of output from `pppstats`:

```
fileevent $fid readable "get_samples $fid"
```

Whenever the file `$fid` becomes readable, the command `get_samples $fid` is executed to handle the data.

Now let's look at `get_samples`:

```
proc get_samples {fid} {
    if {[gets $fid line] >= 0} {
        if {[scan $line "%d %*d %*d %*d %*d | %d" in out] == 2} {
            pppmon_add $in $out
        } elseif {[lindex $line 0] == "in"} {
            gets $fid line     ;# skip cumulative totals
        }
    } else {
        close $fid
    }
}
```

This procedure takes one parameter, which will be the file handle returned when we opened the `pppstats` program. Note that since the value of `$fid` is stored as part of the command, we can avoid having to access the file handle through a global variable.

The first thing the procedure does is read a line of text and check for end-of-file. If the `gets` command returns a negative number, the `pppstats` program has terminated. Detecting this isn't really necessary for our demo program (`pppstats` won't exit unless it has a bug), but it's good form, and it's required when a subprocess is expected to exit at some point.

Once we have read the line of output, processing is simple. If the first word of the line is `"in"`, we have received the header line, and we skip it. Otherwise, we have received a line of data. We use the `scan` command to extract the data from the first and sixth columns (the input and output data transfer rates), and we call the `pppmon_add` procedure to plot it. There's nothing special about using `scan`—we could just as easily have used `regexp`, `lindex`, or any of the other string-manipulation commands to extract the two fields.

Sometimes you can use your knowledge of the invoked program to simplify your processing—especially if you wrote the invoked program! For example, if you knew for certain that `pppstats` prints its header only once, you could add a couple of `gets` statements to skip over the header lines, like this:

```
set fid [open "| pppstats" "r"]
gets $fid ;# eat header line
gets $fid ;# eat cumulative total line
fileevent $fid readable "get_samples $fid"
```

If you wrote `pppstats` or if you have the source code for it, you might even modify it to work this way. Unfortunately, `pppstats` was designed to be run from a terminal, so it repeats the header every so often, and we are forced to work around it.

Using some of the concepts we discussed in Chapter 4, it is a simple matter to write a plotting routine to draw a line chart on a canvas. We won't show the plotting code here, but it is contained in the file `efftcl/apps/pppmon`, which can be obtained from the Web site mentioned on page xiv. When you run this program, it produces a nice PPP monitor, as shown in Figure 7.3.

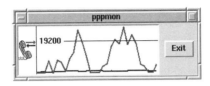

Figure 7.3. Monitoring PPP output by creating a pipe to `pppstats`.

7.3 Driving other programs without temporary files

In the same way that we can open programs for reading, we can also open programs for writing. We open the pipe in "write" mode by changing the access parameter to `"w"`, like this:

```
set fid [open "|program" "w"]
```

Anything written to the file handle `$fid` will be sent to the standard input of *program*.

As an example, suppose you're writing an electronic mail (e-mail) program like the one shown in Figure 7.4. You fill in an e-mail address, a subject line, and a message, and then click on the Send Message button to send out the mail message.

On UNIX systems, you can use the `mail` and `sendmail` programs to send the mail. You might be tempted to write the mail message to a temporary file and then execute `sendmail`, feeding it the file. But with the pipe facility in Tcl, things are much simpler. You can use the `open` command to execute the `sendmail` program and then write the message directly to its standard input. For example, suppose we handle this with a procedure called `email_send`:

```
proc email_send {to from cc subject text} {
    set fid [open "| /usr/lib/sendmail -oi -t" "w"]
    puts $fid "To: $to"
    if {[string length $from] > 0} {
        puts $fid "From: $from"
    }
    if {[string length $cc] > 0} {
        puts $fid "Cc: $cc"
    }
    puts $fid "Subject: $subject"
```

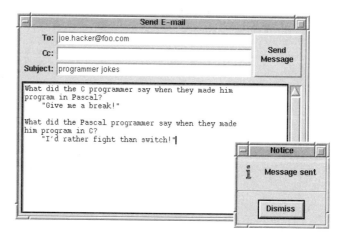

Figure 7.4. Sending mail by creating a pipe to `sendmail`.

```
    puts $fid "Date: [clock format [clock seconds]]"
    puts $fid ""   ;# sendmail terminates header with blank line
    puts $fid $text
    close $fid
}
```

This procedure takes five arguments: e-mail addresses for the recipient and the sender, a comma-separated list of e-mail addresses for anyone else who should get the message, the subject line, and the body of the message. We open the `sendmail` program and write out the message header and its body. When we close the pipe, `sendmail` sends the mail message and terminates.

Notice that we didn't put any error checking in this routine. Since this is a fairly generic procedure, we didn't want to add any application-specific error reporting. That would make it difficult to reuse this procedure in other applications. So there is no point in catching the errors from the `open` or `close` commands. Instead, it is better to let the errors filter back up to the calling routine and handle them there with a single `catch` command. (This is one of the advantages of Tcl's exception-style error reporting—intermediate layers of software can safely defer error handling to calling routines.)

For example, the e-mail application shown in Figure 7.4 uses the following bit of code to send the mail message:

```
    ...
    set cmd {email_send $to $from $cc $subject $text}
    if {[catch $cmd result] != 0} {
        notice_show "ERROR:\n$result" error
```

```
    } else {
        notice_show "Message sent"
    }
```

The `catch` command catches any error that occurs within the `email_send` procedure. If an error is encountered, we pop up a notice dialog to report it. Otherwise, we pop up a notice saying that the message was sent.

7.4 Working around buffering problems

If you are reading output from a program, you may find that it comes in large chunks instead of a little at a time. Many programs keep their output in a buffer and flush it only when it is full. This makes the programs much more efficient, but it causes many headaches when you want to monitor the output of a program in real time.

This problem is sometimes difficult to diagnose. Many programs will refrain from buffering when their output is destined for the screen, since presumably a human will be watching. But the same programs will buffer their output if the destination is a file or another program, since in that case, it's more efficient to conserve system resources. The C standard I/O library does this kind of smart buffering, so the majority of C programs have this behavior built in.

7.4.1 Seeing the problem

Suppose the following C program is stored in a file called `bufdemo.c`:

```
#include <stdio.h>
main() {
    while (1) {
        printf("This is a line of text which might be buffered\n");
        sleep(1);
    }
}
```

On UNIX systems, you can compile this program with a command like this:

```
$ cc bufdemo.c -o bufdemo
```

This produces a program called `bufdemo` that we can use in the following experiment.

To see the effects of buffering, try running this program two different ways. First, run it from the command line without redirecting the output:

```
$ bufdemo
```

You will see that every second, the program prints one line of output. Now try running the program with this command line:

```
$ bufdemo | cat
```

As the program's output is not going directly to the terminal, the output will be buffered. The `cat` program on the receiving end of the pipe will not get any input until the `bufdemo` program's output buffer is filled. The size of the buffer will vary by system, but buffers of 4K to 8K are typical. Assuming a 4K buffer, the program will seem to be idle for about 1.5 minutes, spit out a bunch of text, sit idle for another 1.5 minutes, and so forth. (You can calculate this as follows: 4096-character buffer size / 46 characters per line = 89 lines to fill the buffer. Since one line is printed each second, it takes ~1.5 minutes to fill the buffer.) If you wrote a graphical front end for the `bufdemo` program, you would see the same behavior.

Now suppose that this same program were written in Tcl instead of C. The Tcl version might look like this:

```
while {1} {
    puts "This is a line of text which might be buffered"
    after 1000
}
```

If this program were stored in a file called `bufdemo.tcl`, you could run it like this:

$ tclsh bufdemo.tcl

The program would write out one line each second, like the previous `bufdemo` program. Again, try piping its output to the `cat` program, like this:

$ tclsh bufdemo.tcl | cat

You might think that the output would arrive in chunks, as it did in our previous experiment. But in this case, there doesn't seem to be a buffering problem. By default, Tcl flushes the standard output buffer when you write out each line. Tcl does this whether the output is sent to a terminal or to another program.

But there is still a buffering problem lurking about. Suppose that we modify the program slightly to look like this:

```
set fid [open "| cat" "w"]
while {1} {
    puts $fid "This is a line of text which might be buffered"
    after 1000
}
```

This time, instead of writing to standard output, we open a pipe to the `cat` program and write directly to it. In this case, the output to the `cat` program is fully buffered, so again, the output will appear in chunks every 1.5 minutes.

7.4.2 Fixing the problem

Now that you've diagnosed the problem, what can you do about it? Take a look at the program that is producing the output.

- If the program is under your control and is written in C, C++, or Tcl, just make sure that you flush the output after writing each line.

  In C, you should call the `fflush` procedure (part of the standard I/O library) after printing each line. In C++, you can simply terminate each line with the `endl` manipulator for the `ostream` class, and it will flush automatically. In Tcl, you can call the `flush` command after each `puts`, like this:

```
set fid [open "| cat" "w"]
puts $fid "This line of text is immediately flushed"
flush $fid
```

Or, better yet, you can use the `fconfigure` command to change the buffering mode for a file handle, like this:

```
set fid [open "| cat" "w"]
fconfigure $fid -buffering line
puts $fid "This line of text is immediately flushed"
puts $fid "So is this line"
```

In this example, we set the buffering mode to `line`, so each line of output is flushed automatically.

- If you are using a program written by someone else or if for some reason you can't flush the output (this may be a problem with some FORTRAN compilers), there is still hope.

    If you are on a UNIX system, you can use a program called `unbuffer`, which is provided as part of a popular package called Expect.[*] Expect is a version of Tcl that's been souped up to handle interactive programs. Expect lets you write scripts to control these programs, so you can automate things that would normally require a human operator.

    The `unbuffer` program executes another program and then fools the program into thinking that it is being run interactively from a terminal. Remember, most programs won't buffer their output in this mode, so the buffering problem is solved.

    For example, let's revisit the `bufdemo` program, which we used to demonstrate the buffering problem. When we run it like this, it buffers the output:

    ```
    $ bufdemo | cat
    ```

    Without changing the source code, we can run it like this, and the buffering stops:

    ```
    $ unbuffer bufdemo | cat
    ```

    Suppose you want to read the output from `bufdemo` within a Tcl program. You might open a pipe to the program and read the output, like this:

    ```
    set fid [open "|bufdemo" "r"]
    set line [gets $fid]
    ```

    But `bufdemo` buffers its output, so it would take 1.5 minutes for the first chunk of output to become available for reading. Again, you can solve this problem by adding the `unbuffer` program to the pipe, like this:

---

[*] Don Libes, *Exploring Expect*, O'Reilly & Associates, 1995.

```
set fid [open "|unbuffer bufdemo" "r"]
set line [gets $fid]
```

Each line of output will be available as soon as it is written from `bufdemo`.

7.5 Bidirectional pipes

So far, we've read from pipes in one example and written to pipes in another. These were examples of *unidirectional pipes*, since the output was either coming from or going to another process. Now let's look at *bidirectional pipes*, which can both read from and write to a process on the same file descriptor.

For example, suppose we're writing a calculator-style application and need more precision than Tcl's built-in math library could provide. On many UNIX systems, we can run the binary calculator program `bc`, which handles arbitrary-precision arithmetic. We can execute this program within our Tcl/Tk application and talk to it through a bidirectional pipe. We can write arithmetic commands to its standard input and read the results back from its standard output.

7.5.1 Buffering problems

In the previous section, we showed how to work around the problems that arise when a program buffers its output. With bidirectional pipes, two programs are producing output, as shown in Figure 7.5. One is our Tcl/Tk application, which writes a string, such as "2+2", to the `bc` program. The other is the `bc` program, which writes back a result string, such as "4".

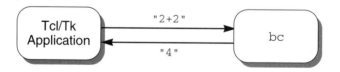

Figure 7.5. Bidirectional pipes have two sources of output and therefore two sources of buffering problems.

If either of these programs buffers its output, our calculator won't work. For example, suppose that the Tcl/Tk application writes out the string "2+2" and then tries to read the response from `bc`. If the Tcl/Tk application buffers its output, `bc` will never receive the string, so it will sit idly, waiting for input. Meanwhile, our Tcl/Tk application will sit idly, waiting for the response.

We can solve half of the problem by making sure that our Tcl/Tk application does not buffer the output to `bc`. As we explained earlier, we can do this by setting the buffering mode for the pipe, like this:

```
set bc [open "|bc" "r+"]
fconfigure $bc -buffering line
```

So each line of output from the Tcl/Tk application will be flushed automatically.

Now suppose that the `bc` program buffers its output. The program may receive a string, such as "2+2", and write out the result, "4", but this result will sit in its buffer. Our Tcl/Tk application will sit idly, waiting for the response, and the `bc` program will sit idly, waiting for more input.

Some implementations of `bc` do indeed buffer their output. If you happen to have one, your options are rather limited. As we discussed in Section 7.4.2, you can do one of the following.

- Obtain the source code for the `bc` program and modify it to flush after printing each result.

- Use Expect to work around the problem. Unfortunately, the simple `unbuffer` solution that we mentioned earlier won't work in this case. The `unbuffer` program blocks the standard input to the target program, so in this example, it would block incoming strings, such as "2+2".

  In a case like this, you should use Expect instead of the normal Tcl/Tk distribution. Exactly how you do this is outside the scope of this book, but it works something like this. Expect is just like Tcl/Tk but has extra commands to deal with interactive programs. You can use Expect's `spawn` command to execute the `bc` program from within your application. Then you can use its `send` command to send a string, such as "2+2", and use its `expect` command to look for the result string, such as "4".

  We have included a simple Expect program in the file `efftcl/fixes/bc`, which can be obtained from the Web site mentioned on page xiv. This program makes the version of `bc` from the Free Software Foundation work for the examples shown in this chapter. The program removes the header lines that this version of `bc` normally prints, and it makes sure that output is not buffered.

7.5.2 Writing and reading

Now that our buffering problem is solved, let's try a simple example. We can start up Tcl and enter commands interactively to talk to the `bc` program, like this:

```
% set bc [open "|bc" "r+"]
⇒ file5
% fconfigure $bc -buffering line
% puts $bc "2+2"
% gets $bc
⇒ 4
```

So far, so good, but now let's consider what will happen when we send an expression that returns a large result. Try starting bc by hand and enter an expression with a large exponent, like this:

```
$ bc
727^210
836038505805331903074868211018095896573235464696982659964239830621390\
987995467327790417122230342223272656480088325745136796097111771390239\
...
280668998576356559531025540620433502646674750606116707480100950572265\
888510191206304132167288269696997520892158042986708901649
```

As you can see, bc splits the result into multiple lines and indicates that the line is being continued, using a trailing backslash on each line. So reading the result back from bc may take more than a single gets command. We can handle this by writing a small procedure to read the output from bc, concatenating lines that are terminated with a backslash:

```
proc getbc {bc} {
    set answer ""
    set line "\\"
    while {{[string last "\\" $line] >= 0} {
        append answer [string trimright $line "\\"]
        set line [gets $bc]
    }
    append answer [string trimright $line "\\"]
    return $answer
}
```

You can start Tcl and open the bc program to test the new procedure. This time, instead of using the gets command to read the result, use getbc. It returns the result as a single (very long!) number, which we have abbreviated as follows:

```
% puts $bc "727^210"
% getbc $bc
```
⇒ *836038505805331903074868211110...58042986708901649*

7.5.3 Graphical interface

Now that our Tcl/Tk application can talk to the bc program, we can build a calculator like the one shown in Figure 7.6. We showed how to create and align the widgets in the calculator when we talked about the grid command in Section 2.2.2. Now we'll discuss how it works.

When you press a number key or the decimal point, we add that character to the string shown in the readout. When you press an operator key, such as +, -, *, or /, we consider that operation to be pending, and we start to build another operand string. Finally, when you press the = key, we write the entire expression out to the bc program, read back the result, and display it in the readout window. If you'd like to see exactly how this is done, you can look at the complete application in the file efftcl/apps/calc, which can be obtained from the Web site mentioned on page xiv.

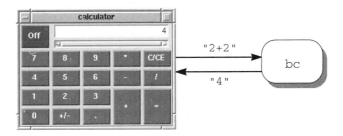

Figure 7.6. Graphical interface for the bc calculator program.

But the important point is this: You can take an existing program, such as bc, and dress it up with a spiffy graphical interface. You can use the program as is and talk to it through a bidirectional pipe. This is a powerful technique for extending many programs. This includes the programs that you're unable to modify and the legacy code that you don't want to modify.

7.6 Client/server architectures

In the previous section, we stumbled onto an important idea. We used two cooperating programs to implement a single application. We started with the bc program, which can do arbitrary-precision arithmetic but has a simple, command-line interface. This program is called the *back-end process*, or *engine*, since it does all of the real work in the application. Then we added a Tcl/Tk program providing a calculator-style interface. This program is called the *front-end process*, or *interface*, since it interacts with the user.

For our simple calculator, the front-end process (Tcl/Tk) and the back-end process (bc) have a master/slave relationship. When you start up a calculator, the Tcl/Tk front end starts up its own bc back end. When you turn off a calculator, the Tcl/Tk front end exits, causing the bc back end to terminate.

You can also have a single back-end process that serves many different front ends. For example, you may have a back end that provides access to a database. Each user could start up a front-end process, connect to the back end, and query information from the database. Usually, this kind of back-end process runs continuously, waiting for new front-end processes to connect and request information. This kind of back-end process is called a *server*, and each front-end process is called a *client*.

7.6.1 Advantages

Using separate front-end/back-end processes has some advantages.

- You may want to run the front end and the back end on different machines. For example, you may have a graphical interface running on a Windows platform, talking to a database server running on a larger, centralized system. This is an example of traditional client/server programming.

  The emergence of the World Wide Web has changed things a bit. These days, you can run your client program from a Web browser and talk to a remote server across the Internet. We'll see an example of this in Section 8.4.

- You may not want to (or be able to) modify the back-end program. For example, you may have a commercial program or some legacy code that you want to wrap with a graphical interface.

There are also advantages related to design and coding:

- This approach is good for a programming team. Programmers can work independently on cooperating programs instead of integrating their code into a single, gigantic program. This is especially useful during the testing and debugging phases. Normally, a piece of code in one subsystem can corrupt ("step on") another subsystem's data area, causing it to fail unexpectedly. But since the front-end and back-end code are in different processes, there are no unexpected interactions between the two and no finger-pointing about whose code might be causing a bug. Recall Figure 7.1, which shows how this pays off.

  Also, you can partition a problem into smaller domains. For example, your database expert can work on the back-end process, and your GUI expert can work on the front end. Neither expert has to know much about the other problem domain. Instead, they communicate by passing strings back and forth. Even inexperienced developers can handle this.

- You can write several front-end programs without modifying the back-end program. So you can have a graphical front end for general use, a batch-style front end for automated system updates, and so on. Also, you can write different front ends for different users, customizing the front end for each user's particular needs.

- There is a well-defined interface to the back-end process, so you get a testing interface at no extra cost. This makes it easy to write test programs to exercise the back end. And if the front end encounters an unexpected error in the back end, the problem is easy to reproduce.

- The front-end and back-end programs can be written in different languages.

7.6.2 Disadvantages

Depending on your application, there are a few drawbacks to consider.

- Extra work may be involved in designing and maintaining the interface for the back-end process.

- A performance penalty may result from crossing processing boundaries. This is usually not the case for a "traditional" graphical interface, since a human being's perception of time is so much slower than a computer's. Adding 10 milliseconds to a typical transaction won't be noticed by anyone but Superman or The Flash.

     However, if you need to download a lot of data from the back end or if you need to send numerous queries back and forth, you may be better off using a single process. For example, suppose you're using a client to plot data from the server. If the server generates a few hundred points, you may not notice the delay. But if it generates a few million points, you certainly will.

- There is an extra program to manage in configuration control and an extra process to keep track of while executing. This by itself shouldn't preclude the front-end/back-end approach, but it helps to take this into account when planning your system.

     If you're wondering whether to use a single program or the front-end/back-end approach, there is no simple answer. Like so many other things in software design, you have to weigh the trade-offs and make the right choice for the project at hand.

7.6.3   A simple server

Now let's see how to create a simple client/server application. Suppose we create a simple math server that can perform two functions: addition and subtraction. For convenience, we'll write both the client and the server in Tcl, but you can write either program in any other language as well. Thus you can use a client written in Tcl with a server written in C, or a client written in C++ with a server written in Tcl.

7.6.3.1   How it works

Our simple math server will perform two functions: add x y will return $x+y$; and subtract x y will return $x-y$. Each request will be sent in the form of a string consisting of a command (either add or subtract), followed by two parameters (the numbers to be added or subtracted). The command and the parameters will be separated by spaces.

     Figure 7.7 shows a request and the response for a typical transaction with the math server. As a first pass, we'll have the client and the server communicate through a bidirectional pipe. Later we'll show how to use a socket connection so that the two processes can live on different machines in a network. But even though the communication channel may change, the requests and responses sent back and forth will stay just the same.

7.6.3.2   A brute-force implementation

Our server will read a line from its standard input, handle the add or subtract operation, and print the result. The server will continue doing this as long as input is available.

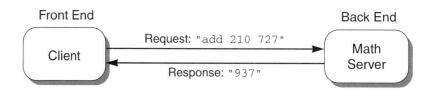

Figure 7.7. Math server, first pass.

How should we implement this? Well, as Ken Thompson, the designer of UNIX, once said, "When in doubt, use brute force."[*] With this in mind, let's take a first cut at our math server:

```
while {[gets stdin request] != -1} {
    set cmd [lindex $request 0]
    switch -- $cmd {
        add {
            if {[llength $request] == 3} {
                set parm1 [lindex $request 1]
                set parm2 [lindex $request 2]
                set result [expr $parm1 + $parm2]
                puts $result
            } else {
                puts "error: add should have 2 parameters"
            }
        }
        subtract {
            if {[llength $request] == 3} {
                set parm1 [lindex $request 1]
                set parm2 [lindex $request 2]
                set result [expr $parm1 - $parm2]
                puts $result
            } else {
                puts "error: subtract should have 2 parameters"
            }
        }
        default {
            puts "error: unknown command: $cmd"
        }
    }
}
```

---

[*] Jon L. Bentley, *Programming Pearls*, Addison-Wesley, 1986.

The `gets` command reads a line from standard input, saving it in the variable `request`. The command returns the number of characters in the line or `-1` at the end-of-file condition. So we use the `while` loop to continue reading until there is no more input.

Each request line has an operation and its arguments, all separated by spaces. As far as Tcl is concerned, this is like any other list, so we can use the `lindex` command to pick it apart. The first element (at index 0) is the operation, which we store in a variable called `cmd`.

Now we look at the operation and handle it accordingly. We use a `switch` command to handle the various cases. For the `add` operation, we get the next two elements in the request, add them, and print the return result. For the `subtract` operation, we get the next two elements, subtract them, and print the return result. If anything goes wrong, we print an error message as the result. Since we are printing to standard output, each line is automatically flushed. So we don't have to worry about output buffering in this case.

Whenever you use a `switch` command, you should always add the `--` argument to guard against unexpected errors. The reason is that the `switch` command has some optional flags that control its behavior.

```
switch -regexp "foo" {
    f.* { ... }
}
```

In this code, the `switch` command will interpret patterns like `f.*` as regular expressions. Now suppose that a math client accidentally sends the request "`-3 + 12`". Our server will think that `-3` is the operation and will feed this to the switch. If we didn't include the `--` argument, the switch would look like this:

```
switch -3 {
    add { ... }
    subtract { ... }
    ...
}
```

Since the argument after the `switch` command starts with a dash, the switch would treat it as an option like `-regexp` and return the following error:

```
bad option "-3": should be -exact, -glob, -regexp, or --
```

By adding the `--` argument, we're telling the switch that there are no more control flags and that the next argument that follows is the string we're trying to match.

7.6.4 A simple client

Now let's turn our attention to the front-end process. We'll build a simple client like the one shown in Figure 7.8. This client has entries for two numbers, with + and - buttons between them. When you click on either of these buttons, it sends a request to the server and displays the result in a label on the right-hand side.

The widget code in this client interface is straightforward. It looks like this:

```
entry .x
pack .x -side left
```

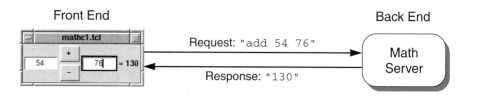

Figure 7.8. Talking to the math server.

```
frame .op
pack .op -side left
button .op.add -text "+" -command do_add
pack .op.add -fill both
button .op.sub -text "-" -command do_subtract
pack .op.sub -fill both
entry .y
pack .y -side left
label .result -text ""
pack .result -side left
```

We'll start by using a bidirectional pipe to communicate with the server. We connect to the server and handle the + and – buttons like this:

```
set backend [open "|tclsh maths1.tcl" "r+"]
fconfigure $backend -buffering line

proc do_add {} {
    global backend
    set x [.x get]
    set y [.y get]
    puts $backend "add $x $y"
    gets $backend num
    .result configure -text "= $num"
}

proc do_subtract {} {
    global backend
    set x [.x get]
    set y [.y get]
    puts $backend "subtract $x $y"
    gets $backend num
    .result configure -text "= $num"
}
```

We open a bidirectional pipe to the math server, storing the file handle in a variable called backend. Remember, the math server was written in Tcl, and the code is stored in a file called maths1.tcl, which we assume to be in the current directory. So we use the command `tclsh maths1.tcl` to start the server. We set the output buffering for this pipe to `line` mode, so each request line that we print to the pipe will be flushed automatically. This avoids any buffering problems.

The + button invokes the `do_add` procedure, and the – button invokes `do_subtract`. These two procedures are very much alike. They both query the numbers from the entry widgets `.x` and `.y` and then print a request to the server. They both read the result and display it in the label called `.result`. The only difference is that `do_add` prints an `add` request, and `do_subtract` prints a `subtract` request.

7.6.5 Smarter parsing

Now let's look at the server program more carefully. It works, but it's not particularly elegant. The bulk of this code (about 80 percent!) handles argument parsing, error checking, and error reporting. Had we written our back end in C or C++, the percentage would be about the same. The bottom line is this: If you write your servers with the brute-force approach, you'll spend 80 percent of your time implementing a new command language for each server.

Did we just say *command language*? Don't we have a nice *tool command language* (Tcl) sitting around? Of course we do. We can use Tcl to handle the request parsing for our server. This will dramatically reduce the amount of code in the server and will give us error checking for free!

For example, we could rewrite our math server like this:

```
proc add {x y} {
    return [expr $x+$y]
}
proc subtract {x y} {
    return [expr $x-$y]
}

while {[gets stdin request] != -1} {
    if {[catch $request result] != 0} {
        puts "error: $result"
    } else {
        puts $result
    }
}
```

This time, we defined `add` and `subtract` as procedures in the Tcl interpreter. The `add` procedure takes two arguments and returns their sum. The `subtract` procedure takes two arguments and returns their difference.

We read each line of input just as we did before. But this time, instead of parsing it ourselves, we execute each request as a Tcl command. The `catch` command executes the request string and returns a status code indicating success or failure. That way, we can trap errors and handle them gracefully.

If anything goes wrong, `catch` returns a nonzero status code, along with an error message in the `result` variable. In that case, we return a result string that says `error:` followed by the error message. If the command is successful, `catch` returns 0, along with a valid result in the `result` variable. In that case, we return the result string directly.

Of course, it was trivial for us to use the Tcl interpreter in our math server, since we were already using Tcl. But it's not much more trouble to do the same thing in C or C++. With just a few lines of code, you can drop a Tcl interpreter into your program and add Tcl commands to handle the important operations.[*] When all is said and done, you'll probably decrease your code size, thereby decreasing your maintenance costs.

Note: *When you think parsing, think Tcl, the Tool Command Language!*

7.6.6   Safer parsing

In the previous section, we built a math server that was smaller, faster, and better. What more could we ask? Well, for starters, we could ask for something *safer*.

Suppose that an unfriendly programmer puts this bit of code in a front-end program:

```
button .b -text "Add" -command "send $backend {exec rm -rf .}"
```

When you click on the Add button, it sends the command `"exec rm -rf ."` to the server, which happily executes the command. On UNIX platforms, this will delete the current working directory for the server! Remember, the `catch` command will execute *any* command in the Tcl interpreter, including `exec`.

You may trust your programmers not to do something nefarious like this, but what if you have an unfriendly user? Suppose that a user enters the following string in one of the number fields:

```
[exec rm -rf .]
```

Our client would package up a command that looks something like this:

```
add [exec rm -rf .] 17.5
```

The client would then send it to the back end to be executed, again with disastrous results. This is a serious security risk, and it must be fixed. Fortunately, Tcl has a simple solution.

7.6.6.1   Safe interpreters

Within each Tcl interpreter, you can create subinterpreters, called *slave* interpreters, and execute code within them. There is a special kind of slave interpreter called a *safe interpreter*. It has most of the usual Tcl commands but none of the dangerous commands, such as `exec` and `open`. So you can use a safe interpreter to execute arbitrary code without worrying that it will harm your environment.

You can create a safe interpreter and have it execute some code, like this:

---

[*] For details, see John K. Ousterhout, *Tcl and the Tk Toolkit*, Addison-Wesley, 1994.

```
set parser [interp create -safe]
set num [$parser eval {expr 2+2}]
```

The `interp create` command creates a safe interpreter and returns its name, which we store in the variable `parser`. We can use this name to access the interpreter. In this case, we're telling the interpreter to evaluate the `expr 2+2` command, and we store the result in a variable called `num` in the main interpreter.

Each interpreter has its own set of commands and global variables. You can add new commands to a slave interpreter by defining a few procedures. For example, we could define `add` and `subtract` procedures in the safe interpreter, like this:

```
$parser eval {
    proc add {x y} {
        return [expr $x+$y]
    }
    proc subtract {x y} {
        return [expr $x-$y]
    }
}
```

Now that it understands the `add` command, the safe interpreter can add two numbers, like this:

```
set num [$parser eval {add 2 2}]
```

At this point, we have a safe interpreter that accepts commands such as `add` and `subtract` but rejects anything unsafe, such as `exec` or `open`. So we can go back and rewrite our math server to use a safe interpreter to handle all incoming commands. Our new math server looks like this:

```
set parser [interp create -safe]
$parser eval {
    proc add {x y} {
        return [expr $x+$y]
    }
    proc subtract {x y} {
        return [expr $x-$y]
    }
}

while {[gets stdin request] != -1} {
    if {[catch {$parser eval $request} result] != 0} {
        puts "error: $result"
    } else {
        puts $result
    }
}
```

We read each request just as we did before. But this time, instead of evaluating a request directly within the `catch` command, we use the safe interpreter to evaluate it. We still catch the result, so we can report any errors.

Should some evil client send a destructive command, it will get an error message, such as this:

```
invalid command name "exec"
    while executing
"exec rm -rf ."
    invoked from within
"add [exec rm -rf .]..."
```

7.6.6.2 Aliases

Let's digress briefly to explore another important feature of safe interpreters. Suppose we want to write an `add` procedure that supports arbitrary-precision arithmetic. We saw how to handle this with the `bc` program in Section 7.5.2. We can open a pipe to the `bc` program and add the numbers as follows:

```
$parser eval {
    proc add {x y} {
        set bc [open "|bc" "r+"]
        puts $bc "$x + $y"
        flush $bc

        set result [gets $bc]
        close $bc

        return $result
    }
}
```

This procedure starts up the `bc` program, writes out the `add` instruction, reads back the result, and shuts down the `bc` program. This may not be the most efficient solution, but we're trying to keep things simple for the current discussion.

If you test out this new `add` command, you'll get the following error:

```
% $parser eval {add 2 2}
```
⇒ *invalid command name "open"*

You see, the `add` procedure executes in the context of the safe interpreter, and there's no way to execute the `open` command in that interpreter. Although the `add` command itself is safe, we need to do something unsafe as part of its implementation.

There is a simple way to solve this problem. If a procedure like `add` is defined in the main interpreter, it will have access to all of the Tcl commands in that interpreter, including `exec` and `open`. So it will execute properly in that context. Instead of adding the procedure to the safe interpreter, you can add it to the main interpreter and in the safe interpreter create an *alias* that points to the real command. For example:

```
proc cmd_add {x y} {
    set bc [open "|bc" "r+"]
    puts $bc "$x + $y"
    flush $bc

    set result [gets $bc]
    close $bc
```

```
        return $result
    }
    $parser alias add cmd_add
```

This defines a procedure called `cmd_add` in the main interpreter and then adds an alias called `add` in the safe interpreter. You execute the `add` command in the safe interpreter, like this:

```
    $parser eval {add 2 2}
```

The command then transfers control to the real `cmd_add` procedure in the main interpreter, which adds the two numbers.

You might be thinking that a malicious client could add its own set of aliases to access things in the main interpreter. But it can't. An alias can be added to a slave interpreter only by its master. As long as the client doesn't have direct access to the main interpreter, it can't break out of its protected environment.

You can use aliases to provide safe versions of otherwise unsafe commands. For example, suppose you want to let clients use the `open` command but want to restrict their access to files in a temporary directory. You could write a procedure called `safe_open` in the main interpreter. It could examine each file name, making sure that it points to the temporary directory, and it could use the normal `open` command to open the file. Then you could add an alias called `open` in the safe interpreter to point to `safe_open` in the main interpreter. Clients would think that they were using the regular `open` command, but any attempt to access a file outside of the temporary directory would be blocked.

7.6.6.3 Using Tcl commands to express data

You should always use a safe interpreter when you're evaluating commands from an outside source. This includes the commands in a data file, if you're using Tcl commands to express data. For example, in Section 4.7, we created a drawing program that saved a drawing as a series of `draw` commands. We showed how you could load a drawing via the `source` command. Now let's revisit this example and see how to load a drawing properly, using a safe interpreter.

First, we create a safe interpreter to handle the `draw` commands:

```
    set canvParser [interp create -safe]
```

We save the name of this interpreter in a global variable called `canvParser`, so we can access it later.

Next, we write a procedure called `canvas_load`, which loads a drawing onto a canvas. The procedure takes the name of a canvas and a script of `draw` commands, and it uses the safe interpreter to execute the script. The procedure is implemented as follows:

```
    proc canvas_load {win script} {
        global canvParser
        $win delete all
        $canvParser alias draw canvas_parser_cmd $win
        $canvParser eval $script
    }
```

We start by deleting all of the items on the canvas, to prepare for the new drawing. Then we configure the safe interpreter to recognize the `draw` command. Each `draw` command creates an item on the canvas. But the canvas isn't available in the safe interpreter. The canvas belongs to the main interpreter, so we create an alias for the `draw` command; the alias transfers control to the `canvas_parser_cmd` procedure in the main interpreter. This procedure will have no problem accessing the canvas.

Notice that when we defined this alias, we added the `$win` argument after `canvas_parser_cmd`. This makes the argument part of the translation. Suppose that `$win` contains the canvas name `.drawing` and that you execute a `draw` command in the safe interpreter:

```
draw rectangle 79.0 24.0 256.0 196.0 -fill red
```

The alias will trigger a call to `canvas_parser_cmd`, like this:

```
canvas_parser_cmd .drawing rectangle 79.0 24.0 256.0 196.0 -fill red
```

As you can see, the canvas name is automatically included as the first argument on the command line. The rest of the arguments follow exactly as they appear in the `draw` command.

The `canvas_parser_cmd` procedure is implemented like this:

```
proc canvas_parser_cmd {win args} {
    eval $win create $args
}
```

This looks a lot like the `draw` procedure that we defined in Section 4.7.9. The procedure passes the item description contained in `$args` to the canvas `create` operation, creating the item on the canvas.

Now that we have the `canvas_load` procedure, we can use it within our drawing program to load a drawing. First, we add an **Open...** option to the **File** menu, like this:

```
.mbar.file.m add command -label "Open..." -command draw_open
```

When you select **Open...**, it calls the following procedure to load the drawing:

```
proc draw_open {} {
    global env
    set file [tk_getOpenFile]
    if {$file != ""} {
        set cmd {
            set fid [open $file r]
            set script [read $fid]
            close $fid
            canvas_load .drawing $script
        }
        if {[catch $cmd err] != 0} {
            notice_show "Cannot open drawing:\n$err" error
        }
        draw_fix_menus
    }
}
```

This procedure uses `tk_getOpenFile` to get the name of the input file. This pops up a file-selection dialog, letting you navigate the file system and select a file. If you click on the Cancel button, `tk_getOpenFile` returns a null string, and the `draw_open` procedure does nothing. Otherwise, `tk_getOpenFile` returns the name you selected for the drawing file.

To load the drawing, we need to open the file, read the script, close the file, and call `canvas_load` to evaluate the script. Any of these operations could fail, so we wrap them up as a small script and execute them, using the `catch` command. If we catch any errors, we use the `notice_show` procedure developed in Section 6.4 to display the error message in a notice dialog. We also use a procedure called `draw_fix_menus`, which we won't show here. It just checks to see whether any items in the drawing are selected and then enables or disables some commands in the Edit menu.

Tcl commands are a powerful way of expressing data. As long as you use a safe interpreter to load the data, you can avoid any mishaps. In the current example, suppose you try to load a drawing file that looks like this:

```
draw rectangle 79.0 24.0 256.0 196.0 -fill red
exec rm -rf .
```

The `canvas_load` procedure will complain that `exec` is an invalid command, and the `draw_open` procedure will notify the user that the operation failed. Your files will remain intact, in spite of someone's best effort to clobber them!

7.6.7 Asynchronous communication

So far, all of the interactions between our front-end and back-end programs have been *synchronous*. The front end sends a request string and then waits for the response string, as shown in Figure 7.9. While the front end is waiting, execution in the front-end program is blocked. If the front end has a graphical user interface, it won't be responsive to the mouse or the keyboard, and its windows won't refresh themselves properly when you cover and uncover them. If the back end doesn't respond quickly, most users will think that the front end has mysteriously locked up.

You can avoid this by using an *asynchronous* communication scheme, as shown in Figure 7.10. In this scheme, the front-end program sends a request and then continues execution. While it is waiting for the response, it might spin the cursor or display an Abort button that you can use to cancel the request. Eventually, the back-end program sends a response, and the front end reads it and handles it at its first opportunity.

For this scheme to work, we can't have the front end send a request and read the response right away, like this:

```
puts $backend "add $x $y"
gets $backend num
```

Instead, we need to make it listen for messages that might appear at any time. We ran into the same problem when we were listening for output from the `pppstats` program in Sec-

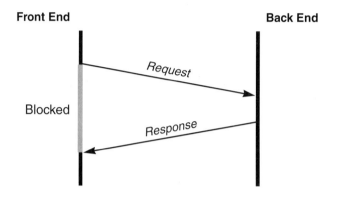

Figure 7.9. For a *synchronous* call, the front end sends a request and does nothing else until the back end sends a response.

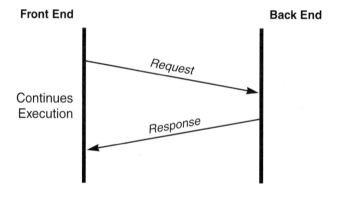

Figure 7.10. For an *asynchronous* call, the front end sends a request and continues execution. When the back end eventually sends the response, the front end handles it.

tion 7.2, and we can use the same solution here. We use the `fileevent` command to determine when the connection to the back end is readable. For example:

```
set backend [open "|tclsh maths4.tcl" "r+"]
fconfigure $backend -buffering line
fileevent $backend readable \
    "front_handler $backend $parser"
```

```
proc front_handler {fd parser} {
    if {[gets $fd request] < 0} {
        catch {close $fd}
        notice_show "Lost backend" error
    } elseif {[catch {$parser eval $request} result]} {
        notice_show $result error
    }
}
```

When a message arrives from the back end, the `front_handler` procedure is called to handle it. This procedure reads a line of input. If for some reason the back-end process has terminated, the `gets` command will return `-1`, indicating an end-of-file condition. In that case, we close the connection (ignoring any errors that we might encounter), and we let the user know that the back end has died. We use the `notice_show` procedure to display the message `"Lost backend"`.

Otherwise, the `gets` command will return the number of characters in the request line. In that case, we try to evaluate the incoming message, and if something goes wrong, we use `notice_show` to notify the user.

We use a safe interpreter, which we refer to as `$parser`, to interpret all incoming messages in the front end. Before seeing how to write the code, we'll explain why this is needed.

Messages can arrive at any time from the back end, so we don't know what to expect. When we send the command `"add 2 2"`, it isn't enough to get back the response `"4"`. By the time we receive that response, it may not be obvious what 4 means. So instead of having the back end send back a simple data value, such as 4, we'll modify it to send back a Tcl command, such as `show_result 4`. This tells us what to do with the result.

This scheme also lets the back-end program send notification messages to the front end. For example, if two clients are connected to a server, one client might want to be notified when the other client changes some data. Since all incoming messages are in the form of commands, the server can "tell" the client that some data has changed. And since the communication is asynchronous, a message like this can be received and processed at any point—even when the front end is waiting for a response, as shown in Figure 7.11.

Our math client is now set up to read incoming messages and interpret them, but one task remains: We need to determine the *protocol*, or the messages that are exchanged between the client and the server. There are several ways of doing this. We'll look at two of them in the following sections.

7.6.7.1 Predefined callbacks

Let's assume that our math server will always respond to an `add` or `subtract` command by sending back the string:

```
show_result value
```

where *value* is the result from the `add` or `subtract` operation. Different math clients could define the `show_result` procedure to do different things. One client might print

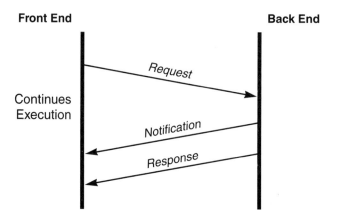

Figure 7.11. With asynchronous communication, the front end can receive a notification while it is waiting for a response.

out the value; another might save it in a log file. In the current example, we'll display the result in a label on the right-hand side of our graphical interface, as we saw in Figure 7.8.

If the server encounters an error, it will send back the following message:

    error_result *message*

Again, different clients could handle this in different ways, but in the current example, we'll display the *message* string in a notice dialog.

We can rewrite our math server to implement this new protocol as follows:

```
set parser [interp create -safe]

$parser eval {
    proc add {x y} {
        return [list show_result [expr $x+$y]]
    }
    proc subtract {x y} {
        return [list show_result [expr $x-$y]]
    }
}

proc back_handler {parser} {
    if {[gets stdin request] < 0} {
        exit
    } elseif {[catch {$parser eval $request} result] == 0} {
        puts $result
```

```
        } else {
            puts [list error_result $result]
        }
    }


    fileevent stdin readable "back_handler $parser"
    vwait enter-mainloop
```

There are just a few places where the code has changed, so we've highlighted them in boldface type.

Our previous version of the server handled requests in a synchronous fashion. In this version, we changed the server to work asynchronously, using the pattern described in the previous section. We set up a file event on standard input, so that when input arrives, the procedure back_handler will be called to handle it. This procedure reads each request, executes it in a safe interpreter, and prints out the result.

In order to receive file events, the program must be executing in the event loop. If you use wish to execute the server program, this happens automatically at the end of your script. However, it is better to use tclsh to execute the server program so that it can run in the background, without a window on the desktop. But tclsh doesn't drop into the event loop automatically. You have to force execution into the event loop, using the vwait command. The vwait command waits for a variable to change. In this case, the variable enter-mainloop will never change, so the server will sit in the event loop as long as it continues to run.

In the previous version of the server, we returned an error message when something went wrong. Now we return error_result, followed by the error message. You might be tempted to use double quotes to build the response string, like this:

```
    puts "error_result $result"
```

But doing so would probably cause an error in the client. Remember, the client will expect the error_result command to have a single argument. If the message in $result is something like invalid command name "foo", using double quotes will produce a response like:

```
    error_result invalid command name "foo"
```

This looks like we're passing four arguments to error_result, so the client will complain.

Instead, we use the list command to build the return string. The list command automatically adds the braces needed to keep the error message together as a single argument. It produces a response string that looks like this:

```
    error_result {invalid command name "foo"}
```

The client can interpret this response string correctly.

Similarly, in the previous version of the add and subtract procedures, we returned a number. Now we return show_result, followed by a number. Again, we could have used double quotes to build the return string, like this:

```
    return "show_result [expr $x+$y]"
```

But instead, we use the `list` command to build the return string. The `list` command isn't really necessary in this case, since the `expr` command won't return a result with spaces in it. But using the `list` command won't hurt, and it's a good habit to get into.

At this point, we've fixed the math server to respond to `add` and `subtract` commands with the new protocol. Now we'll fix the math client to interpret the new protocol.

Since all of the incoming messages are Tcl commands, we can create a safe interpreter to handle them, as we discussed in Section 7.6.6. The safe interpreter will contain the two protocol commands. The `show_result` command will update a label on the graphical interface to show the result value, and the `error_result` command will pop up a notice dialog with an error message. Both of these procedures need to access widgets that exist in the main interpreter. So we need to define these procedures in the main interpreter and add aliases for them in the safe interpreter. For example:

```
proc cmd_show_result {num} {
    .result configure -text "= $num"
}
proc cmd_error_result {msg} {
    notice_show $msg error
}


set parser [interp create -safe]
$parser alias show_result cmd_show_result
$parser alias error_result cmd_error_result
```

When we execute `show_result` in the safe interpreter, it will call `cmd_show_result` in the main interpreter, which will change the text of the `.result` label to display the result. Likewise, when we execute `error_result` in the safe interpreter, it will call `cmd_error_result` in the main interpreter, which will call `notice_show` to pop up a notice dialog.

The client listens for incoming messages and then uses this safe interpreter to evaluate them. We've seen the code that handles this. We described it in detail in Section 7.6.7, but we'll include it again here so you can see how things fit together.

```
set backend [open "|tclsh maths4.tcl" "r+"]
fconfigure $backend -buffering line
fileevent $backend readable \
    "front_handler $backend $parser"

proc front_handler {fd parser} {
    if {[gets $fd request] < 0} {
        catch {close $fd}
        notice_show "Lost backend" error
    } elseif {[catch {$parser eval $request} result]} {
        notice_show $result error
    }
}
```

We set up a bidirectional pipe with the server program and use `fileevent` to watch for incoming messages. Whenever the pipe is readable, the `front_handler` procedure is called to handle the message. The procedure reads a line of input and uses the safe interpreter to evaluate it. We use the `catch` command to look for errors, and if anything goes wrong, we report it in a notice dialog.

Finally, we need to modify the `do_add` and `do_subtract` procedures, which send requests to the back end. We'll still use the `puts` command to send requests to the back end, but we don't need the `gets` command to read the response. We already have code in place to handle the response asynchronously. So these procedures now look like this:

```
proc do_add {} {
    global backend
    set x [.x get]
    set y [.y get]
    puts $backend "add $x $y"
}
proc do_subtract {} {
    global backend
    set x [.x get]
    set y [.y get]
    puts $backend "subtract $x $y"
}
```

Everything is in place to handle the new communication protocol. When you enter some numbers and click on the + button on the client, it sends a message like this to the server:

```
add 2 2
```

The server evaluates this in its safe interpreter and sends back the message:

```
show_result 4
```

The client evaluates this in its safe interpreter, displaying the string "= 4" in the result label on the graphical interface. When you click on the – button, it generates another request and another response, and so on.

7.6.7.2 Command formatting with templates

Having a specific protocol for requests and responses works just fine. But sometimes you need more flexibility in the responses returned by the back end. This becomes an issue when the back end returns several different values in a single response. For example, suppose we add to our math server a `divide` command that returns both the quotient and the remainder. Our standard `show_result` response won't handle this, since it was designed to return only a single value. You might be tempted to define a new response for the `divide` operation, like this:

```
show_divide dividend remainder
```

But adding new responses like this quickly gets out of hand.

Instead, we'll use a different approach: We'll have the client send a *response template* to the server and have the server fill in the return values and send it back. For example, suppose the client sent a response template like:

```
show_result "= %q (remainder %r)"
```

The server could replace `%q` with the quotient, replace `%r` with the remainder, and then send the string back. As far as the client is concerned, it sees an ordinary `show_result` message, which it already knows how to handle.

Let's see how this works for the simple `add` and `subtract` commands in our math server. Suppose we modify these commands to take the response template as a third argument, like this:

```
add x y response
subtract x y response
```

The server will add or subtract the numbers *x* and *y* and then substitute the result in place of `%v` in the *response* template. Now we can send the server a command like:

```
add 2 2 {show_result %v}
```

The server will return the following response:

```
show_result 4
```

Now suppose that we want to change our client to display its results in a notice dialog. We could modify the client to send a different response template, like this:

```
add 2 2 {notice_show "The result is: %v"}
```

The server will return a different response:

```
notice_show "The result is: 4"
```

Of course, the client may read this response, but it won't recognize the `notice_show` command unless we add `notice_show` to its vocabulary of incoming commands. We do this by adding an alias to the client's safe interpreter, like this:

```
$parser alias notice_show notice_show
```

When the `notice_show` message comes in, the client's safe interpreter will transfer control to the real `notice_show` procedure in the main interpreter, which will pop up a notice dialog with the result string.

We were able make this change to the client without changing anything in the server. We simply changed the client's response template and added to its vocabulary of incoming commands.

Using response templates has a few important advantages.

• It eliminates a lot of unnecessary protocol commands, such as `show_divide`, which would otherwise be added to handle the extra arguments. This simplifies the protocol between the client and the server, making the two programs easier to maintain.

• It improves the separation between the client and the server. The client sends the response templates over and interprets them when they come back. All of the response-related code resides within the client, so it is easier to maintain.

- It lets the client use the same server command in many different places, with many different results.

7.6.7.3 Percent substitution

In the previous section, we saw how response templates work. Now let's see how to modify the server to handle the substitutions.

As you'll recall, the server has a safe interpreter to handle incoming commands, such as add and subtract. We can modify these procedures to use a response template, as follows:

```
set parser [interp create -safe]
$parser eval {
    proc add {x y cmd} {
        set num [expr $x+$y]
        set response [percent_subst %v $cmd $num]
        return $response
    }
    proc subtract {x y cmd} {
        set num [expr $x-$y]
        set response [percent_subst %v $cmd $num]
        return $response
    }
}
```

Both of these procedures get the response template via the cmd argument, and they substitute their result by using a procedure called percent_subst. This procedure is much like the usual regsub command in Tcl, but it does something that regsub won't—it ignores characters like &, \0, \1, \2, ... that might be lurking in the result string. You can see why this is important in the following example.

Suppose that you're building a server to access a marketing database. This database contains the names and phone numbers of thousands of people, and it identifies their long-distance telephone carriers. Now suppose that this server has a command to query the long-distance carrier:

    get_carrier *customer response*

You pass in the *customer* name; the server accesses the database, finds the long-distance carrier, and substitutes the result into the %c field of the *response* string.

Now suppose that you send a request like this:

    get_carrier "Hacker, Joe" {notice_show "long-distance: %c"}

Suppose further that the server uses regsub to substitute the result into the %c field, like this:

    regsub -all %c $cmd $company response

The -all flag tells regsub to find all occurrences of the pattern %c in the template $cmd and to replace them with the long-distance carrier name $company. The resulting string is stored in the response variable.

This works fine for company names like `MCI` and `Sprint`, but it fails miserably for a name like `AT&T`. The `regsub` command automatically replaces the `&` character with the pattern `%c`, so you get back the company name `AT%cT`! Using `regsub` directly to perform substitutions is an accident waiting to happen.

Instead, we use the `percent_subst` procedure to handle percent substitutions. It uses `regsub`, but it suppresses the normal substitutions for things like `&`, `\0`, `\1`, `\2`, and so on. The procedure is implemented as follows:

```
$parser eval {
    proc percent_subst {percent string subst} {
        if {![string match %* $percent]} {
            error "bad pattern \"$percent\": should be %something"
        }
        regsub -all {\\|&} $subst {\\\0} subst
        regsub -all $percent $string $subst string
        return $string
    }
}
```

The first `regsub` command suppresses any dangerous characters in the substitution string `$subst`. It adds an extra `\` in front of each `\` or `&`, so the next `regsub` command will ignore them. A complete description of regular expressions is beyond the scope of this book.* But we'll explain briefly how this works. The first `regsub` command tries to match the pattern "`\\|&`", which means "either `\` or `&`". If it finds this pattern, it replaces it with "`\\\0`", which means "backslash (`\\`) followed by the matching character (`\0`)". It stores the resulting string back into the `subst` variable.

Having done this, we can use the second `regsub` command to substitute the `$subst` string in place of each percent field, without worrying about any of the dangerous characters. If `regsub` succeeds, it saves the updated string in the `string` variable. If it fails, it leaves the `string` variable alone. Either way, we return `$string` as the result of the procedure.

We use the `string match` command to make sure that the percent string really starts with a `%` sign. If it does not, we return a usage error. Finally, we pass this whole procedure definition to the safe interpreter, so that the `add` and `subtract` commands will have access to it.

7.6.8 Handling multiline requests

Not all of the commands that we pass to the front end or the back end will fit on a single line. For example, suppose that we send our math server a command like this:

---

* See Alfred V. Aho, Brian W. Kernighan, and Peter J. Weinberger, *The AWK Programming Language*, Addison-Wesley, 1988; and Don Libes, *Exploring Expect*, O'Reilly and Associates, 1995.

```
add 2 2 {
    show_result %v
    notice_show "The server has responded."
}
```

This should be treated as a single Tcl command, but the way the server is currently writ-ten, it will read only the first line, try to execute it, and return an error.

The server needs to keep reading until it has a complete command and then execute that command. Fortunately, we can use the `info complete` command to determine whether a string is syntactically complete. We can modify the `back_handler` procedure to use it as follows:

```
proc back_handler {parser} {
    global buffer
    if {[gets stdin request] < 0} {
        exit
    } else {
        append buffer $request "\n"
        if {[info complete $buffer]} {
            set request $buffer
            set buffer ""
            if {[catch {$parser eval $request} result] == 0} {
                puts $result
            } else {
                puts [list error_result $result]
            }
        }
    }
}
```

We use the global `buffer` variable to store each line of the incoming command. After appending each line, we check to see whether the command is complete. If it is, we handle it as we did before. If it is not, we return from `back_handler` and wait for another line.

Notice that before we evaluate the command, we transfer it from the buffer to the `request` variable, and we clear out the buffer. While the server is evaluating this request, it may handle more input, so we must prepare for this by resetting the buffer. We can make a similar change to the `front_handler` procedure in our math client, so the client can handle multiline responses as well.

7.6.8.1 Prompting for commands

This same code comes in handy in another context: You can add an interactive shell to a Tcl/Tk program that is not being run interactively. Normally, you won't get the usual com-mand prompt when you execute `tclsh` or `wish` with a command script, like this:

```
$ wish script.tcl
```

However, you can implement your own command prompt by adding the following code to the bottom of your script:

```
proc prompt {} {
    puts -nonewline "% "
    flush stdout
}
proc process_cmdline {} {
    global buffer
    if {[gets stdin line] < 0} {
        exit
    } else {
        append buffer $line "\n"
        if {[info complete $buffer]} {
            set cmd $buffer
            set buffer ""
            catch {uplevel #0 $cmd} result
            puts $result
            prompt
        }
    }
}
fileevent stdin readable process_cmdline
prompt
vwait enter-mainloop
```

This registers a file event for the standard input channel so that each line of input triggers a call to the `process_cmdline` procedure. Of course, this will work only if our program enters the event loop to look for file events. The `wish` program will enter the event loop automatically, but `tclsh` won't. So to make this example work in both cases, we've included the `vwait` command to force execution into the event loop. The variable `enter-mainloop` should never change, so the program will stay in the event loop.

When we receive a file event, we read each line, append it onto the buffer, and check for a complete command. When we have one, we transfer it into the `cmd` variable and then execute it.

Instead of using a safe interpreter in this case, we execute the command directly in the main interpreter. However, we use `uplevel #0` to execute the command at the global scope, outside the `process_cmdline` procedure. That way, if the command is something like `set x 0`, it will set a global variable called x, not a local variable in the `process_cmdline` procedure. We use `catch` to suppress any errors that we might encounter. Then we print the result and prompt for another command.

7.7 Network programming with sockets

We've already seen how client/server programs can send commands back and forth to communicate. But so far, our client/server programs have been connected by a bidirectional pipe. In this section, we'll change the communication channel, replacing the bidirectional pipe with a *socket connection*. As far as your Tcl code is concerned, using sockets is a lot like using bidirectional pipes. But sockets have a couple of advantages.

- You can run the client (front end) and the server (back end) on different machines in the network. If your server is running on a system attached to the Internet, you can provide your service to computers all over the world—including the bad guys, so it's extremely important to use safe interpreters!

- One server can service several clients, as shown in Figure 7.12. Clients can share data and send messages to one another via the server.

Tcl provides its networking capabilities at a very high level, so you don't need to do much programming to set up a socket connection. Once you have set up the connection, your client and server programs can communicate as we described in the previous section.

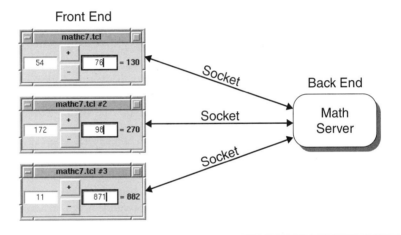

Figure 7.12. A networked server with several client processes. Each client has its own connection to the server.

7.7.1 Overview

Networked client/server applications work something like this.

1. A server process is started on a particular machine (called a *host*) on the network. The server opens a socket with a specific port number, such as 8111, and then listens for clients to connect. You can choose any port number for the server, as long as it isn't being used by another application. Numbers in the range 8100-9999 are usually good choices.

   Normally, the server program runs until the host goes down. That way, clients can connect at any time. When the host comes back up, you can arrange for the server program to be restarted automatically. On UNIX systems, you do this by adding the server program to a file called `rc.local`, which is usually in the `/etc` directory.

2. A client program connects to the server. The client connects to a particular host, using a host name, such as `frame.tcltk.com`, or an Internet Protocol (IP) address, such as `128.92.104.10`. The client then asks for the server at a particular port, which is something like `8111`, as we decided in Step 1.

3. The server recognizes the client connection. A special procedure is invoked within the server to handle each new client. This procedure usually sets up a file event to read input from the client and may also allocate some resources for each client. For example, the server may open a separate data file for each client, to service its requests.

4. The client and the server communicate by sending commands back and forth. This works as we described in Section 7.6.

5. Eventually, either the client or the server disconnects. When this happens, the other side should detect the broken connection and close the socket. Server processes usually live longer than clients, so it is important that the server clean up properly after each client. For example, if the server has opened a file for a client, it must close the file when the client disconnects. Otherwise, the server will run out of file descriptors for future clients.

7.7.2 A networked server

You can create a server by using the `socket` command, like this:

```
socket -server command port
```

The `-server` option tells this command to listen for clients on a particular *port* number on the current host. When each client tries to connect, the server executes the *command* to recognize the new client.

Three parameters are automatically appended to *command*: the file handle for the client's connection, the IP address of the client's host, and the client's port number. Normally, the *command* parameter is simply the name of a procedure that takes three arguments. The procedure usually looks something like this:

```
proc server_accept {cid addr port} {
    fileevent $cid readable "server_handle $cid"
    fconfigure $cid -buffering line
}
```

In this case, we have used the `fileevent` command to handle requests coming from the client. Whenever the client's connection becomes readable, the `server_handle` procedure will be called to read the request and handle it. Also, we have changed the output buffering for the client to `line` mode. That way, each response line we send to the client will be flushed automatically. This avoids any buffering problems, as we discussed in Section 7.4.

Let's see how all of this comes together. We can rewrite our math server to use sockets, as follows:

```
set parser [interp create -safe]
$parser eval {
    ...
}

proc server_accept {cid addr port} {
    fileevent $cid readable "server_handle $cid"
    fconfigure $cid -buffering line
}
proc server_handle {cid} {
    global parser buffer
    if {[gets $cid request] < 0} {
        close $cid
    } else {
        append buffer $request "\n"
        if {[info complete $buffer]} {
            set request $buffer
            set buffer ""
            if {[catch {$parser eval $request} result] == 0} {
                puts $cid $result
            } else {
                puts $cid [list error_result $result]
            }
        }
    }
}
socket -server server_accept 9001
vwait enter-mainloop
```

We start by creating a safe interpreter to handle incoming requests. We left out the code in the $parser eval command. This defines the add and subtract commands, as we saw in Section 7.6.7.3.

Next, we define the server_accept procedure, which is called when each client connects. We also define the server_handle procedure, which is called when a request line arrives. This procedure looks a lot like the back_handler procedure shown in Section 7.6.8. This procedure reads request lines from the socket and assembles them to form a complete command. When the procedure has a complete command, it executes the command in a safe interpreter and then writes the result back to the socket.

Next, we use the socket command to establish a server at port number 9001 on the current host. Finally, we use the vwait command to enter the event loop, as discussed in Section 7.6.7.1. This causes the server to listen for clients to connect.

7.7.2.1 Testing the server manually

One advantage of passing text strings between client/server programs is that it makes the programs easy to test. If you want to verify that a server is running properly, you can connect to the server, send it some commands, and get back human-readable results. On UNIX systems, you can use the `telnet` program to interact with a server. Just give the program the host name and the port number of the server you want to talk to. For example, you could start up our math server and interact with it like this:

```
$ tclsh maths7.tcl &
$ telnet localhost 9001
⇒   Trying 127.0.0.1 ...
    Connected to localhost.
    Escape character is '^]'.
    add 2 3 %v
⇒   5
    add 2 3 "set x %v"
⇒   set x 5
    exec rm -rf .
∅   error_result {invalid command name "exec"}
```

7.7.3 A networked client

Let's rewrite our math client to use sockets, so it can talk to the new math server. Again, most of the client code will remain the same—we need change only the communication channel that we use to talk to the server.

```
proc client_handle {sid} {
    global backend parser buffer
    if {[gets $sid request] < 0} {
        catch {close $sid}
        set backend ""
        notice_show "Lost connection to server" error
    } else {
        append buffer $request "\n"
        if {[info complete $buffer]} {
            set request $buffer
            set buffer ""
            if {[catch {$parser eval $request} result] != 0} {
                notice_show $result error
            }
        }
    }
}
proc client_send {args} {
    global backend
```

```
        if {$backend != ""} {
            puts $backend $args
        }
    }


    set sid [socket localhost 9001]
    fileevent $sid readable "client_handle $sid"
    fconfigure $sid -buffering line
    set backend $sid
```

The `client_handle` procedure is a lot like the `back_handler` procedure shown in Section 7.6.8. The procedure reads response lines from the server and assembles them to form a complete command. When it has a complete command, the procedure executes the command in its safe interpreter. Remember, the server will send back commands like `show_result` or `error_result`. Executing these commands will cause the client to display its results.

We use the `socket` command to connect to the server program. For this simple example, we assume that the client and the server are running on the same machine, so we use `localhost` as the server's host name. If the server were running on a different host, we would replace `localhost` with the name of that machine.

If for some reason we can't connect to the server, the `socket` command will fail, and the client program will terminate. We could use the `catch` command to handle the error more gracefully, but in this simple example, we didn't bother.

If the connection is established, the `socket` command returns a file handle that we can use to communicate with the server. We should configure this connection just as we did on the server side. We set up a file event to handle response lines coming from the server, and we set the output buffering to `line` mode, so each request line we send to the server will be flushed automatically. Finally, we save the file handle in a global variable called `backend`, so we can use it throughout the program.

We've defined a procedure called `client_send` that makes it easy to send requests to the server. You simply append the request as arguments to this command. For example, we might use this to handle the `add` request as follows:

```
    proc do_add {} {
        set x [.x get]
        set y [.y get]
        client_send add $x $y {show_result %v}
    }
```

When you select the + button on the client interface, it invokes this procedure, which extracts the numbers from the two entry fields and then sends an `add` request to the server. The server sends back a `show_result` command, which causes the client to display the result.

7.8 A case study—the Electric Secretary

Let's look at a case study that illustrates many of the concepts we've studied so far. The application, which is shown in Figure 7.13, is a multiuser scheduling/calendar program called the Electric Secretary. Its features include

* A standard perpetual calendar
* A day-by-day appointment minder
* Configurable alarms for appointments
* Group calendar management
* Options for colors, alarm characteristics, and work groups

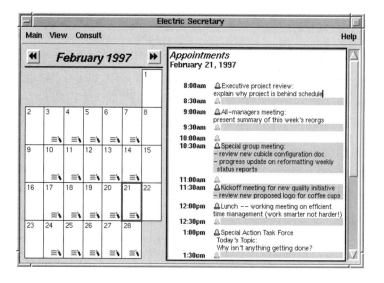

Figure 7.13. Dilbert's boss uses the Electric Secretary.

This application uses our client/server architecture, as shown in Figure 7.14. A networked server keeps the appointment data in a centralized location. Clients connect to the server and display the appointment data in a graphical user interface. Each client has certain configuration options, called *preferences*, that are stored in a file in the user's home directory. Thus each user can configure the client program to customize such things as colors and alarm characteristics.

The server program is about 200 lines long. The client program is about 850 lines long, not counting the components, such as the calendar and the appointment editor, that

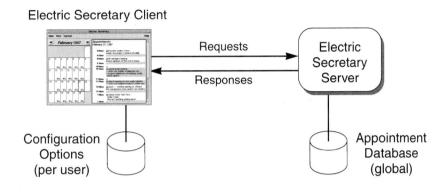

Figure 7.14. Electric Secretary client/server architecture. Multiple clients can be attached to the server at the same time.

we developed in previous chapters. We won't go into the details of this code. Instead, we'll focus on the overall architecture and describe the communication between the client and the server. If you'd like to try out this application or see exactly how it is written, you can find the client in the file `efftcl/apps/electric` and the server in the file `efftcl/apps/elserver`, which can be obtained from the Web site mentioned on page xiv.

7.8.1 Downloading appointments from the server

When each client starts up, it opens a socket to the server and sends the following message:

```
notify $env(USER) {
    receive {%date} {%time} {%alarm} {%comments}
} {
    startup
}
```

This tells the server that the client is interested in the appointments for a particular user. In this case, we're taking the user's name from the environment variable USER. On UNIX and Macintosh systems, this variable contains the current user name. On Windows systems, this variable may not be set, so we'll also provide a way to set the user name in a preferences file.

The server reads the `notify` command and executes it in a safe interpreter. This causes the server to send back appointment data, using two response templates, as shown in Figure 7.15. The first template is returned for each of the user's appointments, with data substituted into the following fields:

`%date`	Appointment date (*mm*/*dd*/*yyyy*)
`%time`	Appointment time (8:00am, 8:30am, and so on.)

```
%alarm              Nonzero means that a reminder alarm is set
%comments           Description for this appointment
%user               User who owns this appointment
```

So in this example, the server returns a series of `receive` commands, like this:

```
receive {03/10/1997} {9:00am} {1} {design review}
receive {03/25/1997} {1:00pm} {1} {conference call}
...
receive {07/15/1997} {8:00am} {1} {Tcl/Tk Workshop '97}
```

The client reads each `receive` command and executes it in its own safe interpreter. This causes the client to store the data for each appointment in its memory.

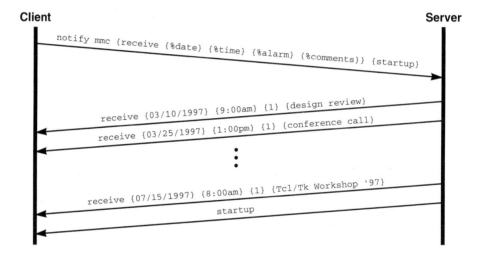

Figure 7.15. The Electric Secretary client sends a `notify` message to the server and gets back appointment data.

The second template is returned after all of the appointments have been sent. This lets the client know that the download is complete. Downloading all of the appointment data may take a minute or two, so while the client starts up, it will display an animated placard, letting the user know that the program is active. We'll see how the placard is implemented in Section 8.1.3.

When the download is complete, the client receives a `startup` command. This triggers an alias in the safe interpreter:

```
set clientParser [interp create -safe]
$clientParser alias startup placard_destroy
...
```

As you can see, the `startup` command invokes a procedure called `placard_destroy`, which takes down the placard and brings up the main application window.

7.8.2 Sending an appointment to the server

Once the client has started up, you can select any date on the calendar and view the appointments for that date. You can modify any appointment by typing your comments right into the appointment window. Whenever you modify an appointment, the client sends an `appointment` command to the server, like this:

```
appointment mmc 02/14/97 8:00am 0 {Valentine's Day}
```

The server reads this command and executes it in a safe interpreter. This causes the server to do two things.

- It adds the appointment to its own database.

- It sends the appointment to all other clients interested in this user, as shown in Figure 7.16. How does the server know which clients are interested? Remember, each client sends a `notify` command when it starts up, registering its interest in a particular user. The server not only sends the appointments for that user but also makes a note of the client's interest and saves the client's response template. When anything changes for that user later on, it notifies the client. With this feature, you can add an appointment to someone else's calendar, and it will instantly appear on that user's screen!

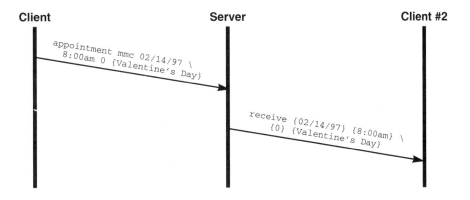

Figure 7.16. One client sends an appointment to the server, which then automatically notifies another client.

7.8.3 Handling schedule conflicts

Many calendar programs let you store appointments. But the Electric Secretary does more than that. It manages the calendars for many people simultaneously, so if you want to arrange a meeting, the Electric Secretary can help you find times when everyone is free. And when you set a meeting date, the server will automatically broadcast the change to each person's screen.

For example, suppose that you want to arrange a staff meeting for the junior executives. First, you bring up the Preferences dialog and create a group called `jrstaff`, as shown in Figure 7.17(a). This will add an entry for jrstaff onto the Consult menu. Next, you select a date for the meeting. Now, if you select the jrstaff entry on the Consult menu, you'll get a composite schedule for that day, as shown in Figure 7.17(b). Conflicting times will be marked in red, showing the names of the people who are busy. If you can find an empty slot, you can enter a new appointment. Clicking on Update will add the appointment to your own calendar, but clicking on Update All will add the appointment to the calendars of everyone in the group! If the group members happen to be looking at their calendars, they'll see the change immediately.

Let's see how this works. When you select a group from the Consult menu, the client sends the server a `consult` message, which looks something like this:

```
consult 03/10/1997 {allegra alex max katie} {conflicts %users}
```

The first two arguments tell the server the desired date and the list of users. The server checks the schedules for these users and builds a list of time conflicts. Then the server substitutes the information into the `%users` field of the response template and sends the client the response, which in this case looks something like this:

```
conflicts 8:00am allegra 8:30am {allegra alex} 9:00am {allegra max} ...
```

When the client receives the `conflicts` command, it pops up a dialog with an appointment editor, showing the conflicts.

When you click on the Update button, the client sends new appointments off to the server, using the `appointment` command that we saw earlier. For example:

```
appointment max 03/10/1997 11:00am 1 {Junior Staff Weekly Meeting}
```

Similarly, when you click on the Update All button, the client sends a series of appointments to the server, one for each user in the group:

```
appointment allegra 03/10/1997 11:00am 1 {Junior Staff Weekly
Meeting}
appointment alex 03/10/1997 11:00am 1 {Junior Staff Weekly Meeting}
appointment max 03/10/1997 11:00am 1 {Junior Staff Weekly Meeting}
appointment katie 03/10/1997 11:00am 1 {Junior Staff Weekly Meeting}
```

7.8.4 Preferences

The Preferences dialog shown in Figure 7.17(a) lets you customize the colors, alarm characteristics, and work groups for the Electric Secretary. When you make any changes, your

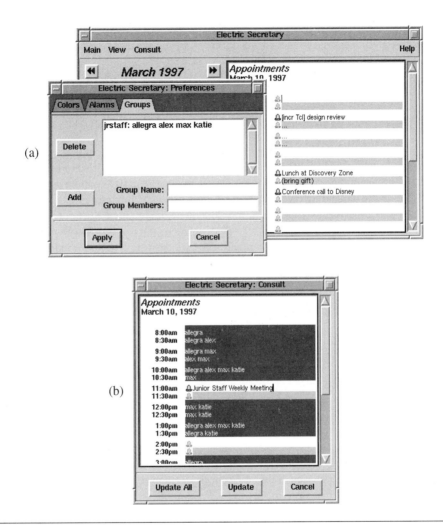

Figure 7.17. (a) The Preferences dialog lets you define groups of users. (b) When you consult the schedule for a group, conflicts are marked in red.

new settings are saved in a file called .esecrc in your home directory. Each time you start up the client application, it loads your settings from this file.

We could make up any format for the preferences file, but following the advice in Section 7.6.5, we'll invent some Tcl commands. A typical preferences file might look like this:

```
# Electric Secretary Preferences
# updated: Mon Mar 10 01:09:23 EDT 1997
user mmc
colors white black red
alarms {All of the above} {Pop-up reminder}
groups {{jrstaff: allegra alex max katie}}
```

Four commands are used to convey the preference values. The `user` command sets the user name, which is stored in the USER environment variable. The `colors` command sets the background, foreground, and selection colors used in the calendar. The `alarms` command sets the alarm characteristics. Each appointment has an alarm bell that can be turned on or off. If it is turned on, the client program will warn the user when the time for that appointment draws near. The client can ring a bell, pop up a reminder notice, or do both, depending on the settings in the `alarms` command. Finally, the `groups` command specifies the user groups in the Consult menu, letting the user check for scheduling conflicts.

We can load the preferences file by executing it in a safe interpreter, like this:

```
set prefsParser [interp create -safe]
$prefsParser alias user esec_prefs_cmd_user
$prefsParser alias colors esec_prefs_cmd_colors
$prefsParser alias alarms esec_prefs_cmd_alarms
$prefsParser alias groups esec_prefs_cmd_groups

set cmd {
    set fid [open [file join $env(HOME) .esecrc] r]
    set script [read $fid]
    close $fid
    $prefsParser eval $script
}

if {[catch $cmd err] != 0} {
    notice_show "Error in preferences file .esecrc:\n$err" error
}
```

If anything goes wrong, we pop up a notice dialog to display the error.

We use aliases to link the four preference commands to the procedures in the main interpreter that store the settings. For example, the `user` command is aliased to `esec_prefs_cmd_user`, which is implemented like this:

```
proc esec_prefs_cmd_user {name} {
    global env
    set env(USER) $name
}
```

This procedure stores the user name in the USER environment variable. The other preference procedures are implemented in a similar manner.

7.8.5 Persistent storage

When the server receives an appointment, it adds that appointment to persistent storage. That way, if the server crashes or its host machine goes down, the appointment data won't be lost. When the server restarts, it can find all of its data on disk.

We could have used a relational database to store the information. There are a few different extensions that you can add to Tcl to access commercial database packages. For example, you can use Oratcl to access Oracle databases, and Sybtcl to access Sybase databases.[*]

But for this simple application, we'll use a plain ASCII file. When our server receives an appointment, it'll echo an `appointment` command to the storage file. Over time, the storage file will build up a complete history of appointments. That history might look something like this:

```
appointment boss 02/21/1997 8:00am 1 {Executive project review:
explain why project is behind schedule}
appointment allegra 03/10/1997 8:00am 1 {Finish Tcl/CORBA interface}
appointment alex 03/10/1997 1:00pm 1 {Call John Ousterhout}
appointment max 03/10/1997 9:00am 1 {[incr Tcl] design review}
appointment katie 03/10/1997 9:00am 1 {[incr Tcl] design review}
```

When the server starts up, it can restore all of its data by executing this file in a safe interpreter. It just so happens that we have a safe interpreter with an `appointment` command—we're using it to filter the client requests. So we can use this same interpreter to load data from persistent storage.

7.8.6 Conclusions

Using a networked, client/server architecture has two advantages.

- It centralizes our data storage.
- It lets clients communicate and share information.

All of the messaging in this application is based on Tcl commands. The client and server programs communicate by exchanging Tcl commands. The client stores its preferences as Tcl commands, and the server handles persistent storage through Tcl commands. Tcl provides a powerful way of expressing information. As long as we're careful to execute these commands in a safe interpreter, we can keep the power of Tcl safely under control.

---

* You can download these extensions from http://www.NeoSoft.com/tcl/ftparchive/sorted/databases.

Client/server programs don't have to be complicated. As you can see, our server is just 200 lines long and has a small vocabulary. It handles three commands: `notify`, `appointment`, and `conflicts`. But when these simple commands are used together, they form a powerful application.

Chapter 8
Delivering Tcl/Tk Applications

The day has come. Your application is finished, and you're eager to ship it to the throngs of customers who will make you rich. But what exactly do you ship? The answer may be more complicated than you think.

In this chapter, we'll see how to put Tcl/Tk applications in the hands of your customers. There are two different ways to handle this.

- *Desktop application*: Customers own this program and install it on their computers. This works well for applications that are large or frequently used. You must send your script, along with any library procedures that it requires. You must include any bitmaps or image files used within the application. And in most cases, you'll need to include the wish program, because your customers may not have it. Your customers won't care to know about these details, so you should send all of this in a single package that's easy to install.

- *Web-based application*: Customers see this program as part of a Web page. Each time they visit the Web page, they download the latest copy of the program. This works well for casual users or for demo programs, and it adds marketing glitz to your Web pages.

You can use either method, depending on the kind of application you're trying to deliver.

We'll also look at some finishing touches for your applications. We'll see how you can customize the look and feel of a program by using the Tk option database. We'll show you how to handle unexpected errors (bugs!) in a graceful manner. We'll even create an introductory placard with an animated logo. These techniques give your products a professional look that your customers will appreciate.

8.1 Adding polish to your application

Finishing the last 10 percent of an application often takes 90 percent of the time. When you're pressed to deliver a product, you may find yourself cutting corners as time runs out. But you should always reserve some time to polish your application. Spend a few days tweaking colors and fonts; add some padding to make your widget layouts look nice; include an introductory placard with some splashy graphics. If you do, you'll be richly rewarded.

In this section, we'll look at three techniques that will make your applications sparkle.

8.1.1 Handling widget resources

You may be tempted to set the colors and fonts for widgets as you develop an application. However, it's usually best to leave these decisions to the very end. After all, you may spend hours fiddling with the colors for a dialog and then redesign or eliminate the dialog later in the development cycle.

8.1.1.1 Tk option database

When the time comes to polish your application, you can set colors, fonts, and other resources by using the *Tk option database*. This database sets the default values for all widget configuration options. For example, suppose you want to change the background color for your application. Instead of setting the -background option for each widget individually, you can add a single entry to the database to set the default background color for the entire application. If you handle things properly, your customers can override your choices with their own values, to customize the program to their liking.

Let's revisit the desktop calculator described in Section 2.2.2 and Section 7.5.3. We could add the following commands to our script to customize the look of this application:

```
option add *Entry.background white startupFile
option add *Scrollbar.width 8 startupFile
option add *readout.justify right startupFile
option add *Button.background DimGray startupFile
option add *Button.foreground white startupFile
option add *quit.background red startupFile
option add *quit.foreground white startupFile
```

Each of these commands adds a default value to the option database. These settings apply only to the program that contains them, so the settings in one program will not interfere with the settings in another. Also, these commands affect only the widgets created *after* they're in place, so it's best to put them at the start of your script.

The string *Entry.background describes a widget configuration option, which is also referred to as a *resource*. Each resource is identified by a series of names separated by either the "*" or the "." character. The names form a path that describes how the resource applies to the widget hierarchy. When you're reading a particular resource name, you can translate "*" as "any" and "." as "that has a...". For example, the resource name

`*Entry.background` means "any entry widget that has a background option." In our example, we set this resource to `white`, so all of the entry widgets in our application will have a white background. Similarly, all of our scrollbars will have a width of 8 pixels, all of our buttons will have a background color `DimGray`, and so on.

Notice that some parts of the resource names start with uppercase letters, whereas other parts start with lowercase letters. The option database is case sensitive, so the distinction is important. Any name that starts in uppercase refers to a class of widgets. Any name that starts in lowercase refers to a specific widget. For example, the name `Entry` refers to the class of entry widgets, which affects all the entry widgets in an application; however, the name `entry` refers to a particular widget named `entry`. This may or may not be an entry widget. In this example, we set `*quit.background` to `red`, so any widget named `quit` that has a `-background` option will be red. In the calculator, we have only one such widget—the Off button in the upper-left corner. But instead of tracing the particular path through the widget hierarchy that leads to this widget, we simply refer to it as `*quit`.

The uppercase/lowercase distinction applies to configuration options as well. For example, the name `Background` refers to a class of background-style options. This includes the usual `-background` option, as well as `-activebackground`, `-selectforeground`, and `-troughcolor`. However, the name `background` refers specifically to the `-background` option.

The last value on each line is the keyword `startupFile`. This assigns a priority to each setting in the database. We'll see why this is important shortly.

8.1.1.2 Handling color resources

It's quite common to use resources to set the colors of an application. But what if a customer has a monochrome display? In that case, color values are mapped to either black or white, according to their intensity. Thus a color like red becomes black, and yellow becomes white.

Automatic color mappings don't always work properly. If you have black text on a red background, for example, it will look completely black on a monochrome display. You can handle this by setting different resources for color and monochrome displays. In our calculator, for example, we could rewrite the option commands like this:

```
option add *Entry.background white startupFile
option add *Scrollbar.width 8 startupFile
option add *readout.justify right startupFile
option add *printTape off startupFile

if {[string match *color [winfo screenvisual .]]} {
    option add *Button.background DimGray startupFile
    option add *Button.foreground white startupFile
    option add *quit.background red startupFile
    option add *quit.foreground white startupFile
```

```
    } else {
        option add *Button.background black startupFile
        option add *Button.foreground white startupFile
        option add *quit.background white startupFile
        option add *quit.foreground black startupFile
    }
```

We use the `winfo screenvisual` command to determine the kind of display that contains the main window ".". If it's a color display, this command will return a name, such as `truecolor`, `directcolor`, `staticcolor`, or `pseudocolor`. (The different names indicate how many different colors the display can show at once, providing some measure for the quality of the display. Right now, we're looking for color support of any kind.) If we find any kind of color support, we set certain resources to color values. Otherwise, we set the same resources to black/white values.

8.1.1.3 Inventing new resources

The option database will accept anything as a resource name, so you must be careful to spell things correctly. For example, the following command won't cause an error, but it won't change the application in any way:

```
        option add *Entry.borderwidth 4 startupFile
```

It looks as though we're trying to set the border width of all entry widgets to 4 pixels. But the -borderwidth option is controlled by the `borderWidth` resource. We accidentally misspelled `borderWidth` with a lowercase w, so this setting will have no effect.

If you need to double-check the spelling for a particular resource name, you can consult the `options` manual page. You can also query the information directly from a widget, like this:

```
        $ wish
        % entry .test
    ⇒   .test
        % .test configure -borderwidth
    ⇒   -borderwidth borderWidth BorderWidth 2 2
```

The `configure` operation returns a list of five values. The first value is the name of the option—in this case, -borderwidth. The second and third values are the resource name and the resource class for the option database. So the -borderwidth option is controlled by the `borderWidth` resource, which belongs to a class of `BorderWidth` options. The resource names must be spelled exactly as they are reported here, or they will have no effect.

This may seem like a bug, but it's really more of a feature. Since the option database will accept anything as a resource name, you can invent new resources to control certain features of an application. For example, suppose we add a "paper tape" feature to our calculator. Each time you press the = key, we could print the current operation and the result to the screen, like this:

```
8 + 3
= 11
11 * 5
= 55
55 - 12
= 43
. . .
```

Some users would like this feature, since they could look back through the history of a long calculation to spot an error. Others would say that it's a lot of extra noise that they don't need. You can keep both kinds of users happy by adding a resource to control this behavior.

Suppose we add the following resource to the top of our calculator script:

```
option add *printTape off startupFile
```

This says that the `printTape` resource is set to `off` for every widget in our application. None of the Tk widgets have a `printTape` resource, so by itself, this won't do anything. But we can use the `option get` command to query the `printTape` resource and then handle things accordingly. For example, we could add the following code to the bottom of the calculator script:

```
set val [option get . printTape PrintTape]
switch -- $val {
    1 - true - yes - on {
        proc print_tape {mesg} {
            puts $mesg
        }
    }
    0 - false - no - off {
        proc print_tape {mesg} {
            # do nothing!
        }
    }
    default {
        puts stderr "bad printTape value \"$val\""
    }
}
```

We use the `option get` command to look for a `printTape` setting on the main window ".". The print tape feature belongs to the application as a whole, so it makes sense to query the resource from the main window. Whenever you query a resource value, you must supply both a resource name and a resource class. There are only a few useful classes, such as `Background` or `Font`. If none of the standard classes apply, you can make the resource class the same as the resource name but starting with a capital letter.

Once we have the value of the `printTape` resource, we use a `switch` command to handle it. A positive or negative Boolean value will turn the print tape feature on or off. Any other value is flagged as an error. As we'll see shortly, customers can override the `printTape` setting, so error checking here is extremely important.

The print tape feature is controlled by a `print_tape` procedure. During each calculation, the `print_tape` procedure is called with an operation string and a result string. Thus we can turn on the print tape by defining `print_tape` to print its result, and we can turn off the print tape by defining `print_tape` to do nothing.

8.1.1.4   Resource priorities

The last argument for the `option add` command sets the priority of a resource setting. In all of the examples in this section, we've used the `startupFile` priority, like this:

```
option add *Button.background DimGray startupFile
```

This priority is low enough that a customer can easily override the setting. By default, we supply a calculator with dim gray buttons, as shown in Figure 8.1(a). But a customer can override our settings to produce the calculator shown in Figure 8.1(b).

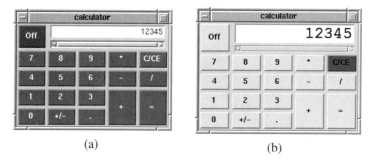

(a)   (b)

Figure 8.1. A simple calculator application. (a) The calculator's default appearance. (b) Its appearance with a set of customized resources.

For this to work properly, you must supply a priority value, such as `startupFile`. If you leave it off, the setting is given an extremely high priority that the customer can't override:

```
option add *Button.background DimGray
```

This statement sets the background of all buttons to dim gray, regardless of the settings that a customer may provide.

On UNIX systems, each customer can add resource settings to a file called `.Xresources` or `.Xdefaults` in the home directory. We'll describe how this is handled on other platforms in Section 9.1.5. Within this file, the resources for the calculator program might look like this:

```
calc*Button.background: yellow
calc*Button.foreground: black
calc*clear.background: red
calc*Scrollbar.borderWidth: 1
```

```
calc*readout.font: -*-courier-bold-r-normal--*-240-*
calc*readout.width: 10
calc.printTape: yes
```

The format of this file is quite similar to the `option add` command. Each line has a resource name, followed by "`:`" and the resource value. This file contains resources for many different applications, so each resource should start with an application name. In this case, we're setting resources for our calculator. This script resides in a file named `calc`, so all of these resources are prefixed with the name `calc`. Setting the resource `calendar*background` would affect only an application named `calendar`. Setting the resource `*background` would change the background color for all of the applications on the desktop.

In this example, we've given all of the buttons in the calculator a yellow background, except for the C/CE button, which is red. We've enlarged the font for the readout window and reduced its width to ten characters. We've also turned on the print tape feature.

You should use the `startupFile` priority whenever you're setting defaults for an entire application. But when you're developing library code that may be used in many different applications, you should use a lower priority, such as `widgetDefault`. That way, you can set defaults for the library and override them with other defaults for an application, and the customer can override them yet again.

For example, we included the following resources in the tabnotebook library developed in Section 4.5:

```
option add *Tabnotebook.tabColor #a6a6a6 widgetDefault
option add *Tabnotebook.activeTabColor #d9d9d9 widgetDefault
```

We gave these settings the low-priority `widgetDefault`, so an application that uses the tabnotebook can override them, like this:

```
option add *Tabnotebook.tabColor LimeGreen startupFile
option add *Tabnotebook.activeTabColor PaleGreen startupFile
option add *Tabnotebook.notebook*background PaleGreen startupFile
option add *Tabnotebook.notebook*highlightBackground PaleGreen \
    startupFile
```

In this application, unselected tabs will have a lime green background, and the selected tab will have a lighter, pale green color. We want the notebook page to match the selected tab color, so we added some resources to control the notebook. The name `*Tabnotebook.notebook*background` means "any widget in class `Tabnotebook` that has a widget called `notebook`, and any background option under that." This resource sets the background color of the notebook assembly itself, all of the pages in the notebook, and all of the widgets on each page. We're careful to set the `highlightBackground` resource along with the regular background. If we didn't do this, many of the widgets inside the tabnotebook would have funny gray rings around them, due to the focus highlight border. Each gray ring would turn black when its widget received keyboard focus. As a rule, the focus highlight border should be kept in sync with the normal backgound color.

Finally, a customer could supply settings for the tabnotebook by including the following resources in the `.Xresources` or `.Xdefaults` file:

```
*Tabnotebook.tabColor: SteelBlue
*Tabnotebook.activeTabColor: LightSteelBlue
*Tabnotebook.notebook*background: LightSteelBlue
*Tabnotebook.notebook*highlightBackground: LightSteelBlue
```

These settings would override the `startupFile` priority, changing the color scheme from green to steel blue.

8.1.1.5   When to use the option database

You shouldn't use resources to control everything in your application. It's a good idea to hard-code the options that affect the functionality of widgets and to soft-code the options that control their appearance.

In our calculator, for example, we create the Off button like this:

```
button .quit -text "Off" -command exit
```

We hard-code the values for the label and the command, since there is no need for a customer to change them. Then, as we're polishing the application, we add some resources to control the appearance of the button:

```
option add *quit.background red startupFile
option add *quit.foreground white startupFile
```

We might change the `option add` commands to try out a few different color schemes before we ship the program. If the customers grumble about our colors (they usually do!), they can supply their own values.

8.1.2   Handling unexpected errors

When you encounter an error in a Tcl/Tk application, you get a dialog box like the one shown in Figure 8.2(a). If you click on the Stack Trace button, you get another window, which describes the code that was executing when the error occurred. To the developer, this is an extremely handy feature; to the customer, it is an eyesore.

No matter how carefully you test your application, a customer may encounter an error. If that happens, the customer should not confront the horrors of a complete stack trace. You should replace the usual Tk error dialog with something like the dialog shown in Figure 8.2(b). That dialog lets the customer know that something went wrong, and with the click of a button, it sends a bug report back to the developer.

If you look carefully at this dialog, you'll notice that it looks just like the confirmation dialog that we developed in Section 6.5. In fact, we can use our `confirm_ask` procedure to pop up this dialog and wait for a response. The following procedure handles all of this. You call it with an e-mail address and an error message, and it prompts the user and then sends the bug report. Of course, you would never call this explicitly. We'll see how to plug this in as an error handler, so it gets called automatically when an error occurs.

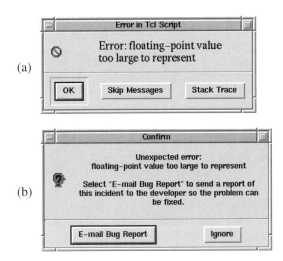

(a)

(b)

Figure 8.2. (a) The default dialog that appears when an unexpected error is encountered in your application. (b) An improved dialog that lets the user send a bug report via e-mail.

```
proc email_bug_report_send {bugAddress error} {
    global errorInfo env argv argv0
    set bugReport $errorInfo

    set question "Unexpected error:\n$error\n\n"
    append question "Select \"E-mail Bug Report\" to send "
    append question "a report of this incident to the developer "
    append question "so the problem can be fixed."

    if {[confirm_ask $question "E-mail Bug Report" "Ignore"]} {
        if {[info exists env(REPLYTO)]} {
            set from $env(REPLYTO)
        } else {
            set from ""
        }
        set body [format {
While the following program was executing...
------------------------------------------------------------
  %s %s
------------------------------------------------------------
...the following error was detected:

%s} $argv0 $argv $bugReport]
```

```
        catch {
            email_send $bugAddress $from "" \
                "BUG REPORT ($argv0)" $body
        }
    }
}
```

The global `errorInfo` variable contains the stack trace for the most recent error. We start by copying this information into the `bugReport` variable. That way, we'll have the information even if another error occurs before we finish sending this bug report.

Next, we build up a message for the dialog, and we call `confirm_ask` to pop it up. If the customer selects **E-mail Bug Report**, the `confirm_ask` procedure returns 1, and we send the bug report. As a developer, you'll want to see a few important things in the e-mail message: the name of the script, which is stored in the global variable `argv0`; the command-line arguments, which are in the global variable `argv`; and the stack trace, which we saved earlier, in the `bugReport` variable. The `format` command substitutes these things in place of the `%s` fields in a stock message, forming the body of an e-mail message.

We send the message using the `email_send` procedure developed in Section 7.3. This procedure takes the e-mail address for bug reports, the e-mail address of the customer, a subject line, and the body of the message. We determine the e-mail address for the current customer by looking for the `REPLYTO` environment variable. On UNIX systems, this is often set with the preferred e-mail address for the user. If this variable doesn't exist, we set the `from` address to `""`, and `email_send` won't bother to include a `From:` line in the message.

Notice that we wrap the `email_send` call in a `catch` command. If something goes wrong as we're sending the message, we don't want another **Unexpected** error dialog to pop up. Instead, we'll ignore any errors that come from the mailer.

Whenever an error occurs in the event loop, a procedure named `bgerror` is called to handle it. The default `bgerror` procedure pops up the error dialog shown in Figure 8.2(a), but you can redefine this procedure to do anything you like.

If you want to save error messages in a log file, for example, you might define the `bgerror` procedure like this:

```
proc bgerror {error} {
    set fid [open "/tmp/log.txt" a]
    puts $fid $error
    close $fid
}
```

Notice that this procedure takes one argument—a brief message describing the current error. In this case, we open the log file in "append" mode and write the error message to the file.

Now let's change the default error handler to use our `email_bug_report_send` procedure:

```
proc bgerror {error} {
    email_bug_report_send efftcl-bugs@aw.com $error
}
```

This time, when an error occurs, we call `email_bug_report_send`. It pops up the dialog and waits for the user's response. If the user selects **E-mail Bug Report**, it sends off the bug report. In this case, the bug reports will be sent to `efftcl-bugs@aw.com`.

If you like our error handler, you may find yourself flipping back to this page in the book from time to time, to copy out the `bgerror` procedure. We can prevent a lot of wear and tear on your book by adding the following procedure to our library:

```
proc email_bug_reports {addr} {
    proc bgerror {error} "
        email_bug_report_send [list $addr] \$error
    "
}
```

You can call this procedure with an e-mail address for your bug reports, like this:

```
email_bug_reports efftcl-bugs@aw.com
```

Doing so installs the proper `bgerror` procedure automatically. That way, you can use our error handler without having to remember the details of `bgerror`.

This procedure uses the `proc` command to redefine the `bgerror` procedure. But this isn't your run-of-the-mill `proc` definition. We use some special quoting to expand the e-mail address `$addr` but not the error variable `$error`. Specifically, we wrap the entire body in double quotes, so `$addr` will be expanded. But we put a backslash in front of `$error`, so it won't be expanded. We also wrap `$addr` in the `list` command, so it will be properly formatted even if it contains spaces, quotes, or braces. The result is a `bgerror` procedure that looks just like the one we coded by hand.

8.1.3   Animated placard

Some applications take a moment to load before they pop up on the desktop. For example, consider the Electric Secretary application described in Section 7.8. When the application starts up, it connects to an appointment server, downloads all of the data for a particular user, then pops up on the desktop. While the application is downloading the data, we can put up an introductory placard like the one shown in Figure 8.3. This isn't absolutely necessary, but it adds a bit of polish to the application, and it makes the download time much more tolerable.

We saw a simple way to create a placard in Section 6.7.1. Now let's take things one step further. Suppose you want to animate the Electric Secretary logo while the application is busy downloading data from the server. That way, the user knows that the application hasn't locked up but instead is busy doing something.

The `wish` program is single-threaded—it can't do two things at once. If it's busy reading data, it won't be able to handle the animation for the placard. We can get around this problem by starting a second `wish` process to handle the placard. While our application is busy, the second `wish` can pop up the placard window and handle its animation.

Figure 8.3. Introductory placard with an animated logo. Lights flash across the Electric Secretary logo while the application downloads data from the server.

When our main application is ready to continue, we can terminate the second `wish` and continue.

We'll write a few procedures that make it easy to add a placard to any application. The `placard_create` procedure hides the main application window and pops up a placard window in its place. This procedure is implemented as follows:

```
proc placard_create {script} {
    global env placard
    wm withdraw .
    set placard [open "| wish" w]
    puts $placard {
        wm overrideredirect . 1
        . configure -borderwidth 4 -relief raised
        after idle {
            update idletasks
            set maxw [winfo screenwidth .]
            set maxh [winfo screenheight .]
            set x0 [expr ($maxw-[winfo reqwidth .])/2]
            set y0 [expr ($maxh-[winfo reqheight .])/2]
            wm geometry . "+$x0+$y0"
        }
    }
    puts $placard $script
    flush $placard
}
```

First, we withdraw the main window of the current application—we don't want it to appear while we're setting things up. Then we open a new `wish` program in "write" mode, so we can write commands directly to its standard input. We store the file handle for the new `wish` in a global variable called `placard`, so we can access it later.

The first `puts` command tells the new `wish` to configure its main window as a placard. We've already seen this code in Section 6.7.1, so we won't bother to explain it here. The second `puts` command sends some extra code passed in via the `script` argument. You can use this code to create widgets within the placard to customize its appearance.

Finally, we flush the output to make sure that all of this code reaches the new `wish`. This gets around the buffering problems described in Section 7.4.

Once the placard is up, you might want to change something within it. For example, you might change a status message from time to time, letting the user know that things are progressing. We can write a procedure called `placard_eval` to send a script over to the placard application. The implementation of this procedure is trivial:

```
proc placard_eval {script} {
    global placard
    puts $placard $script
    flush $placard
}
```

We write the `script` argument to the standard input of the placard process. And again, we flush the output to make sure that the code reaches the process. You may be tempted not to write such seemingly trivial procedures. But having this procedure is important. It insulates you from things like the `placard` variable, which is really a detail of the implementation.

At some point, our main application will be ready to start up. We can take down the placard and display the main application window, using a procedure like this:

```
proc placard_destroy {} {
    global placard
    update
    puts $placard "exit"
    flush $placard
    close $placard
    wm deiconify .
}
```

We use the `update` command to finalize all of the changes in the main window, so it will come up cleanly when we deiconify it. Then we take down the placard and put up the main window. If we merely close the placard process, it won't go away. Instead, we must send it the `exit` command and then close the pipe to terminate the process.

We can use all of these procedures to create an animated placard, like this:

```
placard_create {
    package require Efftcl
    set images {}
    set counter 0
    for {set i 1} {$i <= 9} {incr i} {
        set file [file join $env(EFFTCL_LIBRARY) images esec$i.gif]
        set imh [image create photo -file $file]
        label .l$i -image $imh
        lappend images $imh
    }
    ...
    label .movie -image [lindex $images 0]
    pack .movie -side left -padx 8 -pady 8
```

```
    ...
    label .status -text "Connecting to server..."
    pack .status -fill x -pady 8
    ...
    animate_start 100 $images ".movie configure -image %v"
    update
}
```
...connect to server...
```
placard_eval {
    .status configure -text "Loading appointments..."
}
```
...load appointments...
```
placard_destroy
```

This is how the code looks in the Electric Secretary application. Of course, we've left out some of the code so we can focus on the important parts for this example.

The `placard_create` command appears near the start of the main application. This command puts up the placard, using the code shown here to handle the animation. After accomplishing some things in the main application, we call `placard_eval` to update the status message on the placard. Finally, when the application is ready, we call `placard_destroy` to take down the placard.

8.2 Creating Tcl/Tk libraries

After you've written a few hundred lines of Tcl/Tk code, you'll notice the same combinations of widgets appearing again and again. You don't have to build the same dialog too many times before you start to think about better ways to organize your applications. You may be tempted to copy code from one project to another. But you'll get much better results if you create *code libraries* that can be shared across all of your applications.

In this section, we'll show you how to design libraries and how to include them in your applications. If you look back through the examples in this book, you'll notice that they follow the conventions described here.

8.2.1 Designing library components

Let's begin with an example. Suppose we're building an "install" program and want to give the user some options. We might build a set of radiobuttons like the one shown in Figure 8.4. We'll call this widget assembly a *radiobox*.

The code required to build this is not terribly complicated. Just create a label and a few radiobuttons and pack them all together, like this:

```
frame .rbox
pack .rbox -padx 4 -pady 4
```

Figure 8.4. A simple radiobox with three options.

```
label .rbox.title -text "Installation Options:"
pack .rbox.title -side top -anchor w

frame .rbox.border -borderwidth 2 -relief groove
pack .rbox.border -expand yes -fill both

radiobutton .rbox.border.rb1 -text "Full install" \
    -variable current -value "Full install"
pack .rbox.border.rb1 -side top -anchor w

radiobutton .rbox.border.rb2 -text "Demo only" \
    -variable current -value "Demo only"
pack .rbox.border.rb2 -side top -anchor w

radiobutton .rbox.border.rb3 -text "Data files" \
    -variable current -value "Data files"
pack .rbox.border.rb3 -side top -anchor w

.rbox.border.rb1 invoke
```

But if we write the code this way, we'll have to rewrite it for each new radiobox. Instead, we can put this code in a procedure and pass in the bits that change for each radiobox.

We make a procedure to create the widget assembly for a radiobox, like this:

```
proc radiobox_create {win {title ""}} {
    frame $win -class Radiobox

    if {$title != ""} {
        label $win.title -text $title
        pack $win.title -side top -anchor w
    }
    frame $win.border -borderwidth 2 -relief groove
    pack $win.border -expand yes -fill both
```

```
        return $win
    }
```

You'll notice several important things.

- The procedure name follows a convention. The name starts with `radiobox`, which is what we're trying to build, and it ends with `create`. All of our library procedures follow this convention.

- This procedure creates a frame that we'll call the *hull*, which contains the widget assembly. Instead of using a hard-coded name for the hull, it uses a name that's passed in to the procedure. This makes it work like the rest of the Tk commands. You can create one radiobox like this:

```
    radiobox_create .install
```

and another like this:

```
    radiobox_create .cleanup
```

- This procedure sets the class of the hull to `Radiobox`, with a capital "R." This lets you set default values for the radiobox in the option database. For example, you could add the following line to your application:

```
    option add *Radiobox*selectColor ForestGreen startupFile
```

Then all of your radioboxes would have a green diamond that marks the selected option. This setting will affect only the radioboxes, not the rest of the radiobuttons in your application.

- This procedure does not pack the hull frame. It packs only the widgets inside the hull. Whoever calls this procedure will decide how to pack or grid the overall radiobox. Again, this makes it work like a normal Tk widget. You can create a radiobox and pack it with an extra command, like this:

```
    radiobox_create .flavors
    pack .flavors -padx 4 -pady 4
```

- This procedure returns the name of the hull as its result. Again, this makes it work just like a normal Tk widget.

The rest of the procedure is quite straightforward. After we create the hull, we create the widgets that go inside it. The `title` argument is optional. If it's not specified, it's set to the null string (`" "`), and we do nothing. Otherwise, we create a label for the title and pack it at the top of the hull. So if you want to add a title to the radiobox, you can do it like this:

```
    radiobox_create .flavors "Select your favorite flavor:"
```

We also create an empty frame with a grooved border to contain the options for the radiobox. But you'll notice that we didn't create the options themselves. Each radiobox will have a different number of options, so we can't just hard-code three radiobuttons into this procedure. We need a flexible way of adding options to the radiobox.

In addition to the creation procedure, you may write other procedures to support a widget assembly. For example, we could make a `radiobox_add` procedure to add options to an existing radiobox. We could use it to build the radiobox shown in Figure 8.4 like this:

```
radiobox_create .options "Installation Options:"
pack .options -padx 4 -pady 4


radiobox_add .options "Full install"
radiobox_add .options "Demo only"
radiobox_add .options "Data files"
```

Each call to `radiobox_add` creates a radiobutton and packs it into the grooved frame in the radiobox. This design makes it easy to set up a radiobox, and it also lets us change a radiobox on the fly.

We could add another procedure that lets you set the current choice. For example, if we want the default choice to be Demo only, we could use the following command after we create the radiobox:

```
radiobox_select .options "Demo only"
```

This selects Demo only as if the user had clicked on this option.

Finally, we could add a procedure that lets you query the current choice. After all, at some point, we'll do the installation, and we'll need to know what option the user selected. We can query the current choice like this:

```
set opt [radiobox_get .options]
```

If you look at these radiobox procedures, you'll notice a few important things.

- All of the procedures follow a naming convention. Their names start with `radiobox` and end with an action that describes what they do.

- All of the procedures take the name of the hull as their first argument. Inside each procedure, we'll need to know which radiobox to add to or which radiobox to select.

  This is a little different from the Tk convention. If this were a normal Tk widget, we would use it like this:

```
radiobox .flavors
.flavors add "Vanilla"
.flavors add "Chocolate"
```

Instead, we've set things up to work like this:

```
radiobox_create .flavors
radiobox_add .flavors "Vanilla"
radiobox_add .flavors "Chocolate"
```

In both cases, the idea is the same. We've just rearranged the words on the command line a bit so that we could implement the commands as Tcl procedures. Once you get used to our convention, you'll find that it works quite well.

8.2.2 Synthesizing data structures

At this point, we know how the radiobox should work, so we can write the procedures outlined in the previous section. But as soon as we start to do this, we'll hit a snag. A radiobox is more than a collection of procedures. Each radiobox has some data associated with it, and we need to manage that data.

Each radiobox needs two variables: one for the option that's currently selected and another to keep track of the number of options. In Tk, you use a global variable to tie a group of radiobuttons together. We saw this earlier when we first looked at the radiobox. We created the radiobuttons like this:

```
radiobutton .rbox.border.rb1 -text "Full install" \
    -variable current -value "Full install"
pack .rbox.border.rb1 -side top -anchor w

radiobutton .rbox.border.rb2 -text "Demo only" \
    -variable current -value "Demo only"
pack .rbox.border.rb2 -side top -anchor w

radiobutton .rbox.border.rb3 -text "Data files" \
    -variable current -value "Data files"
pack .rbox.border.rb3 -side top -anchor w
```

All of these radiobuttons are tied to the global variable `current`. When one is selected, the variable is set to the value for that radiobutton, and the others pop out. If we have more than one radiobox in an application, each one will need its own global variable for the current choice. Otherwise, if they all use the same variable, all of the radioboxes will be tied together.

Also, we need to keep track of the number of options so that we can give each radiobutton a unique name. Each radiobox can have a counter, like this:

```
set count 0
```

When we add a radiobutton, we can generate its name automatically, like this:

```
set name ".rbox.border.rb[incr count]"
radiobutton $name -text "Full install" \
    -variable current -value "Full install"
pack $name -side top -anchor w
```

Each time we do this, we'll get such names as `.rbox.border.rb1`, `.rbox.border.rb2`, and so on.

Thus you can see that each radiobox needs two variables: one for the current choice and one to act as a counter. If we were programming this example in C language, we might define a data structure for the radiobox as follows:

```
struct RadioboxData {
    char *current;
    int count;
};
```

We'd allocate memory for one of these structures whenever we created a radiobox.

There are no data structures in Tcl, but we can synthesize something like a data structure by using an array. In this example, we'll create one global array named `rbInfo` to contain all of the information for radioboxes. Each time we create a radiobox, we'll allocate two slots in this array with the following commands:

```
set rbInfo($win-current) ""
set rbInfo($win-count) 0
```

Together, these two fields act like the data structure shown earlier for C language.

Here, `$win` is the name of the hull, which uniquely identifies each radiobox. So each slot is parameterized by two names: the name of the radiobox (`$win`) and the name of the field that we're interested in (such as `current` or `count`). These two names are separated by a punctuation character, so they're easy to spot. We've chosen -, but you could also use . or , or something else.

At this point, we should fix our `radiobox_create` procedure to allocate the data when we create each radiobox:

```
proc radiobox_create {win {title ""}} {
    global rbInfo
    set rbInfo($win-current) ""
    set rbInfo($win-count) 0

    frame $win -class Radiobox

    if {$title != ""} {
        label $win.title -text $title
        pack $win.title -side top -anchor w
    }
    frame $win.border -borderwidth 2 -relief groove
    pack $win.border -expand yes -fill both

    bind $win <Destroy> "radiobox_destroy $win"
    return $win
}
```

We'll use this data later, when we add each option to the radiobox.

Notice that before we return, we bind to the `<Destroy>` event on the hull frame. When each radiobox is destroyed, the following procedure will be called automatically to remove data from the `rbInfo` array:

```
proc radiobox_destroy {win} {
    global rbInfo
    unset rbInfo($win-count)
    unset rbInfo($win-current)
}
```

It's a good idea to make a destruction procedure like this for each component that you create. If you don't, you may introduce a memory leak into your programs. For most of the applications that use the radiobox, this wouldn't be a significant leak. But even so, having the destruction procedure is good practice.

Now let's look at the radiobox_add procedure:

```
proc radiobox_add {win choice {command ""}} {
    global rbInfo

    set name "$win.border.rb[incr rbInfo($win-count)]"
    radiobutton $name -text $choice -command $command \
        -variable rbInfo($win-current) -value $choice
    pack $name -side top -anchor w

    if {$rbInfo($win-count) == 1} {
        $name invoke
    }
}
```

We generate the name of each radiobutton as we showed earlier, but now a bit more syntax is needed to access the count variable. We tie the radiobuttons together with the -variable option the same way, too, but again, more syntax is required to access the current field in the data structure.

In addition to having the radiobox name and the choice string as arguments, we've added a command string as an optional argument. If a command is not specified, it's set to the null string. But in any case, it's assigned to the -command option of the radiobutton. When you click on the radiobutton, it will invoke this command. So you can have each option do something when it's selected, or it can do nothing, and you can query the current choice later on.

We do one other thing at the end of this procedure. When the first option is added to the radiobox, we automatically invoke it to make it the default selection.

If you want to change the current selection, you can call radiobox_select. Let's see how this is implemented:

```
proc radiobox_select {win choice} {
    global rbInfo
    set rbInfo($win-current) $choice
}
```

This procedure merely sets the current field for the radiobox to whatever choice you specify. The radiobuttons react to this automatically. The one that's selected lights up, and the others go dim.

If at some point, you want to query the current choice, you can call radiobox_get, which also is trivial to implement:

```
proc radiobox_get {win} {
    global rbInfo
    return $rbInfo($win-current)
}
```

This procedure merely returns the value of the current field for the radiobox.

The `rbInfo` array is shared by all of these radiobox procedures, so it must be a global variable. You'll notice that we were careful to declare it with the `global` command in each radiobox procedure.

8.2.3 Adding callbacks to components

Many of the Tk widgets have actions associated with them. When you click on a button, for example, it invokes the code in the `-command` option. This code is often referred to as a *callback*, since the widget uses it to "call back" into your program to do something.

It's a good idea to design callbacks into all of your library components. Doing so gives them more flexibility, making them useful for many different applications. Let's revisit the color menu that we started to develop in Chapter 1. This time, we'll design a callback feature into the component.

You can create a colormenu component as follows:

```
colormenu_create .pen -text "Pen Color"
pack .pen
```

Then you can call `colormenu_action` to assign some callback code:

```
colormenu_action .pen {puts "pen color: %c"}
```

Whenever you select a color from the menu, the colormenu component will substitute the color name into the %c field and will then execute the callback code. When you select red, for example, the colormenu will execute the following command:

```
puts "pen color: red"
```

Now let's see how this is implemented. We'll start by writing a procedure to create the widget assembly for a colormenu. You pass in a widget name and some configuration options, and it creates the colormenu:

```
proc colormenu_create {win args} {
    global cmInfo

    frame $win -class Colormenu
    eval menubutton $win.cb $args
    $win.cb configure -menu $win.cb.clist -borderwidth 2
    pack $win.cb -expand yes -fill both

    menu $win.cb.clist
    $win.cb.clist add command -label "Off" \
        -command [list colormenu_select $win ""]
    $win.cb.clist add command -label "More..." \
        -command {wm deiconify $cmInfo(colorSelector)}
    ...
    set cmInfo($win-colors) ""
    set cmInfo($win-current) ""
    set cmInfo($win-command) ""
```

```
colormenu_add $win black
colormenu_add $win white
colormenu_add $win red
colormenu_add $win green
colormenu_add $win blue
colormenu_add $win yellow
colormenu_select $win black


return $win
    }
```

This procedure follows the pattern that we described in Section 8.2.1. We start by creating a hull frame in class `Colormenu`. Then we create a menubutton and pack it into the hull. We take any configuration options that are passed in to this procedure and apply them to the menubutton. So when you create a colormenu, you can supply a label for the menu-button, as we saw in the example.

Next, we create the pop-up menu for the menubutton. We start with two choices on this menu. The Off entry sets the current color to the null string. We'll use this to represent an invisible color in our applications. The More... option brings up a dialog box with a color selector, letting you add new colors to the menu. Since we saw how the color selector is implemented in Section 4.4 and how dialogs are created in Chapter 6, we'll skip over this code for now.

Next, we initialize the data structure for the colormenu. Each colormenu has three slots in the `cmInfo` array: the `colors` field contains the list of colors on the menu; the `current` field contains the current color choice; and the `command` field contains the callback code for this component. Initially, all of these fields are null.

You can use the `colormenu_action` procedure to change the callback code for a colormenu. This procedure is implemented as follows:

```
proc colormenu_action {win command} {
    global cmInfo
    set cmInfo($win-command) $command
}
```

You pass in the name of a colormenu and the callback code, and we store this code in the `command` field of the data structure. We'll see how this code is used shortly.

Before we return from `colormenu_create`, we add a series of default colors to the menu. We use the following procedure to add each color:

```
proc colormenu_add {win color} {
    global cmInfo

    if {[lsearch $cmInfo($win-colors) $color] < 0} {
        set imh [image create photo -width 40 -height 10]
        $imh put $color -to 0 0 40 10
        set last [$win.cb.clist index end]
        $win.cb.clist insert [expr $last-1] command -image $imh \
            -command [list colormenu_select $win $color]
```

```
            lappend cmInfo($win-colors) $color
        }
    }
```

This procedure checks the `colors` field for the colormenu to see whether the color is already on the menu. If it is not, the procedure adds an entry to the menu and adds the color name into the `colors` field. Each entry is labeled with a color sample. We create the sample by creating an image with a fixed width and height and by copying the color value over the entire area of the image.

Notice that we use the `list` command to format the callback for each entry. This is a good habit to get into. As we explained in Section 3.1.5, the `list` command adds braces as needed around each argument. Thus if the color value is `navy blue`, for example, the menu entry will have a command such as this:

```
    colormenu_select .pen {navy blue}
```

Now let's see how the callback part of this example works. When you select a color on the colormenu, it triggers a call to the following procedure:

```
    proc colormenu_select {win color} {
        global cmInfo

        if {$color == ""} {
            $win.cb configure -relief flat \
                -background white -activebackground white
        } else {
            $win.cb configure -relief raised \
                -background $color -activebackground $color
        }
        set cmInfo($win-current) $color

        if {$cmInfo($win-command) != ""} {
            set cmd [percent_subst %c $cmInfo($win-command) $color]
            uplevel #0 $cmd
        }
    }
```

If the new color is the null string, we flatten the menubutton and set its background color to white. This indicates that the colormenu is in the Off state. Otherwise, we give the menubutton a raised relief, and we set its background color to the current color choice. We also store the color in the `current` field for the colormenu, so we can keep track of the current color.

Then we look for the callback code in the `command` field of the data structure. If we find it, we substitute the current color in place of `%c` and execute the command. We use the `percent_subst` procedure developed in Section 7.6.7.3 to handle the substitution.

Notice that we're careful to use `uplevel #0` to execute the callback code. If the code contains any variable references, this is an important detail. For example, suppose that we have a colormenu called `.pen` and set its callback code like this:

```
    colormenu_action .pen {set pencolor "%c"}
```

We want the colormenu to save the current pen color in a global variable called `pencolor`. If we evaluate this command in the context of `colormenu_select`, we'll get a *local* variable, called `pencolor`, and that variable will disappear as soon as we return from `colormenu_select`. Instead, we evaluate the command in the global scope, so any variables that it references will be treated as global variables. This mimics the usual behavior of the Tk widgets, as discussed in Section 3.1.4.

Callbacks add flexibility to your components. For example, we can use our colormenus in two different modes.

- In *active mode*, we assign a callback to the colormenu. Whenever the color changes, the callback is executed to handle the new color choice.

- In *passive mode*, we don't use the callback. When the color changes, nothing happens. At some point later in the program, we use the following procedure to query the current color choice:

```
proc colormenu_get {win} {
    global cmInfo
    return $cmInfo($win-current)
}
```

This simply returns the color from the `current` field of the colormenu's data structure.

If you support value substitutions in the callback code, you can add even more flexibility to your components. In the colormenu, for example, we substitute the current color into the `%c` field of the callback. This lets you access the color value anywhere in the callback code—as the first argument, as the last argument, or at several different places in a large code paragraph.

For example, we can use colormenus to control a label, as shown in Figure 8.5. Changing the fill color sets the label's background color, but changing the pen color sets both the foreground color and the text.

Figure 8.5. A colormenu component uses callback code to update the color of a label.

This example is implemented as follows:

```
label .sample -width 30 -height 3 -text "Sample Text"
pack .sample -side right -expand yes -fill both

set imh [image create bitmap -foreground black -background white \
    -file [file join $env(EFFTCL_LIBRARY) images pen.xbm] \
    -maskfile [file join $env(EFFTCL_LIBRARY) images penm.xbm]]
colormenu_create .pen -image $imh
pack .pen -padx 4 -pady 4

set imh [image create bitmap -foreground black -background white \
    -file [file join $env(EFFTCL_LIBRARY) images paint.xbm] \
    -maskfile [file join $env(EFFTCL_LIBRARY) images paintm.xbm]]
colormenu_create .fill -image $imh
pack .fill -padx 4 -pady 4

colormenu_action .pen {
    .sample configure -foreground "%c" -text "%c"
}
colormenu_action .fill {
    .sample configure -background "%c"
}
colormenu_select .pen black
colormenu_select .fill white
```

Notice that when we set the callback for the pen color, we were able to substitute the color value in two places, which is particularly convenient for this example.

8.2.4 Autoloading

Both the radiobox and the colormenu are ready to use. We can collect these procedures together and keep them on hand for future projects. We'll put the radiobox procedures in a file called `radiobox.tcl` and the colormenu procedures in a file called `clrmenu.tcl`. When we need them, we could copy them in and make them part of a script. Or, we could leave them in their separate files and use the `source` command to load them into a script. But there is an even better way to handle your code libraries.

Tcl has a facility called *autoloading* that you can use to bring in libraries as they're needed in an application. It sounds complicated, but it's extremely easy to use. You can set up a library for autoloading in two steps.

1. Make a directory to represent your library, and collect your Tcl code files into this directory. For example, we could make a directory called `/usr/local/efftcl` that contains all of the code that we've developed in this book. Each file in this directory represents one component in the library. For example, the file `radiobox.tcl` contains

procedures such as `radiobox_create` and `radiobox_add`. The file `clrmenu.tcl` contains procedures such as `colormenu_create` and `colormenu_select`.

2. Generate an index for the library, using the `auto_mkindex` command in `tclsh` or `wish`. We could generate an index for our library by starting `wish` and typing:

```
auto_mkindex /usr/local/efftcl *.tcl
```

This finds all of the files that match the pattern `*.tcl` in the directory `/usr/local/efftcl` and generates a list of procedures found in these files. This list is stored in a file named `tclIndex` in the `/usr/local/efftcl` library directory.

Note: *Whenever you make changes to the library code, you must repeat the second step to keep the index file up to date.*

At this point, the library is ready for autoloading. When you want to use it, you append the directory name onto the `auto_path` variable. For example, the following script uses our newly created library in `/usr/local/efftcl`:

```
lappend auto_path /usr/local/efftcl

radiobox_create .options "Installation Options:"
pack .options -padx 4 -pady 4

radiobox_add .options "Full install"
radiobox_add .options "Demo only"
radiobox_add .options "Data files"

button .go -text "OK" -command {
    notice_show "Installed: [radiobox_get .options]"
}
pack .go -fill x
```

This script gives you a list of installation options in a radiobox, as shown in Figure 8.6. When you click on the OK button, it pops up a notice dialog telling you that the installation is done. Of course, a real install program has a little more code, but this shows the basic idea.

Autoloading works like this. Tcl encounters a command such as `radiobox_create` for the first time. Instead of immediately returning an error, Tcl visits each of the directories listed in the `auto_path` variable and looks for a `tclIndex` file. If it finds this file, Tcl looks for the `radiobox_create` procedure on the list and, if that procedure is found, loads the file that contains the procedure. This loads the `radiobox_create` procedure, as well as all of the other procedures in that file. At that point, the program is all set up to use radioboxes. The next time a procedure such as `radiobox_create` or `radiobox_add` is used, it is known, so everything works smoothly.

You might think that autoloading would slow down your application with all of this extra searching. But in most cases, it speeds things up. The searching is done only once—the first time that an unknown procedure is encountered—so there is relatively little overhead. And autoloading lets you load only what you use in a particular script. In the code

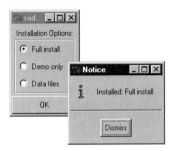

Figure 8.6. A simple application using the radiobox and the notice dialog from a library.

shown here, for example, we have the entire library in /usr/local/efftcl at our fingertips. But we use only the radiobox and the notice dialog, so we load only that much
code.

8.2.5 Packages

Autoloading is extremely useful, but it has one drawback: You have to append a directory
name onto the auto_path variable, so you have to know where the library directory is
installed. Suppose that we install our library in the directory /usr/local/efftcl. Now
suppose that we send a script to someone else. That person may have our library, but it
may be installed in a different directory. If the person doesn't have our library, we can send
it, but the person may not be able to install it in /usr/local/efftcl. If we hard-code a
particular directory name into our script, the person will have to change it.

   Tcl has a package facility that sits on top of autoloading, making it much easier to use.
You don't have to request a library in a particular directory, like this:

```
lappend auto_path /usr/local/efftcl
```

You can instead request a package by name, like this:

```
package require Efftcl
```

Tcl will search for the package; if it is found, its directory will be added to the auto_path
variable automatically.

   You can use a procedure called pkg_mkIndex to create a package, but we recommend that you avoid it. It generates messy files that are difficult to read, and it makes the
whole package mechanism much more complicated than it needs to be. Instead, you can
set up a package as follows.

1. Decide on a name for your package. The package name should start with a capital letter.
   For example, we'll make a package called Efftcl that contains all of the library procedures in this book.

2. Make a directory to represent your package. Within that directory, make a subdirectory called `scripts` that contains all of the library scripts. Make a subdirectory called `images` that contains all of your bitmaps and image files. Make other subdirectories for any other files that are required for your package.

We'll make a directory called `efftcl/lib` for the `Efftcl` package. We'll put all of our library files in `efftcl/lib/scripts` and all of our bitmaps in `efftcl/lib/images`.

3. Set up autoloading in the `scripts` directory. Enter that directory, start up `wish`, and use the `auto_mkindex` command as described in the previous section:

```
$ cd efftcl/lib/scripts
$ wish
% auto_mkindex . *.tcl
```

4. Create a file called `pkgIndex.tcl` in the `efftcl/lib` directory. This file contains a single Tcl command that describes how to load the package. For our `Efftcl` package, the `pkgIndex.tcl` file looks like this:

```
package ifneeded Efftcl 1.0 \
    [list source [file join $dir efftcl.tcl]]
```

All of the parts that are specific to this example are shown in boldface type: **Efftcl** is our package name; **1.0** is the current version number; and **efftcl.tcl** is a file that's executed whenever the package is loaded.

The `package ifneeded` command declares a package. In this case, the command says that if anyone requests version `1.0` of the `Efftcl` package, Tcl should respond by sourcing the file `efftcl.tcl`. The `dir` variable contains the name of the directory that contains the `pkgIndex.tcl` file. So no matter where this file is installed, we can refer to its directory as `$dir`.

You can treat the rest of the code as boilerplate. Each time you create a new package, substitute the appropriate information into the boldface areas.

5. Create the file that will be executed when the package is loaded. For our package, that file is called `efftcl/lib/efftcl.tcl`. It looks like this:

```
package provide Efftcl 1.0
set efftcl_version 1.0
set env(EFFTCL_LIBRARY) [file dirname [info script]]
lappend auto_path [file join $env(EFFTCL_LIBRARY) scripts]
```

This file must include a `package provide` command with the package name and the version number. This tells the package facility that the package was loaded successfully. If you forget the `package provide` command, Tcl will complain that it can't find the package.

This file should also set up autoloading for the `scripts` directory. To do this, we append the `scripts` directory onto the `auto_path` variable. But instead of hard-coding the directory name, we use Tcl commands to deduce its name automatically. The `info script` command returns the name of the script that is currently being executed. In this example, it might return the name `/usr/local/efftcl/efftcl.tcl`. The `file dirname` command extracts the package directory name from this result. Then we build the full name for the `scripts` directory and append it onto the `auto_path` variable. From that point on, all of the library procedures are available for autoloading.

Notice that along the way, we update the environment variable `EFFTCL_LIBRARY` to point to the package directory. As you'll recall, we've used this environment variable throughout our library to find things related to the package. For example, in Section 4.4 we created a color editor that required a special background image. We loaded the image with the following code:

```
set fname [file join $env(EFFTCL_LIBRARY) images colors.gif]
set imh [image create photo -file $fname]
```

So again, without using any hard-coded file names, we can refer to files that belong to the package.

The package initialization file can include other commands, too. In our example, we set a variable called `efftcl_version` with the version number for our package. This mimics the `tcl_version` and `tk_version` variables created by Tcl and Tk. We could also open a log file, connect to a database, or do anything else needed to initialize the package.

6. Install the package directory in a place where Tcl will find it automatically. Both `tclsh` and `wish` look to a certain directory for library files. It's easy to figure out where this is on your system. Just start up an interpreter and query it, like this:

```
$ wish
% file dirname [info library]
⇒ /usr/local/tcltk/lib
```

In this case, Tcl will search for packages in the directory `/usr/local/tcltk/lib`. If we copy our `efftcl/lib` directory into this library directory, it will be recognized by our `wish` as an official Tcl/Tk package.

Later on, we may make improvements to the package and release version 1.1 of our `Efftcl` package. When we install this, we don't want to clobber the old release. It's a good idea to include the version number as part of the directory name whenever you install a package. So we'll install our `efftcl/lib` directory with the name `/usr/local/tcltk/lib/efftcl1.0`. That way, we can install later releases in other directories, such as `efftcl1.1`, `efftcl1.2`, and so on.

Once a package is installed, you can use it in many different scripts. Just include a `package require` command at the start of each script, like this:

```
package require Efftcl

radiobox_create .options "Installation Options:"
pack .options -padx 4 -pady 4
```

```
radiobox_add .options "Full install"
radiobox_add .options "Demo only"
radiobox_add .options "Data files"

button .go -text "OK" -command {
    notice_show "Installed: [radiobox_get .options]"
}
pack .go -fill x
```

If several different versions of the package are installed, you'll automatically get the latest version.

You can request a specific version, like this:

```
package require Efftcl 1.2
```

You'll get that version or a later release.

If your script will work only with a particular version, you can ask for that version specifically:

```
package require -exact Efftcl 1.2
```

If it's not available, your script will abort with an error.

8.3 Desktop applications

Suppose you've just finished an application, such as the calculator or the drawing program that we've developed in this book. Now you want to ship it off to customers, who are eager to install it on their desktops. In this section, we'll see what it takes to distribute and install a Tcl/Tk application.

If you're developing for Windows or Macintosh systems, many commercial tools are available that will create a self-installing program, but on UNIX systems, they are few and far between. So we'll focus our discussion on UNIX systems, although the same concepts apply to all three platforms.

8.3.1 Creating a distribution

Suppose you have a single script file that contains the code for your application. Suppose further that you're delivering it to other Tcl/Tk developers, who already have the `wish` program installed. In that case, it's easy to distribute your application. You can send out your script by e-mail.

But for any other scenario, it's a bit more complicated. You have to collect all of the files needed to run your application and put them together in one place. You'll probably want to build a distribution directory like the one shown in Figure 8.7. The distribution directory includes many different files.

- If you've developed your own library of components, you may have many different scripts for your application. Put these files in the `scripts` directory.

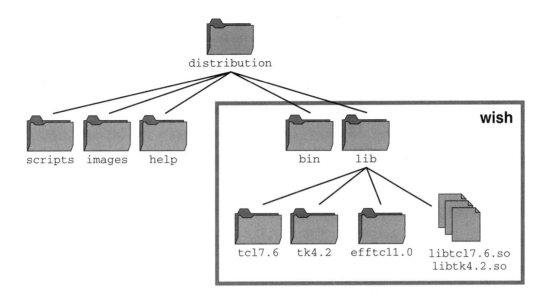

Figure 8.7. The distribution for a Tcl/Tk application may have many different files, including a complete distribution of the `wish` program.

- You may use special bitmaps, cursors, or color images in your application. Put these files in the `images` directory.
- You may have an online help facility that displays help files. Put these files in the `help` directory.
- You should probably include the `tclsh` program or the `wish` program as part of your distribution. Otherwise, your customers will have to install it themselves, and that can lead to problems. Customers may botch the installation or may install a version that's incompatible with your code.

    When you include `tclsh` or `wish`, you need to include two things: the executables, which are normally kept in the `bin` directory; and the support library, which is kept in the `lib` directory. The support library must include the directories that you'd have in a normal `wish` installation. You can find these and copy them into your distribution, like this:

```
$ wish
% file copy $tcl_library distribution/lib
% file copy $tk_library distribution/lib
```

If you rely on other packages, you must copy their support libraries, too. For example, if you use the `Efftcl` package that we've created in this book, you must copy its library directory into the distribution:

```
$ wish
% set lib [file dirname [info library]]
⇒ /usr/local/tcltk/lib
% file copy $lib/efftcl1.0 distribution/lib
```

If the `tclsh` or `wish` programs require shared libraries, you must include them in the `lib` directory as well. If you don't know how these programs were built, you can use the `ldd` program on some UNIX systems to check for library dependencies:

```
$ ldd /usr/local/tcltk/bin/wish
⇒     libtk4.2.so => /usr/local/tcltk/lib/libtk4.2.so.4.2
      libtcl7.6.so => /usr/local/tcltk/lib/libtcl7.6.so.7.6
      libX11.so.6 => /usr/X11R6/lib/libX11.so.6.1
      libdl.so.1 => /lib/libdl.so.1.7.14
      libm.so.5 => /lib/libm.so.5.0.6
      libc.so.5 => /lib/libc.so.5.3.12
```

In this case, the `wish` program requires `libtcl7.6.so` and `libtk4.2.so` as shared libraries. It requires a few other shared libraries as well, but these are likely to be installed on the customer's machine.

Once you've finished putting together the distribution directory, you can copy it onto a floppy or a CD-ROM. If you're distributing your application on the Internet, you'll probably want to wrap everything up in a single file. On UNIX systems, you can create a compressed `tar` file like this:

```
$ tar cvf mydist.tar ./distribution
$ compress mydist.tar
```

Then you can put the distribution file `mydist.tar.Z` on an `ftp` site for downloading.

8.3.2   Making scripts into executable programs

When you're developing a script, you're continually starting up `wish` and loading the code either like this:

```
$ wish calc
```

or like this:

```
$ wish
% source calc
```

For you, this may seem perfectly natural, but your customers won't want to bother with this. They'll want to double-click on an icon or type in a simple program name to start your application.

Suppose we have the following script:

```
button .b -text "Hello, World!" -command exit
pack .b
```

On a Windows platform, it's easy to make this script look like a program. Just save it in a file with a `.tcl` extension, such as `hello.tcl`. When you double-click on the script, Windows will start up `wish` to execute the script.

On Macintosh systems, the Tcl/Tk distribution comes with a utility called Drag & Drop Tclets. Dropping a script on this utility will create a separate application icon that you can use to execute the script.

On UNIX platforms, it's a little more complicated. First, you put a line starting with `#!` at the very top of your script, like this:

```
#!/bin/wish
button .b -text "Hello, World!" -command exit
pack .b
```

The rest of the line specifies the complete file path for your `wish` executable. Then you change the permission bits on the script to make it executable. For example, if this script is stored in a file called `hello`, you can set its permission bits like this:

```
$ chmod 755 hello
```

At this point, the script will act like a program. As long as it sits somewhere in your command path, you can invoke it by name, like this:

```
$ hello
```

When UNIX sees `#!` as the first two characters in this file, it identifies the file as a shell script and uses the program specified after the `#!` characters to interpret the script.

You can supply command-line arguments to the program, like this:

```
$ hello -geometry +50+50 x y z
```

Some of these arguments are recognized by `wish` and handled automatically. The rest are passed on to your script in a global variable called `argv`. In this example, `wish` recognizes `-geometry +50+50` as a geometry specification for the main window, removes these arguments from the list, and stores the remaining arguments `x y z` in the variable `argv`. If you need these arguments, you can use list commands to pick apart the values in `argv`. Of course, our current script just ignores the arguments.

There is one important caveat about the `#!` trick: On some UNIX systems, the file name following `#!` is limited to 30 characters. If you exceed that length, you may get an error. For example, suppose our `wish` is installed in a different location, so the `hello` script looks like this:

```
#!/usr/local/tcltk/sunos4.1.3/bin/wish
button .b -text "Hello, World!" -command exit
pack .b
```

On some systems, you'll get a mysterious `not found` message when you run this script. If you encounter this problem, you can use the following trick to work around it. Modify your script to look like this:

```
#!/bin/sh
# /bin/sh interprets this part, but wish ignores it...
#\
exec /usr/local/tcltk/sunos4.1.3/bin/wish "$0" "$@"
```

```
# The rest of this is interpreted by wish...
# ------------------------------------------------------
button .b -text "Hello, World!" -command exit
pack .b
```

Be careful to include the #\ comment line above exec.

When you execute this script, UNIX sees the #! characters and executes the Bourne shell program to interpret the script. The name /bin/sh is short enough that there is never a problem invoking this shell. The Bourne shell starts executing the script. It treats the first three lines as comments and then performs the exec command to start up the wish program. The 30-character limit doesn't apply in this context, so the complete file path for wish can be arbitrarily long. The Bourne shell replaces "$0" with the script name (which is hello in this example), and replaces "$@" with the command-line arguments, and it starts up wish to replace the shell process.

The wish program interprets the same script but handles things differently. It treats the #\ line as a comment that's being continued on another line. So wish sees the exec command as part of a comment and ignores it. It skips over the remaining comments as well and starts execution with the button command.

8.3.3 Making a self-installing program

Once your customers have received your software, they'll have to install it. All of the files in the distribution will have to be copied to a permanent location. Some of the files may have to be edited slightly. For example, if the wish program is installed in /usr/local/bin/wish, any scripts that reference it will have to use this new path.

On Windows and Macintosh systems, many commercial tools are available that you can use to automate the installation process. If you don't have one of these tools, you may be tempted to write out a list of instructions or to make a shell script to handle the installation. But stop and think. All of your customers have the wish program—either you're counting on them to have it, or you're sending it with the distribution. So you can write a simple Tcl/Tk script to handle the entire installation.

For example, Figure 8.8 shows a simple "install" program for the code examples in this book. You can use the checkbuttons to request certain parts of the overall package. If you choose to install the application programs, you can specify the directory where they should reside. When you click on the INSTALL button, the installation is carried out, and a notice dialog appears, telling you that the software is installed.

We use the following procedure to install the Efftcl library package:

```
proc install_lib {} {
    global efftcl_version
    set libDir [file dirname [info library]]
    set installDir [file join $libDir efftcl$efftcl_version]
```

Figure 8.8. Simple "install" program for the `Efftcl` package and the examples in this book.

```
if {[file exists $installDir]} {
    set mesg "Package \"Efftcl\" is already installed."
    append mesg "\n\nOverwrite?"
    if {![confirm_ask $mesg]} {
        return
    }
    file delete -force $installDir
}
file copy lib $installDir
}
```

When we created the index files for the `Efftcl` package in Section 8.2.5, we carefully avoided any hard-coded file paths. So we can install the package by copying it into the Tcl library directory. We use the `info library` command to determine the location of the Tcl library directory, and we use the `file copy` command at the bottom of the procedure to copy the package directory. We also check to see whether the package already exists, maybe as the result of an earlier install. If it does and if the customer wants to overwrite it, we use the `file delete` command to delete the old installation.

We handle the application scripts in much the same way. But there is one important difference. Let's assume that we're installing on a UNIX system, so each of the application scripts includes the `#!` trick described in Section 8.3.2. Somehow, we need to substitute the full path name for the `wish` program into the `exec` line at the top of each script:

```
#!/bin/sh
# /bin/sh interprets this part, but wish ignores it...
#\
exec wish "$0" "$@"
```

```
# The rest of this is interpreted by wish...
# --------------------------------------------------------
. . .
```

We handle that in the following procedure. We pass in the name of an application script and the full path name for `wish`. The procedure loads the script, substitutes the `wish` name into the `exec` line, and returns the entire script:

```
proc fix_app {program wish} {
    set fid [open $program r]
    set contents [read $fid]
    close $fid
    regsub {exec wish \"\$0} $contents "exec $wish \"\$0" contents
    return $contents
}
```

We use this in the following procedure, which installs all of the example applications included with the package:

```
proc install_apps {dir} {
    global tcl_platform

    if {![file isdirectory $dir]} {
        set mesg "Directory $dir does not exist."
        append mesg "\n\nCreate it?"
        if {![confirm_ask $mesg]} {
            return
        }
        file mkdir $dir
    }
    foreach program [glob [file join apps *]] {
        if {![file isdirectory $program]} {
            set contents [fix_app $program [info nameofexecutable]]
            set tail [file tail $program]
            set file [file join $dir $tail]
            switch $tcl_platform(platform) {
                unix {
                    save_app $file $contents
                    exec chmod 755 $file
                }
                windows {
                    save_app $file.tcl $contents
                }
                macintosh {
                    save_app $file $contents
                }
            }
        }
    }
}
```

First, we check to see whether the target directory exists; if necessary, we create it. Then we loop through all of the programs found in the `apps` directory and install them.

For this package, all of our customers will be Tcl/Tk developers. So we assume that each customer already has `wish` and is using it to run this "install" script. We use `info nameofexecutable` to get the full path name of the customer's `wish` program, and we call `fix_app` to substitute it into the application script. Then we use a procedure called `save_app` to save the script in a file. That procedure is implemented as follows:

```
proc save_app {file script} {
    if {[file exists $file]} {
        set mesg "Program \"$file\" already exists."
        append mesg "\n\nOverwrite?"
        if {![confirm_ask $mesg]} {
            return
        }
    }
    set fid [open $file w]
    puts -nonewline $fid $script
    close $fid
}
```

The procedure warns you if the target program already exists, so we don't accidentally clobber another program by the same name. Then the procedure opens the file, writes out the script, and closes the file.

You may have to handle some things differently on each of the different platforms. When we install the application scripts, for example, we want to make them into executable programs. Each platform handles this differently, as we discussed in Section 8.3.2. You can use the `tcl_platform` variable to get information about the platform where `wish` is currently executing. In the `install_apps` procedure, for example, we get the platform type from `$tcl_platform(platform)`. Then, on Windows systems, we save the scripts in a file with a `.tcl` extension. On UNIX systems, we use the `chmod` program to set the permission bits.

When you're writing an installation program like this, you must be careful how you bootstrap things. In our script, for example, we've used procedures, such as `confirm_ask` and `notice_show`, that come with the `Efftcl` library package. But the whole point of our installation script is to install this library. So how do we access these procedures?

Near the top of the installation script, we include the following code:

```
if {![file isdirectory [file join lib scripts]]} {
    cd [file dirname [info script]]
}
set auto_path [linsert $auto_path 0 lib]
package require Efftcl
```

We look for the `efftcl/lib/scripts` directory that comes with our distribution. If we can't find it, the customer must have started this script in the wrong directory context. No problem. We use `info script` to get the name of the install script, and we use `cd` to

change to the proper directory context. Then we add the `lib` directory into the
`auto_path` variable and request the package. Notice that we insert our `lib` directory at
the front of `auto_path`. This ensures that we get the right package, even if the customer
has some other `Efftcl` package already installed.

If you're distributing `wish` and using it for the installation program, there's another
problem as well. When `wish` starts up, it looks for certain library files. The location of
these files is compiled into the executable. These files won't be properly installed until
after the installation program is finished.

You can use the `TCL_LIBRARY` and `TK_LIBRARY` environment variables to tell `wish`
where to find these files. Before the installation, they'll be sitting in your distribution
directory. The customer doesn't have to know this. You can make a shell script to start the
installation program. On UNIX systems, it might look like this:

```
#!/bin/sh
TCL_LIBRARY=./lib/tcl7.6; export TCL_LIBRARY
TK_LIBRARY=./lib/tk4.2; export TK_LIBRARY
exec ./bin/wish ./install.tcl "$@"
```

Then you tell the customer to install your package as follows:

```
$ tar xf mydist.tar
$ cd distribution
$ ./install
```

At that point, the installation program will appear, and the rest of the installation will be
automated.

You may encounter a similar problem with the library directories, even after `wish` is
installed. Suppose that you compiled `wish` for an installation in `/usr/local`. But suppose the customer installs your entire package in another directory. When `wish` starts up,
it will look for its libraries in `/usr/local/lib`, unless you tell it to look somewhere else.
You can solve this problem by telling the customer to set some environment variables. Or,
you can set these variables automatically at the top of each script.

For example, suppose you're using the `#!` trick that we described in Section 8.3.2.
You can add a few lines to set the environment variables in the shell area at the top of each
application script:

```
#!/bin/sh
# /bin/sh interprets this part, but wish ignores it...
#\
TCL_LIBRARY=/usr/tools/lib/tcl7.6; export TCL_LIBRARY
#\
TK_LIBRARY=/usr/tools/lib/tk4.2; export TK_LIBRARY
#\
exec /usr/tools/bin/wish "$0" "$@"

# The rest of this is interpreted by wish...
# -----------------------------------------------------
...
```

The installation program can substitute the proper directory names in place as it installs each application script.

Again, you must include each of the #\ lines exactly as they're shown here. The Bourne shell treats each #\ line as a comment, but it executes the line beneath it. So the Bourne shell sets the TCL_LIBRARY and TK_LIBRARY environment variables and then starts up wish. The wish program treats both #\ and the line beneath it as a single comment. So wish skips over the lines shown here and executes the rest of the script.

8.4 Web-based applications

More and more businesses are advertising their services and setting up shop on the Internet. Clients can visit their Web pages, find out about the company, and perhaps even place an order online. The Web started out as a way of viewing information on the Internet. But these days, you don't just read a Web page; you interact with it. The Web is filled with animated advertisements, survey forms, and interactive programs. If you're interested in developing active content for the Web, Tcl/Tk can help.

In this section, we'll see how you can embed your Tcl/Tk applications in a Web page so users can access them online. If you have a large audience of casual users, the Web can be a powerful distribution channel. You don't have to mail out floppy disks or CD-ROMs. You don't have to bundle up the wish program or create a fancy installation script. You can embed your program in a Web page and let users download it and execute it on the fly.

Embedded applications are called *applets*, to distinguish them from ordinary applications. The distinction is important. An application is installed on your computer and has full access to the machine. An application can create files, delete files, access the Internet, and so on. You trust the application because you trust the company that sold it to you. An applet, however, is downloaded and executed on the fly in your Web browser. You may not know or trust whoever put it up, and you certainly don't want a rogue applet to wipe out your files or crash your machine. So applets run in a protected environment controlled by strict security policies. Applets can't wipe out your files or steal your intellectual property, but they can do a lot of other useful things. We'll see how useful they can be in the following example.

8.4.1 Simple example

Let's revisit the Electric Secretary application developed in Section 7.8. Suppose we want to put this application up on the Web. There are a few good reasons for doing this.

- This may be a demo version of the program. Customers could try it before they buy it.

- This may be a way of communicating a calendar of events to a group of customers. For example, they could use this to find training dates in their area or to request a sales meeting.

- This may be available only on an intranet, so secretaries all over the company can coordinate the schedules of the management team.

We'll assume that we've already built the application. Let's look at the steps needed to embed it in a Web page:

1. Modify your script to work within the restricted environment of an applet. If your script is simple enough, it may already be suitable for the Web. But chances are, you'll have to make some modifications before it will run properly as an applet. We'll discuss these modifications further in the next section and see how they affect the Electric Secretary program.

2. Make a Web page that references your script. Somewhere in the Web page, include an embed tag of the following form:

```
<embed src=script-name width=wsize height=hsize>
```

The *script-name* is the name of the script that represents your applet. This file name must have a .tcl extension, or it won't be recognized as a Tcl/Tk applet. The *wsize* and *hsize* parameters set the size of the applet window on the Web page. Unlike an ordinary Tcl/Tk application, an applet can't determine the proper size for itself; you must set its size explicitly.

A simple Web page for the Electric Secretary might look something like this:

```
<html>
<head> <title>
Effective Tcl/Tk Programming: Example Applet
</title> </head>
...
<p>
For example, here is the <i>Electric Secretary</i> application
described in our book:
<p>
<embed src="elplugin.tcl" width=600 height=350>
...
</html>
```

In this case, our applet script is called elplugin.tcl, and we set the overall size of the applet to 600×350 pixels.

3. Make the Web page and the applet script available on a Web server. Both the Web page and the applet script should be stored in the same directory on the Web server.

4. Bring up the Web page. Once the Web page is loaded, the browser will download the applet script and try to execute it. The first time you encounter any Tcl/Tk applet, your browser will tell you that you need a special plug-in module to view it. You can obtain the Tcl/Tk plug-in from http://sunscript.sun.com/products/plugin.html. Follow this link, download the Tcl/Tk plug-in, and install it. You do this once; from then on, you'll be able to run Tcl/Tk applets all over the Web.

If you bring up the Electric Secretary page, it will appear as shown in Figure 8.9. You can use this applet the same way that you'd use the regular Electric Secretary application. Click on the arrows to change the current month, and click on a particular day to display its appointments. Edit the appointments, set the alarm bells, consult the schedules for other users—all from the convenience of your Web browser.

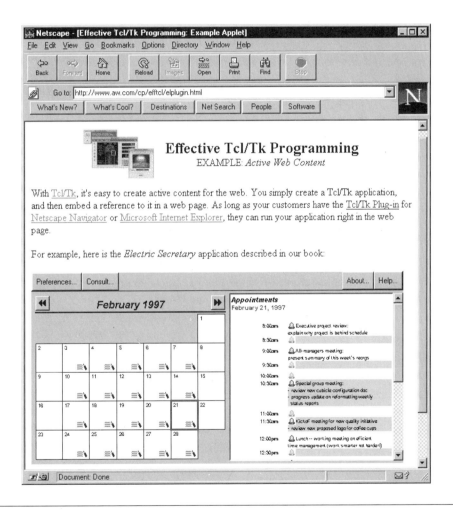

Figure 8.9. The Electric Secretary application is embedded in a Web page.

8.4.2   A few important caveats

Embedding a Tcl/Tk application in a Web page is easy to do. But making a Tcl/Tk application work properly as an applet is a bit more difficult. Applets have several restrictions that may require you to rework your code. In this section, we'll look at these restrictions and see how they impact the Electric Secretary application. As you'll see, we had to make a lot of changes to the Electric Secretary. However, it didn't take long to make these changes. With less than 4 hours of work, the Electric Secretary was up on the Web.

8.4.2.1   Gather everything into a single script

We spent a lot of time in Section 8.2 learning how to set up autoloading and packages. But unfortunately, you can't depend on libraries for a Web-based application. After all, the customer who downloads your applet probably won't have your libraries installed. All of the code needed to run your script must be gathered together in a single file so it can be downloaded to the customer's Web browser in one shot.

For the Electric Secretary applet, we have a single script, called `elplugin.tcl`, which contains all of the code, including the client code that was originally in the `electric` script, along with library code from files such as `radiobox.tcl`, `clrdial.tcl`, `calendar.tcl`, and so on.

All of the bitmaps and images files must be included in the applet script as well. For example, the calendar component uses bitmaps for the buttons that control the month. The bitmaps reside in files that we've been referencing like this:

```
button $win.cal.back \
    -bitmap @[file join $env(EFFTCL_LIBRARY) images back.xbm] \
    -command "calendar_change $win -1"
```

For the applet script, we define a bitmap image that includes the entire bitmap file in line, and we configure the button to use that image:

```
image create bitmap calendar-back -data {
#define back_width 16
#define back_height 16
static unsigned char back_bits[] = {
    0x00, 0x00, 0x00, 0x00, 0x00, 0x00, 0xc0, 0x30, 0xe0,
    0x38, 0xf0, 0x3c, 0xf8, 0x3e, 0xfc, 0x3f, 0xfc, 0x3f,
    0xf8, 0x3e, 0xf0, 0x3c, 0xe0, 0x38, 0xc0, 0x30, 0x00,
    0x00, 0x00, 0x00, 0x00, 0x00};
}
...
button $win.cal.back -image calendar-back \
    -command "calendar_change $win -1"
```

We use a similar technique to handle color images as well. For example, the Electric Secretary uses a pencil image that we've been referencing like this:

```
image create photo pencil-image \
    -file [file join $env(EFFTCL_LIBRARY) images pencil.gif]
```

For the applet script, we include the image data in line, like this:

```
image create photo pencil-image -data {
R0lGODdhEgAMAMIAAP///zAwMAAAAP+uZQAA/wAATQAAAAAACwAAAAEg
AMAAADLAi63P4gQAEolXU4WzsdIPSABNFwnFKUDOqppSk2q6y41FLLeKez
M8YqKEoAADs=
}
```

The image data is a `base64` encoding of the original `pencil.gif` file. On UNIX systems, you can use the `mimencode` program to encode the image, like this:

```
$ mimencode pencil.gif
```

⇒ *R0lGODdhEgAMAMIAAP///zAwMAAAAP+uZQAA/wAATQAAAAAACwAAAAEg*
  AMAAADLAi63P4gQAEolXU4WzsdIPSABNFwnFKUDOqppSk2q6y41FLLeKez
  M8YqKEoAADs=

8.4.2.2 Convert menus to buttons

Applets are not allowed to have pop-up menus. This may seem surprising, but it's a security issue. When a menu pops up, it places a grab on the desktop and doesn't let go until you select an option or dismiss the menu. Malicious applets could exploit this feature to lock up your desktop, so menus are not allowed.

When you're creating an applet, you must use buttons instead of menu entries. You can see how we handled this for the Electric Secretary applet in Figure 8.9. In the original application, we had a Main menu with the entries About... and Exit. In the applet, we made a button for About..., but we dropped Exit. After all, you can exit the applet by changing the Web page. In the original application, we had a View menu with the entries Today, +6 Months, -6 Months, and Preferences... . In the applet, we made a button for Preferences..., but we dropped the other choices. They were handy but not really necessary.

If you have any menus that change during the course of execution, you must replace them with equivalent dialogs. For example, in our original application, we had a Consult menu with entries for various user groups. Whenever you defined a new group in the Preferences dialog, it appeared on the menu. In the applet, we replaced the Consult menu with a Consult... button. This brings up a dialog with a listbox showing the various user groups. You can select a group from the listbox and click on the OK button to perform a consultation.

8.4.2.3 Convert toplevels to frames

Applets are not allowed to create top-level windows. This may seem *really* surprising, but again, it's a security issue. A malicious applet could create a really big top-level window that obscures everything on your desktop. Or, it could mimic another application and trick you into divulging some important information, such as your credit card number or your password.

When you're creating an applet, you must use frames instead of toplevel widgets to implement your dialogs. In the Electric Secretary applet, for example, the Preferences dialog appears as shown in Figure 8.10. It has the same widgets as the original dialog, but they're contained in a frame instead of a toplevel. This dialog isn't controlled by the window manager, so it doesn't have the usual title bar or a border with resizing handles. And you can't use the wm command to control it. The frame sits on top of the applet window until you click on Apply or Cancel to remove it.

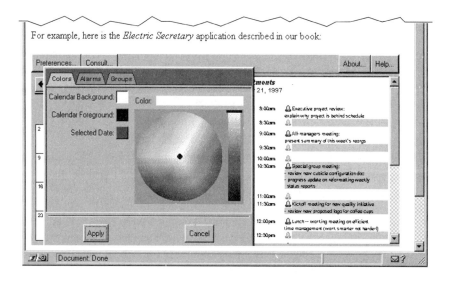

Figure 8.10. Dialogs can be synthesized by using the place command to position a frame on the main application window.

Let's see how this is implemented. In the original application, we created a toplevel called .prefs that's controlled by a menu entry:

```
toplevel .prefs
...
.mbar.view.m add command -label "Preferences..." -command {
    wm deiconify .prefs
}
```

In the applet, we create a frame called .prefs that's controlled by a button:

```
frame .prefs -borderwidth 4 -relief raised
...
button .mbar.prefs -text "Preferences..." -command {
    place .prefs -x 20 -y 20
    raise .prefs
    focus .prefs.cntls.ok
}
```

Instead of using wm deiconify to pop it up, we use the place command to position the frame, and we use the raise command to put it on top of the applet window. At some point, we'll need to take this dialog down. Instead of using `wm withdraw`, we use the `place forget` command to remove it, like this:

```
place forget .prefs
```

In the original application, we also used commands such as `wm title`, `wm protocol`, and `wm group` to configure the toplevel. In the applet, we remove these commands, since there's no equivalent functionality for an ordinary frame.

Handling modal dialogs is a little trickier. In Section 6.5, we presented the following code:

```
proc dialog_wait {win varName} {
    dialog_safeguard $win

    set x [expr [winfo rootx .]+50]
    set y [expr [winfo rooty .]+50]
    wm geometry $win "+$x+$y"

    wm deiconify $win
    grab set $win

    vwait $varName

    grab release $win
    wm withdraw $win
}
```

Unfortunately, this code has two strikes against it.

- Applets are not allowed to use `grab`. You can synthesize a grab by covering the applet with an empty frame. When you pop up a dialog on top of that the user can interact with the dialog, but not with the underlying window.

- Applets are not allowed to use `vwait`. We're forced to split the `dialog_wait` procedure into two parts: a procedure called `dialog_lock`, which handles everything before `vwait`, and a procedure called `dialog_unlock`, which handles everything after.

This changes the way that we control the dialog. We call the `dialog_lock` procedure to pop up the dialog:

```
proc dialog_lock {win} {
    frame .lock -background white
    place .lock -x 0 -y 0 -relwidth 1 -relheight 1
    raise .lock

    place $win -in .lock -x 20 -y 20
    raise $win
}
```

We create an empty frame called `.lock` to synthesize the grab. We place the frame at the upper-left corner of the applet window and then stretch it across the window by setting its relative width and height to `1`. Then we place the dialog window `$win` on top of that.

At some point, you click on the OK or Cancel button, and we call the following procedure to take the dialog down:

```
proc dialog_unlock {win} {
    place forget $win
    destroy .lock
}
```

We use `place forget` to remove the dialog, and we destroy the `.lock` frame, thereby exposing the applet.

8.4.2.4 Strip out comments

If you have a lot of comments in your applet script, you might want to strip them out. Comments increase the size of your script and therefore increase the time required to download it.

8.4.3 Security policies

The commands available to an applet are tightly controlled, so you can use applets without worrying that they'll harm your system. By default, there's no `open` command, so an applet can't open files. There's no `socket` command, so an applet can't connect to the network. And as we saw in the previous section, there are no `menu`, `toplevel`, or `grab` commands, either.

To an applet user, all of this security is quite comforting. But to an applet developer, it can be quite frustrating. What if your applet really needs to open a file? What if it needs to connect to a server? As you'll recall, the Electric Secretary application connects to a server that stores all of its appointment data. Since it manages many different calendars, the server can easily check for scheduling conflicts, as we discussed in Section 7.8.3. So what's the point of making an Electric Secretary applet if it can't connect to the appointment server?

Fortunately, the Tcl/Tk plug-in provides a way to access files and sockets in a controlled manner. Depending on what you need for your applet, you can use the `package require` command to request one of the following security policies.

- `package require Browser`

  This policy provides access to functions in the browser. This policy lets the applet display status messages, fetch Web pages, send e-mail messages, and execute Javascript commands.

- `package require Http`

  This policy provides access to the client-side protocol of `HTTP/1.0` and supports proxy servers, so the applet can fetch Web pages even if it's running within a firewall.

- `package require Safesock`

  This policy lets the applet open a socket connecting back to the machine that served it. If you want to give an applet more freedom, you can let it connect to other machines as well. You can add a list of trusted machines to the `safesock.data` file for your Tcl/Tk plug-in.

- `package require Tempfile`

  This policy lets the applet create and delete files in a temporary storage area on your machine.

- `package require Trusted`

  This policy lets the applet access all of the usual Tcl/Tk commands, without any restrictions. So the applet can open files, execute other programs, open a socket to any machine on the network, and so on. It can also create menus and toplevels, eliminating the need for the workarounds discussed in Section 8.4.2. An applet is allowed to run in "trusted" mode only if it appears on a list of trusted applets in the `trusted.data` file for your Tcl/Tk plug-in.

  The `Trusted` policy works well in an intranet environment, where applets are developed and used internally and therefore can be trusted. If you're creating an applet in this environment, running in "trusted" mode can save you a lot of development headaches. But if you're creating an applet that will be accessed by people all over the Internet, don't expect anyone else to trust it.

For the Electric Secretary applet, we need to open a socket to an appointment server, so we need to request the `Safesock` policy. After that, we can open a socket in the usual manner:

```
package require Safesock
set server $env(SERVER)
set port 8823
...
if {[catch {socket $server $port} sid] != 0} {
    esec_error "Cannot connect to server"
}
```

Notice that instead of hard-coding a particular network address, we use the address in the `SERVER` environment variable. This is the address of the machine that served the applet. As we mentioned earlier, an applet can connect back to the machine that served it. So if we run the appointment server on that same machine, there will be no problems opening the socket.

Chapter 9
Developing Cross-platform Applications

Your customers may use various platforms—UNIX, Windows 95/NT, or Macintosh systems. With Tcl/Tk, you can write one script that works properly on all of these platforms.

For the most part, you can achieve this portability with very little effort. Tcl/Tk insulates you from many details of the underlying system. The same Tcl/Tk code that creates a Motif-style button on UNIX systems, for example, will create a Windows-style button on Windows systems and a Macintosh-style button on Mac systems. So you may develop a script under UNIX and be pleasantly surprised when it runs on the other platforms without any modifications.

But more than likely, you'll encounter a few problems when you test on other platforms. These problems usually arise from assumptions that you've made during development.

- Suppose you've included a binding for `<ButtonPress-3>`. We used a binding like this when we added a pop-up menu to a text widget in Section 5.2. Macintosh systems have only one mouse button, so there is no way to trigger such a binding.

- Suppose you've used a command such as `exec mkdir` to create a directory in the file system. This works fine on UNIX systems, but there is no `mkdir` program to execute on Windows and Macintosh platforms.

- Suppose you've used Avant Garde or Chicago fonts. Your application will look great on Windows and Macintosh platforms, but it will look very different on UNIX systems, where those fonts don't exist.

In this chapter, we'll look at the solutions to the problems and show you ways to make your scripts truly portable. Unlike in the rest of this book, we'll use features that are available only in Tcl/Tk 8.0 and beyond.

Cross-platform support continues to improve with each new release. If you're serious about developing cross-platform applications, you should plan on using the latest release of Tcl/Tk.

9.1 User interface issues

For the moment, let's set aside issues involving the operating system and focus on the user interface. We'll see how to create menu bars, handle file-selection dialogs, and use fonts in a portable manner.

9.1.1 Menu bars

If you've used Tcl/Tk before version 8.0, you may be in the habit of synthesizing a menu bar with a frame and some menubuttons, like this:

```
frame .mbar -borderwidth 1 -relief raised
pack .mbar -fill x


menubutton .mbar.file -text "File" -menu .mbar.file.m
pack .mbar.file -side left
menu .mbar.file.m
.mbar.file.m add command -label "Exit" -command exit


menubutton .mbar.edit -text "Edit" -menu .mbar.edit.m
pack .mbar.edit -side left
menu .mbar.edit.m
.mbar.edit.m add command -label "Clear" -command {
    .sketchpad delete all
}
```

This is the same code that we used in Section 1.2.3 to create the menu bar for the sketch application. This code works fine on UNIX and Windows platforms, where the menu bar appears at the top of the main window. But on the Macintosh, the menu bar is supposed to appear in the system area at the top of the screen, as shown in Figure 9.1.

In Tcl/Tk 8.0, there is a different way of creating a menu bar that works properly on all three platforms. Instead of creating a frame full of menubuttons, you create a menu full of cascaded menu entries. Then you assign the menu to the -menu option of the main window, like this:

```
. configure -menu .mbar
menu .mbar

.mbar add cascade -label "File" -menu .mbar.file
menu .mbar.file
.mbar.file add command -label "Exit" -command exit
```

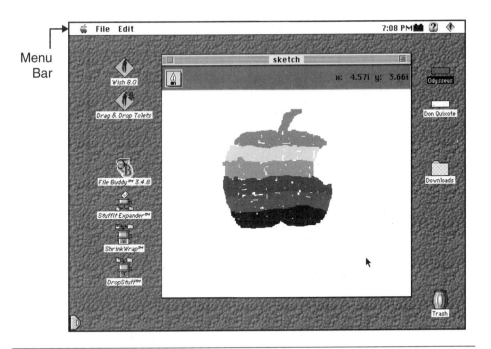

Menu
Bar

Figure 9.1. On Macintosh systems, menu bars should be installed in the system area at the top of the screen.

```
.mbar add cascade -label "Edit" -menu .mbar.edit
menu .mbar.edit
.mbar.edit add command -label "Clear" -command {
    .sketchpad delete all
}
```

The menu .mbar doesn't appear as an ordinary menu in the application. Instead, its entries are used to construct the menu bar for the main window. The File entry represents the File menubutton, and the Edit entry represents the Edit menubutton. Each of these entries has a cascaded menu. These menus will appear as normal menus below the menubuttons.

Toplevel widgets also have a -menu option, so each toplevel can have its own menu bar. On the Macintosh, a menu bar is installed in the system area whenever its top-level window is active. On UNIX and Windows systems, a menu bar appears along the top of the window that contains it, so it is always visible.

9.1.2 Common dialogs

Each platform has characteristic dialogs that users have come to expect. In this section, we'll see how these dialogs can be used to add native look and feel to your applications.

9.1.2.1 Notices and confirmations

All three platforms have some sort of notice dialog like the one that we created in Section 6.4. You can see what they look like in Figure 9.2. The one that we created is appropriate for UNIX systems, but it looks out of place on a Windows or Macintosh desktop.

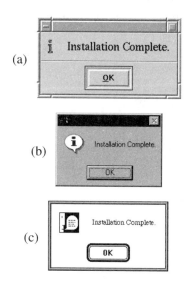

Figure 9.2. Standard message boxes for the three platforms: (a) UNIX, (b) Windows, and (c) Macintosh.

For cross-platform applications, you should use the standard notice dialog that is supplied with Tk. This dialog is called a *message box*, and it is activated as follows:

```
tk_messageBox -icon info -message "Installation Complete."
```

The message box is a modal dialog with the behavior that we described in Section 6.5. While it appears on the screen, the other windows in the application are inactive. When the user dismisses the dialog, the application becomes responsive again, and the call to `tk_messageBox` returns.

The `tk_messageBox` procedure has other configuration options that you can use to control its behavior. In particular, you can use the `-type` option to control the buttons at the bottom of the dialog. The default type is `ok`, so normally you get a single OK button. If you change the type to `yesno`, the message box becomes a confirmation dialog. You can use it to prompt the user and handle the response, like this:

```
set response [tk_messageBox -type yesno -title "InstallMagik" \
    -icon question -message "File exists.  Overwrite?"]


if {$response} {
    tk_messageBox -icon info -message "Installation Complete."
} else {
    tk_messageBox -icon error -message "Installation Aborted."
}
```

Here, we've created a message box of type `yesno` displaying the `question` icon. The message box asks the user whether a file should be overwritten, waits for the response, and returns either `yes` or `no`. If the answer is `yes`, we pop up another message box saying that the installation is complete. Otherwise, we pop up a message box with the `error` icon saying that the installation was aborted. You'll find a complete explanation of other types and configuration options on the manual page for `tk_messageBox`.

9.1.2.2 File selection

Many applications need to read or write files in the file system. For example, the drawing editor that we developed in Section 4.7 manipulates drawing files. You can open a drawing by selecting the Open... entry on the File menu. When you do this, the program pops up a dialog that you can use to select the drawing file.

We could write our own file-selection dialog for this application, but it's a lot of work. Instead, it's better to use the standard file-selection procedures supplied with Tk. They produce dialogs with the proper native look and feel, as shown in Figure 9.3.

On UNIX systems, Tk has two file selectors. The one that you get by default has a quirky "Windows" look and feel. This is fine for some applications, but if you're trying to achieve the Motif look and feel, this dialog is an eyesore. You can request the Motif file selector shown in Figure 9.3(a) by setting the `tk_strictMotif` variable, like this:

```
set tk_strictMotif 1
```

Now let's see how these dialogs work. In our drawing editor, we use the following procedures to read and write drawing files:

```
proc draw_open {} {
    global env

    set file [tk_getOpenFile]
    if {$file != ""} {
        ...
    }
}
proc draw_save {} {
    global env
```

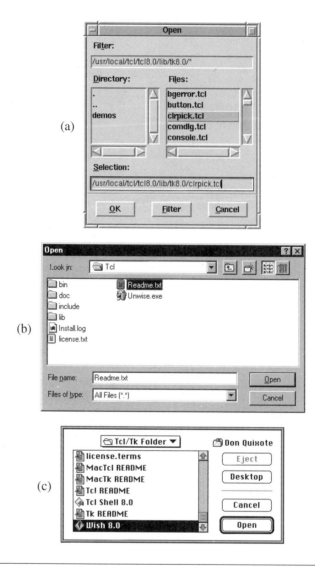

Figure 9.3. Standard file-selection dialogs for the three platforms: (a) UNIX, (b) Windows, and (c) Macintosh.

```
          set file [tk_getSaveFile]
          if {$file != ""} {
             ...
          }
       }
```

We've left out the details in these procedures so you can focus on the file selection. You'll find the rest of the code in the file efftcl/apps/draw, which can be obtained from the Web site mentioned on page xiv.

In draw_open, we use tk_getOpenFile to activate the file selection dialog. When the user has selected a file and clicked on **OK** or **Cancel**, tk_getOpenFile returns. If the user clicked on **OK**, the command returns the name of the selected file; otherwise, the command returns the null string. We look at the result, and if a file was selected, we load that drawing file.

The tk_getSaveFile procedure works much the same way, with one important difference: If the user selects a file that already exists, a confirmation dialog appears, asking whether the file should be overwritten. The user can confirm the choice or go back and select another file.

These procedures have some handy configuration options to control their behavior. For example, suppose we're creating an editor for color images. Our program may be able to load only certain image formats. We can use the -filetypes option to limit the file-selection dialog to display certain types of files. For example, we can add filters for GIF and PPM/PGM image formats as follows:

```
label .image -image [image create photo]
pack .image

button .load -text "Load Image..." \
    -command {load_image .image}
pack .load

proc load_image {win} {
    set types {
        {{GIF Files} {.gif}      }
        {{GIF Files} {}      GIFF}
        {{PPM Files} {.ppm}      }
        {{PGM Files} {.pgm}      }
    }
    set file [tk_getOpenFile -title "Load Image" \
        -filetypes $types]

    if {$file != ""} {
        set imh [$win cget -image]
        $imh configure -file $file
    }
}
```

The `types` variable contains a list of file types. Each type is a list with the following elements: a descriptive name for the file-selection dialog, a file extension for UNIX and Windows platforms, and a four-character Macintosh file type, which is optional.

Notice that we supplied two records for GIF files—one with a file extension and the other with a Macintosh file type. This acts as an "or" operation. The file selector will display files with a `.gif` extension *or* a Macintosh `GIFF` type. If we had supplied both the extension and the Macintosh type in one record, it would signify an "and" operation. On Macintosh systems, the file selector would display files with a `GIFF` type *and* a `.gif` extension, which is much too limiting.

9.1.2.3   Color selection

Many applications have color choices. For example, the fractal generator that we developed in Section 3.1.3 has a certain color scheme. The fractal shown in Figure 3.4 appears in shades of blue. If you like, you can click on the color sample to change the color scheme.

Tk comes with standard dialogs to handle color selection, as shown in Figure 9.4. The dialogs for Windows and Macintosh systems are quite good. The one for UNIX systems is not, but it is adequate for simple applications.

The `tk_chooseColor` procedure handles color selections. In our fractal generator, we use this procedure as follows:

```
...
label .controls.colorl -text "Color:"
button .controls.color -command {
    set color [.controls.color cget -background]
    set color [tk_chooseColor -initialcolor $color]
    if {$color != ""} {
        .controls.color configure \
            -background $color -activebackground $color
    }
}
...
.controls.color configure -background blue -activebackground blue
...
```

We've left out some code to focus on the problem at hand. You'll find the rest of the code in the file `efftcl/lib/demos/busy.tcl`, which can be obtained from the Web site mentioned on page xiv.

In this example, we've created the Color: label and the color sample button for the main window. The button doesn't display any text. Instead, it displays the current color choice as its background color.

When the color sample button is selected, we call `tk_chooseColor` to activate the color selector. We pass the current background color to the `-initialcolor` option, giving the user a starting point for the color selection. The user can spend some time adjusting the color and then click on OK or Cancel. If the user clicks on OK, `tk_chooseColor`

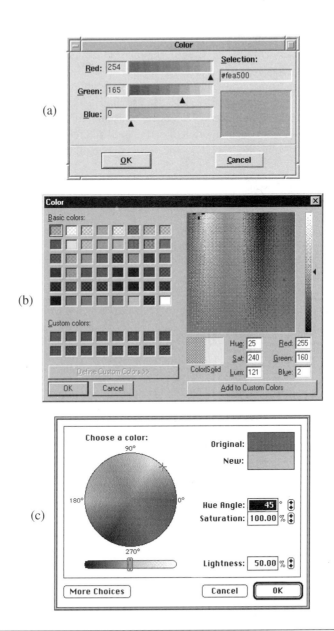

Figure 9.4. Standard color-selection dialogs for the three platforms: (a) UNIX, (b) Windows, and (c) Macintosh.

returns a new color selection; otherwise, it returns a null string. If we detect a color setting, we change the background of the button. The next time the fractal is generated, it will take its color from the -background option of this button.

The standard color selectors are quite handy, but if you have a more demanding application—such as a drawing program or a Web authoring tool—you should consider building your own color selector. You can use the HSB editor that we developed in Section 4.4 as a starting point. Color selectors are nonstandard across many applications anyway, so you won't lose much in terms of native look and feel. Also, your users may like the fact that your color selector works the same way on all three platforms.

9.1.3   Virtual events

Different platforms have different conventions for the behavior of a program—the "feel" part of the native look and feel. For example, on Windows systems, the keyboard shortcut for the paste operation is Control-v. On the Macintosh, it's Command-v, and for some UNIX applications it's Control-y. If you add the following binding to your program, the shortcut will work properly on Windows, but not on the other platforms:

```
bind . <Control-v> do_paste
```

Tk solves this problem through *virtual events*. A virtual event is a symbolic name for an event specification. For example, Tk recognizes the name <<Paste>> as the generic event specification for a paste operation. Instead of binding to a particular event, such as <Control-v>, you can bind to the <<Paste>> virtual event, like this:

```
bind . <<Paste>> do_paste
```

If you do this, the binding will be handled correctly on all three platforms. Tk also handles <<Cut>>, <<Copy>>, and <<Clear>> as standard virtual events.

You can define your own virtual events to handle other behaviors as well. For example, at the beginning of this chapter, we pointed out a problem in the e-mail editor that we developed in Section 5.2. We added a pop-up menu to a text widget by binding to the <ButtonPress-3> event. So when you click the third mouse button, it pops up a menu of text editing options. This works fine on UNIX and Windows systems. (All Windows systems have a two-button mouse. But in that case, the two buttons are treated as numbers 1 and 3. The missing button 2 can be synthesized by clicking both mouse buttons at the same time.) A Macintosh mouse, however, has only one button!

We can solve this problem by using a virtual event to post the menu and by defining the event differently on the various platforms:

```
    ...
    switch $tcl_platform(platform) {
        unix - windows {
            event add <<PopupMenu>> <ButtonPress-3>
        }
```

```
            macintosh {
                event add <<PopupMenu>> <Control-ButtonPress-1>
            }
        }
        ...
        bind .message.text <<PopupMenu>> {
            tk_popup .message.text.edit %X %Y
        }
        ...
```

We use a virtual event called <<PopupMenu>> to post the menu on the text widget.
The event add command defines one or more event specifications that correspond
to this virtual event. On UNIX and Windows systems, we define <<PopupMenu>>
as <ButtonPress-3>. But on Macintosh systems, we define it as
<Control-ButtonPress-1>, which means that holding down the Control key and
clicking the mouse button will activate the menu. Notice that we use the global
tcl_platform array to determine the current platform type. We'll talk more about
this array in Section 9.4.

9.1.4 Fonts

If you've used early releases of Tcl/Tk, you may have gotten used to the quirky X window
syntax for font specifications:

```
        label .l -text "Hello, World!" \
            -font -*-lucida-bold-o-normal--*-140-*
```

A particular font is specified as a series of dash-separated fields. If the value of a particular
field is not important, the * character can be used to match any available font. In this
example, lucida is the font family; bold, the weight; o, oblique or italic; normal, normal width (not compressed); and 140, 14 point.

In Tcl/Tk 8.0, these font specifications still work, but they have been superseded by a
richer font mechanism. A particular font can be specified in several ways, which are all
much easier to use. For example, we could specify the same 14-point Lucida font as follows:

```
        label .l -text "Hello, World!" \
            -font {Lucida 14 bold italic}
```

In this case, the font name is a list of values. The first value is the font family. If a second
value is included, it is treated as the point size. Any remaining values are treated as style
hints.

We could also create a font object to represent the font, like this:

```
        set token [font create -family Lucida \
            -size 14 -weight bold -slant italic]
        label .l -text "Hello, World!" -font $token
```

The `font create` command creates a new font object and returns a token that identifies the object. In this case, we created a font and set its family, size, weight, and slant options. We saved the font token in the variable `token` and then assigned this font to the label.

Using a font object like this has one important advantage. We can assign a particular font to many widgets. If we change the font options, all of the widgets that use the font will be updated automatically. For example, we could change our Lucida font back to a normal (roman) slant, like this:

```
font configure $token -slant roman
```

The label would be updated automatically.

If we request a font that is not available on a particular platform, Tk will use the closest available font. For example, we might create a label like this:

```
label .l -text "Hello, World!" \
    -font {"AvantGarde Bk BT" 18}
```

On a Windows system, we would see the Avant Garde font. But on a UNIX system, that font is not available. Instead, Tk will substitute a system font, such as the standard fixed-width font.

We can create a library procedure called `font_best` to make font choices more portable. This procedure works like the `font create` command but lets you specify a list of font families. The procedure uses the first family it can find and, as a last resort, defaults to the system font.

```
set fancyFont [font_best "AvantGarde Bk BT" Geneva Helvetica \
    -size 24 -weight bold -slant italic]
button .b -text "Hello, World!" -font $fancyFont
pack .b
```

In this case, `font_best` creates a 24-point bold italic font. If at all possible, it will use the Avant Garde face, defaulting to Geneva, Helvetica, and a system font as a last resort.

We can implement this procedure as follows:

```
proc font_best {args} {
    set fname [font create]
    set family ""
    while {[llength $args] > 0} {
        set arg0 [lindex $args 0]
        if {[string index $arg0 0] == "-"} {
            break
        }
        set args [lrange $args 1 end]

        if {$family == ""} {
            font configure $fname -family $arg0
```

```
                    if {[font actual $fname -family] == $arg0} {
                        set family $arg0
                    }
                }
            }
        eval font configure $fname $args
        return $fname
    }
```

We start by using `font create` to create a font in a default state. Then we scan through the command-line arguments and pick out the font family names. We assign each family to the font and use the `font actual` command to check the result. If the font exists, the family will be the same as the requested family; otherwise, it will be the name of a system font. When we find a particular font, we save its name in the `family` variable and skip over the remaining family names.

If an argument starts with the – character, it signals the start of configuration options, such as `-size` or `-weight`, so we break out of the loop. Then we use the remaining arguments to configure the font. The `eval` command is needed to handle the arguments properly. It breaks out the elements of the `$args` string so they're treated as separate arguments on the command line:

```
      eval font configure $fname $args
➡    eval font configure font12 {-size 24 -weight bold -slant italic}
➡    font configure font12 -size 24 -weight bold -slant italic
```

Without `eval`, the `$args` string would be interpreted as a single, rather strange-looking option name. Finally, we return the new font token as the result of `font_best`.

The Tk `font` command also has a `families` operation that returns the list of fonts available on a system. We can use this to build a font selector like the one shown in Figure 9.5. The font selector displays the complete list of families and provides controls for the all of the font characteristics, such as the size, the weight, the slant, and so forth. The font selector also displays a bit of sample text, providing an example of the selected font.

We'll make a procedure called `font_select` to activate the dialog. This procedure pops up the dialog and lets the user adjust the font. If the user clicks on OK, the procedure returns a list of font characteristics:

```
      -family Helvetica -size 14 -weight normal -slant italic
```

If the user selects Cancel, the procedure returns the null string.

We might use this procedure in a simple example, as follows:

```
    button .b -text "Change Font" -command {
        set options [font_select "Change Font"]
        if {$options != ""} {
            .b configure -font $options
        }
    }
    pack .b
```

Figure 9.5. Font-selection dialog.

In this example, we've used the result from `font_select` as a font specification. Tk parses the options within the specification automatically. We could also assign the font characteristics to a font object, thereby updating all of the widgets that use that particular object.

This font dialog is constructed much like the printer dialog that we discussed in Section 6.6.3. So we'll skip over many of the details and concentrate on how the fonts are handled.

We create the dialog and initialize its list of fonts like this:

```
set fnInfo(dialog) [dialog_create Fontselect]
...
set win [dialog_info $fnInfo(dialog)]
...
listbox $win.families -height 1 -exportselection 0 \
    -yscrollcommand "$win.sbar set"
pack $win.families -side left -expand yes -fill both
...
eval $win.families insert 0 [lsort [font families]]
$win.families selection set 0
```

We use the `font families` command to query the list of families available on the current system. We pass the list through `lsort` to sort the names alphabetically, and then we insert the names into the listbox. The listbox will insert many strings at once, as long as they appear as separate arguments on the command line. So we use the `eval` command to treat the result from `lsort` as a series of separate strings.

We display a sample of the current font characteristics in a text widget, which is created as follows:

```
set win [dialog_info $fnInfo(dialog)]
frame $win.sample -height 1i
...
text $win.sample.text -width 1 -height 1 -wrap none \
    -font $fnInfo(font) \
    -yscrollcommand "$win.sample.sbar set"
```

The text widget uses a font object that's created like this:

```
set fnInfo(font) [font create]
```

When the user selects a different font family or changes any of the font characteristics, we update this object, and the sample changes immediately. When the user clicks on OK, we query the characteristics from this font object and return them from font_select as follows:

```
proc font_select {{sample ""}} {
    global fnInfo

    ...pop up the dialog and wait for a selection...

    if {$fnInfo(ok)} {
        return [font configure $fnInfo(font)]
    }
    return ""
}
```

Of course, there's lots more code that creates the dialog and handles the font controls. You'll find it in the file efftcl/lib/scripts/font.tcl, which can be obtained from the Web site mentioned on page xiv. But the code presented here shows the power of the new font mechanism—not only for specifying fonts but also for manipulating them.

9.1.5 Option database

In Section 8.1.1, we saw how the Tk option database can be used to customize an application. This database came from the X window heritage of Tcl/Tk, but that doesn't mean that it's only for UNIX platforms. The option database works on Windows and Macintosh systems as well, and it provides a handy way to configure applications on all three platforms.

On UNIX systems, the option database automatically loads resources from a file called .Xdefaults or .Xresources in the user's home directory. Windows and Macintosh systems have no such convention, but you can support your own configuration file, if you like.

For example, suppose we're distributing the sketch program that we developed in Chapter 1. Along with it, we might include an example resource file called sketch.rdb that contains the following:

```
sketch*sketchpad.background: OldLace
```

```
sketch*style*foreground: white
sketch*style*background: NavyBlue
sketch*style*highlightBackground: NavyBlue
sketch*style*font: "ZapfHumnst BT" 12 bold
```

This file gives the users some idea of the resources that are available in the `sketch` program. Users can edit this file, adding their own choices for colors and fonts.

On UNIX systems, users normally add these resources to their `.Xdefaults` or `.Xresources` file. But instead of relying on this mechanism, we can have the program load resources directly from the `sketch.rdb` file. That way, the resources will work on all three platforms.

We can add the following code near the top of the `sketch` script to load the resources:

```
set file [file join $env(INSTALL_DIR) sketch.rdb]
option readfile $file userDefault
```

We've assumed that an environment variable called `INSTALL_DIR` contains the name of the installation directory. This environment variable may be set by the installation program or by some script that invokes the program, as we discussed earlier in Section 8.3.3. We use the `file join` command to build a proper file path for `sketch.rdb`. Then we use the `option readfile` command to load the resources. We give these resources a priority of `userDefault`, which is what they would have if they had come from the `.Xresources` file. This priority is a bit higher than the `startupFile` priority that we use at the application level. So the resources in the `sketch.rdb` file will override other resources that we've included in the application.

9.2 File system issues

UNIX, Windows, and Macintosh systems all share the notion of a hierarchical file system. These files systems are very much alike, but each has its own idiosyncrasies. This becomes obvious when you try to reference a file. On a UNIX system, a file name might look like this:

```
/usr/local/lib/tcl/tcl8.0/init.tcl
```

On a Windows system, a similar file name might look like this:

```
C:\Program Files\Tcl\tcl8.0\init.tcl
```

And on the Macintosh, it might look like this:

```
Don Quixote:Tcl/Tk Folder:tcl8.0:init.tcl
```

The different file systems use different separator characters, and they have different conventions for the directories where files are commonly stored.

Tcl/Tk includes some special commands for manipulating files. If you're careful to use them, you can handle files in a portable manner. In this section, we'll take a look at those commands.

9.2.1   File names

If you've used early versions of Tcl/Tk on UNIX systems, you may be in the habit of writing code like this:

```
set fid [open $dir/$file "r"]
```

This command opens a file called `$file` in a directory called `$dir`. This command works fine on UNIX systems and will also work on Windows systems, provided that `$dir` contains a sensible name for a Windows directory. But the command fails miserably on Macintosh systems. On the Macintosh, the file separator character is : instead of /. So a name such as the following looks like an ordinary file name in the current working directory—not a file path:

```
$dir/$file
```
➥ `Don Quixote/script.tcl`

Instead of joining names with the / character, you should use the `file join` command to build a proper file path, like this:

```
set fid [open [file join $dir $file] "r"]
```

The `file join` command joins any number of file components with the proper separator for the current platform.

Notice that in this example, the directory name `Don Quixote` has a space in it. This is a common occurrence on Windows and Macintosh systems, and it can happen under UNIX as well. You must keep this in mind whenever you write code that uses file names. If you're not careful, you may introduce a subtle bug, as we'll see in the following example.

Suppose we're building a simple text editor like the one shown in Figure 9.6. Each time the user opens a file, it is added to the list of recent documents near the bottom of the File menu. The user can return to a particular file by selecting its name from the menu.

The Open... option on the File menu is implemented as follows:

```
.mbar.file add command -label "Open..." -command {
    set file [tk_getOpenFile]
    if {$file != ""} {
        open_doc $file
        add_doc $file
    }
}
```

We use `tk_getOpenFile` to select a file, as we discussed in Section 9.1.2. Then we call one procedure, named `open_doc`, to load the document and another procedure, named `add_doc`, to add it to the File menu.

If we weren't thinking clearly, we might implement the `add_doc` procedure as follows:

```
proc add_doc {file} {
    set name [file tail $file]
    if {[catch {.mbar.file index $name}] != 0} {
        set pos [expr [.mbar.file index "Print..."]+2]
```

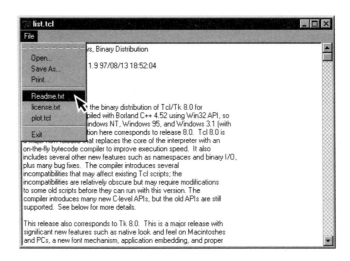

Figure 9.6. In this simple text editor, files are added to the **File** menu for easy access.

```
                .mbar.file insert $pos command -label $name \
                    -command "open_doc $file"
        }
    }
```

This seems to make sense. We start by using `file tail` to get the simple file name at the end of the file path. Then we ask the menu for the index of this entry, to see whether the file is already on the menu. If this operation fails, we add the file to the menu. We use the `index` operation again to locate the Print... entry, and we add the file two slots below that. We give the file entry a command that calls `open_doc`, so when the file is selected, it is loaded into the editor. And of course, we use double quotes to make sure that the `$file` argument is substituted into the command.

Therein lies the problem. Suppose that the file path contains a space, like this:

```
C:/Program Files/Tcl/lib/tcl8.0/init.tcl
```

Then the menu entry will have a command that looks like this:

```
open_doc C:/Program Files/Tcl/lib/tcl8.0/init.tcl
```

This command will produce an error, since it looks as though we're calling `open_doc` with two arguments—`C:/Program` and `Files/Tcl/lib/tcl8.0/init.tcl`.

Instead of using double quotes, we should have used the `list` command, like this:

```
                .mbar.file insert $pos command -label $name \
                    -command [list open_doc $file]
```

The `list` command preserves `$file` as a single argument on the command line, as we explained in Section 3.1.5.

9.2.2 File manipulation

Until recently, Tcl had no commands to make directories, copy files, rename them, or delete them. If you've grown up with Tcl/Tk on UNIX systems, you've probably written code like this:

```
exec rm -rf install.tmp
exec mkdir install.tmp
exec cp -rp src install.tmp
exec mv install.tmp install
...
```

Programs such as rm, mkdir, and cp don't exist on Windows and Macintosh systems, so this code is not at all portable.

Instead of relying on these external programs, you should use the built-in file-manipulation commands as follows:

```
file delete -force install.tmp
file mkdir install.tmp
file copy src install.tmp
file rename install.tmp install
...
```

If you look back at the installation program we developed in Section 8.3.3, you'll notice that we used these same commands. These commands are portable, so the installation program works properly on all three platforms.

9.2.3 End-of-line translations

The UNIX, Windows, and Macintosh file systems use different conventions to mark the end of each line in a text file. On UNIX, lines are marked with the newline character, \n; on Windows, with a carriage return, \r, followed by \n; and on the Macintosh, by \r alone. If you create a file on one system, it may be garbled when you view it on another. For example, if you write a script under UNIX, copy it over to a Windows machine, and open it with the Notepad utility, the entire script will appear on one long line. This is bothersome, to say the least.

You might think that Tcl would have the same problem reading your scripts, but it handles the platform differences with relative ease. When reading any file, Tcl automatically translates sequences of \n and \r to a single \n character. So no matter what system was used to create the file and no matter what system is currently reading the file, the lines are understood correctly.

The conversion to a single \n marker meshes nicely with everything else in Tcl/Tk. For example, suppose you read a file and load its contents directly into a text widget. The text widget recognizes each \n as the end of a line, so no matter what system created the file, the text widget will display the lines correctly.

When writing out a file, Tcl automatically translates each \n back to the appropriate end-of-line marker for the current platform. So output files have the proper convention for the local file system.

You can take advantage of the automatic file translation to create a handy file-conversion utility. If you're moving text files from one platform to another, you can use the following program to convert them:

```
catch {console hide}
button .convert -text "Convert Text File..." -command do_conversion
pack .convert -padx 4 -pady 4
proc do_conversion {} {
    set file [tk_getOpenFile -title "Convert Text File"]
    if {$file != ""} {
        set fid [open $file "r"]
        set contents [read $fid]
        close $fid

        set fid [open $file "w"]
        puts -nonewline $fid $contents
        close $fid

        tk_messageBox -icon info -message "Conversion complete"
    }
}
```

We perform the file conversion in do_conversion simply by reading the file in and writing it back out.

Tcl's automatic end-of-line translation is normally quite handy. But when you're reading and writing binary files, you must be careful to disable this feature, using the fconfigure command:

```
set fid [open $file "r"]
fconfigure $fid -translation binary
```

If you don't do this, your binary data may be corrupted.

9.3   Program invocation issues

Each platform manages its processes in a different way. In this section, we'll see how these differences affect your Tcl/Tk programs.

9.3.1   Communicating with other programs

Tcl is not a system programming language like C or C++; it's a "glue" language. You'd never write Tcl code to compute the stress contours on an aircraft. But you might use another program to compute the contours and have Tcl/Tk display the results.

There are various ways to communicate with other programs, as we discussed in Chapter 7. But when you devise a solution for one platform, you may have difficulty moving your application to the others.

For example, suppose that someone else has created a program for computing stress contours and that we want to create an interface for it with Tcl/Tk. Suppose that the program has been developed and tested on UNIX systems and that it runs like this:

```
$ aircad -file plane12.geom -contours 50
```

We could use a file-selection dialog to select the input file and a scale widget to select the number of contours. Once we've gathered all of the input parameters, we could use exec or open to execute the program.

So we have a solution for UNIX systems. Now suppose that we have some customers with Windows machines. Windows and UNIX are similar in many respects. Both have a notion of programs with command-line options, and both support the exec and open commands in Tcl/Tk. If we can arrange for aircad to be ported to Windows, we may be able to handle both platforms quite easily.

Now suppose that we also have customers on the Macintosh. Mac programs don't have a command-line interface, so there is no exec command in the Mac version of Tcl/Tk. Instead, there is an AppleScript command that you can use in place of exec to drive other programs. Let's take a moment to see how this works.

Suppose that we're adding online help to a Tcl/Tk application on the Mac. If we have help files written in HTML format, we could use Internet Explorer to display them as follows:

```
package require Tclapplescript
proc open_html {file} {
    set script {
        tell application "Internet Explorer 3.0"
            open(file "%s")
            Activate -1
        end tell
    }
    AppleScript execute [format $script $file]
}
```

The package require command brings in the AppleScript facility. This package exists only in the Mac version of Tcl/Tk, so we'll have a problem porting this code back to UNIX and Windows platforms. But let's ignore that problem for now. We'll get back to it in Section 9.4.

The open_html procedure uses the format command to build a script that looks something like this:

```
tell application "Internet Explorer 3.0"
    open(file "Don Quixote:HTML Docs:index.html")
    Activate -1
end tell
```

This script is written in the AppleScript language, which has a different syntax from Tcl/Tk.[*] The first line identifies the application that we want to talk to—in this case, Internet Explorer. The second line tells the application to open a certain HTML file. The third line tells the application to activate itself, which brings it to the foreground. When the `AppleScript execute` command executes this script, the help file pops up on the desktop.

You can use the same technique to communicate with many other Macintosh applications. The trick is knowing what to say to them. A utility called Script Editor, which normally resides in the `AppleTalk` folder, can help in this regard. This program has an **Open Dictionary...** option under the **File** menu that lets you view the dictionary of commands an application will recognize. If you open the dictionary for Internet Explorer, for example, you'll see the `open` and `Activate` verbs that we used in this example.

Let's get back to our original example. If the `aircad` program were ported to the Macintosh, we could use the `AppleScript execute` command to drive it. We might have to write some special-purpose code for each of the platforms, but in theory, we could support all three.

In reality, it is quite difficult to find a program that runs on all three platforms. But there's a better solution that often solves the portability problem once and for all: We can use the client/server architecture described in Section 7.6. We can set up a server somewhere in network. If the server is running on a UNIX machine, for example, it would have no problem executing the original `aircad` program. Clients could connect to the server from any platform, request computations, and display the results. The client code wouldn't have any dependencies on the operating system, so it would be completely portable.

Of course, this solution assumes that our customers have access to a network and that we have a machine that can handle the computational load of the server. If these assumptions apply to the problem at hand, the client/server solution works quite well.

9.3.2 Environment variables

Tcl/Tk grew up on UNIX systems, so it has the notion of environment variables. These variables are stored in the `env` array, and they contain information about the program (usually a shell) that invoked Tcl/Tk.

The `env` array also exists in the Windows and Mac versions of Tcl/Tk and serves more or less the same purpose. So you can use the `env` array in your Tcl/Tk programs, but you must use it carefully. Each platform stores different information in this array. When you're looking for a particular slot, there is no guarantee that it will exist.

---

* To learn more about AppleScript, see Danny Goodman, *Danny Goodman's AppleScript Handbook,* 2d ed., Random House, 1995.

For example, on UNIX and Macintosh systems, the slot `env(USER)` contains the name of the current user, but on Windows systems, it doesn't exist. If you want to access the user name, you should guard against an undefined value as follows:

```
if {[info exists env(USER)]} {
    set user $env(USER)
} else {
    set user "unknown"
}
```

9.4   When all else fails

When all else fails, you can write some special-purpose code for each platform. You can determine the current platform type, the machine type, and information about the operating system by examining a global array called `tcl_platform`. So you can write one bit of code to handle UNIX, and a different bit of code to handle Windows. You may even have special-purpose code that handles Windows 95 differently from Windows NT.

Let's return to the example that we discussed in Section 9.3.1. Suppose that we have some HTML files containing help information and that we want to display these files in a Web browser. We've already seen how to use the `AppleScript` command to handle this problem on the Macintosh. But we'll need a different solution for UNIX and Windows environments.

We'll wrap up all of these solutions in a procedure called `open_html`. That procedure is implemented as follows:

```
proc open_html {file} {
    global tcl_platform

    switch $tcl_platform(platform) {
        unix {
            set cmd "exec netscape -remote \"openFile($file)\""
            if {[catch $cmd] != 0} {
                exec netscape &
                while {[catch $cmd] != 0} {
                    after 500
                }
            }
        }
        windows {
            set cmd [list exec netscape $file &]
            if {[catch $cmd] != 0} {
                set prog [tk_getOpenFile -title "Where is Netscape?"]
```

```
                    if {$prog != ""} {
                        exec $prog $file &
                    }
                }
            }
        macintosh {
            package require Tclapplescript
            set script {
                tell application "Internet Explorer 3.0"
                    open(file "%s")
                    Activate -1
                end tell
            }
            AppleScript execute [format $script $file]
        }
    }
}
```

We determine the platform type by examining the `tcl_platform` array. On UNIX machines, we invoke Netscape Navigator with the `-remote` option, which tells an existing browser to open a file. If a browser isn't running on the desktop, this command will fail. In that case, we start a new browser and attempt to communicate until the file has been displayed.

On Windows machines, Netscape doesn't support the `-remote` option. Instead, we can supply the file name as an argument, and the browser will display that file. The `netscape.exe` program may not be on the user's command path. So if we have any trouble starting Netscape, we ask the user to find the program, and then we try one last time to bring up the browser.

On Macintosh machines, we use `AppleScript execute` to send commands to Internet Explorer, as we explained earlier in Section 9.3.1.

Having special-purpose code like this requires more work to develop and maintain. But if you encapsulate it as we did here, it's manageable. When push comes to shove, it may be the only solution.

Appendix A
Getting Started with Tcl/Tk

You'll need to have two programs to execute Tcl/Tk scripts: `tclsh`, a command shell for Tcl-only scripts; and `wish`, which is like `tclsh` but includes the Tk widgets. In this appendix, we'll show you how to obtain and install these programs. Once you've done that, you can download the examples presented in this book. Visit our Web site for details: http://www.awl.com/cseng/books/efftcl/.

If you'd like to learn more about Tcl/Tk and extensions, you can visit any of the following Web sites.

- **http://sunscript.sun.com**   This site is run by the Tcl/Tk development group at Sun Microsystems and is the official source for Tcl/Tk distributions.

- **http://www.NeoSoft.com/tcl**   This site, the Tcl/Tk Contributed Sources Archive, contains source code for packages and extensions contributed by developers all over the world. Like Tcl/Tk, many of these packages and extensions can be used in commercial applications without licensing fees or royalties.

- **http://www.tcltk.com**   This site has many useful pointers for Tcl/Tk information all over the Web. You'll find information about training seminars, special-interest groups, extensions, and so on.

A.1   Installing on Windows 95/NT

The easiest way to get started with Tcl/Tk is to install it under Windows 95/NT. Just follow these steps.

1. Visit the Sun Web site (http://sunscript.sun.com) and follow the link to the Download page. Then follow the link for the latest release of Tcl/Tk, which should be version 8.0 or higher. In the section on binary releases, download the release titled Windows 95 and Windows NT self-extracting installer.

2. Run the self-extracting installer. This program will guide you through the rest of the installation.

3. When the installer has finished, the `tclsh` and `wish` programs will be ready to use. They're normally installed on the Start menu under Programs → Tcl. Start up the `wish` program and try out this simple script:

```
% button .b -text "Hello, World!" -command exit
⇒ .b
% pack .b
```

Or, start up the Widget Tour program and explore some of the demos.

A.2   Installing on UNIX

You can download the Tcl/Tk source distribution and compile it on all of the major UNIX platforms. This requires a bit more work than the Windows 95/NT installation does, but it is still relatively easy.

1. Visit the Sun Web site (http://sunscript.sun.com) and follow the link to the Download page. Then follow the link for the latest release of Tcl/Tk, which should be version 8.0 or higher. In the section on UNIX source releases, download both the Tcl and Tk source distributions.

2. Unpack the distributions. The files containing these distributions include the version numbers. In the following example, we'll assume that you've downloaded version 8.0:

```
$ zcat tcl8.0.tar.Z | tar xf -
$ zcat tk8.0.tar.Z | tar xf -
```

3. Build and install the Tcl distribution. You'll find detailed instructions in the README file that's included with the Tcl sources, but it works as follows. First, run the `configure` script to configure the Makefiles for your system:

```
$ cd tcl8.0/unix
$ ./configure
```

By default, Tcl will configure itself to be installed in `/usr/local`. If you can't write to that directory, you should use the `--prefix` option to change the installation directory:

```
$ ./configure --prefix=/home/joehacker/tcltk
```

In this case, Tcl will install itself the directory `/home/joehacker/tcltk`, creating the directories `bin`, `lib`, and `man` underneath it.

If you want to use the GNU compiler `gcc`, add the `--enable-gcc` option:

```
$ ./configure --prefix=/home/joehacker/tcltk --enable-gcc
```

If you want to use shared libraries and dynamic loading, add the `--enable-shared` option:

```
$ ./configure --prefix=/home/joehacker/tcltk --enable-shared
```

Once the `configure` script has finished, you can build the distribution:

```
$ make all
```

When this has finished, you can run the built-in regression tests:

```
$ make test
```

Don't be alarmed if some of the tests fail. This is not uncommon, and it doesn't mean that the build has failed. Quite often, problems arise due to minor differences between UNIX platforms, but the underlying error is benign. (Of course, if the program dumps core, that is another matter!)

Finally, you can install the Tcl distribution, like this:

```
$ make install
```

This creates `bin`, `lib`, and `man` directories under the install directories and populates them with `tclsh`, its libraries, and its manual pages. The name of the `tclsh` executable includes its version number. So if you've installed version 8.0, the name of the executable is `tclsh8.0`. It's a good idea to create a symbolic link called `tclsh` that points to this version:

```
$ cd /home/joehacker/tcltk/bin
$ ln -s tclsh8.0 tclsh
```

That way, you can always use `tclsh` as the program name, even if you upgrade to another version.

If you've included the `bin` directory on your command path, you should be able to start up `tclsh` and enter some commands, like this:

```
$ tclsh
% info tclversion
```
⇒ *8.0*

4. Build and install the Tk distribution. This is quite similar to the way that we built Tcl in the previous step. First, run the `configure` script with the appropriate options. For example:

```
$ cd tk8.0/unix
$ ./configure --prefix=/home/joehacker/tcltk --enable-shared
```

Once the `configure` script has finished, you can build the distribution:

```
$ make all
```

When this has finished, you can run the built-in regression tests:

```
$ make test
```

This will bring up a series of windows that dance furiously as their options are tested. Again, don't be alarmed if many of the tests fail. The tests have hard-coded numbers for the expected size and placement for the windows. The numbers may be off by 1 pixel on some platforms. So a test may fail, but the problem is harmless.

Finally, you can install the Tk distribution, like this:

```
$ make install
```

This adds to the `bin`, `lib`, and `man` directories that were created when Tcl was installed. It adds `wish`, its libraries, and its manual pages. The name of the `wish` executable includes its version number. Again, it's a good idea to create a symbolic link for the executable:

```
$ cd /home/joehacker/tcltk/bin
$ ln -s wish8.0 wish
```

If you've included the `bin` directory on your command path, you should be able to start up `wish` and enter some commands, like this:

```
$ wish
% button .b -text "Hello, World!" -command exit
⇒ .b
% pack .b
```

5. At this point, Tcl/Tk is installed. You may want to start up the widget tour and explore some of the demos:

```
$ cd /home/joehacker/tcltk/lib/tk8.0/demos
$ wish widget
```

A.3 Installing on Macintosh

Installing on the Macintosh is almost as easy as installing under Windows 95/NT.

1. Visit the Sun Web site (http://sunscript.sun.com) and follow the link to the Download page. Then follow the link for the latest release of Tcl/Tk, which should be version 8.0 or higher. In the section on binary releases, download the release titled Macintosh 68K and PowerPC self-extracting installer.

2. This file is in binhex format, so you'll need the StuffIt program to decode it. You can obtain StuffIt from the following site: http://www.aladdinsys.com/.

3. Once you've decoded the installer, double-click on it to perform the install. This will create a folder containing the `wish` program, its libraries, and its documentation.

4. Double-click on the `wish` program and try out this simple script:

```
% button .b -text "Hello, World!" -command exit
⇒ .b
% pack .b
```

Appendix B
Annotated Bibliography

This appendix lists some of the books that we've found to be helpful in developing Tcl/Tk applications.

Graphical design and human interfaces

- Norman, Donald A., *The Psychology of Everyday Things*, Currency-Doubleday, 1989.

  Published in paperback as *The Design of Everyday Things*, this book has become a classic in the design field. The book discusses the thought processes behind everyday actions and explains how designs can benefit from an understanding of the mental models users create when using a particular tool or product.

- Tognazzini, Bruce ("Tog"), *Tog on Interface*, Apple Computer/Addison-Wesley, 1992.

  Before moving to Sun, Tog was Apple's Human Interface Evangelist. This book presents clearly spelled-out principles and guidelines to help you create intuitive, clear human interfaces.

- Tufte, Edward R., *The Visual Display of Quantitative Information*, Graphics Press, 1983; and *Envisioning Information*, Graphics Press, 1990.

  These books review the graphical practices of the last two centuries and present a "practical theory of data graphics," with an emphasis on "turning data into information." These books are generally credited with creating a renaissance in visual design and information display.

Programming

- Aho, Alfred V, Brian W. Kernighan, and Peter J. Weinberger, *The AWK Programming Language*, Addison-Wesley, 1988.

  AWK is generally regarded as the grandfather of the current batch of scripting languages. The examples in this book, ranging from text processing to little languages and algorithm experimentation, are still timely and informative.

- Harrison, Mark, ed., *Tcl/Tk Tools*, O'Reilly and Associates, 1997.

  With contributions by both of us, this book covers the most useful and popular extensions to Tcl and Tk.

- Kernighan, Brian W., and P. J. Plauger, *Software Tools*, Addison-Wesley, 1976.

  This book was largely responsible for spreading the concept of reusable software components packaged as "tools." It introduced the idea of component-based development, whereby small, discrete pieces were integrated to make a variety of useful applications. A second version of the book, *Software Tools in Pascal*, updates and presents the examples in Pascal.

- Libes, Don, *Exploring Expect*, O'Reilly and Associates, 1994.

  Expect, a program for dealing with interactive software, uses Tcl for its scripting interface. In addition to covering Expect, the book has a good introduction to Tcl.

- Ousterhout, John K., *Tcl and the Tk Toolkit*, Addison-Wesley, 1994.

  Ousterhout is the original developer of Tcl/Tk, and this is the Tcl/Tk book. Although somewhat dated (it covers Tcl 7.3 and Tk 3.6), it is still a good introduction to the subject.

- Welch, Brent, *Practical Programming in Tcl and Tk,* 2d ed., Prentice Hall, 1997.

  This is a comprehensive introduction to the latest versions of Tcl and Tk. Welch is a member of the Tcl team at Sun.

Computer graphics

- Foley, James D., Andries van Dam, Steven K. Feiner, and John F. Hughes, *Computer Graphics, Principles and Practice—Second Edition in C*, Addison-Wesley, 1996.

  This is one of the standard texts for computer graphics. The color wheel in Section 4.4 of our book is based on algorithms presented in Chapter 13 of this book.

Index

Procedures are defined on pages shown in boldface.